"*North American Integration* makes a compelling point: the growing interaction between Canada, Mexico, and the United States has been beneficial to all three countries, but it is now endangered by an "institutional void." This book is a clarion call to build continental institutions to manage the policy intersection of migration, security, and development and forge a more equitable, secure and prosperous North America.
—Robert A. Pastor, *American University,* author of *The North American Idea: A Vision of a Continental Future*

# North American Integration

The course of events since the implementation of NAFTA has had unexpected elements with significant impacts on North American integration. First has been the rise of China as a larger source of imports and production partner than Mexico. Second has been the rise of security concerns since September 11, 2001. The result has been much stronger integration between Canada and the US than with Mexico. Migration issues are now linked with security, which has risen to a top priority in the international agenda. While liberalization has furnished strong economic incentives for integration, it has not provided a sufficient guide for the political process, which requires leadership and appropriate institutions to coordinate and regulate special interest groups. A coherent and effective North American integration would be a valuable asset in the context of global integration and competition, yet the issues involved are quite complex and varied.

*North American Integration: An Institutional Void in Migration, Security and Development* examines the current state of North American integration. Editors Gaspare M. Genna and David A. Mayer-Foulkes gather an international group of experts to give a broad, coherent picture of the current, multifaceted process of integration, and find that institutional development is an essential component. Divided into three sections, the book:

- Discusses the determinants of integration and shows that the institutional characteristics of the three countries, including democracy and basic rights, are the most important.
- Provides examples of institutional building in contexts for which institutions are lacking, specifically labor, migration and health issues.
- Examines issues such as overall security arrangements, trade, drug related violence, and the continuing wage gap among the countries, which have an important bearing on integration.

**Gaspare M. Genna** is an associate professor of political science at the University of Texas at El Paso. His work is found in *International Politics, Journal of European Integration, Comparative European Politics, Latin American Perspectives, Journal of Developing Societies, International Interactions, International Political Economy, European Union Politics* and numerous book chapters. He is an associate editor of *Politics & Policy*, senior research fellow at the TransResearch Institute and associate research fellow at the Institute on Comparative Regional Integration Studies, United Nations University.

**David A. Mayer-Foulkes** has conducted research for CIDE, Mexico, for many years, as well as PAHO, UNDP, World Bank and the Mexican Commission on Macroeconomics and Health, among others. His main interest is economic development, including the role of long-term intergenerational health, nutrition and educational poverty traps, and multiple steady-state models of endogenous technological change.

# Routledge Studies in North American Politics

1 **Political Institutions and Lesbian and Gay Rights in the United States and Canada**
*Miriam Smith*

2 **Black Women, Cultural Images and Social Policy**
*Julia S. Jordan-Zachery*

3 **How Courts Impact Federal Administrative Behavior**
*Robert J. Hume*

4 **State Failure, Underdevelopment, and Foreign Intervention in Haiti**
*Jean-Germain Gros*

5 **Mexico-United States Relations: The Semantics of Sovereignty**
*Arturo Santa-Cruz*

6 **Federalism, Secession, and the American State: Divided, We Secede**
*Lawrence M. Anderson*

7 **The State and Security in Mexico: Transformation and Crisis in Regional Perspective**
*Edited by Brian Bow and Arturo Santa-Cruz*

8 **North American Integration: An Institutional Void in Migration, Security and Development**
*Edited by Gaspare M. Genna and David A. Mayer-Foulkes*

# North American Integration
An Institutional Void in Migration, Security and Development

**Edited by
Gaspare M. Genna
David A. Mayer-Foulkes**

NEW YORK AND LONDON

First published 2013
by Routledge
711 Third Avenue, New York, NY 10017

Simultaneously published in the UK
by Routledge
2 Park Square, Milton Park, Abingdon, Oxfordshire OX14 4RN

First issued in paperback 2015

*Routledge is an imprint of the Taylor & Francis Group,
an informa business*

© 2013 Taylor & Francis

The right of the editor to be identified as the author of the editorial material,
and of the authors for their individual chapters, has been asserted in accordance
with sections 77 and 78 of the Copyright, Designs and Patents Act 1988.

All rights reserved. No part of this book may be reprinted or reproduced or
utilized in any form or by any electronic, mechanical, or other means, now
known or hereafter invented, including photocopying and recording, or in any
information storage or retrieval system, without permission in writing from
the publishers.

**Trademark Notice:** Product or corporate names may be trademarks or
registered trademarks, and are used only for identification and explanation
without intent to infringe.

*Library of Congress Cataloging-in-Publication Data*

North American integration : an institutional void in migration, security and
    development / edited by Gaspare M. Genna, David A. Mayer-Foulkes.
        pages cm. — (Routledge studies in North American politics)
    ISBN 978-0-415-82353-1 (hardback) — ISBN 978-0-203-55126-4 (ebk)
    1. North America—Economic integration.   2. North America—Emigration
and immigration.   3. Canada. Treaties, etc. 1992 October 7.
I. Genna, Gaspare M.   II. Mayer-Foulkes, David.
    HC95.N675   2013
    337.1'7—dc23
    2012049459

ISBN13: 978-1-138-94306-3 (pbk)
ISBN13: 978-0-415-82353-1 (hbk)

Typeset in Sabon
by Apex CoVantage, LLC

**The book is dedicated to the peoples of North America**

# Contents

| | | |
|---|---|---:|
| | *List of Tables* | xi |
| | *List of Figures* | xiii |
| | *List of Contributors* | xv |
| **1** | **Introduction** | 1 |
| | GASPARE M. GENNA AND DAVID A. MAYER-FOULKES | |

## PART I
## Determinants of Integration

| | | |
|---|---|---:|
| **2** | **What Will It Take to Build a North American Community?** | 15 |
| | GASPARE M. GENNA | |
| **3** | **The Mess They Made: How Conservatism Is Wrecking North America** | 34 |
| | JULIÁN CASTRO-REA | |
| **4** | **Immigration and Institutional Voids: North American Citizenship and Human Rights in Conflict** | 51 |
| | EMMA R. NORMAN | |
| **5** | **Democracy and Development for Mexico** | 78 |
| | DAVID A. MAYER-FOULKES AND RAÚL GARCÍA-BARRIOS | |

## PART II
## Examples of Institutional Building in North America

| | | |
|---|---|---:|
| **6** | **The Evolution of US-Mexico Labor Cooperation and the NAALC Institutions** | 99 |
| | KIMBERLY A. NOLAN GARCÍA | |

x *Contents*

7 Citizenship at the Margins: The Canadian Seasonal
Agricultural Worker Program and Civil Society Advocacy     115
CHRISTINA GABRIEL AND LAURA MACDONALD

8 Organizing the Mexican Diaspora: Can It Strengthen
North American Integration?     136
JANE H. BAYES AND LAURA GONZALEZ

9 What Does the 2010 Affordable Care Act Mean for Securing
Immigrant Health in North America?     152
NIELAN BARNES

## PART III
## Economic and Security Issues in Integration

10 Obstacles to Security Cooperation in North America     177
ROBERTO DOMÍNGUEZ AND RAFAEL VELÁZQUEZ

11 Secure Borders and Uncertain Trade     198
CORAL R. SNODGRASS AND GUY H. GESSNER

12 Drug-Related Violence and Forced Migration from
Mexico to the United States     211
EVA OLIMPIA ARCEO-GÓMEZ

13 Wage Differentials, Public Policies and Mexico-US Migration     231
ERNESTO AGUAYO-TÉLLEZ, ARUN K. ACHARYA AND CHRISTIAN I.
RIVERA-MENDOZA

14 Conclusion     254
GASPARE M. GENNA AND DAVID A. MAYER-FOULKES

*Index*     259

# Tables

| | | |
|---|---|---|
| 2.1 | Variable Values for Select Cases of Regional Integration Organizations (2004) | 21 |
| 2.2 | Time Series (AR1) Regression with Correlated Panels Corrected Standard Errors | 23 |
| 2.3 | Time Series (AR1) Regression with Correlated Panels Corrected Standard Errors | 23 |
| 2.4 | North American Integration Scenarios | 25 |
| 6.1 | NAALC Petitions Filed 1994–2012 | 104 |
| 7.1 | Profile of Civil Society Organizations Interviewed | 121 |
| 9.1 | Im(migrant) Access to Health Care: Policies, Programs and Services Pre- and Post-2010 ACA | 162 |
| 10.1 | Comparison of the Three North American Countries | 179 |
| 12.1 | Characteristics of Mexican Immigrants: Border versus Nonborder States | 217 |
| 12.2 | Characteristics of Mexican Migrants Living in Border States by Distance to the Border | 218 |
| 12.3 | Growth Rates in the Number of Establishments | 218 |
| 12.4 | Growth Rates in the Number of Establishment in Border States | 219 |
| 12.5 | Effect of Violence on Mexican Migration to the United States | 220 |
| 12.6 | Robustness Checks | 221 |
| 12.7 | Effect of Mexican Violence on the Number of Business Establishments in the United States | 222 |
| 12.8 | Effect of Mexican Violence on the Number of Business Establishments on Southern US Border (fake experiment) | 223 |
| 12.9 | Effect of Violence on Mexican Migration to US Southern Border States | 224 |
| 12.10 | Robustness Checks of Model with Interactions | 225 |
| 12.11 | Effect of Mexican Violence on the Number of Business Establishments on Southern US Border | 226 |

xii *Tables*

| | | |
|---|---|---|
| 13.1 | Mexico and US Descriptive Statistics (2008) | 237 |
| 13.2 | Mincer Wage Regressions: Equations (1) and (2) | 239 |
| 13.3 | Mean US-Mexico Wage Ratios, Corrected for Self-Selection: 2008 | 240 |

# Figures

| | | |
|---|---|---|
| 1.1 | Imports to the United States from various countries and regions. | 3 |
| 2.1 | North American power ratios and institutional homogeneity. | 24 |
| 5.1 | Evolution of mean and standard deviation of autocracy and democracy across human development country groups, 1970–2010. | 82 |
| 5.2 | When a group of countries undergoes a transition in $x$ through time, this can be observed in the $(\mu,\sigma)$ plane. | 87 |
| 12.1 | Trends in homicide rates along the Mexico-US border. | 215 |
| 13.1 | Mexican migration to the United States, yearly migrants as share of total population. | 233 |
| 13.2 | National income per capita, US-MEX ratio. | 234 |

# Contributors

**Arun K. Acharya,** Professor, Instituto de Investigaciones Sociales, Universidad Autónoma de Nuevo León, Monterrey, Mexico

**Ernesto Aguayo-Téllez,** Professor, Facultad de Economía, Universidad Autónoma de Nuevo León, Monterrey, Mexico

**Eva Olimpia Arceo-Gómez,** Assistant Professor, División de Economía, Centro de Investigación y Docencia Económicas, Mexico City, Mexico

**Nielan Barnes,** Associate Professor, Department of Sociology, California State University, Long Beach, USA

**Jane H. Bayes,** Professor, Department of Political Science, California State University, Northridge, USA

**Julián Castro-Rea,** Associate Professor, Department of Political Science, University of Alberta, Edmonton, Canada

**Roberto Domínguez,** Jean Monnet Fellow, Robert Schumann Center at the European University Institute, Florence, Italy and Associate Professor, Department of Government, Suffolk University, Boston, Massachusetts, USA

**Christina Gabriel,** Associate Professor, Department of Political Science, Carleton University, Ottawa, Ontario, Canada

**Raúl García Barrios,** Professor, Centro Regional de Investigaciones Multidisciplinarias, Universidad Nacional Autónoma de México, Cuernavaca, Mexico

**Gaspare M. Genna,** Associate Professor, Department of Political Science, The University of Texas at El Paso, USA

xvi  *Contributors*

**Guy H. Gessner,** Associate Professor, Department of Marketing/Information Systems, Canisius College, Buffalo, USA

**Laura Gonzalez,** Associate Researcher, Mid-Atlantic Addiction Research and Training Institute, Indiana University of Pennsylvania, Indiana, Pennsylvania, USA

**Laura Macdonald,** Professor, Department of Political Science, Carleton University, Ottawa, Ontario, Canada

**David A. Mayer-Foulkes,** Professor, División de Economía, Centro de Investigación y Docencia Económicas, Mexico City, Mexico

**Kimberly A. Nolan García,** Assistant Professor, Division de Estudios Internacionales, Centro de Investigación y Docencia Económicas, Mexico City, Mexico

**Emma R. Norman,** Professor, Department of International Relations, Alliant International University, Mexico City, Mexico

**Christian I. Rivera-Mendoza,** Graduate Student, Facultad de Economía, Universidad Autónoma de Nuevo León, Monterrey, Mexico

**Coral R. Snodgrass, Professor,** Department of Management, Canisius College, Buffalo, USA

**Rafael Velázquez,** Professor, Facultad de Economia y Relaciones Internacionales, Universidad Autonoma de Baja California, Tijuana, Mexico

# 1 Introduction

*Gaspare M. Genna and*
*David A. Mayer-Foulkes*

Little progress has been made between Canada, Mexico, and the United States in deepening regional integration since the implementation of the North American Free Trade Agreement (NAFTA) and the labor and environmental side agreements in 1994. This fact is contrasted by efforts in other regions around the world that at least speak to the desire to deepen cooperation in vital areas or regions that are actually increasing their levels of cooperation and interdependence. The lack of advancement among North American political leaders is not due to the lack of common problems facing the three countries. The continent still faces problems, that to date have been remedied unilaterally, leaving multilateral solutions the least utilized tools. Among the policy issues addressed in this book are two vital and, some would argue, interrelated policy areas—namely, migration and security. The chapters by scholars from all three North American countries explore the fundamental questions regarding cooperation in the region, and each recommends potential policy solutions based on an institutional analysis. They do so by examining the North American institutional void among the three partners concerning migration, security, and development. Some demonstrate that this void is sometimes filled by political forces while others speak to the dilemmas this void brings.

Regional integration is a process that merges the economies and political decision making of countries that neighbor one another. Examples outside of North America include the European Union, the Association of Southeast Asian Nations, the Economic Community of West African States, and the Common Southern Market. The degree of integration can take the form (from the lowest to the highest degree) of a free-trade area, a customs union, a common market, an economic union, and complete economic integration.[1] Each of these levels includes an agreed-upon merger of economies, but also associated levels of multilateral decision making. For example, in order for a product to move freely from one country to another, some regulatory coordination may be important. This can include issues related to the content of the product or how it was manufactured. Regulations are harmonized by either a specific treaty or through the establishment of multilateral agencies. Either way, there exists a multilateral settlement of important issues. These

## 2 Gaspare M. Genna and David A. Mayer-Foulkes

multilateral decisions increase in number and importance as we move up through the degrees of integration. The economic merging and multilateral political decision-making dimensions of integration occur simultaneously.

The political and economic perspective on which NAFTA was based, liberalization, was based on the belief that the lifting of restrictions on economic activity would itself produce solutions to a series of problems. For example, proponents of NAFTA argued that by bringing wealth and jobs to Mexico, free trade would stem the flow of undocumented workers to the United States. By moving investment into Mexico, manufacturing would increasingly absorb surplus labor. Labor mobility was therefore largely left out of the NAFTA agreement.[2] However, the economic benefits for Mexico have not created enough jobs, and Mexicans continue to travel to the United States in large numbers and under increasingly dangerous conditions, despite stronger US attempts to stem migration. Sizeable numbers of Mexicans are also traveling to Canada, many of them brought under the Canadian Seasonal Agricultural Workers Program (SAWP). Only the recent economic crisis in the United States has slowed down the migration flow.

The same philosophy was supposed to hold in the political arena. The political expression of special interest groups would serve as sufficient guide for the political process. In fact, the successful negotiation of NAFTA demonstrated the ability of the three governments to coordinate the preferences of their domestic constituencies.[3] However, the short-term spike in political and economic energy liberated by NAFTA has essentially run its course and new obstacles emerged for economic growth and political harmony. Issues such as security and migration require long-term perspectives and solutions, which tend to be hindered rather than furthered by special interest groups. These solutions require political leadership through effective institutions.

NAFTA itself was part of a broader policy of liberalization that began in the 1980s with Reagan and Thatcher. This broad movement for global free trade, investment, and deregulation coincided with China's introduction of market mechanisms in its economy in December 1978 and the fall of the Berlin Wall in 1989, and led to a resurgence of globalization whose depth and extent were unexpected. However, while imports from Mexico multiplied by 4.6 between 1994 and 2010 (the factor was 2.2 for Canada), the corresponding factor was 9.4 for China, which overtook Mexico as a US import partner in 2003 and Canada in 2009. Figure 1.1 shows US imports for these three countries as well as the newly industrialized countries (NICs), Europe, and the Organization of the Petroleum Exporting Countries (OPEC). While both Mexico and Canada both became much more important partners for the United States than the NICs, China approached the importance of Europe for the United States. What this meant was that, even in the presence of a considerable degree of free trade in North America, the overriding economic forces pulled away from North American integration, because of the essentially unanticipated strength of globalization (US imports multiplied by 2.9 between 1994 and 2010), in particular the

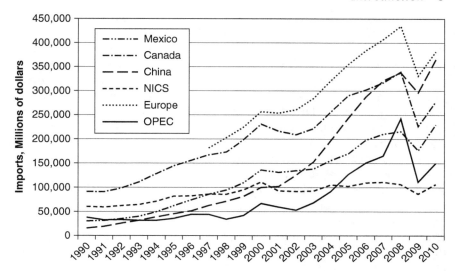

*Figure 1.1* Imports to the United States from various countries and regions.
*Source*: US Census Bureau, http://www.census.gov/foreign-trade/balance/.

strength of trade with China, all of which also contributed to the current unprecedented economic crisis in the United States. In a context in which policy priorities were defined according to large economic interests, one consequence of these economic trends was placing integration with Mexico and Canada on a back burner, each according to their own status quo.

Another unexpected change in the policy climate was that the issue of migration is no longer of purely economic concern. The terrorist attacks of September 11, 2001, shifted the political agenda of the North American region to one dominated by security issues and migration was no longer viewed as a pressing social problem. Like NAFTA, the meetings composing the Security and Prosperity Partnership of North America (SPP) do not contain discussion of the easement of labor mobility for migrants to the richer countries of the region. Instead the focus is on increased surveillance to detect illicit activity, such as smuggling of contraband and individuals associated with international terrorism. The noticeable avoidance of discussion on immigration, however, may still have a good deal to do with security. Some have concluded that a state's immigration and security policies are linked since policies that determine who can enter a country will affect the country's social, economic, and political stability, with the latter three forming the foundation of state security.[4] Therefore one conclusion that can be made is that stricter immigration policies, in both the United States and Canada regarding Mexican nationals, are also part of the increased emphasis on security. Migration is thus a critical and politicized issue, one that threatens to damage intergovernmental relationships and that may jeopardize the future of North American regional integration.

4  *Gaspare M. Genna and David A. Mayer-Foulkes*

Security issues, more recently combined with drug related violence,[5] thus further put integration, in particular with Mexico, under a negative light. Recently we have also seen a new wave of anti-immigration laws enacted in the United States. Arizona's SB 1070 is one example of an attempt to decentralize national law enforcement in an effort to maintain a strong unilateral policy against Mexican migration. Another US-related issue is repeated difficulties in passing the DREAM Act.[6] This legislation would allow children of undocumented immigrants to apply for permanent residency after the age of eighteen. Opponents to this law argue that it would delegitimize aspects of current immigration law and therefore condone criminal activity.

Of course tying migration, security, and development together with North American cooperation begs a simple yet relevant question: Why is there a need for the three countries to cooperate? North American cooperation is an expression of contemporary global trends that compel countries to join efforts in a strategic search for a better position in the world economy. The development of the European Union and the economic advances of China and India require a coherent policy for North America, especially for the United States, if it wishes to continue to play a leading role in world affairs. In a partnership with Canada and Mexico, the United States can better position itself competitively. This comes out of the benefits generated by economies of scale that can be realized by easing the barriers of the manufacturing supply chain. Also deeper cooperation can release underutilized labor and increase demand. If cooperative policies on migration and security reflect advantages for all three countries, then the United States will not be alone in reaping rewards. As a result, the destinies of Canada, Mexico, and the United States are tied. It is in the best interest of all parties involved to find a balance between their respective interests, instead of yielding to the priorities of the strongest partner, or yielding to strong economic interests that tend not to act in the best national interest of any of the countries. Unfortunately, immigration policy is often viewed and discussed as zero-sum competition among both high-skilled and low-skilled workers in the United States[7] and/or negatively impacting welfare policies.[8,9]

Why are the North American partners having trouble cooperating in these interlinked areas? A complete answer to this question would be quite complex because it would have to address not only the legacies of the three countries' joint and individual histories, but also the current social realities. Nevertheless, this book gives a coherent picture of the underlying difficulties in the process of integration. The authors find that beyond some level of economic integration, institutional development is essential for integration. The low levels of cooperation in solving the joint problems of migration, security, and development are due to inadequate or, in some cases, the sheer lack of institutions, tied to the lack of overriding, constructive policy agendas that move beyond the simplistic agenda of liberalization. While the institutional examination of regional cooperation is not new, the chapters in the book offer a detailed and current analysis that includes general perspectives on the determinants of integration, case studies of institutional building in contexts for which institutions are lacking, such as labor, migration, and health issues, and examples of economic and security issues that have and will continue to have an important bearing on integration.

What is meant by institutions and what importance do they have in explaining patterns of regional cooperation? March and Olsen define institutions in broad terms by stating that they are the norms, rules, understandings, and routines found in society.[10] Scott defines institutions as structures and activities that provide meaning to social behavior.[11] Institutions, therefore, reflect society's preferences through these structures. Different types of institutions would also influence behavior.[12] This way of conceptualizing institutions produces the following observations. First, societies that lack institutions experience a void in efficient decision making, lacking structures with which political groups can articulate and aggregate preferences and debate potential solutions. Also the lack of institutions would indicate that there is a lack of consensus on legitimate rules or norms. In the case of North America, the lack of continental or trilateral institutions speaks to the lack of legitimacy regarding migration, security, and development as a common set of problems in need of common solutions.

Second, inefficient institutions lead to suboptimal outcomes. If institutions allow only a subset of preferences to be expressed, then societies will not consider all of the potential solutions available. This can be the case in situations in which there are strong national institutions but weak regional ones. Without continental institutions, we see the lack of a venue where state leaders can negotiate with each other and supply regional solutions using the preferences of domestic constituencies.[13] The result is the desire for each actor to seek out solutions that would benefit it while potentially ignoring the nonzero-sum solutions. Zero-sum solutions come about because there are poor conduits for the exchange of information across countries, but strong conduits of information within countries that reinforce unilateral policies.

Last, we should also consider institutionalization. This is the process of creating values and cognitive frames.[14] If institutions are lacking or if the available institutions are inefficient, the simple remedy is to create them. Of course this is easier said than done. Institutionalization requires a foundation of shared values. These values would include ideas associated with identity and procedure. Identity is important because it creates the boundaries of who can and cannot participate in institutionalization. Procedure is closely related to identity because it speaks to institutional jurisdiction: who has the right to make decisions and at what level of governance?

The book is divided into three sections. The first section discusses the determinants of integration. As discussed earlier, these turn out to be institutional characteristics of the three countries involved. The different chapters corroborate the importance of institutions, underline the role of differences across the political spectrum, examine the role of basic rights, and point to the importance of such institutions as democracy. The second section gives

## 6 Gaspare M. Genna and David A. Mayer-Foulkes

examples of institutional building in contexts for which institutions are lacking, specifically labor, migration, and health issues. The third section gives examples of economic and security issues that have an important bearing on integration, such as overall security arrangements, trade, drug-related violence, and the continuing wage gap among the countries. The three sections together give a broad, coherent picture of the current, multifaceted process of integration, and of the level of cooperation in North America. One of the features that emerges is a much faster pace of integration between the United States and Canada, contrasted with a slower one with Mexico.

Institutional and economic differences with Mexico appear hard to bridge. But an important aspect of policy becomes apparent. Current integration efforts, based on NAFTA, have emphasized economic policy. Born as NAFTA was in a period of market policies, these efforts have not been strongly supported by complementary public policies. Put together, the various authors show that such complementary public policies not only are necessary but also could yield promising results.

The first section of the book examines the determinants of integration. Gaspare M. Genna examines where North America sits in the overall picture of regional integration worldwide. He examines two variables that explain the level of regional integration, homogeneity of domestic institutions, and economic asymmetry. He finds that regional integration and homogeneity of domestic institutions mutually promote each other. Thus, while low levels of institutional homogeneity serve to explain the current low level of North American cooperation, including institutional compatibility in the international agenda can promote a virtuous cycle towards integration. In sum, Genna's chapter serves to show that there is a broad scope for public policy in promoting the homogenization of institutions across North America that will yield benefits in integration.

Castro-Rea argues that the uneven actions regarding North American integration are mostly due to the inherent contradictions of conservatism, an ideology that combines market goals with nonnegotiable social concerns, such as hypernationalism and xenophobia. These ideas are borne out of the domestic political struggles and as a result provide critical disincentives for cooperation. This is another example of how stronger national institutions prevent an institutionalization of trilateral norms.

Norman discusses Hannah Arendt's notion of superfluousness and her critique of human rights. Given that human rights are generally guaranteed by a state, the lack of transnational or supranational institutions dealing with labor mobility in North America effectively leaves undocumented workers as "stateless people." Therefore any rights afforded to them are at the mercy of national institutions in which the undocumented have no voice. The lack of an identity required to have a say in laws that affect them renders these people as superfluous. The chapter uses Arizona's SB 1070 to demonstrate how undocumented workers play this role in the domestic politics of a country as special interests wish to further strip their rights.

*Introduction* 7

García-Barrios and Mayer-Foulkes discuss the economic paradigms that are available to advance democracy and development in Mexico. In particular they discuss neoclassical, Keynesian, and Marxist economics as well as the modern theory of economic growth. They discuss a hierarchical ethical perspective that distinguishes between ethical levels: E0 indicates no ethical level (typical of an abusive government); E1 indicates individual rights and Pareto efficiency (typical of a market economy); E2 indicates individual rights and pursuit of equality; and E3 indicates a nonutilitarian E2 including extensive human rights and community values. By recognizing that general equilibrium is unstable, they are able to synthesize the economic paradigms and reach the following conclusions. First, economic liberalization is not enough to promote economic growth and development. It needs to be complemented with government policies making technological change, human capital accumulation, urbanization, and economic equality available for all. Second, democracy is essential for effective economic policy, but difficult to achieve. This is especially so when emerging from an authoritarian status quo. The basic lines of power that have run from top to bottom need to run from the bottom to the top. Third, ethical governance, based on a strengthened, participative democracy, is essential for an egalitarian Mexico, and essential for its economic development. As is discussed in this book, institutional improvements in the three North American countries are essential ingredients of integration.

The second section of the book gives detailed examples of institutional building in contexts in which institutions are lacking—for example, effective rights—and in which local actors get involved in remedying the situation. This process would be more effective in the presence of concerted institutional building promoted by the three governments.

Nolan García examines the US-Mexico cooperation in the area of labor, as it originated with the signing of the NAFTA labor side agreement. She argues that cooperation has diminished over time since then. By examining the roles civil society and labor unions have had in this diminishment, she provides implications on the effect it will have on migration policy. As Nolan García points out, complementary policies to NAFTA such as cooperation in the area of labor have not turned out to be sufficiently well structured, with cooperation in this area diminishing over time.

Turning to a guest worker program allowed by NAFTA, Gabriel and Macdonald look at the role nonstate actors in four Canadian cities have played in promoting and upholding migrant workers' access to social rights. They argue that access to Canadian welfare benefits are circumscribed by the SAWP, but obtaining them is difficult given the structural conditions of their employment. As a result, these conditions provide workers disincentives to access social rights and instead lead to their exploitation. Therefore immigrant advocacy groups create institutions in order to fill a need not supplied due to the lack of effective Canadian institutions. Gabriel and Macdonald go further when they demonstrate that the lack of effective domestic institutions

## 8   Gaspare M. Genna and David A. Mayer-Foulkes

requires additional state and nonstate action in promoting and upholding migrant workers' rights.

In contrast, Bayes and Gonzalez analyze the *Consejo Consultivo del Instituto de los Mexicanos en el Exterior*, a Mexican government-funded initiative designed to organize and service the Mexican diaspora in the United States and Canada. In response to demands by migrant communities, the home country established an institution to promote interregional advocacy in all three countries, one that has subsequently spawned other independent community-based grassroots organizations in both Canada and the United States. The authors focus on how transnational citizens negotiate their dual identities and loyalties, and creativity in addressing health, education, and business service problems related to migrants, and find that these efforts have tended to expand horizons and networks, helping to unite and construct the communities.

Institutional development is also required with regard to health care. Mexican migrants to the United States are often left without adequate health care given their low-income status and the lack of an universal US health care system. Nielan Barnes explores how the adoption of the Patient Protection and Affordable Care Act of 2010 (PPACA) would address this problem. Assuming that the PPACA will survive the numerous court challenges, it can help noninsured immigrants by requiring employers to provide health insurance and expand local and federal assistance to this population.

The last section of the book examines economic and security issues that have an important impact on integration. Security has become an overriding concern for integration. Dominguez and Velazquez examine the institutionalization of the three partners' security arrangements. They argue that the understanding of security in North America should include the regional and bilateral levels of analysis, because the different arrangements reflect how the interests and security concerns of the three countries vary. They conclude that while the institutionalization of economic interdependence is moving forward, North America is not producing similar actions on the security front due to differing security cultures. Without a trilateral institutionalization of a security agreement, economic interdependence may not deepen.

Security has an everyday impact on trade. The chapter authored by Snodgrass and Gessner analyzes the interaction of trade and security on the Canada-US border. Once touted as the largest unprotected land border in the world, this border has witnessed greater barriers for the movement of goods and in some cases services. The unilateral action associated with the "thickening" of this border requires the buyers and sellers in the links of the supply chains that support this massive movement of goods and services to make new decisions and calculations. Firms are required to react and transform business practices, especially on the Canadian side, due to the lack of transnational institutions that could include greater input from stakeholders.

While the United States and Canada are very concerned with the impact of terrorism on security, the narco war that has resulted from the unenforced criminalization of drug consumption in the United States has had a

*Introduction* 9

huge impact on security in Mexico. Arceo-Gómez's chapter looks at the impact of the escalating violence associated with Calderón's war on drug trafficking. This is an example of how the ineffectiveness of national institutions produces policy concerns for regional partners. The increase in violence has promoted the exodus of Mexicans who do not fit the usual migrant's demographic. Instead, current patterns of migration include more middle-class entrepreneurs, who also bring with them similar or, in many cases, the same businesses they established in their home cities.

Finally, the last chapter notes that the economic pressures for migration will continue to be an important driver of economic relations in North America. Aguayo-Téllez, Acharya, and Rivera-Mendoza's chapter corroborates that wage differences between Mexico and the United States continue to be very high, pointing to lower-than-expected results from NAFTA. Since the wage differences have not diminished, the agreement did not lead to a reduction in migration. They look at the wage gap experienced by Mexican workers seeking employment in the United States. Their findings show that, on average, Mexican-born workers in the United States with no schooling earn about seven times more than their Mexican counterparts. The gap descends with schooling and for women, recently arrived, non-citizen and non-English speaking migrants. Within the US-Mexico border region, wage differentials are smaller for all migrants. Thus even in the economic sphere policies oriented exclusively to markets have not yielded the desired fruits.

The research in this volume was supported by several sources. Participants benefited from a joint grant awarded by the three North American governments under the North American Mobility Program in Higher Education, which seeks to exchange knowledge among university faculty and students in order to build a North American community.[15] The grant helped create a consortium titled, "Beyond Borders: Migration, Security and Cooperation in North America."[16] Those participants wish to thank Human Resources and Social Development Canada, *Dirección de Desarollo Universitario (Secretaría de Educación Pública, México)*, and the Fund for the Improvement of Postsecondary Education (US Department of Education). The authors presented their initial research at the Access, Boundaries, and Cooperation: The ABC's of North American Security colloquium held at Florida International University, which was funded with the assistance of the government of Canada. The editors wish to thank David Twigg and Hector Cadavid of the Jack D. Gordon Institute for Public Policy and Citizenship Studies for producing this successful workshop.

## NOTES

1. B. Balassa, *The Theory of Economic Integration* (Homewood, IL: Richard D. Irwin, 1961).

## 10  *Gaspare M. Genna and David A. Mayer-Foulkes*

2. Except for chapter 6, which created visa provisions for some categories of business people and highly skilled workers.
3. Frederick W. Mayer, *Interpreting NAFTA: The Science and Art of Political Analysis* (New York: Columbia University Press, 1998).
4. Christopher Rudolph, "Security and the Political Economy of International Migration," *American Political Science Review* 97, no. 4 (2003) pp 603–620.
5. Strong economic interests also lie behind these anti-immigration laws and the drug war. Miron and Waldock (2010) estimate drug consumption in the United States at $121 billion dollars in 2010. UNINCB (2011) estimates the income of Mexican drug cartels at about $14 billion dollars. Sullivan (2010) documents the role of the US prison lobby in promoting the Arizona SB 1070 anti-immigration law.
6. Development, Relief and Education for Alien Minors Act.
7. J. Hainmueller and M.J. Hiscox, "Attitudes towards Highly Skilled and Low-Skilled Immigration: Evidence from a Survey Experiment," *American Political Science Review* 104, no. 1 (2010) pp 61–84.
8. R. Hero and R. Preuhs, "Immigration and the Evolving American Welfare State: Examining Policies in the US States," *American Journal of Political Science* 51, no. 3 (2007) pp 498–517.
9. P. Nannestad, "Immigration and Welfare States: A Survey of 15 Years of Research," *European Journal of Political Economy* 23, no. 2 (2007) pp 512–532.
10. James G. March and Johan P. Olsen, "The New Institutionalism: Organizational Factors in Political Life," *American Political Science Review* 78 (1984) pp 734–749.
11. W. Richard Scott, *Institutions and Organizations* (Thousand Oaks, CA: SAGE, 1995).
12. March and Olsen, "New Institutionalism."
13. Andrew Moravcsik, *The Choice for Europe: Social Purpose and State Power from Messina to Maastricht* (Ithaca, NY: Cornell University Press, 1998); Robert Putnam, "Diplomacy and Domestic Politics: The Logic of Two-Level Games," *International Organization* 42 (1988) p 427.
14. B. Guy Peters, *Institutional Theory in Political Science: The New Institutionalism* (London: Pinter, 1999).
15. US Department of Education Grant, Fund for the Improvement of Postsecondary Education, #P116N080010.
16. Carleton University, the University of Alberta, the University of Texas at El Paso, Florida International University, *Centro de Investigación y Docencia Económicas*, and *Universidad Autónoma de Nuevo León*.

## REFERENCES

Balassa, B. *The Theory of Economic Integration*. Homewood, IL: Richard D. Irwin, 1961.

Hainmueller, J., and M.J. Hiscox. "Attitudes towards Highly Skilled and Low-Skilled Immigration: Evidence from a Survey Experiment." *American Political Science Review* 104, no. 1 (2010) pp 61–84.

Hero, R., and R. Preuhs. "Immigration and the Evolving American Welfare State: Examining Policies in the US States." *American Journal of Political Science* 51, no. 3 (2007) pp 498–517.

March, James G., and Johan P. Olsen. "The New Institutionalism: Organizational Factors in Political Life." *American Political Science Review* 78, no. 3 (1984) pp 734–749.

Mayer, Frederick W. *Interpreting NAFTA: the Science and Art of Political Analysis*. New York: Columbia University Press, 1998.

Miron, Jeffrey A., and Katherine Waldock. "The Budgetary Impact of Ending Drug Prohibition." Cato Institute. Washington, DC. 2010. http://www.cato.org/pubs/wtpapers/DrugProhibitionWP.pdf.

Moravcsik, Andrew. *The Choice for Europe: Social Purpose and State Power from Messina to Maastricht.* Ithaca, NY: Cornell University Press, 1998.

Nannestad, P. "Immigration and Welfare States: A Survey of 15 Years of Research." *European Journal of Political Economy* 23, no. 2 (2007) pp 512–532.

Peters, B. Guy. *Institutional Theory in Political Science: The New Institutionalism.* London: Pinter, 1999.

Putnam, Robert. "Diplomacy and Domestic Politics: The Logic of Two-Level Games." *International Organization* 42 (1988) pp 427–460.

Rudolph, C. "Security and the Political Economy of International Migration." *American Political Science Review* 97, no. 4. (2003) pp 603–620.

Scott, W. Richard. *Institutions and Organizations.* Thousand Oaks, CA: SAGE, 1995.

Sullivan, Laura. "Prison Economics Help Drive Ariz. Immigration Law." National Public Radio. October 28, 2010, http://www.npr.org/2010/10/28/130833741/prison-economics-help-drive-ariz-immigration-law.

United Nations International Narcotics Control Board (UNINCB). *Report of the International Narcotics Control Board for 2010.* Vienna, Austria: United Nations, 2011, http://www.incb.org/documents/Publications/AnnualReports/AR2010/AR_2010_English.pdf.

# Part I
# Determinants of Integration

# 2 What Will It Take to Build a North American Community?

*Gaspare M. Genna*

## INTRODUCTION

Why is it important to assess North America's integration potential? Regional integration is one method countries use to solve commonly held problems. In North America, many of the issues and problems among the three countries boil down to migration, security, and development. Migration, security, and development are interrelated problems because they have in common the quest for stable economic and political environments where individuals' and states' objectives can be realized. Individuals will choose to exit when they perceive the lack of economic opportunities and/or physical security in their home countries and believe that there are ample quantities of these two items in a neighboring country.[1] Countries seek to control immigration in order to maximize security and development in their countries.[2] Political development also helps in the area of security by reducing the likelihood of civil conflict[3] and external threats.[4] Economic development reduces the likelihood that individuals will seek the exit strategy. It also increases the likelihood that states will experience domestic stability and favorable relations with neighboring countries. Economic development, therefore, becomes the linchpin in solving the associated problems of migration and security. Political leaders can develop policies, laws, and regulations to solve these problems unilaterally. Another approach is to develop solutions in a trilateral manner. The aim of this chapter is to assess the probability of increasing trilateral cooperation.

If the three partners do not view the migration-security-development issue as a common problem, then North America will lack a unified strategy and a set of effective institutions to solve these problems. As was argued in the introduction, North America will persist in having an institutional void. However, the three North American partners can view them as a common problem and thereby conceptualize solutions as collective goods because benefits are spread to all those involved, although not necessarily equally. Collective goods are achieved through collective action, which is often difficult to carry out.[5] What are the main problems for achieving collective action and what form would this action take? Although there are many views

## 16 *Gaspare M. Genna*

associated with the collective action problem,[6] I will focus on transaction costs and uncertainty with attention on how homogeneity and power asymmetries among countries will lower them.

Transaction costs are costs borne by individuals when they operate in a foreign political and economic environment. Differences between the home and foreign environment increase costs due to the need to adjust in the new environment. In addition to increased transaction costs, individuals have greater uncertainty for success since they will be departing from what is known to what is unknown. Transaction costs and uncertainty can discourage individuals from integrating regionally. The lowering of the levels of these variables can result from homogeneity because of the effect on compatibility. In order to assess North America's current and future state of integration, it is important to examine the compatibility of the three partners in light of transaction costs and uncertainty.

Collective action can take the form of regional integration. Regional integration is the establishment of collective decision making among states for the intention of establishing and regulating market flows.[7] Market flows are the entries and exits of the factors of production (except land), as well as goods and services. The degree of integration refers to the degree of collective decision making. At one end is an intergovernmental arrangement in which states make common decisions but are autonomous in regulating those decisions. If a regional authority does exist, it serves at the pleasure of the individual states. On the opposite end is the supranational arrangement, in which regional institutions do exist and make decisions alongside intergovernmental arrangements or supersede member states' authority.

The possibility of solving the problems of migration, security, and uneven development in North America through regional integration requires us to first discover the general conditions under which integration develops. The optimal conditions, I will argue, are regional leadership and homogeneity. After making the argument and testing if homogeneity and regional leadership do promote integration, I assess North American integration today and then examine what conditions are needed for various levels of integration. The final step is to analyze the likelihood of homogeneity in the North American context.

## CONDITIONS OF REGIONAL INTEGRATION

The literature provides several important variables for explaining the levels of integration. The power theories indicate that an asymmetric distribution of power produces a more favorable condition for integration than a grouping of similarly powerful countries.[8] This is due to the ability of the preponderant power to coordinate efforts and distribute incentives to other members. In other words, the region must include a capable leader.

*What Will It Take to Build a North American Community?* 17

The coordination of efforts begins with negotiating treaties and continues with treaty implementation and amendments. The attainment of a collective good, like regional integration, requires partners to come together and negotiate terms. Although all actors will recognize the need for the collective good, they may not wish to accept the cost of organizing the negotiations for several reasons. The actor may not have the resources to participate in negotiations and may therefore need a partner to assume the initial cost. In addition, some actors may perceive an asymmetrical distribution of the collective good's potential benefits. With this perception, they may not wish to assume the costs of coordinating the negotiations. Therefore, a regional leader that is willing and capable would overcome these barriers by assuming the initial costs of coordination.

A regional leader's capabilities would also be useful in providing incentives in the bargaining process. These incentives can be directly or indirectly associated with the regional integration negotiations. The direct incentives can include asymmetric concessions during the bargaining process. For example, a regional leader may agree to delay the timing of implementing parts of a treaty in order to alleviate concerns that potential benefits will be asymmetric. The regional leader can do this given its larger economy and therefore its ability to absorb asymmetric treaty implementation. Indirect incentives involve side terms that directly influence the terms of negotiations but are outside the treaty. The regional leader can promise developmental aid in exchange for a concession.

The need for a regional leader is also necessary in treaty implementation and amendment. Free riders may appear in the implementation process. These would be partners that may not be able or, politically, may not want to implement agreements after ratification. A regional leader would be one that would have the resources to effectively prevent or change a free rider's behavior. If the behavior is unintentional, as is often the case, then the leader can provide aid or coordinate efforts among the other partners to provide aid. If the behavior is intentional, the leader can enforce sanctions either on its own or through coordination with other partners. A regional leader's role in amending agreements would follow the same logic as in the production of the initial agreement(s).

Next is the compatibility of countries. Having a powerful regional leader alone cannot help the development of integration if there are wide preferences leading to irresoluble disagreements.[9] Although the powerful country could force preferences on others in the region, the outcome would resemble an empire rather than a voluntary association of countries. In order to form a cohesive unit, political and economic environments must be similar in order to reduce transaction costs[10] and reduce uncertainty. Without compatibility, individuals will assume a cost of having to adjust to new partnerships and have greater uncertainty that the new partnerships will be successful. Therefore, individuals would prefer that regional integration develop between compatible actors so that the costs are low. This explanation follows

## 18  *Gaspare M. Genna*

theories involving interactions between domestic groups and the interests represented in government policies.[11]

Homogeneity can deepen integration for two reasons. One is the perceived reduction of the costs and uncertainties due to the effects that identity politics has on cooperation. Prior research demonstrates that countries that have a similar political identity also have similar policy preferences.[12] Institutions can be defined as the set of rules and procedures that are deemed appropriate by the political leaders.[13] Given this definition, individuals are assumed to make decisions based on institutionalized values.[14] Since values are closely related to the economic development of a country, research has empirically demonstrated a close association between economic development, values, and institutional preferences.[15] Similar institutions breed ideological similarities since they share a "co-evolutionary process."[16] Norms and institutions reinforce one another, and therefore a country's institutions are viewed as the expected expression of their norms.[17] Similar institutions and levels of development, therefore, will correlate with similar preferences.

The identity factor also provides a decision-making shortcut that would facilitate cooperation because it greatly simplifies a rather complex set of cognitive processes. Research into the dynamics of in-group and out-group behavior has shown that cooperation is easier among those that share an identity than those that do not.[18] Simply being viewed as "one of us" will elicit the type of cooperation that would also include resource allocations.[19] This holds not only for individuals, but for states as well. For example, Werner and Lemke[20] demonstrate that alliances are more likely among similar countries. With a similar identity, actors believe that cooperation is easier due to lower transaction costs.

Another reason that similar institutions can improve the deepening of integration is based on material concerns. Individuals are faced with an important reality: there is one set of factors in life that they can control and then there are those that they cannot. Controllable factors are inward and include only those in their immediate environments. Uncontrollable factors are external. What is and is not controllable varies among individuals, but I assume that issues in the national political and economic realms are outside the control of any one individual. When institutions vary greatly from what an individual is accustomed to, then adjustment costs are needed and uncertainty regarding outcomes increases. Adjustment costs can involve acquiring new information about and adaptation to the new circumstances. Uncertainty about the outcomes can involve the likelihood or degree of success. Also, uncertainty can involve the degree of fair play.

Take the case of entrepreneurs. They have control within their firms and operations. Such factors include personnel, marketing, physical operations, etc. Uncontrollable factors are found outside the firm. These include the political, economic, and social factors of a country. For example, a firm cannot control the economic climate at any given time. Also, it cannot control the

## What Will It Take to Build a North American Community? 19

institutional arrangement of a foreign country. There have been examples of large firms influencing regulations, especially in small countries, but most firms in general can at best lobby for their preferences at the margin. They are not assumed to have the ability to produce revolutionary institutional change in a given country. As a result, firms are less likely to demand regional integration with neighbors that do not have similar institutions because needing to adapt to new environments introduces greater costs and uncertainty. Firms instead would either demand regional integration with neighbors that are similar or attempt to change institutions to match their home institutions.

In sum, power preponderance and compatibility are the main conditions associated with the deepening of regional integration. A regional leader is needed for guiding the processes, using available capabilities. Compatibility promotes the idea that states are similar enough in either perceived or material terms not to add additional transaction costs nor increase uncertainty.

### HYPOTHESIS TESTING

I test the hypotheses using a time series linear regression technique that assumes correlated panels. Since such data properties produce inaccurate standard errors, a correction method is used.[21] AR(1) autocorrelation is assumed and the unit of analysis is the regional integration organization during 1975–2004. The time period is bounded by data availability. The variables measuring power preponderance and institutional homogeneity are lagged by five years given the hypothesized direction of association.[22] Five-year lags were chosen in order to reduce endogeneity problems, to work with some data issues (see ahead), and to focus on a long-term examination. Control variables (see ahead) are lagged by one year while regional dummy variables are not lagged. The remainder of this section describes the variables used in the model with the following specifications:

$$Level\ of\ Integration_t = \alpha_1 + \gamma_1 Power\ Preponderance_{t\text{-}5} + \gamma_2 Homogeneity_{t\text{-}5} + \gamma_n Controls_{t\text{-}1} + \gamma_m Regional\ Dummies_t + \varepsilon_t$$

The operationalization of regional integration is a systematic coding so that the analysis can distinguish varying levels while still comparing similar attributes. This is done by using a multidimensional measurement referred to as the integration achievement score (IAS), which was first developed by Hufbauer and Schott[23] and later refined and applied by Efird and Genna.[24] It gauges the level of regional integration by looking at six categories commonly attributable to regionalism: (1) trade in goods and services, (2) degree of capital mobility, (3) degree of labor mobility, (4) level of supranational institution importance, (5) degree of monetary policy coordination, and (6) degree of fiscal policy coordination. Each of the six categories is also

20   *Gaspare M. Genna*

broken down into five levels along a Guttman scale. The measure is an equal weighted average of the six categories. The potential range of the score is from zero to five. Zero represents no formal regional integration in place, and five represents a complete merger of markets, including all economic factors, and political decision making.

Power preponderance is relatively simple to operationalize using GDP data (in constant US dollars) from the World Development Indicators.[25] I calculate the variable by dividing the GDP of the largest economy by the sum of the GDPs of all remaining members.

I operationalize institutional homogeneity two ways. The first uses a measurement of economic institutions, the Economic Freedom of the World (EFW) index.[26] EFW index includes (1) size of government (expenditures, taxes, and enterprises), (2) legal structure and security of property rights, (3) access to sound money, (4) freedom to trade internationally, and (5) regulation of credit, labor, and businesses. Since item four is a proxy for regional integration, it was removed from the index. The data are yearly starting from 2000. Prior to 2000, the data are reported in five-year intervals beginning in 1975. The gaps in time were filled by interpolating averages, but recall that panel error correlation and AR(1) will be used. If a country experienced an extraordinary change in regime or other social, political, and economic instability during the five-year gap, it was coded as missing. I summed the index value for each regional integration organization member and calculated the standard deviation. Since larger standard deviation translates to greater institutional *heterogeneity*, the values were multiplied by negative one. Further, I added one to each value so that the maximum value is one instead of zero, and thereby aiding in the interpretation of the results. The range is −0.566 to 1, with larger values translating to larger levels of institutional homogeneity.

The second homogeneity method uses the Human Development Index (HDI) created by the United Nations Development Programme.[27] HDI measures a country's level of development using indicators of health, education, and living standards. Homogeneity in HDI is an indicator of how similar countries are regarding values and approaches to problems they individually face. The HDI homogeneity measurement is calculated like the measure for EFW homogeneity: the standard deviation of the regional integration organization's HDI values were multiplied by negative one and then added to one in order to create a range in which higher values indicate greater levels of homogeneity. The range for the transformed HDI standard deviation is 0.504 to 0.995.

Table 2.1 displays the values of the integration achievement score and the primary explanatory variables (power preponderance and the two homogeneity variables) for select cases of regional integration organizations in 2004.[28] The Gulf Cooperation Council (GCC; Bahrain, Kuwait, Oman, Qatar, Saudi Arabia, and United Arab Emirates) has the highest integration score among the selected cases, and the Association of Southeast Asian

*What Will It Take to Build a North American Community?*   21

Nations (ASEAN; Brunei, Cambodia, Indonesia, Laos, Malaysia, Myanmar, the Philippines, Singapore, Thailand, and Vietnam) has the lowest score. The GCC integration score is higher because it has formed a customs union (free trade among members and a common external tariff); it allows full capital mobility among its members except for large-scale mergers and acquisitions; citizens of member countries can transfer professional qualifications; the regional institutions gather information and have an advisory role for the organization's principal decision-making body; and they have a formal commitment to maintain a fixed exchange rate system.

Table 2.1 also displays the economic power ratios and transformed EFW index and HDI standard deviations. The North American Free Trade Agreement (NAFTA) is the organization with the largest power asymmetry, since the US economy is approximately seven times larger than Canada's and Mexico's economies combined. The smallest asymmetry is found in ASEAN (Indonesia's economy is approximately half as large as the remaining countries combined). The greatest institutional homogeneity is found among the members of the GCC and the least is found in ASEAN. NAFTA is in the middle with a value close to zero for EFW homogeneity, but higher for HDI homogeneity.

The data analysis also includes the following control variables. The first is the presence of an ongoing crisis between members of the regional integration association. Intuitively, one would suspect that integration would not deepen under such circumstances. The data come from the International Crisis Behavior data set.[29] The variable has a value of zero for the absence

*Table 2.1*   Variable Values for Select Cases of Regional Integration Organizations (2004)

| Regional integration organization | Integration score | Power reponderance | EFW Index SD (transformed) | HDI SD (transformed) |
| --- | --- | --- | --- | --- |
| North American Free Trade Agreement | 1.67 | 6.96 | 0.008 | 0.931 |
| Common Market for Eastern and Southern Africa | 1.67 | 0.799 | −0.124 | 0.866 |
| Common Southern Market (MERCOSUR) | 1.33 | 3.75 | 0.569 | 0.938 |
| Association of Southeast Asian Nations | 0.667 | 0.491 | −0.488 | 0.876 |
| Gulf Cooperation Council | 2.50 | 1.12 | 0.846 | 0.965 |

## 22   *Gaspare M. Genna*

of an ongoing crisis and one otherwise. The second control, which is also found in the International Crisis Behavior dataset, is the presence of a new crisis during the year. Like an ongoing crisis, a new crisis may threaten current or future integration efforts. The variable has a value of zero for no new crisis and one otherwise. The age of the regional integration organization is also included because older organizations are more likely to have deeper integration. Integration may deepen due to the political will or persistent effort. The number of members is also included. Larger memberships may encounter greater collective action problems, which makes coordination among member states challenging. Finally, regions could possess specific attributes that may influence the level of integration. I include regional dummy variables for Europe, the Americas,[30] the Middle East, and Africa. Asia is the baseline region.

## RESULTS

The regression model estimates the relationship of regional integration around the world with power asymmetry and homogeneity while controlling for other factors. Overall the results support the hypotheses.

Table 2.2 presents the estimation results using the EFW homogeneity measurement. The model supports the hypothesis that a regional leader and homogeneity among members are positively associated with the level of integration. If the regional leader is *as large as* all other member states combined (a ratio equal to one) then the level of integration is small. At the maximum value of the power preponderance variable found in the data (~11), the effect would be 0.67. At the smallest value of preponderance found in the data (~0.17), the effect would be almost nonexistent (0.0104). EFW homogeneity also has statistically significant explanatory power. From the variable's lowest value to its highest value, the level of integration increases from –0.413 to 0.729.

Table 2.3 presents the estimation results using the HDI homogeneity measurement. We again see support for the hypothesis that a regional leader and homogeneity among members are positively associated with the level of integration. If the regional leader is as large as all other members combined (a ratio equal to one) then the level of integration is small. The effect would be 0.20 at the maximum value of the power preponderance, while it is almost nonexistent (0.0003) at the smallest value of preponderance. From the variable's lowest value to its highest value, the level of integration increases from 0.485 to 0.958.

Among the control variables, the organization's age and membership size as well as its geographic location are consistently significant in explaining the level of the regional integration in the two models. An ongoing crisis is significant in the EFW model, but not the HDI model. A new crisis is not statistically significant in either model.

## What Will It Take to Build a North American Community? 23

*Table 2.2* Time Series (AR1) Regression with Correlated Panels Corrected Standard Errors

|  | $IAS_t$ | Standard error |
|---|---|---|
| Power preponderance$_{t-5}$ | 0.036*** | 0.009 |
| EFW Index, standard deviation$_{t-5}$ | 0.126** | 0.048 |
| *Controls* | | |
| ICB on going crisis$_{t-1}$ | −0.036* | 0.019 |
| ICB new crisis$_{t-1}$ | −0.021 | 0.015 |
| Regional organization age$_{t-1}$ | 0.027*** | 0.003 |
| Regional organization membership size$_{t-1}$ | −0.014*** | 0.003 |
| Europe | 1.37*** | 0.108 |
| The Americas | 0.879*** | 0.061 |
| Middle East | 0.831*** | 0.162 |
| Africa | 0.449*** | 0.106 |
| Constant | 0.172* | 0.076 |
| Observations | 390 | |
| $R^2$ | 0.517 | |

*Note*: *** $p < 0.000$; ** $p < 0.01$; * $p < 0.05$; the EFW standard deviation variable was transformed (the negative of the standard deviation plus one) so that the indices now measure institutional homogeneity using the EFW index.

*Table 2.3* Time Series (AR1) Regression with Correlated Panels Corrected Standard Errors

|  | $IAS_t$ | Standard error |
|---|---|---|
| Power preponderance$_{t-5}$ | 0.018* | 0.008 |
| HDI, standard deviation$_{t-5}$ | 0.963** | 0.346 |
| *Controls* | | |
| ICB ongoing crisis$_{t-1}$ | −0.033 | 0.018 |
| ICB new crisis$_{t-1}$ | −0.018 | 0.013 |
| Regional organization age$_{t-1}$ | 0.025*** | 0.003 |
| Regional organization membership size$_{t-1}$ | −0.011** | 0.003 |
| Europe | 1.29*** | 0.144 |
| The Americas | 0.848*** | 0.099 |
| Middle East | 0.748*** | 0.199 |
| Africa | 0.400** | 0.141 |
| Constant | −0.616* | 0.293 |
| Observations | 390 | |
| $R^2$ | 0.416 | |

*Note*: *** $p < 0.000$; ** $p < 0.01$; * $p < 0.05$; the UNDP standard deviation variable was transformed (the negative of the standard deviation plus one) so that the indices now measure institutional homogeneity using the HDI.

## IMPLICATIONS FOR NORTH AMERICAN INTEGRATION

The prior section indicates that the optimal conditions for regional integration to develop are the presence of a preponderant power and homogeneity among the members. The model demonstrates that the larger the GDP ratios (between the regional leader and the sum of all other members), the greater the regional integration score. The necessary condition of homogeneity was also demonstrated by the findings. Recall that these tests demonstrate a *general relationship* and not one that is exclusive to North America. Assuming that North American integration is not unique and is therefore comparable to all other cases, the general results give us an opportunity to see how North America compares with all other cases of regional integration. From this comparison, it becomes possible to make recommendations for deepening integration. The next step is to examine the estimated model in the North American case.

One of the key variables, power asymmetry, is clearly present in the region. The GDP ratio between the United States and Canada during 1989–1993, under the Canada-US Free Trade Agreement, was between 9.8 and 10.8. After the implementation of NAFTA in 1994, the ratio between the United States and the other two partners varies between 6.8 and 8.4 (see Figure 2.1). The data indicates a fairly wide variation in the homogeneity variables. NAFTA's EFW homogeneity values range from −0.169 to 0.809, and the HDI values range from 0.913 to 0.995 (see Figure 2.1). This section will examine the effect that the two homogeneity variables have on North American cooperation.

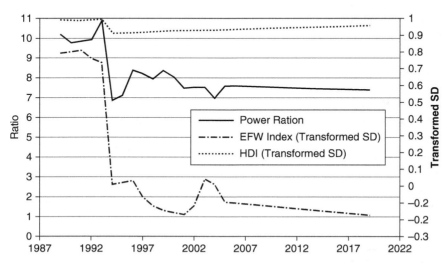

*Figure 2.1* North American power ratios and institutional homogeneity.

*What Will It Take to Build a North American Community?* 25

*Table 2.4* North American Integration Scenarios

| Scenarios | Integration score |
| --- | --- |
| 2004 (EFW; HDI) | 1.57; 1.49 |
| Low-end Values (EFW; HDI) | 1.26; 1.23 |
| High-end Values (EFW; HDI) | 1.77; 1.60 |
| Institutional homogeneity (EFW; 25 years) | 2.08 |
| Institutional homogeneity (HDI; 25 years) | 1.92 |

Table 2.4 displays calculated North American integration scenarios using varying values of power preponderance and homogeneity indicators. We begin with a baseline examination before discussing potential scenarios that could deepen North American integration. The 2004 estimated value for NAFTA is 1.57 for the EFW model and 1.49 for the HDI model, while the actual value is 1.67. Therefore we will need to keep in mind that the model underestimates the integration score's value when examining future estimated values. The next entry includes North American values at the low end of the range for all the independent variables, while the third entry includes high-end values. Note that these entries represent hypothetical scenarios; the actual data do not have these combinations of values. The point is to determine the bounded values of integration given historical precedence before looking at other scenarios. At the historically lowest values, the predicted integration score is approximately 1.26 (EFW) and 1.23 (HDI). We can use the European Union as a substantive comparison. The EU scored a value of one just before the implementation of the Treaty of Rome (1957). At this time the EU was a partial free-trade area that also allowed foreign capital withdrawal. Regional institutions were limited to information gathering and had advisory roles. At NAFTA's historically highest values, the estimated score is 1.77 (EFW) and 1.60 (HDI). This value represents a substantive change in the level of integration because it requires a one-point increase in at least three categories of composite index. For example, the score increase could represent a change to a full free-trade area, the ability for full access for foreign investment and capital withdrawal (except for national government procurement), and the ability for regional institutions to amend member state proposals.

The next entries in Table 2.4 provide results given improvements to homogeneity between the three countries at different ages of NAFTA. I keep the power ratio at seven and also hold the membership at three. *If* the three achieve perfect EFW homogeneity when NAFTA turns 25 years old, it is estimated that the integration value would be 2.08. If the three achieve perfect HDI homogeneity, it is estimated that the value would be 1.92. Recall that the model underestimates the values, so this is a conservative estimate. What

# 26   Gaspare M. Genna

could such a value represent? Let's again use the EU as a comparative example. It achieved this value in 1958 as the members began their earliest integration efforts. The EU was a full free-trade area, provided full access for foreign investment (except for national government procurement), allowed capital withdrawal from member states, labor mobility among nationals of member states, included regional institutions that had the ability to amend proposals, and required member states to consult with each regarding monetary policy. Therefore, a one half–point increase in the integration score represents a great deal of change from NAFTA's 2004 score.

The predicted values all pivot on the notion that homogeneity would take place. However, what are the current differences and what would need to change? In 2004 the three countries' level of EFW homogeneity was 0.008 and HDI homogeneity was 0.931. Recall that the EFW index includes four components. Of these, the three partners display the largest differences in two components: the legal structure and security of property rights and regulation of credit, labor, and business. I will examine each of these components in order to account for the differences.

In the areas of legal structure and security of property, there is a large disparity between Canada and the United States on one side and Mexico on the other. With regard to the judicial system, the northern partners have greater judicial independence than their southern partner. Also, Canada and the United States score high on the impartiality of the courts and integrity of the legal system, while Mexico is coded at the lower end of the scale. Without independence, impartiality, and integrity, cooperation can be hampered by the uncertainty of rulings. This uncertainty is not a moral judgment of the Mexican judicial system, but instead an "unknown" or extra costs for those that come from diverse systems, such as the Canadian or US judicial systems. This uncertainty is a salient concern given the issue of protecting intellectual property, where we see the same pattern: Canada and the United States are higher on this scale than Mexico.

The second highest gap between the partners is in the area of regulation of credit, labor, and business. Of these three subcomponents, the smallest gap is in the area of credit market regulation. While Mexico does score lower than either Canada or the United States, the difference is not very large. The large differences are found in labor and business regulation. Regarding labor, there is a large divergence among all three with respect to flexibility in hiring and firing. The flexibility in this area refers to the mix of government regulation and private contracts. The more a private contract is the source behind these decisions, the higher the score. The United States scores high on this scale, followed by Canada with a value in the mid-range. Mexico scores near the bottom. This divergence introduces risk among firms and therefore uncertainty of success. This also introduces long-term economic uncertainty because labor markets are not competitive. The other large difference is in business regulation. With this indicator, we return to the familiar pattern of greater similarity between Canada and the United States

*What Will It Take to Build a North American Community?*   27

and a gap between them and the southern partner. The level of regulation in Canada and the United States is very small compared to Mexico. Price controls and high levels of bureaucratic control are prevalent in Mexico as is the need to provide "irregular payments" to government officials.

Like the EFW index, a comparison of the HDI for the three countries indicates a large gap between Canada and the United States on one side and Mexico on the other. The HDI values for Canada and the United States in 2004 were 0.892 and 0.902 respectively, while Mexico was at 0.741. The Canadian and US values are considered very high, while Mexico ranks as high according to the UN Development Programme's *Human Development Report*.[31]

The largest gap between the northern partners and the southern partner is in education and per capita income. Life expectancy among the three does vary, but not to a large degree.[32] Two measures make up the educational component of the HDI: mean years of formal education for individuals aged 25 years and the mean expected number of years for children entering school, with the highest value set at 18. Canada and the United States have similar mean attainment values (16 and 15.7 years, respectively), but Mexico is on the low side with 13 years. The expected educational attainment values for Canada and the United States are also similar (11 and 12.5 years), while Mexico is far behind (7.8 years). The per capita income is the largest gap among the three. Canada and the United States are clearly on the higher end ($34,380 and $43,130) while Mexico's is $12,380.[33]

The foregoing description exposes the problem of North America's compatibility; we see a greater amount of compatibility between Canada and the United States and less so with Mexico. Scores among the northern partnership indicate a high level of homogeneity, while the partnership with Mexico displays less homogeneity. Since North America is a trilateral partnership, the findings lead us to expect that the southern partnership would be the limiting factor when it comes to deepening integration unless we witness homogenization. In other words, most policy recommendations are going to spotlight the changes needed in the southern relationship.

But are such recommendations realistic? What are the trends in the important variables that predict the level of integration? Figure 2.1 plots the trend in power preponderance and the two homogeneity variables. Trends were calculated based on values from 1994–2004. The almost flat trend line of the power ratio indicates that over time the GDP ratio will remain at the same approximate proportion. EFW homogeneity, however, is trending slightly downwards. If the current changes continue, the three will have a value of –0.2 by 2020. This value is smaller than the 2004 value of 0.008. By including these two values, the model predicts the NAFTA integration score to be 2.09 in 2025. The HDI homogeneity values are trending upwards and by 2020 we can see a value of 0.96. The predicted value in 2025 is similar to the one calculated by the EFW homogeneity value: 2.03. At a minimum, the years leading to 2025 can introduce *one* of the following changes to North American integration: 1) the creation of a customs union; 2) unrestricted

## 28  *Gaspare M. Genna*

capital mobility expect for large-scale mergers and acquisitions; 3) full right of movement for all North American workers; 4) the ability for a regional institution to amend proposals; 5) a commitment to a fixed currency exchange rate; or 6) consolations among the three governments regarding fiscal policies. Neither the theory nor the results can predict with any certainty which of the six changes will occur—only that one of these changes is likely to occur.

## CONCLUSION

The literature on regional integration presents various theories and empirical findings. The conditions distilled in this paper are power asymmetry and partner compatibility. First, I evaluated the empirical validity of these conditions and then compared the general model with the North American experience. My goal was to assess North America's potential for deepening integration; does it have the ability to fill the institutional void discussed in the book's introduction? The rationale is that collective action through trilateral agreements would be the most effective way to solve the migration-security-development issue.

The general findings confirm that specific conditions are needed. First is the presence of a regional leader. The statistical results show that greater asymmetry is associated with greater levels of integration in general. The presence of the leader was theorized to be necessary in order to solve some problems of collective action (coordinate efforts and distribute incentives). However, valid as this variable is in general, it does not extensively help us to explain North American integration since the United States has been a regional (and global) preponderant power for some time.

The second condition is compatibility of members. The results indicate that homogeneity is a good predictor of integration. It is in this area that we see a good deal of variation among the North American states. Homogeneity is stronger in the northern partnership than the southern partnership, which produces an unbalanced compatibility problem. Therefore, the policy recommendations are geared to improving the compatibility between Mexico and Canada/United States in order to fill the North American institutional void.

The first recommendation is to reduce the differences involving legal structures, the security of property rights, and regulation of labor and business. Regarding the legal structures, the deepening of integration would benefit from the Mexican judiciary becoming more independent and impartial, and increasing its integrity. Also, there will need to be some sort of convergence in the protection of property rights. Regarding the regulation of labor and business, there needs to be a convergence in the regulation of workers' rights regarding hiring and terminating employment. Work also needs to be done in converging business regulations and the reduction of the use of bribes in Mexico.

## What Will It Take to Build a North American Community? 29

The second recommendation involves improving Mexico's education and per capita income levels. Education is the backbone of any economy because the human capital developed translates into higher value production. A workforce based mostly on low- or semi-skilled labor can lead to a manufacturing platform for the other partners, but not a dynamic partnership that introduces firm competition. Also, the lack of human capital development in one partner reduces the potential for innovation and discovery through public and private research and development. Income can follow educational attainment, but only if employment opportunities are present. Otherwise Mexico will see either a brain drain to the north and/or dissatisfaction from a growing number of educated individuals.

The two sets of recommendations can be addressed unilaterally, but they can also be addressed trilaterally. Using the theoretical mechanism described earlier, Canada and the United States can help develop changes in Mexico through the development of regional institutions. These institutions can develop plans and strategies and provide pooled funding in order to promote homogeneity and therefore foster greater levels of integration. Unfortunately, North America does not currently have the appropriate conditions that can fill the institutional void. While a power asymmetry is in place, homogeneity, and therefore compatibility, of the three partners is low. But a two-pronged policy of improving homogeneity while increasing integration can very well promote a virtuous cycle that continues to unite the economies and decision making of the three countries. The need to solve problems like the migration-security-development issue requires collective action because unilateral action thus far has proven to be unsuccessful.[34] The limiting factor of the three issues is development, which integration has the potential to solve. By recognizing that the problem is a commonly held one, the three partners can begin to seek out the conditions, and make the appropriate adjustments, for cooperation to develop. Otherwise an institutional void among the three partners cannot be filled.

## NOTES

1. Howard F. Chang, "Migration as International Trade," *UCLA Journal of International Law and Foreign Affairs* 3 (1998): 371.
2. Christopher Rudolph, "Security and the Political Economy of International Migration," *American Political Science Review* 97 (2003): 603.
3. Paul Collier and Anke Hoeffler, "On the Incidence of Civil War in Africa," *Journal of Conflict Resolution* 46 (2002): 13.
4. Jacek Kugler, Michelle Benson, Andy Hira, and Dimitry Panasevich, "Political Capacity and Violence," in *Political Capacity and Economic Behavior*, ed. Marina Arbetman and Jacek Kugler (Boulder, CO: Westview Press, 1997) pp 221–234.
5. Mancur Olson, *The Logic of Collective Action: Public Goods and the Theory of Groups* (Cambridge, MA: Harvard University Press, 1965).

30 *Gaspare M. Genna*

6. Ibid.; Elinor Ostrom, *Governing the Commons: The Evolution of Institutions for Collective Action* (Cambridge, UK: Cambridge University Press, 1990).
7. Ernest B. Haas, *The Uniting of Europe* (Stanford: Stanford University Press, 1958); Leon N. Lindberg, "Political Integration as a Multidimensional Phenomenon Requiring Multivariate Measurement," in *Regional Integration: Theory and Research*, ed. Leon N. Lindberg and Stuart A. Scheingold (Cambridge, MA: Harvard University Press, 1970) pp 149–232.
8. Stephen D. Krasner, "State Power and the Structure of International Trade," *World Politics* 28 (1976): 317; Walter Mattli, *The Logic of Regional Integration: Europe and Beyond* (Cambridge, UK: Cambridge University Press, 1999); Robert Gilpin, *The Political Economy of International Relations* (Princeton: Princeton University Press, 1987); Gilpin, *Global Political Economy: Understanding the International Economic Order* (Princeton: Princeton University Press, 2001); Brian Efird and Gaspare M. Genna, "Structural Conditions and the Propensity for Regional Integration," *European Union Politics* 3 (2002): 267; Gaspare M. Genna and Taeko Hiroi, "Power Preponderance and Domestic Politics: Explaining Regional Economic Integration in Latin America and the Caribbean, 1960–1997," *International Interactions* 30 (2004): 143; Genna and Hiroi, "The Effects of Unequal Size: Costs and Benefits of Unilateral Action in the Development of Mercosur," *Journal of Developing Societies* 21 (2005): 337; Genna and Hiroi, "Brazilian Regional Power in the Development of Mercosul," *Latin American Perspectives* 34 (2007): 43.
9. Efird and Genna, "Structural Conditions."
10. Yi Feng and Gaspare M. Genna, "Regional Integration and Domestic Institutional Homogeneity: A Comparative Analysis of Regional Integration in the Americas, Pacific Asia, and Western Europe," *Review of International Political Economy* 10 (2003): 278.
11. Genna and Hiroi, "Power Preponderance."
12. Mark Souva, "Institutional Similarity and Interstate Conflict," *International Interactions* 30 (2004): 263.
13. James G. March and Johan P. Olsen, "The New Institutionalism: Organizational Factors in Political Life," *American Political Science Review* 78 (1984): 734.
14. B. Guy Peters, *Institutional Theory in Political Science: The New Institutionalism* (London: Pinter, 1999).
15. Ronald Inglehart, *Modernization and Postmodernization: Cultural, Economic, and Political Change in 43 Societies* (Princeton: Princeton University Press, 1997); Inglehart and Christian Welzel, *Modernization, Cultural Change and Democracy* (New York: Cambridge University Press, 2005); Inglehart and Welzel, "Changing Mass Priorities: The Link between Modernization and Democracy," *Perspectives on Politics* 8 (2010): 551.
16. Arthur T. Denzau and Douglass C. North, "Shared Mental Models: Ideologies and Institutions," *Kyklos* 47 (1994): 3.
17. Zeev Maoz and Bruce Russett, "Normative and Structural Causes of Democratic Peace, 1946–1986," *American Political Science Review* 87 (1993): 624–638.
18. Henri Tajfel, "Interindividual Behaviour and Intergroup Behaviour," in *Differentiation between Social Groups: Studies in the Social Psychology of Intergroup Relations*, ed. Henri Tajfel (London: Academic Press, 1978) pp 27–60.
19. Ibid.
20. Susan Werner and Douglas Lemke, "Opposites Do Not Attract: The Impact of Domestic Institutions, Power, and Prior Commitments on Alignment Choices," *International Studies Quarterly* 41 (1997): 529.

## What Will It Take to Build a North American Community? 31

21. Nathaniel Beck and Jonathan N. Katz, "What to Do (and Not to Do) with Time-Series Cross-Section Data in Comparative Politics," *American Political Science Review* 89 (1995): 634.
22. Lagged dependent variables were not used because lagged dependent variables will dominate the results, thereby destroying the effect of other variables when included with heavily trending exogenous variables and disturbances, regardless of whether the lagged dependent variable has any true causal power. In addition, the interest in this study is not in the change or growth in the level of integration, but in the level of integration at a given time period. The lagged independent variables were included to better account for causality. Christopher Achen, "Why Lagged Dependent Variables Can Suppress the Explanatory Power of Other Independent Variables," Center for the Study of Democratic Politics, Princeton University, 2001, http://www.princeton.edu/csdp/events/Achen121201/achen.pdf.
23. Gary C. Hufbauer and Jeffrey J. Schott, *Western Hemisphere Economic Integration* (Washington, DC: Institute for International Economics, 1994).
24. Efird and Genna, "Structural Conditions," Feng and Genna, "Regional Integration," Genna and Hiroi, "Power Preponderance," Brian Efird, Gaspare M. Genna, and Jacek Kugler, "From War to Integration: Generalizing the Dynamic of Power Transition Theory," *International Interactions* 29 (2003): 293.
25. United Nations Development Programme, *Human Development Report* (New York: United Nations, 2005), http://hdr.undp.org/en/reports/global/hdr2005/.
26. James Gwartney and Robert Lawson, *Economic Freedom of the World: 2008 Annual Report* (Vancouver, BC: Economic Freedom Network, 2008).
27. United Nations Development Programme, *Human Development Report.*
28. There are a total of 36 regional integration organizations in the data set.
29. Michael Brecher and Jonathan Wilkenfeld, *A Study of Crisis* (Ann Arbor: University of Michigan Press, 2000).
30. I code NAFTA in the Americas regional dummy.
31. United Nations Development Programme, *Human Development Report*, p 21.
32. Canada's is 80.1, the United States' is 77.6, and Mexico's is 75.6 years.
33. The figures are in constant US PPP dollars.
34. Robert A. Pastor, *The North American Idea: A Vision of a Continental Future* (New York: Oxford University Press, 2011).

## REFERENCES

Achen, Christopher. "Why Lagged Dependent Variables Can Suppress the Explanatory Power of Other Independent Variables." Center for the Study of Democratic Politics, Princeton University. 2001 http://www.princeton.edu/csdp/events/Achen121201/achen.pdf.

Beck, Nathaniel, and Jonathan Katz. "What to Do (and Not to Do) with Time-Series Cross-Section Data in Comparative Politics." *American Political Science Review* 89, no. 3 (1995) pp 634–647.

Brecher, Michael, and Jonathan Wilkenfeld. *A Study of Crisis.* Ann Arbor: University of Michigan Press, 2000.

Chang, Howard F. "Migration as International Trade." *UCLA Journal of International Law and Foreign Affairs* 3, no. 2 (1998) pp 371–414.

Collier, Paul, and Anke Hoeffler. "On the Incidence of Civil War in Africa." *Journal of Conflict Resolution* 46, no. 1 (2002) pp 13–28.

## 32 Gaspare M. Genna

Denzau, Arthur T., and Douglass C. North. "Shared Mental Models: Ideologies and Institutions." *Kyklos* 47, no. 1 (1994) pp 3–31.

Efird, Brian, and Gaspare M. Genna. "Structural Conditions and the Propensity for Regional Integration." *European Union Politics* 3, no. 3 (2002) pp 267–295.

Efird, Brian, Gaspare M. Genna, and Jacek Kugler. "From War to Integration: Generalizing the Dynamic of Power Transition Theory." *International Interactions* 29, no. 4 (2003) pp 293–313.

Feng, Yi, and Gaspare M. Genna. "Regional Integration and Domestic Institutional Homogeneity: A Comparative Analysis of Regional Integration in the Americas, Pacific Asia, and Western Europe." *Review of International Political Economy* 10, no. 2 (2003) pp 278–309.

Genna, Gaspare M., and Taeko Hiroi. "Brazilian Regional Power in the Development of Mercosul." *Latin American Perspectives* 34, no. 5 (2007) pp 43–57.

———. "The Effects of Unequal Size: Costs and Benefits of Unilateral Action in the Development of Mercosur." *Journal of Developing Societies* 21, nos. 3–4 (2005) pp 337–355.

———. "Power Preponderance and Domestic Politics: Explaining Regional Economic Integration in Latin America and the Caribbean, 1960–1997." *International Interactions* 30, no. 2 (2004) pp 143–164.

Gilpin, Robert. *Global Political Economy: Understanding the International Economic Order*. Princeton: Princeton University Press, 2001.

———. *The Political Economy of International Relations*. Princeton: Princeton University Press, 1987.

Gwartney, James, and Robert Lawson. *Economic Freedom of the World: 2008 Annual Report*. Vancouver, BC: Economic Freedom Network. 2008.

Haas, Ernest B. *The Uniting of Europe*. Stanford: Stanford University Press, 1958.

Hufbauer, Gary C., and Jeffrey J. Schott. *Western Hemisphere Economic Integration*. Washington, DC: Institute for International Economics, 1994.

Inglehart, Ronald. *Modernization and Postmodernization: Cultural, Economic, and Political Change in 43 Societies*. Princeton, NJ: Princeton University Press, 1997.

Inglehart, Ronald and Christian Welzel. *Modernization, Cultural Change and Democracy* (New York: Cambridge University Press, 2005).

———. "Changing Mass Priorities: The Link between Modernization and Democracy," *Perspectives on Politics* 8 (2010) p 551.

Krasner, Stephen. "State Power and the Structure of International Trade." *World Politics* 28, no. 3 (1976) pp 317–347.

Kugler, Jacek, Michelle Benson, Andy Hira, and Dimitry Panasevich. "Political Capacity and Violence." In *Political Capacity and Economic Behavior*, edited by Marina Arbetman and Jacek Kugler pp 221–234. Boulder, CO: Westview, 1997.

Lindberg, Leon N. "Political Integration as a Multidimensional Phenomenon Requiring Multivariate Measurement." In *Regional Integration: Theory and Research*, edited by Leon N. Lindberg and Stuart A. Scheingold pp 149–232. Cambridge, MA: Harvard University Press, 1970.

Maoz, Zeev, and Bruce Russett. "Normative and Structural Causes of Democratic Peace, 1946–1986." *American Political Science Review* 87, no. 3 (1993) pp 624–638.

March, James G., and Johan P. Olsen. "The New Institutionalism: Organizational Factors in Political Life." *American Political Science Review* 78, no. 3 (1984) pp 734–749.

Mattli, Walter. *The Logic of Regional Integration: Europe and Beyond*. Cambridge, UK: Cambridge University Press, 1999.

Olson, Mancur. *The Logic of Collective Action*. Cambridge, MA: Harvard University Press, 1965.

## What Will It Take to Build a North American Community? 33

Ostrom, Elinor. *Governing the Commons: The Evolution of Institutions for Collective Action.* Cambridge, UK: Cambridge University Press, 1990.

Pastor, Robert A. *The North American Idea: A Vision of a Continental Future.* New York: Oxford University Press, 2011.

Peters, B. Guy. *Institutional Theory in Political Science: The New Institutionalism.* London: Pinter, 1999.

Rudolph, Christopher. "Security and the Political Economy of International Migration." *American Political Science Review* 97, no. 4 (2003) pp 603–620.

Souva, Mark. "Institutional Similarity and Interstate Conflict." *International Interactions* 30, no. 3 (2004) pp 263–280.

Tajfel, Henri. "Interindividual Behaviour and Intergroup Behaviour." In *Differentiation between Social Groups: Studies in the Social Psychology of Intergroup Relations*, edited by Henri Tajfel pp 27–60. London: Academic Press, 1978.

United Nations Development Programme. *Human Development Report.* New York: United Nations, 2005 http://hdr.undp.org/en/reports/global/hdr2005/.

Werner, Susan, and Douglas Lemke. "Opposites Do Not Attract: The Impact of Domestic Institutions, Power, and Prior Commitments on Alignment Choices." *International Studies Quarterly* 41, no. 3 (1997) pp 529–546.

# 3 The Mess They Made
## How Conservatism Is Wrecking North America[1]

*Julián Castro-Rea*

Over the last twenty years, North America has been through a strange process. In the early 1990s, the region bombastically inaugurated what was supposed to become a fully integrated market, pooling together the economic strengths of three member countries and foreshadowing increased political cooperation. In the early 2000s, however, market integration and political cooperation were clouded by an overarching concern with security. Under the pressure of the strongest partner, all North American countries rebuilt their domestic and foreign security apparatuses, adopting muscular antiterrorism legislation for internal threats—often to the detriment of civil liberties—and creating stronger police and military capabilities, while spending impressively unprecedented amounts of public funds in the process. Yet paradoxically these measures seem unable to solve a pressing North American security issue: the drug war quagmire that persists in Mexico, clearly originated by this country's closeness to the biggest illegal drug market in the world.

Simultaneously, the trilateral spirit of the North American Free Trade Agreement (NAFTA) has been for all practical purposes destroyed, and replaced by two dual-bilateralisms, mostly over measures to increase border security to even higher levels. Overall, during this period of time, internal borders in North America became thicker, not lighter as promised. This is especially true for most people traveling or moving from one North American country to another.[2] Yet, the flow of unauthorized migrants from Mexico to the United States keeps increasing, under the double pressure of demand for their labor in the north, and shrinking opportunities for economic improvement in the south. Canada also contributed to making North America's borders thicker, by imposing visa requirements for Mexican visitors in June 2009 and controlling the flows of temporary workers in an arbitrary manner. Strongly nationalist, even xenophobic positions run amok throughout North America, often legitimized by mainstream politicians, justifying exclusionary views of each other rather than mutual understanding among the peoples of the region.[3] This is especially true in the United States, where variations of ideologies building on exceptionalism are used as the basis for exclusionary and unilateral actions against the supposed partners in North America.

The Mess They Made    35

Smooth economic and political cooperation among the three countries in the region also remains an elusive goal twenty years after it was announced. North American governments did not react to the economic crisis unleashed in the fall of 2008 in a coordinated way, choosing instead to implement piecemeal emergency measures with no regard for the consequences for their neighbors.[4] The benefits of trade liberalization have not been evenly distributed, creating strong regional contrasts in terms of prosperity and worsening the concentration of household income measured in Gini coefficient terms.

Common theoretical explanations of these developments, based on IR realist assumptions, have a hard time making sense of what happened. Their main limitation, I would argue, is that these explanations use the state as their unit of analysis for explaining international behavior, thus neglecting the role of domestic political actors and their political struggles within each state, which end up producing the observed outcomes. Additionally, realism tends to take government policy justifications at face value, without questioning the fundamental motivations and assumptions underlying them.

Giving back to ideologies their important place in domestic and continental politics, this chapter proposes an alternative theoretical explanatory framework for the current state of the continent. I will argue that the ebbs, flows and paradoxes of North American integration are mostly due to the prevalence of right-wing conservative ideologies and their inherent contradictions. Indeed, these ideologies attempt to reconcile contradictory objectives, such as free market goals with nonnegotiable social policy concerns, tainted with hypernationalism and xenophobia; massive security spending with tax cuts; libertarian principles with social conservatism and intrusive and violent law enforcement, and so on. To the extent that conservatism has been a determinant factor in the construction of North America, these incompatible objectives eventually conflicted, thus creating the current uneven, chaotic North American architecture.

This is, I would argue, the main reason why there is an institutional void in North America. Right-wing conservatism, especially in its US version, strongly distrusts the state, regulations and public institutions in general. It is also congenial with the neoclassical economic paradigm that García Barrios and Mayer-Foulkes discuss in their chapter in this volume. Because of the important power asymmetries that exist in North America, this vision has become prevalent every step of the way in the process of North American integration. The vision was present, for instance, in the refusal of US NAFTA negotiators to accept the creation of permanent tribunals for dispute resolution, the adoption of an enforceable single competition policy, and common mandatory targets for the protection of workers and the environment, among many other aspects. This vision was also behind the adoption of a narrow understanding of security, as an exclusively military matter, after 9/11, thus rejecting Mexico's government proposals for a comprehensive approach to security incorporating policies and institutions to deal with migration, development and quality of life.[5]

## 36  *Julián Castro-Rea*

North America's institutional void is a clear projection of the ideals of the conservative right: minimal state, solidarity and regulation; maximum market, security and competition. This is not, as some may argue, the intrinsic North American approach to governance, as history shows that the three sovereign states in the region have been heavily involved in promoting economic development at different points in time, by funding infrastructure, providing cheap credit to emerging companies, investing directly in strategic sectors, shielding infant industries from foreign competition, favoring monetary policies that enhance competitiveness and so on and so forth. Guided by conservative convictions, the three North American governments seem to have forgotten how crucial state intervention at the right time can be to protect countries' interests and avoid economic catastrophes, and they have instead relied on the market, fallaciously believed to favor equilibrium and optimize resource allocation and efficiency, to do the job. Moreover, promarket, antistatist conservative policies have over time created an institutional habit, which feeds even more conservative policies through path dependence. As a result, they have created an environment in which the strongest economic and political actors prevail, contrary to what sound governance would require, as explained in the introduction to this volume.

In order to make my case, this chapter will first discuss the incongruous shape of the main right-wing actors in the three North American countries. Then it will illustrate how their contradictions have had negative impacts on public policy by focusing on three areas of particular importance for North America: migration, security and trade.

## THE PARTIES OF THE RIGHT: AN UNEASY ALLIANCE OF BUSINESS AND MORAL IMPERATIVES

North American integration is a direct product of the end of the Cold War and the process of neoliberal globalization that followed. The collapse of the Soviet Union emboldened global capitalism into believing that there was no alternative left to unrestrained markets, so the only task that governments should reasonably accomplish within the realm of economic policy was to make those markets even freer. Neoliberalism and the policies that flowed from it became conventional wisdom, the hegemonic way of reorganizing economic relations among countries.[6]

In North America, conservative actors thus acquired a hegemonic position. Conservative politicians, NGOs, economists, think tanks, media, parties, etc. ended up shaping the continent's plans and priorities. Their agenda advanced by leaps and bounds whenever they directly ran the federal governments. This occurred especially during three years, from the beginning of 2006 to the end of 2008, when conservative parties were simultaneously at the helm of governments across North America.

The mainstream parties that are the standard bearers of the right in Canada, Mexico and the United States are respectively the Conservative Party of Canada, the National Action Party (PAN) and the Republican Party. They have some important features in common. For the purposes of this chapter, the most important commonality is that all three parties resulted from the convergence of all kinds of promarket, conservative and religious political interests that came together in an effort to maximize their electoral leverage. The second important commonality is that at different points in time they have directed the federal government of their respective country of origin, giving momentum to promarket policies such as trade liberalization, privatizations, deregulation and fiscal austerity.

Canada's present-day Conservative Party was born in 2003, from the merger of two preexisting parties: the Progressive Conservative Party (PCP) and the Canadian Alliance (CA). The respective origins of these parties are very different, even contrasting. The PCP was the heir of traditional conservatism in Canada, strongly influenced by British conservative thought. This brand of conservatism, commonly known as Toryism, played a leadership role in the very creation of the Dominion of Canada in 1867. Later on, it developed a distinctive brand of conservatism known as "red Toryism," which blended political conservatism with social responsibility of the state towards the masses.[7] The PCP was able to form several governments through the twentieth century until it faced a crushing defeat in 1993, which reduced its presence in Parliament to only two seats.

In contrast, the Canadian Alliance originated from the Reform Party, created in 1987 on the wave of Western Canadian discontent with the way Canada's federation was run. From the start, the new party adopted a platform that blended populist appeals to reinventing government with market-based policy solutions to Canada's challenges.[8] It also attracted large numbers of Christian evangelists, who found in the party a way to make their values heard in Ottawa. The new party was not conservative in the traditional Canadian sense, but rather right-wing, closely resembling the Republican Party in the United States (see ahead). Because at the time of the merger the Canadian Alliance was in a stronger parliamentary position than the PCP, its cadres and ideology became predominant and immediately displaced Toryism.

The National Action Party was created in 1939, as a reaction to the radical reforms then operated by Mexico's postrevolutionary regime. It resulted from the collaboration between Catholic militants and technocratic, business interests, both disgruntled with their marginalization from meaningful political participation.[9] The coexistence between those two main groups was not always easy, and it reached a confrontational high point in the 1970s, when the Catholic faction imposed a Christian humanist platform on the party. The business wing rebelled, and created a pragmatic current called "neopanismo," which was dead serious in competing and winning elections. It found the opportunity to prevail when it led the opposition to the nationalization of the

## 38 Julián Castro-Rea

banks, decreed in 1982. After a series of regional victories, the PAN established itself as a serious political competitor, able to capitalize on popular discontent against the postrevolutionary regime, and eventually won the 2000 presidential elections.

In the United States, the Republican Party also amalgamated a disparate array of conservative and right-wing interests, building on the systemic incentives to bipartisan politics existing in that country. The party was able to accommodate social conservatives and corporate interests under a single organization. As explained by Jeff Faux:

> The organizing genius of conservative Republicans was to compartmentalize the two opposing value systems so they reinforced each other against what was perceived as a common liberal enemy. The social conservatives would bring grassroots energy. The corporations would bring the money.[10]

In particular, Republicans benefited from

a) The business backlash against the welfare state launched in the early 1970s, symbolized by the Powell Memorandum[11]
b) The religious right, mobilized with explicit electoral purposes first in 1980, with Jerry Falwell's "Moral Majority," then in 1989 with Pat Robertson's "Christian Coalition"[12]
c) The generous use of populism, aimed at convincing the masses of the superior democratic qualities of market competition over party politics.[13]

The Republican newfound strength was first decisively manifested in Ronald Reagan's victories in the early 1980s, surfing on a tidal wave of popular support.[14] The Democratic administrations of Clinton (1993–2000) and Obama (2009–present) have been arguably unable to reverse the right turn in US politics that started with Reagan.[15]

In sum, in all three North American countries we witness a decades-long process of gradual, sometimes uneasy amalgamation of promarket, business right-wing and socially, religion-inspired conservative organizations. In principle, these factions have been able to coexist, to the extent that they share some core values, such as the rejection of state intervention in the private lives of people, seen both as economic and moral subjects. By the same token, they generally praise the primacy of the market over society. They are equally pessimistic about human nature, thus supporting a heavy-handed approach to the preservation of law and order as a condition for peaceful coexistence. Finally, they pragmatically agree that they need each other to gain the necessary political momentum to win elections and thus implement public policy.

However, quite often, when it comes to putting specific public policies into practice, the different conservative right factions aim at goals that not only are

## The Mess They Made   39

incompatible with one another but also end up undermining the very effectiveness of these policies. In order to illustrate this paradox—political expediency destroying policy effectiveness—I will briefly discuss three broad public policy areas that affect North America as a whole: migration, security and trade.

## MIGRATION POLICY

Mexican migrants into the United States have historically been an important economic factor. Since the building of the railroads two centuries ago to intensive agriculture, retail, fast food, manufacturing and the hospitality construction and hospitality industry today, countless business operations in the United States have relied on the supply of abundant and affordable labor flowing from the south.[16] This labor has been important since the accumulation phase of these economic activities, providing what amounts to a net subsidy that made these industries viable and competitive. Its importance has not waned, since, as explained by Wendy Brown, "Northern capital today requires labor that is maximally cheap and exploitable—hirable at subminimum wage, without benefits or regard for regulations on overtime, health, environment or safety, and easily dispatched when not needed."[17]

Yet, despite their crucial economic importance, migrants are socially and politically rejected as undesirables. Migrants from Mexico have commonly been constructed in the United States as the epitome of the Other, as invading hordes that not only violate regulations but also abuse public services and threaten to destroy the host society's social fabric.

Demonization of migrants is, paradoxically, very politically and economically convenient to some specific interests. Many a politician[18] has built a successful career by portraying themselves as the defenders of the country's integrity against the onslaught of illegal immigration. Anti-immigrant policies also justify the preservation and continuous growth of the surveillance complex, a multibillion-dollar industry paid with public monies that provides employment to thousands of officials and other employees. Both contractors and border enforcers have a vested interest in preserving and even enhancing this surveillance complex.

Most people who hire migrants and/or portray them as undesirables, all the while reaping the political and economic benefits of their presence in the United States, are Republicans, or at least identify themselves politically with that party. Economic interest leads them in one direction, social conservatism in the opposite sense. A telling example clearly illustrates this irony: Golden State Fence Company, a private subcontractor installing sections of the wall along the Mexico-US border mandated by the Secure Fence Act (2006), hired hundreds of undocumented workers to do the job.[19]

Recently, international migration has become a politicized issue in Canada too, as it has been reframed as a security matter.[20] Since 2006, successive conservative governments have advanced an increasingly restrictive agenda that is

## 40 Julián Castro-Rea

changing the basic tenets of this country's migration policy. In February 2012, the Harper government introduced an omnibus bill styled "Bill C-31, Protecting Canada's Immigration Act."[21] The new bill consolidates and strengthens partial, negotiated reforms introduced in the recent past, allegedly aimed at controlling the flow and stay in Canada of refuge claimants and deterring human smuggling into this country.

Bill C-31 is adding more restrictive features, such as: a) giving the minister the ability to unilaterally determine which countries are safe and democratic, thus automatically rejecting claimants coming from those countries,[22] b) speeding the refugee claim process, limiting the possibilities for investigation and appeal, c) refugee claimants who were somehow assisted to reach Canada are subject to a discriminatory treatment, accused of being complicit with human trafficking, and d) the government gives to itself the power to collect biometric information on anyone coming to Canada, either as visitor or worker, allegedly as a measure intended at deterring future frivolous refugee claims. The parliamentary opposition sees the new bill as a betrayal of previously negotiated compromises for migration reform, aimed at ramming the government's conservative agenda now that the Conservative Party is leading a majority government. They also accuse the government of scapegoating immigrants, without really making Canada securer for that action.

Migrants leaving Mexico are also judged under a double discourse in their country of origin. On the one hand, especially since the PAN government led by Vicente Fox (2000–2006), they are praised and courted as a part of the Mexican nation that provides an important economic contribution to their country of origin through the money they send to their relatives (the so-called remittances). On the other hand, however, migrants are also seen in Mexico as a handy solution to the pressures, both real and potential, derived from the increasing abandonment to unemployment of impoverished peasants, the urban poor and, more recently, the society at large. The notion of emigration to the United States as an "escape valve" was conveniently adopted by the Mexican government to avoid defending or actually protecting migrants, other than through rhetorical references.[23]

## SECURITY POLICY

Although cooperation on security matters was not part of NAFTA's original design, 9/11 put this policy area decidedly at the center of the North American agenda. As a result, all three governments, to different extents, implemented antiterrorism strategies, boosted their defense expenditures and engaged in muscular illegal drug enforcement. This extraordinary diversion of public attention, institutional effort and government monies built on fear of repeated terrorist attacks instilled in the population, conservative law and order priorities, social conservative concerns about the use of drugs and a general sense of insecurity felt by many.

*The Mess They Made*   41

However, providing a sense that the government is doing something to increase people's security and safety comes at a high cost. The consequences of the security apparatus buildup are vast and alarming,[24] especially from fiscal conservative and libertarian points of view. There are at least three troubling developments associated with it:

1. Exponential increase of government expenditure, which directly violates the priority of fiscal conservatives of keeping expenses and state economic intervention to a minimum. In the United States, defense-related spending was at least $1 trillion for fiscal year 2008 (defense budgets are typically never fully disclosed),[25] the same year when the economic crisis hit that country. That same year, Canada spent C$20.583 billion on defense, as well as additional expenses of close to $35 billion planned over five years. In the future, defense expenditure may become even more onerous if Canada's conservative government has it its own way. The policy document "Canada First Defence Strategy," introduced in 2008, consolidates existing and planned expenditures, expecting to spend C$490 billion over the following twenty years.[26]

   Security expenditure has reached such levels that it might soon become unsustainable, especially during this era of economic crisis,[27]

2. Antiterrorism measures resulted in important restrictions to civil rights and freedoms, promptly justified by their proponents as necessary given the emergency situation, but clearly violating individual freedom. The USA PATRIOT Act, adopted in October 2001, expanded governmental capacities for surveillance, and detention of suspects. It also limited judicial review and increased controls over immigration. A newly created Department of Homeland Security has been put in charge of most of the enforcement of this act, sometimes bypassing Congress and the judiciary. Canada followed suit with the adoption of Bill C-36 (Anti-Terrorism Act, December 2001) and the Public Safety Act (November 2002), which additionally created the infamous mechanism of issuing "security certificates" to suspend the rights of detainees suspected of terrorist activities. In 2008, Mexico embraced a similar approach, adopting the expansive definition of terrorism that had been coined in the United States.[28]

   All limits imposed on individual freedom and the rule of law should be a major concern for the right, in particular for libertarians, constantly wary of the state's intrusion in the private lives of citizens. Paradoxically, then, assuaging the fears of conservatives comes at the price of violating basic tenets of supporters of right-wing ideologies, two constituencies that usually overlap within North America's conservative parties.

3. Illegal drug control policies have been a monumental failure throughout North America. The death toll provoked by the drug war in Mexico

# 42 *Julián Castro-Rea*

has reached horrific levels. Starting in December 2006, it claimed the lives of at least 47,000 people in only five years.[29] Despite the escalating militarization and violence that it creates, the drug war has had limited effects in curbing the cartels' power or actually reducing the potency, production and distribution of illegal substances. It has, in contrast, substantially contributed to the dramatic increase of the incarceration rate in the United States,[30] reaching 743 inmates per 100,000 of national population in 2009, the highest per capita prison population in the world.[31] In 2002, the US government spent US$19 billion in drug control policies, while Canada spent $454 million in 2001, most of which was spent on enforcement.[32] Canada is poised to spend much more, now that a newly minted Omnibus Crime Bill C-10 requires mandatory minimum prison sentences for minor drug offenses.[33]

Despite their clear failure and dramatic costs, drug enforcement policies are upheld by conservative-inspired governments because they fulfill ideological functions: they focus on punishing people considered deviant (consumers, producers, racialized minorities), and they promote the law-and-order agenda so cherished by the right. Additionally, they serve powerful economic interests by supporting the surveillance-enforcement apparatus, closely associated with conservative actors in the three countries considered here.

Requests made by the Mexican government to Washington to do something to stop the traffic of guns that end in the hands of drug dealers are rebuffed with the argument that unlimited gun possession and sale are constitutional rights in the United States. Andrew Arulanandam, spokesperson for the US National Rifle Association, recently declared that his country's Congress should do nothing about these requests because "Simply, this is a Mexican problem."[34]

## TRADE POLICY

Trade liberalization was at the center of the launch of trilateral cooperation in North America in the early 1990s. Trade liberalization was sold as a sure path to prosperity for all countries involved. The increased wealth it was supposed to produce would improve everyone's standards of living, from business people to workers. In order for that to occur, a regime of full national treatment for trade and investment was proposed, and NAFTA was a decisive step in that direction. Deregulation and tax cuts were supposed to entice corporations to invest more, to the extent that less governmental intervention was supposed to help them become more competitive and productive.

*The Mess They Made*  43

These conservative dogmas were very useful excuses for the governments to shy away from implementing positive remedies to alleviate the impacts of trade liberalization, enforced by supranational institutions. However, the dogmas did not live up to reality. Contrary to the ideological expectations, NAFTA in fact promoted the following:

1. Stagnation of real wages throughout North America. According to Organisation for Economic Co-operation and Development (OECD) figures, real hourly minimum wages in Canada barely moved from $6.16 to $7.08 in PPP terms from 2000 to 2010, from $0.78 to $0.79 in Mexico, and from $5.84 to $6.50 in the United States.[35] This progress is clearly a long way from the lofty promises of unlimited prosperity made by NAFTA supporters. Furthermore, the average standards of living of Mexican workers did not catch up with those of the two other North American partners—the chasm between them actually deepened.
2. Increase of socioeconomic inequalities, measured in Gini coefficient terms. In Canada, the coefficient went from 31.5 in 1994 to 32.1 in 2005, while in the United States it increased from 40.8 in 1997 to 45 in 2007. In Mexico, the coefficient improved slightly, going from 53.1 in 1998 to 51.7 in 2008,[36] but this is small consolation for the average worker in an economy with sluggish real wage growth, as discussed in the previous point.
3. Decline of manufacturing production across the continent. Between 1994 and 2003, the contribution of manufacturing to Canada's GDP went from 17.1% to 16.5%, and in Mexico it declined from 18.7% to 18% from 1994 to 2006, after having peaked at 21.5% in 1996. The decline was even more dramatic in the United States, where it went from 18.8% in 1994 to 14.4% in 2005.[37] Ironically, China became the top manufacturing provider to all three North American countries, who under NAFTA were supposed to supplement each other to create more competitive manufactures.
4. Devastation of Mexico's agriculture, with the resulting impoverishment of the population in the countryside. The agricultural sector in that country fell prey to the higher productivity of food producers in Canada and the United States and the massive government support available to them. Worst, the Mexican government contributed to the onslaught, by prematurely eliminating barriers to sensitive agricultural imports (corn, beans, sugar) and supporting only the limited number of domestic products that are competitive internationally (fruits, vegetables, flowers, seafood, beer and tequila).[38]
5. Increased migration of Mexican workers to the United States, authorized or not, as an expression of the crisis in the countryside and, overall, of the limited opportunities available in Mexico for economic advancement of the average worker. This way, contrary to the offer made by NAFTA

## 44  *Julián Castro-Rea*

proponents, who claimed that the agreement would put an end to migration thanks to the new employment opportunities it would create in Mexico, NAFTA itself became a source of pressure for Mexicans to migrate.[39] According to the Pew Hispanic Center, the unauthorized immigrant population from Mexico living in the United States went from 4.8 million in 2000 to an estimate of at least 7 million in 2007.[40] So, far from being solved, the issue of illegal migration is getting bigger and more complex thanks to the conservative approach chosen to deal with it.

Because of the risks involved, previously explained in this article, international migration is a last-resort survival strategy. Most impoverished people do not migrate; they end up swelling the domestic informal economy, including drug-trafficking–related activities. Therefore, NAFTA's inability to provide substantial opportunities and benefits to Mexican displaced workers is fuelling two of North America's major security challenges: drug trafficking and migration.

Assumptions of automatic growth once the market was fully liberalized acted as a deterrent for government action aimed at improving distribution measures (better minimum wages, progressive fiscal regimes and the like).[41] Additionally, nationalism crept in, creating important exceptions to the regime of national treatment, the most blatant of which are the "Buy American" policies put in place since 2009 to stimulate economic recovery in the United States.[42]

The response that the three governments offered to the economic crisis manifested since the fall of 2008 was belated, hesitant, piecemeal, short-term and thus only partially effective. Prime Minister Harper's "Canada Action Plan" was implemented in early 2009, and discontinued after three years, leaving infrastructure works halfway through at a time when the economy is not still sitting on firm ground. Across North America, cuts to government spending, particularly in social programs, are already being made, putting the fragile economic recovery in jeopardy. The three governments have been unwilling to acknowledge that "fiscal austerity in a depressed economy is probably self-defeating; by shrinking the economy and hurting long term revenue."[43]

Right-wing ideologies are an obstacle to the sustained adoption of alternative approaches to economic policy making. The market is supposed to create in due time what the governments refuse to do to reboot the North American economy towards a more sustained growth, and to alleviate the urgent needs of marginalized populations across North America.


## CONCLUSIONS

The casual observer may be tempted to interpret the constant policy contradictions found among right-wing, conservative political actors in North America as a clever conspiracy to achieve their real goals while deceiving

The Mess They Made    45

the public into believing they are doing something else. For example, the combination of tax cuts to corporations and wealthy individuals with out-of-bounds expenditure on security and defense is so blatantly absurd that it seems guided by a hidden, unacknowledged objective. Is this apparent incoherence a cunning strategy to "starve the beast" of big government, making even deeper cuts inevitable once public finances are in crisis?[44]

My foregoing discussion suggests a different, more mundane explanation: conservative actors seem to be victims of their own success in creating effective political machines, amalgamating very disparate factions under a single umbrella. These coalitions work well during election times, animated by the common goal of reaching power. Once in power, these actors feel compelled to please their different constituencies simultaneously. Yet different conservative supporters have contrasting priorities, which sooner or later clash when the time comes to put them into concrete action, producing incoherent and ultimately ineffective policies.

This piecemeal, patchwork approach to public policy is clearly inimical to institutional development. The strength of conservatism in the three countries of North America is a major reason why there is an institutional void in the cooperation efforts attempted in this part of the world.

Are conservative political actors bothered by their dismal policy performance? It is highly unlikely. Looking at the sorry state of the three policy areas discussed earlier, and the way they fulfill political goals, we must come to the alarming conclusion that conservative actors do not seem to care about the internal coherence or the effectiveness of the policies they implement. In their view, what really matters is the political success they get, keeping their supporters content and getting them reelected.

We witness then a clear case of what Peter Andreas described as "policy failure, political success,"[45] which has become the hallmark of conservative governance throughout the continent. In the process, conservatism is indeed wrecking North America.

The only way to undo the damage done by conservatism is by reframing the policy areas discussed in this paper with alternative approaches in mind, which steer away from the conservative understandings on how these policy areas are to be dealt with. This is not the purpose of this paper, although the discussion herein contained certainly is an invitation to think differently.

## NOTES

1. After completing two preliminary versions of this chapter, I became aware of the existence of a work bearing a similar title: Gwynne Dyer's book *The Mess They Made: The Middle East after Iraq* (Toronto: McClelland & Stewart, 2007). I nonetheless decided to keep my original title intact because of the strong parallels existing between Dyer's analysis and mine, only applied to vastly different geographical regions. Indeed, the subtitle of Dyer's work could as well be: "How Conservatism Is Wrecking the Middle East."

## 46 Julián Castro-Rea

2. The exception to this general rule is business people and professionals benefiting from NAFTA's chapter 16, or the programs made available for a fee to frequent travelers (called "Nexus"). The extremely reduced number of people who benefit from eased travel requirements only underscores the exclusionary nature of the migratory regime in North America. See Yasmeen Abu-Laban, "Migration in North America," in *Politics in North America: Redefining Continental Relations*, ed. Y. Abu-Laban et al. (Peterborough: Broadview, 2008) p 342.

3. Nationalism has recently grown while being reframed in all three North American countries. Some examples are in order. In the United States, a backlash against Barack Obama's election gave birth to the hyperpatriotic Tea Party movement. Also in that country, Arizona's SB 1070 law, passed in March 2010, made legal the racial profiling of people who "don't look like US citizens." In Canada, the military engagement in Afghanistan and policy reforms promoted by subsequent conservative governments since 2006 have stressed the country's European, colonialist roots to the detriment of its multicultural reality. In Mexico, the election of PRI's presidential candidate in July 2012 is a testimony of the rebirth of state-centered nationalism, compounded with clientelism and authoritarian nostalgia. See Chip Berlet, "Collectivists, Communists, Labor Bosses, and Treason: The Tea Parties as Right-Wing Populist Counter-Subversion Panic," *Critical Sociology* 38, no. 4 (2012) pp 565–587; Ronald L. Mize and Alicia Swords, *Consuming Mexican Labour: From the Bracero Program to NAFTA* (Toronto: University of Toronto Press, 2011); Sedef Arat-Koc, "The Disciplinary Boundaries of Canadian Identity after September 11: Civilizational Identity, Multiculturalism, and the Challenge of Anti-imperialist Feminism," *Social Justice* 32, no. 4 (2005) pp 32–49; and Lorenzo Meyer, "El tiempo postelectoral," *Reforma*, July 19, 2012.

4. The American Recovery and Reinvestment Act (P.L. 111–5), adopted in 2009, requires nonfederal entities (states, municipalities) benefiting from public recovery funds to spend them with suppliers based in the United States, thereby allowing those entities to bypass NAFTA's ch. 10 national treatment rules for government procurement.

5. This approach, nicknamed NAFTA Plus or "the whole enchilada," was formally proposed by Mexico's government in 2001. See Stephen Clarkson and Maria Banda, "Does 'NAFTA Plus' Have a Common Denominator? The Prospects for Mexico and Canada Achieving a Joint Position on Deepening North America" (paper presented to the NAFTA & After: Looking Forward & Back from a Decade of Free Trade conference, Carleton University, January 23, 2004). http://homes.chass.utoronto.ca/-clarkson/publications/Does%20NAFTA%20 Plus%20Have%20a%20Common%20Denominator%20-%20The%20 Prospects%20for%20Mexico%20and%20Canada%20Achieving%20a%20 Joint%20Position%20on%20Deepening%20North%20America.pdf.

6. Alain Noël and Jean-Philippe Thérien, *Left and Right in Global Politics* (Cambridge: Cambridge University Press, 2008) pp 137–165.

7. Charles Taylor, *Red Tories: The Conservative Tradition in Canada* (Toronto: Anansi, 1982).

8. David Laycock, "Populism and the New Right in English Canada," in *Populism and the Mirror of Democracy*, ed. Francisco Panizza (London: Verso, 2005) pp 172–201.

9. Soledad Loaeza, "The National Action Party (PAN): From the Fringes of the Political System to the Heart of Change," in *Christian Democracy in Latin America: Electoral Competition and Regime Conflicts*, ed. Scott Mainwaring and Timothy R. Scully (Stanford: Stanford University Press, 2003) pp 196–246.

The Mess They Made   47

10. Jeff Faux, *The Global Class War: How America's Bipartisan Elite Lost Our Future and What It Will Take to Win It Back* (Hoboken: John Wiley, 2006) p 82.
11. The Powell Memorandum (August 1971, sometimes also named Powell Manifesto) is a call to probusiness, conservative actors to unite their forces against a mounting welfare state and liberalism. Lewis F. Powell, "The Powell Memo (Also Known as the Powell Manifesto)," Reclaim Democracy!, August 23, 1971, http://reclaimdemocracy.org/corporate_accountability/powell_memo_lewis.html.
12. William Martin, *With God on Our Side: The Rise of the Religious Right in America* (New York: Broadway Books, 1996).
13. Thomas Frank, *One Market under God: Extreme Capitalism, Market Populism, and the End of Economic Democracy* (New York: Anchor Books, 2000) pp 23–50.
14. Faux, *Global Class War*, 76–89.
15. Susan George, *Hijacking America: How the Religious and Secular Right Changed What Americans Think* (Cambridge: Polity, 2008) pp 1–12, 243–254. Obama's re-election in November 2012 may mean a lasting reverse of fortunes for the Republican party, but it is too early to tell.
16. Mize and Swords, *Consuming*, xxviii–xxxi.
17. Wendy Brown, *Walled States, Waning Sovereignty* (New York: Zone Books, 2010) p 111.
18. Including Tom Tancredo, Jesse Helms, John McCain, Jim Sensenbrenner, among many others.
19. Brown, Walled States, loc. cit.
20. François Crépeau and Delphine Nakache, "Controlling Irregular Migration in Canada: Reconciling Security Concerns with Human Rights Protection," *IRPP Choices* 12, no. 1 (2006) p 4.
21. See Tobi Cohen, "Tories Beef Up Refugee Legislation," *Edmonton Journal*, February 17, 2012.
22. Notably, refugee claimants coming from Mexico and Hungary, where real dangers exist for people threatened respectively by the drug cartels and extreme right anti-Roma militias, have been turned over and even deported back to their countries of origin, sometimes with tragic consequences.
23. Jorge A. Bustamante, "A Dialectical Understanding of the Vulnerability of International Migrants," in *Our North America: Social and Political Issues beyond NAFTA*, ed. Julián Castro Rea (Farnham: Ashgate, 2012) pp 114–118.
24. A comprehensive discussion of those impacts is found in Julián Castro-Rea, "Assessing North American Politics after September 11: Security, Democracy, and Sovereignty," in *Contentious Politics in North America: National Protest and Transnational Collaboration under Continental Integration*, ed. Jeffrey Ayres and Laura Macdonald (London: Palgrave, 2009) pp 35–53.
25. Chalmers Johnson, *Dismantling the Empire: America's Last Best Hope* (New York: Henry Holt, 2011) pp 137–139.
26. Julián Castro-Rea, "Delirios de grandeza: La agenda de Norteamérica y la política de seguridad nacional de Canadá," in *La seguridad de América del Norte reconsiderada*, ed. Athanasios Hristoulas (Mexico City: Miguel Ángel Porrúa-ITAM, 2011) pp 163–164.
27. C. Johnson, *Dismantling*, 139–147.
28. Castro-Rea, "Assessing," 46.
29. The government estimate of victims is 47,500 (from December 2006 to December 2011). Independent estimates, based on reports by federal, state and local law enforcement agencies, claim a much larger total of 60,420 for

48  *Julián Castro-Rea*

the same period—that is, an average of 12,000 deaths per year. See Enrique Mendoza Hernández, "Cinco años de guerra, 60 mil muertos," *Proceso*, December 11, 2011.

30. Michelle Alexander, *The New Jim Crow: Mass Incarceration in the Age of Colorblindness* (New York: New Press, 2010) pp 52.
31. International Centre for Prison Studies, *World Prison Brief* (London: University of Essex). Available at http://www.prisonstudies.org/info/worldbrief/.
32. These are the most recent years for which reliable data are available. It is estimated that the US government has spent US$1 trillion on drug enforcement since it declared the "war on drugs" in 1971. See Evan Wood, Moira McKinnon, Robert Strand and Perry Kendall, "Improving Community Health and Safety in Canada through Evidence-Based Policies on Illegal Drugs," *Open Medicine* 6, no. 1 (2012): e35–e40.
33. Postmedia News, "Tory Crime Bill Will Overburden Court System: Retired Judges," *National Post*, February 23, 2012.
34. Tim Johnson, "Who's Arming Mexican Cartels? Maybe Joe Average," *Edmonton Journal*, November 21, 2010.
35. See OECD statistical database available at http://stats.oecd.org/.
36. All Gini coefficient data taken from the CIA database, available at https://www.cia.gov/library/publications/the-world-factbook/fields/2172.html.
37. Data provided by the World Resources Institute, available at http://earthtrends.wri.org/searchable_db/results.php?years=all&variable_ID=217&theme=5&country_ID=all&country_classification_ID=all.
38. Sergio Zermeño, "Desolation: Mexican Campesinos and Agriculture in the 21st Century," *NACLA Report on the Americas* 41, no. 5 (2008) pp 28–32.
39. David Bacon, "Displaced People: NAFTA's Most Important Product," *NACLA Report on the Americas* 41, no. 5 (2008) pp 23–27.
40. Data available at http://www.pewhispanic.org/2011/02/01/ii-current-estimates-and-trends/. The number of unauthorized migrants declined slightly over the following years, to 6.5 million in 2010—not as a reflection of improved opportunities in Mexico but of *decreasing* opportunities in the United States due to the economic crisis.
41. Faux, *Global Class War*, 35–37, 126–154.
42. See note 4.
43. Paul Krugman, "Confidence Fairy Laid to Rest but Reign of Error Stumbles Along," *Edmonton Journal*, April 29, 2012.
44. Stephen Maher, "Harper Channelling Reagan with 'Starve the Beast' Strategy," *Edmonton Journal*, February 2, 2012.
45. Peter Andreas, "US-Mexico: Open Market, Closed Borders," *Foreign Policy*, no. 103 (summer 1996) pp 51–70.

## REFERENCES

Abu-Laban, Yasmeen. "Migration in North America." In *Politics in North America. Redefining Continental Relations*, edited by Abu-Laban, Y., et al., 339–352. Peterborough: Broadview, 2008.

Alexander, Michelle. *The New Jim Crow: Mass Incarceration in the Age of Colorblindness*. New York: New Press, 2010.

American Recovery and Reinvestment Act (APRA). P. L. 111–5. 111th Cong. (2009).

Andreas, Peter. "US-Mexico: Open Market, Closed Borders." *Foreign Policy*, issue 103 (summer 1996): 51–70.

Arat-Koc, Sedef. "The Disciplinary Boundaries of Canadian Identity after September 11: Civilizational Identity, Multiculturalism, and the Challenge of Anti-imperialist Feminism." *Social Justice* 32, no. 4 (2005): 32–49.

Bacon, David. "Displaced People: NAFTA's Most Important Product," *NACLA Report on the Americas* 41, no. 5 (2008): 23–27.

Berlet, Chip. "Collectivists, Communists, Labor Bosses, and Treason: The Tea Parties as Right-Wing Populist Counter-Subversion Panic." *Critical Sociology* 38, no. 4 (2012): 565–587.

Brown, Wendy. *Walled States, Waning Sovereignty.* New York: Zone Books, 2010.

Bustamante, Jorge A. "A Dialectical Understanding of the Vulnerability of International Migrants." In *Our North America: Social and Political Issues beyond NAFTA*, edited by Julián Castro Rea, 109–135. Farnham: Ashgate, 2012.

Castro-Rea, Julián. "Assessing North American Politics after September 11: Security, Democracy, and Sovereignty." In *Contentious Politics in North America: National Protest and Transnational Collaboration under Continental Integration*, edited by Jeffrey Ayres and Laura Macdonald, 35–53. London: Palgrave, 2009.

———. "Delirios de grandeza: La agenda de Norteamérica y la política de seguridad nacional de Canadá." In *La seguridad de América del Norte reconsiderada*, edited by Athanasios Hristoulas, 157–177. Mexico City: Miguel Ángel Porrúa-ITAM, 2011.

Central Intelligence agency (CIA). *The World Factbook.* https://www.cia.gov/library/publications/the-world-factbook/.

Clarkson, Stephen, and Maria Banda. "Does 'NAFTA Plus' Have a Common Denominator? The Prospects for Mexico and Canada Achieving a Joint Position on Deepening North America." Paper presented to the NAFTA & After: Looking Forward & Back from a Decade of Free Trade conference, Carleton University, January 23, 2004. http://homes.chass.utoronto.ca/~clarkson/publications/Does%20NAFTA%20Plus%20Have%20a%20Common%20Denominator%20-%20The%20Prospects%20for%20Mexico%20and%20Canada%20Achieving%20a%20Joint%20Position%20on%20Deepening%20North%20America.pdf.

Cohen, Tobi. "Tories Beef Up Refugee Legislation." *Edmonton Journal.* February 17, 2012.

Crépeau, François, and Delphine Nakache. "Controlling Irregular Migration in Canada: Reconciling Security Concerns with Human Rights Protection." *IRPP Choices* 12, no.1 (2006): 1–39.

Dyer, Gwynne. *The Mess They Made: The Middle East after Iraq.* Toronto: McClelland & Stewart, 2007.

Faux, Jeff. *The Global Class War: How America's Bipartisan Elite Lost Our Future and What It Will Take to Win It Back.* Hoboken: John Wiley, 2006.

Frank, Thomas. *One Market under God: Extreme Capitalism, Market Populism, and the End of Economic Democracy.* New York: Anchor Books, 2000.

George, Susan. *Hijacking America: How the Religious and Secular Right Changed What Americans Think.* Cambridge: Polity, 2008.

International Centre for Prison Studies, *World Prison Brief* (London: University of Essex). http://www.prisonstudies.org/info/worldbrief/.

Johnson, Chalmers. *Dismantling the Empire: America's Last Best Hope.* New York: Henry Holt, 2011.

Johnson, Tim. "Who's Arming Mexican Cartels? Maybe Joe Average." *Edmonton Journal.* November 21, 2010.

Krugman, Paul. "Confidence Fairy Laid to Rest but Reign of Error Stumbles Along." *Edmonton Journal.* April 29, 2012.

Laycock, David. "Populism and the New Right in English Canada." In *Populism and the Mirror of Democracy*, edited by Francisco Panizza, 172–201. London: Verso, 2005.

## 50 Julián Castro-Rea

Loaeza, Soledad. "The National Action Party (PAN): From the Fringes of the Political System to the Heart of Change." In *Christian Democracy in Latin America: Electoral Competition and Regime Conflicts*, edited by Scott Mainwaring and Timothy R. Scully, 196–246. Stanford: Stanford University Press, 2003.

Maher, Stephen. "Harper Channelling Reagan with 'Starve the Beast' Strategy." *Edmonton Journal*. February 2, 2012.

Martin, William. *With God on Our Side: The Rise of the Religious Right in America*. New York: Broadway Books, 1996.

Mendoza Hernández, Enrique. "Cinco años de guerra, 60 mil muertos." *Proceso*. December 11, 2011.

Meyer, Lorenzo. "El tiempo postelectoral." *Reforma*. July 19, 2012.

Mize, Ronald L., and Alicia Swords. *Consuming Mexican Labour: From the Bracero Program to NAFTA*. Toronto: University of Toronto Press, 2011.

Noël, Alain, and Jean-Philippe Thérien. *Left and Right in Global Politics*. Cambridge: Cambridge University Press, 2008.

OECD. Stat Extracts. http://stats.oecd.org/.

Pew Hispanic Center database. http://www.pewhispanic.org/data-and-resources/.

Postmedia News. "Tory Crime Bill Will Overburden Court System: Retired Judges." *National Post*. February 23, 2012.

Powell, Lewis F. "The Powell Memo (Also Known as the Powell Manifesto)." Reclaim Democracy! August 23, 1971. http://reclaimdemocracy.org/corporate_accountability/powell_memo_lewis.html.

Taylor, Charles. *Red Tories: The Conservative Tradition in Canada*. Toronto: Anansi, 1982.

Wood, Evan, Moira McKinnon, Robert Strand, and Perry Kendall. "Improving Community Health and Safety in Canada through Evidence-Based Policies on Illegal Drugs." *Open Medicine* 6, no. 1 (2012): e35–e40.

World Resources Institute database. http://earthtrends.wri.org/searchable_db

Zermeño, Sergio. "Desolation: Mexican Campesinos and Agriculture in the 21st Century." *NACLA Report on the Americas* 41, no. 5 (2008): 28–32.

# 4 Immigration and Institutional Voids
## North American Citizenship and Human Rights in Conflict

*Emma R. Norman*

## INTRODUCTION

Regional integration promises to open up borders, expand the mobility of persons and resources, institutionalize multilateral cooperation fostering security and prosperity, and multiply arenas of belonging, encouraging more inclusive collective identities. In the North American case at least, these promises have rung increasingly hollow.[1] Unequal relationships between states were built into regional agreements at their inception, and the priority of national interests, especially security, has continued to confound cooperation. Harsh attempts to resolidify borders have ensued. In consequence, large groups remain excluded, are becoming progressively marginalized, or find themselves caught in a web of tensions created by the confrontation between transnational forces encouraging migration on one hand, and reassertions of local or national sovereignty emphasizing security on the other. Bridging the gaps in this web to extricate such groups before they fall into the void beneath is proving to be extremely difficult for national and transnational institutions in the region. On the contrary, some national and subnational governments are actively pursuing blatantly exclusionary policies in their efforts to fill the ruptures in their institutional framework that deterritorialization and global restructuring have opened up, or exposed anew.

Explaining the varied and complex reasons behind the difficulty the three partners are experiencing in cooperating on mobility and security issues has become a central task of recent literature in the area. A principal source of the problem naturally concerns the current lack of strong, formal regional institutions that could encourage or, if necessary, enforce trilateral cooperation. Several scholars also focus attention on the deeper voids or disconnects at the level of institutional norms and values that continue to obstruct regional cooperation and its inclusive ideals of free movement across boundaries and equal access to resources and rights.[2] The broad contention of this chapter is that many of those disconnects at both the formal and normative institutional levels are rooted in a more pervasive conceptual confusion that is not often taken into account in contemporary debates on the problems surrounding regional inclusion.

## 52  Emma R. Norman

I suggest that a reading of one of Hannah Arendt's lesser-known discussions offers an additional dimension to our understanding of why North American cooperation on immigration and security is proving to be so elusive. Arendt identified a significant confusion in grounding inalienable rights in the idea of humanity, which led to her disturbing notion of "human superfluousness." This notion depicts a process whereby certain groups who lack (or are divested of) functional legal protection are increasingly excluded politically, juridically, socially, physically, and eventually morally from the world—often as a conscious result of policies designed to reinforce state sovereignty. Human rights should activate at precisely this moment, yet Arendt claimed they frequently fail to do so because of the way they were legally misconceived at their inception. In their absence, the isolation experienced by excluded groups escalates all too quickly to the point where they can be viewed as essentially disposable, and treated by the state accordingly.

Arendt's critique of human rights and the concept of superfluousness are invaluable for the alternative light they shed on the exclusionary dimensions of the region's current wave of restrictive immigration laws. They also contain a grave warning of the potentially severe consequences that could transpire if unilateral, zero-sum solutions to regional problems concerning migration and security continue unrestrained. I hope to show that, despite the differences between Arendt's context and that of contemporary North America, several underlying similarities indicate that it is a warning we ignore today at our considerable peril.

I first outline[3] the logical and conceptual confusions Arendt identified at the foundation of a deep rivalry between citizenship rights and human rights, a rivalry that lies at the heart of the continuing debate over the Arizona Immigration Law and cognate legislation in the region. Section two sketches the notion of human superfluousness she develops from this critique. The remainder of the chapter develops the argument that several elements of Arendt's account of the production of superfluousness appear in modified, but nevertheless alarming form in recent US, Canadian, and subnational immigration policies in the region. I conclude by exploring what an Arendtian perspective indicates for the future of North American cooperation concerning the dilemmas that stem from the conflict between security and mobility as they apply to immigration policy and human rights.

## THE PARADOX OF HUMAN RIGHTS

> If a human being loses his political status, he should, according to the implications of the inborn and inalienable rights of man, come under exactly the situation for which the declarations of such general rights provided. Actually the opposite is the case. It seems that a man who is nothing but a man has lost the very qualities which make it possible for other people to treat him as a fellow-man.[4]

## Immigration and Institutional Voids   53

In Arendt's view, the whole idea of grounding rights in a notion of human-ity contains a conceptual confusion at its base that at certain historical junctures—for her in the aftermath of World War I (WWI) and in totalitar-ian regimes, but also now in times of globalization—can make safeguarding human rights extremely challenging even if the political will to do so is very strong. Her worry was not with rights *per se*, but the way in which human rights were grounded: the alleged universal and inalienable basis of the Rights of Man and the Citizen, which was later reproduced in the Universal Declaration of Human Rights (UDHR).

To serve as a safety net against government mistreatment or negligence, the Rights of Man were designed in 1789 in a way that tied them to hu-manity: to people, not to states. It was believed that only this could render them truly "inalienable"—that is, irreducible to other rights and laws, and "independent of all governments."[5] However, the functioning of any rights system is predicated on the legal system—which requires, rather than by-passes, the state system. "[I]t turned out that the moment human beings lacked their own government and had to fall back upon their minimum rights, no authority was left to protect them and no institution was willing to guarantee them."[6] Arendt thus identified an institutional void of the most fundamental order stemming from the confusion inherent in this paradox: human rights are meant to trigger when the state fails in its duties to its people(s), but they nevertheless require the state system to be guaranteed and claimed. Such rights therefore are not independent from the sovereign state. Just like citizenship rights, they are altogether reliant on it.

> The . . . right of every individual to belong to humanity should be guaranteed by humanity itself. It is by no means certain whether this is possible. For, contrary to the best-intentioned humanitarian attempts to obtain new declarations of human rights from international organi-zations, it should be understood that this idea transcends the present sphere of international law which still operates in terms of reciprocal agreements and treaties between sovereign states.[7]

Human rights, then, were imperfectly designed at the outset since they were conceived in the absence of the kind of suprastate legal framework neces-sary for their enforcement. Instead, they piggy-backed upon the same state-based legal scaffold on which citizenship rights are grounded—both sets of rights are thus thoroughly entangled with each other and with state sover-eignty. Human rights consequently remain dependent on the state's respon-sible treatment of the people(s) within its territory. When that responsibility is upheld, human rights generally appear to function adequately and com-patibly with the political rights associated with citizenship status. However, when the state relinquishes its responsibility to some or all of its denizens, the protective power of human rights evaporates at the very moment it is needed most.

54  *Emma R. Norman*

Arendt observed that the most devastating effects of the paradox of rights were suffered by those made stateless almost overnight when borders across Europe were redrawn in the treaties following WWI. In the face of the sheer numbers of refugees at the time, the long-standing right to asylum was effectively abandoned and the legal process of naturalization broke down internationally. Millions were dispossessed of either a home territory to be repatriated to, or a new state that would offer them naturalization—to the point where even naturalizations that had already been accepted were cancelled.[8]

The international dilemma of stateless persons in interwar Europe threw the tensions between several political and legal idea(l)s into sharp relief. First, what Arendt called "people's sovereignty" (freedom from colonial despotism embodied in the right of a people to collective self-determination) was seen to clash with "state sovereignty" "in which each state has absolute jurisdiction within its own borders and only within them."[9] The enormous number of refugees after WWI meant that, if it were not trumped, people's sovereignty was in danger of constantly threatening the established legal and political order, challenging state sovereignty in the process.

Second, depriving persons of legal membership in a state after the war did not merely dispossess them of their physical homes, and lead to the loss of their identity, a sense of belonging to a rooted homeland, or the cultural world they had carved for themselves there. It also ruled out the possibility of them ever finding another home or territory of their own.[10] Arendt saw this as the most primary deprivation of all: the loss of a place in this world, a loss that renders opinions insignificant and actions ineffective.[11]

A third tension stems from this. Arendt's worry was that the loss of social, cultural, and emotional ties to a territory involved a further juridico-political loss precisely because of the way human rights were grounded. Being stateless ultimately deprives one of occupying a clear "niche in the framework of the general law,"[12] the basis of which rests not on human rights, but on citizenship status and the political rights that accompany it.

A fundamental conceptual confusion between the notions of *homme* and *citoyen* thus permeated the Declaration of the Rights of Man and the Citizen at its inception,[13] and was replicated in a similar confusion over the relation between the individual and the state in the 1948 UDHR. The lack of a clear definition of the right to citizenship and its relation to the right to nationality in Article 15 of the UDHR[14] clouds the conceptual picture further.[15] Adding to Arendt's argument here, it might make intuitive sense to consider the biological status and needs of humans as more fundamental than other statuses and privileges, including political ones. Yet if the protection of these needs is expressed in the form of rights, it is predicated on the *prior* existence of a functional legal and political artifice, not the other way around. Logically (and historically) speaking, then, the exclusive concept of the citizen precedes and is necessary for articulating the inclusive concept of "the human." And, contrary to the reverse derivation found in

Immigration and Institutional Voids   55

Enlightenment social contract theories, the state precedes and is necessary for conceiving and protecting "the individual."

Arendt's work on totalitarianism, first published in 1951, highlights the grave practical consequences created by placing human rights prior to political rights and the ensuing problems with conflating citizenship, nationality, and humanity, or basing rivalrous and conflicting conceptions of rights on any or all of these grounds. The stateless lack the only entity that could guarantee a set of minimum rights, a juridico-political loss that renders them highly vulnerable to many kinds of abuse. It is here that human superfluousness begins to emerge.

## HUMAN SUPERFLUOUSNESS

Arendt's idea of human superfluousness is rooted in the inherent confusions of the paradox she identified at the base of human rights and is a notion that remains highly pertinent today, though I hope to show that new contexts are leading it to be generated and experienced in different ways. The predicament in which the stateless find themselves "is not that they are not equal before the law, but that no law exists for them."[16] The failure to occupy a defined niche in the legal system means that the stateless are deprived of the most fundamental right of all: "the right to have rights."[17] In its absence, human rights cease to function and the stateless are all but condemned to plunge into a gaping void in the legal system to the point where they can be rendered superfluous—and treated in a way that reflects their perceived superfluity. The implications of this radical claim are profound and hold much contemporary significance when reflecting on the exclusionary features of recent immigration policy trends, particularly in North America.

With no state to guarantee their human rights, or to make claims against those who might violate them, the stateless begin to slip through the fissures between institutions, anomalies that no longer fit the ethico-legal-political framework embedded in the state system. If such groups cannot be assimilated, Arendt reflected, it is easier to view them as less worthy of the ethico-political status that citizens possess, or even to see them as threatening. Indeed, the mere presence of anomalous groups poses a serious challenge to the coherence of the juridico-political edifice that, in the interwar period, was already destabilized by the effects of WWI on the territories of Europe and the sovereign authority of the defeated nations. In the 1920s, 1930s, and beyond, the states of Europe responded by soundly re-exerting their shaken authority over the stateless—an authority that was constrained, in Arendt's view, only by pragmatic concerns until the rise of totalitarianism swept even those restrictions away.[18] In a context in which globalization is producing concomitant challenges to the solidity and permanence of territorial boundaries, and thus to state sovereignty, it is not difficult to see the spate of immigration legislation in Arizona, Alabama, Georgia, and elsewhere in North

## 56   Emma R. Norman

America or recent nationalist rhetoric in Europe couched in claims about the failure of multiculturalism[19] as contemporary responses to precisely the kind of perceived "threat" Arendt highlighted.

In Arendt's argument, the move from "threat," which clearly designates some importance to a group, to superfluousness, which does not, begins by slipping through the fissures in the legal system.[20] This paves the way to a continuum of distancing, ostracism, ghettoization, social, cultural, political, and physical isolation, and eventually disappearance from "the world of men" (for her, those who possess functional rights) via internment.[21] Unable to divert the endless flow of refugees back to their nonexistent home countries after WWI, and unwilling to channel and assimilate them into their own nations, internment camps to contain large pools of "the unwanted" became the "routine solution" for numerous states in interwar Europe, along with a temptation to resort to excessive policing and arbitrary rule.[22] Similar "routine solutions" have survived to the present day.[23]

Moving along the continuum, successive layers of deprivation coalesce into total exclusion from the international "family of nations," first juridically, then morally, and ultimately through the destruction of individuality.[24] Exclusion finally culminates in erasure. If "the superfluous" are not claimed by an authority able to enforce the protection of their minimum rights, the extreme end of the continuum intensifies the physical distancing from the "world of men": civilian concentration or labor camps, deportation, evacuation, or, in certain cases where this may not be possible, extermination.

In Arendt's account, the failure of the stateless to occupy a niche in the legal framework and their ensuing degrees of isolation escalated in the 1930s and 1940s to the point where large groups could be "treated as if they no longer existed, as if what happened to them were no longer of any interest to anybody, as if they were already dead."[25] And so she contends that a certain logic was visible in the evolution of interwar internment camps for the stateless to more extreme or "perfect" forms of superfluousness.[26] Arendt was referring to the dehumanization tactics that produced the "living dead" of the Nazi extermination camps (*Vernichtungslager*) where once-human individuals were turned into replaceable, forgettable nonpersons, indistinguishable from each other and stripped of any solidarity. This unclaimed, unwanted, "superfluous human material"[27] was condemned to be shunted between authorities from one place to another, cordoned off from the general population, and ultimately to be liquidated if circumstances were judged to require it.[28] Nevertheless, the relevance of her observations is not limited to such extreme cases, or to conventional forms of statelessness—especially in a world that is becoming progressively deterritorialized. Indeed, the challenges to the traditional Westphalian view of state sovereignty brought about by contemporary global forces share significant parallels with the territorial and juridical upheaval that followed WWI. It is, therefore, not entirely surprising that the context of North America has been similarly throwing the conceptual paradox of human rights into sharp relief for some time.

## NATIONAL IMMIGRATION POLICY:
## CANADA AND THE UNITED STATES

The deterritorialization that accompanies globalization is impacting the ways the paradox of human rights can lead to contemporary variants of superfluousness that apply to more than those who have no state to return to, no clear niche in the legal system. Since the North American Free Trade Agreement (NAFTA), the increased mobility of persons and resources (and violence, information, and contraband) across permeable borders has highlighted the decreased control the North American states can wield over the populations residing in their territory. Political reactions to this reduced control by the three states not only reveal a strong resistance to "deep" integration at the level of regional identity. They likewise reflect an attempt to reassert a notion of state sovereignty that is more consonant with the idea of territorialized, nationally based citizenship rights than human rights.[29] This is evident in the United States' and Canada's reassertion of authority concerning their sovereign right—recognized in international law—to determine who should and should not be granted full citizen status with the legal protection that goes with it. "It is in this respect that immigration has become central to the exercise of state sovereignty," according to Gabriel and Macdonald.[30] In fact, matters of immigration have always been central to the exercise of sovereignty, but certain contexts render the restrictive state machinery at work behind it more salient than others. Perhaps the most worrying consequence is that immigration is a site that is primed for the systematic generation of various degrees of superfluousness, which, under contemporary conditions, is proving difficult to counter at the institutional level for the very reasons Arendt identified.

The range and flexibility of labor, mobility, and attendant expanded rights of citizens built into European integration at its base[31] were, and are, simply not present in the North American model. Inclusion is far from equal across the three states. For example, NAFTA offers a visa permitting temporary free mobility and labor rights across the region to a limited group of professionals and investors. While the number of Canadians who can enter the United States under this visa is not restricted, "For Mexicans, a limit was set at 5,500 initial approvals per year for a transition period of ten years (until 2004)."[32]

Two further examples of the crackdown on North American mobility also emphasize the legal inequality. As part of the US war on terror, in June 2009 the Western Hemisphere Travel Initiative made it compulsory for American citizens to show a passport, passport card, Enhanced Driving License, or Trusted Traveler Card when entering the country's land or maritime borders. This greatly affects the freedom of many Mexican-Americans to visit their families in Mexico, deposit funds there, or engage in other social or professional business south of the border. Six weeks later, in response to a substantial rise in Mexican refugee claims since 2005, Canada also tightened its

## 58 *Emma R. Norman*

initially permissive NAFTA immigration measures. Canadian Citizenship, Immigration, and Multiculturalism Minister Jason Kenney stated in 2009 that, "In addition to creating significant delays and spiraling new costs in our refugee program, the sheer volume of these claims is undermining our ability to help people fleeing real persecution."[33] All Mexicans entering the country now require a Temporary Residence visa.

The temporary visa tightened the 2004 Canada-US Safe Third Country Agreement controls on those attempting to claim refugee status at the Canadian border, by closing it to Mexican claimants if they had already passed through a "safe" country (the United States) in which they could claim asylum from persecution, or a well-founded fear of it, at home. Together with the new visa requirement, this essentially closed access by air or land to the Canadian border for all Mexican refugee claimants who failed to meet the strict exemptions of the Agreement. This occurred even though the US asylum system had already been questioned in Canada for its non-compliance with the UN Convention against Torture and the UN Refugee Convention, and the potential risk to refugee and human rights that could ensue if claimants were forced to seek asylum in the United States.[34]

An Arendtian reading belies any superficial promise contained in such a formal, institutional attempt to express a shared bilateral responsibility concerning what to do about the influx of immigrants and refugees, and where to shunt the large groups of "unwanted" persons next. The question of—and protection of—state sovereignty expressed through immigration control patently overshadows that of human rights here. This is manifestly problematic for Mexican refugee applicants to both countries. The Mexican state might be willing to receive them, but it is in many cases unable to fully "claim" them in the sense Arendt highlighted by guaranteeing their human rights in the face of overwhelming narcoviolence, institutionalized corruption, and extreme economic disparity at home. Stiffer Canadian border controls have also been a contributing factor in the heightened perception of "threat" that "the unwanted" are generating in the United States. And, as we shall see, if no country in the region is prepared to fully claim these groups, certain forms of superfluousness can ensue despite the best efforts of human rights actors seeking to plug this legal void in the regional state system.

The reassertion of state sovereignty has focused on tougher controls, and more funding for policing and surveillance of the region's borders.[35] In the United States, earlier narcotics and border-crossing policies have been tailored to terrorism prevention, cementing the now-pervasive connection between migration policy and security concerns in the region. This is most flagrantly expressed in efforts to resolidify territorial borders very literally via the US-Mexico border fence, 649 miles of which had been completed in August 2011.[36] The combination of attempts by the undocumented to avoid falling afoul of drug gang presence on one side of the frontier, or greatly augmented patrols on the other, seriously increases the risk of death in the most inhospitable parts of the desert or in the sea around the coastal border area. The cumulative effect has been less of a deterrent to illegal crossing and more of an impetus forcing the use of certain routes across the border.[37] The connection between the basic objective of this policy and the logic of super-fluousness is clear: one way or another, far fewer illegal immigrants should enter. These trails towards the remaining gaps in the fence also channel the surviving undocumented migrants into specific areas *en masse*, which again has amplified the perception of "threat" in specific areas.

## STATE IMMIGRATION LAWS: ARIZONA AND BEYOND

The 2010 Arizona Immigration Law (SB 1070) and related legislation in other US states have combined a reassertion of the authoritative value of cit-izenship rights over human rights, with augmented state police muscle—one symptom that Arendt correlated with the production of superfluousness in interwar Europe. "Theoretically," she wrote, "in the sphere of international law, it had always been true that sovereignty is nowhere more absolute than in matters of emigration, naturalization, nationality and expulsion."[38] This led her to muse on such "weapon[s] of denaturalization"[39] and the probable correlation between how far a regime had been "infected" with totalitarian-ism and how often it exercised its sovereign right to denationalize.

Illegal immigrants are obviously not stateless in the sense Arendt dis-cussed. They generally belong to a state to which they can be deported, and, in the case of the eleven million illegal Mexican immigrants much of the recent US and Canadian legislation has targeted, that state does not pro-hibit their return. However, the difficulties the Mexican state is experiencing in its ability and willingness to guarantee the observation of their human rights at home[40] are certainly not offering substantial incentives to remain in Mexico for those who have been deported back, or those contemplating emigration because their basic needs are not being met. In the absence of such incentives, deterrents abroad are escalating in response. The recent US state legislative reaction to illegal immigration exemplifies the ongoing ri-valry between citizenship rights and human rights, while also reflecting new forms of superfluousness that, despite their lower-grade character, remain disturbingly insidious.

It is well known that SB 1070, which criminalizes being in the state with-out applying for and carrying valid documentation, has perturbing implica-tions for human rights by increasing the likelihood of arbitrary arrest and detention and promoting discrimination on the basis of racial appearance. It is in danger of contravening Article 9 of the UDHR concerning arbitrary arrest, detention, or exile and also may transgress international law's stipu-lation that detention is " 'a measure of last resort' . . . deemed appropriate only when states can demonstrate that it is 'necessary and proportionate' to the objective being achieved."[41] It finally risks not just blurring the dis-tinction between civil and criminal law, but also dispensing with it.[42] The

## 60 Emma R. Norman

human rights of the most vulnerable—notably asylum seekers, victims of human trafficking, and women—are hit the hardest.[43] These cases also flag the institutional failures that spring from such control measures in the conflict that emerges between US state immigration legislation and the prior responses that institutions of human rights have established to protect the most susceptible.

As Mayer and others[44] point out, SB 1070 is unclear on what documents constitute valid proof of lawful presence in pending petitions for asylum. The broad latitude and lack of instructions to enforcement officials could result in the "unjustified detention of individuals who have initiated the process to legalize their status in the U.S. . . . [which] contravenes Article 31 of the 1951 Convention Relating to the Status of Refugees, as modified by the 1967 Protocol."[45] A similar lack of clarity applies to escaped victims of human trafficking. "By criminalizing the failure to produce this proof, the Act punishes the victims instead of the traffickers" while jeopardizing the effectiveness of the T and U visa programs the federal government offers to protect trafficking victims.[46] Women are also less likely to report crimes to police (notably violent crimes and domestic abuse) if this would require them to produce documentation and lead to possible detention, criminal prosecution, and eventual deportation. This relates back to the idea of a loss of a place in the world—the loss of a voice. The combination of institutional fissures into which the vulnerable are increasingly likely to fall in Arizona quite evidently renders opinions insignificant and actions ineffective. Mayer and others[47] also underline the conflict with the waiver furnished by the prior federal Immigration and Nationality Act designed to protect the human rights of victims of domestic violence who enter the country illegally.

The conflict here between state interests, federal law provisions, and international legal obligations is patent. So too is the conflict between citizenship rights and human rights, especially when prioritizing the former is used (bio)politically as an expression of state sovereignty.[48] Such instances of institutional failure do not necessarily imply that a total legal void exists. Federal and international provisions for protecting basic human rights are there. Illegal immigrants are not quite the "forgotten" stateless, for whom there exists no law, no juridical niche. But the rivalry between citizenship rights and human rights on one hand and the rivalry over the boundaries between state and federal sovereignty in the United States on the other are rendering the niche they can claim progressively narrow, unclear, and unstable.

While the Supreme Court blocked several of SB 1070's provisions in June 2012, it unanimously upheld the law's "show me your papers" linchpin.[49] The undocumented consequently remain "the unwanted," "the outlawed," and in many respects "the unclaimed." In Arizona, Alabama, Georgia, Indiana, Utah, and to some extent Oklahoma, federal and international laws created for their protection are clearly trumped by tough recent state laws created against them, making it more difficult for existing political or human rights institutions to extricate them from their position caught in the middle.

Part of the reason lies unmistakably in the low level of cooperation between the North American states in resolving migration and security issues in the region, which obstructs institutional success in "claiming" immigrants or rights on their behalf. Such low cooperation is reinforced in its stark contrast to the way the European Union deals with potentially conflicting national and regional policies on immigration and mobility. A particularly salient example concerns the expulsion of over one thousand Roma by France from July to early September 2010. The instant, region-wide public outcry led to the European Parliament Resolution of September 9, calling for the immediate suspension of all deportations of the Roma.[50] The European Commission quickly launched infringement proceedings, setting a two-week deadline for the French government to cease violations of the 2004 European Directive on Freedom of Movement and the regional ban on ethnic discrimination in the European Charter of Fundamental Rights. After ten days, France complied.[51] Recalling the quotation from Arendt at the beginning of the first section of this chapter, in this case at least,[52] the regional government, the publics of several member states, and international human rights organizations cooperated effectively to "claim" the Roma as "fellow" European citizens—if not Arendt's "fellow men"—and the basic rights they hold in a way that is proving far more difficult in North America.

To an extent, the expanded, postnational, transterritorial view of regional citizenship adopted by the European model bridges some of the legal voids created by the conflict between national citizen rights and human rights. If European states fail in their responsibility to respect the rights of those residing in their territory, regional citizenship rights can be invoked to catch vulnerable individuals and groups before they slip through the gaps in the legal safety net. Yet, as with national citizenship rights, the protection of regional citizenship rights (and the human rights they proxy for) remains thoroughly dependent on the ability and willingness of regional institutions to intervene successfully to claim the "unwanted" and to enforce member state accountability. Such intervention by the European Parliament has not always been forthcoming.[53]

Perhaps most importantly for the present argument, the very need in Europe for additional, regional citizenship rights to do the job that human rights were designed to accomplish implies two important things. First, it is at least a tacit recognition by Europe that human rights are not functioning as originally intended, and that the malfunction needs to be addressed at the level of the legal framework. Second, it suggests that, to be functional, existing conceptions of rights may *require* a ground in governments or other (national, regional, potentially even international) sovereign authorities if those rights remain dependent on the current legal framework. Both points hold implications for the future protection of human rights in North America—a point to which I return shortly.

## 62  Emma R. Norman

## THE ESCALATION OF SUPERFLUOUSNESS

In contrast to the European case, North America lacks a regional political identity. It also lacks effective regional institutions that can help build transnational solidarity or at least frame and solve problems as common rather than particularistic ones. Taken together, the absence of these features suggests that it is harder to treat undocumented migrants as "fellow men" and women, and easier to treat the "unwanted" as "legal nonpersons subjecting them to a kind of legal exile,"[54] to quote from one federal court testimony pertaining to recent legislation in Alabama. In the examples discussed so far in this chapter, most treatment of illegal (or otherwise marginalized) immigrants is located relatively early on the continuum of superfluousness. However, as the recent "management" of the Roma and the previous observation concerning the Alabama law reveal, definite signs of escalation are emerging on both sides of the Atlantic.[55]

In the United States, the policy of self-deportation, or attrition-through-enforcement, that occupied debates in the run-up to the 2012 presidential election reinforces that the escalation is continuing. The strategy deliberately aims to render everyday life so wretched for unauthorized immigrants that they choose to go home regardless of how embedded they are in the community, as well as acting as a deterrent to those contemplating unlawful entry.[56] Intentionally creating not just discomfort but misery lies at the core of the 2011 Alabama law (HB 56) by "shutting off access for those in the state illegally to virtually every facet of regulated life, from water utilities to rental agreements to dog tags."[57] Despite the blocks in August 2012 of some of its harshest provisions by the US Court of Appeals for the 11th Circuit, HB 56 has already stimulated much fear and fleeing—its intended consequences. For unauthorized immigrants, the situation has borne enough resemblance to initial experiences in those Mexican states affected severely by narcoviolence to be cause for alarm.

> Unauthorized parents took their kids out of school, they refuse to seek medical services, fear going to church, they don't drive anywhere, their access to water service has been threatened. Some employers have refused to pay their workers, judges and court interpreters threatened to report suspected unauthorized immigrants.[58]

The policy of making life unbearable for illegal aliens in parts of the United States has been packaged as a "kinder, gentler alternative to the harsh, expensive, and unworkable strategy of mass deportation."[59] No Arendtian reading seems necessary to belie this kind of claim, given the misery and fear the policy *is designed to cause*. Yet her arguments do underscore the ease and speed with which such restrictive immigration policies can escalate "the unwanted" along the continuum of superfluousness (particularly concerning its isolating tendencies), and gain at least partial acceptance legally,

*Immigration and Institutional Voids* 63

socially, and politically. The undocumented are formally cast as undeserving not merely of the same kind of political attention citizens enjoy, but of basic social and family needs and human consideration. Being a citizen under such conditions trumps being human on almost every front, and, confirming the continued existence of Arendt's paradox of rights, lacking possession of the former status places the effective protection of the latter in considerable danger. Regarding the many shocking tales of the trials and deaths involved in crossing the Mexican-US border, which, as I noted earlier, recent laws and practices have made even more perilous, the following remark from a retired Border Patrol sector chief is revealing of how higher grades of superfluousness are being generated today. "The strategy is a failure. All it's accomplished is killing people . . . But since these people are Mexicans, no one seems to care."[60]

In Arizona, deportations skyrocketed under Obama's first presidency[61] and the projected increase of legal arrests and incarcerations exhibits disturbing parallels with Arendt's claim that "the internment camp . . . has become the routine solution for the problem of domicile of the 'displaced persons.' "[62] International law considers administrative detention to be nonpunitive. Yet detainees are often jailed in the same space as convicted criminals, are similarly attired and restrained, and subject to the same risks of physical harm despite the stipulation of international law that they should be separated for this reason.[63]

The fact that SB 1070 has spurred even tougher legislation in other states reinforces the gravity of Arendt's observation that, in the absence of political rights, the effective power of human rights evaporates at the very moment they are needed the most. As we have seen, in the European case, transnational citizenship status has been employed as one way around this problem since regional political rights can be used as partial anchors for human rights and transnational solidarity if national political rights are withheld.[64] The contemporary consensus is that too many differences exist between Europe and North America in the conditions and objectives of integration to contemplate a shared regional citizenship in the latter case any time soon. Yet even if it were possible in the future, Arendt's paradox of rights is still likely to apply if the conceptual confusions at the base of human rights and its fundamental conflicts with citizenship rights remain unresolved.[65]

I mentioned earlier that the very need in Europe for regional citizenship rights to do the job that human rights were originally designed to achieve suggests at least a tacit recognition that the "inalienable" ground of human rights is untenable. Human rights have therefore been given additional political support in the form of regional citizenship rights based on a legal framework analogous to that of the state. Insofar as North American integration has prioritized national self-interest and unilateral problem solving far ahead of stimulating a shared regional identity reinforced by effective regional institutions, it seems a similar recognition is conspicuously absent in North America. For Arendt, it is precisely this lack of recognition—lack

## 64  *Emma R. Norman*

of thought in her parlance[66]—that makes the idea of rendering persons superfluous possible. Continued lack of thought enables the practices associated with superfluousness to become increasingly accepted and routinized in the face of more pressing national prosperity and security concerns that obstruct inclusive solidarity.

Also emphasizing the escalating and routinizing tendencies of superfluousness, the biopolitical management of bodies encapsulated in Arizona's SB 1070 was shadowed by the 2011 corollary law HB 2281—which imposes a curriculum banning ethnic studies programs in Arizona public schools and colleges.[67] In teaching students "to treat or value each other as individuals,"[68] the reduced importance this law gives to different ethnic identities indicates a clear reversion to the presumed "leveling effect" of the liberal principles underpinning a view of citizenship that is assumed to be at its best as a culturally unified, homogenous whole. This is a telling example of the earlier point concerning the many basic legal, political, and social deprivations that the vulnerable are subject to, including specific group identity. But here it is not merely the "anomalous" identities of refugees and illegal immigrants that such policies seek to banish from our familiar juridico-socio-political map. The identities and differences of many citizens are also exposed.

The basic point indicates just how broad and routinized the new remit of superfluousness could potentially become in contemporary contexts. It is not only suffered by those who are arrested or fear detainment. It touches the lives and diminishes the rights, freedoms, and human dignity of many: US citizens who are or appear to be Hispanic or who have undocumented family members, legal immigrants who are or appear to be Hispanic, the students affected by HB 2281, and the many employers the new wave of immigration legislation now forces to use E-Verify[69] to check the legal status of their employees, to identify but a few. Indeed, the US House of Representatives voted almost unanimously (412–3) to extend the E-Verify program for a further three years in September 2012 after the bill was approved by the Senate. It was passed on the basis that it would preference the 23 million unemployed American citizens in their search for work[70] and in anticipation of further mandatory state laws and a possible future national mandatory E-Verify law.

Taken together, the examples discussed in this chapter provide fairly strong evidence that those affected by recent immigration measures in the region are being shunted along the continuum of superfluousness increasingly transparently. Recalling the end result of the paradox of human rights, if political status disappears, "human" status and solidarity apparently disappear with it. Current immigration laws in Arizona, Alabama, South Carolina, Indiana, Oklahoma, and Utah, and similar bills introduced in Missouri, Mississippi, Tennessee, and Virginia in 2012 suggest this disappearance will continue in North America, despite probable Supreme Court blocks of some of the more extreme tenets of this legislation in the near future.

## IMPLICATIONS FOR THE FUTURE OF HUMAN RIGHTS IN NORTH AMERICA

The quote from Arendt at the beginning of section one begs the question: what *can* encourage the members of regional community to "treat a (hu) man" like a "fellow (hu)man"? This basic enquiry underpins the kind of multilateral cooperation and regional integration that penetrates deeper than the mere optimization of national economic interests on the world stage. The present argument provides few clearly positive answers. But it does indicate that a satisfactory response is unlikely to be found in human rights alone, at least as they are currently articulated in North America and beyond.

Valuing and institutionalizing a regional respect for the equal application of human rights independently of national citizenship status, and an inclusive political space to express it, are as crucial as providing functional institutional regional state and nonstate human rights enforcement. All these criteria need to be addressed seriously at the subnational, national, and regional policy levels; but, as the examples throughout this chapter suggest, any real success in these areas will have to contend with the continuing fact of state sovereignty. And there is little doubt it is winning in North America.

One strong implication of the arguments in this chapter is that to more effectively protect human rights—at least as they are now conceived—would require a reduction in the priority of, and unilateral exercise of, state sovereignty. This might be engendered legally through what Anthony Burke,[71] following Arendt in some crucial respects, has called the " 'cosmopolitanisation' of international law (such that its subjects are individual humans as much as states)." This would nevertheless require external institutional support by transnational organizations possessing the functional capacity to supersede state sovereignty. Regional institutions have attempted this with some (albeit uneven) success in Europe alongside a postnational, regional view of citizenship. Alternatively, a reduced emphasis on sovereignty might, in theory, be achieved internally, through more objective self-regulation of each state's exclusionary policies.

A major strand of arguments for "deep" regional integration reflects these ideas. Deep integration aims to promote the norms underpinning a more inclusive regional political we-community, while also supplying the supranational institutional machinery to forge a common perspective on regional problems and solutions, and enforce political responses that serve the interests of all wherever narrow national self-interest threatens to obstruct them. In practice, attempts to elevate an adequately institutionalized "people's sovereignty" over state sovereignty in this way have proved to be wildly unrealistic in the North American context. Yet, at least in the case of immigration policy and human rights, Arendt's contentions point to a cause for the region's cooperation failures that runs deeper than Hobbesian self-interest, international *realpolitik*, or even a desperate fear of leaving the Westphalian state system behind. They also suggest that any lasting solution will require

## 66 Emma R. Norman

more than formal institutional redesign intending to ameliorate national self-interest.

The fundamental issue is that the paradox of human rights remains unresolved at the conceptual level. Arendt's wider point was not merely that guaranteeing human rights in a notion of humanity may be impossible in an international system founded on the concept of state sovereignty. Even if it were possible, it generates an uncomfortable predicament: Thinking about the concept of humanity seriously forces us to confront the human capacity for political evil[72] and, at some point, requires us to assume collective responsibility for it.

> The idea of humanity, purged of all sentimentality, has the very serious consequence that in one form or another men must assume responsibility for all crimes committed by all men, and that eventually all nations will be forced to answer for all the evil committed by all others. Tribalism and racism are the very realistic, if very destructive, ways of escaping this predicament of common responsibility.[73]

The recent spate of immigration laws in North America and their obstructive effect on regional integration and cooperation are very clear examples of this escape mechanism in full operation. Perhaps most poignantly, they also reveal a continued ambivalence toward the profound implications that thinking seriously about the "inalienable" ground of human rights eventually unravels. When understood not merely (and in Arendt's view, naively) as either positivistic legal mechanisms[74] or protective shields for the individual to wield against the state,[75] but also as generators of grave collective responsibilities and duties, their demands are sobering. For Arendt, taking human rights seriously involves "the almost-unbearable burden of global political responsibility."[76] And so it may well be that the misconceptions characterizing their origin were born less from a misunderstanding of their requirement of a legal framework functionally distinct from that of the state, than from an unwillingness to face up to "the speechless horror of what man may do and what the world may become"[77] that this concept ultimately requires us to acknowledge. In view of Arendt's position here, taking the appropriate responsibility for human rights would certainly require not just a radical overhaul of the global state system, of international law and its relation to state law, and of the way different sets of rights can be expressed harmoniously on both these levels. It also requires a radical rethinking of the way humanity was, and is, understood and articulated.

The logical confusion in the relation between human rights and citizenship rights seems to be rooted in the unfounded assumption that humanity is somehow morally prior to citizenship because it is biologically prior to it. This biological element to some extent lies behind the general global conception of human rights today and the conceptual confusion in the Rights of Man and the UDHR. Yet Arendt's conceptual precision led her to argue

*Immigration and Institutional Voids* 67

consistently throughout her work that "humanity, politically speaking, does not reside in the natural fact of being alive; politically, humanity depends on artificial legal and political institutions to protect it."[78] The concept of humanity may be biologically categorized. And it is certainly an expression of collective moral responsibility when couched in the language of rights. But it is also ineluctably entangled in "the political"—and thoroughly "alienable" in consequence. Insofar as this conceptual confusion persists, it appears doubtful that either nonstate actors or transnational governmental institutions can be fully successful in stretching far enough across the institutional fissures in the legal safety net that the rivalry between human and citizen rights creates—fissures toward which millions of illegal immigrants are now being so deliberately herded.

## CONCLUSION

There is a tendency in Arendtian scholarship to view the concept of human superfluousness as ancillary to some of her more central arguments concerning the nature of political evil,[79] the origins of totalitarianism,[80] the concept of violence,[81] and the tensions between the life of the mind[82] and the *vita activa*.[83] Yet her critique of rights and views on superfluousness pinpoint and magnify the wider nexus of fundamental conceptual contradictions she identified in the way the relationships between the individual, the political community, and the state operate in the western tradition. This suggests not only that superfluousness might be a more principal element of her work than is often acknowledged by Arendtian scholars. It also reveals that the deeper tenets of this concept apply in contexts much wider than the narrow historical milieu in which Arendt first articulated it. As such, Arendt's work offers a valuable set of perspectives to empirical research on immigration and citizenship, international cooperation, regionalization, and the juridical and normative facets of the study and promotion of human rights.

In this chapter I have argued that the underfunctionality of human rights in the context of contemporary North American immigration is underscored and illuminated by multiple strands of Arendt's arguments concerning superfluousness. An important part of a plausible explanation for their underfunctionality lies in the conceptual confusion at the heart of the paradox of human rights she identified in 1951. The practical consequences of this paradox—then, as now—are significant, for if she is right, the implications for the success of future North American cooperation are profound—and worrying. Certain elements of globalization have meant superfluousness is no longer a condition restricted to the stateless, and capitalized on by totalitarian regimes in death camp scenarios. It is one tactic that can be utilized by otherwise democratic regimes in their attempts to reconcile the sovereignty requirements of the Westphalian state system with globalized conditions of migration, economic and political interdependence, heightened security

68  *Emma R. Norman*

measures, international legal obligations, and technological advances. One point to add here is that weak regional cooperation, self-interested unilateral or subnational problem solving, and radically unequal national status appear to provide many conditions for the systematic proliferation of new forms of superfluousness. The forms being generated in the region today are less extreme than those in Arendt's arguments. Yet, as we have seen, this does little to detract from their insidious character or potential spread.

Arendt highlighted that the way citizenship rights and human rights have been articulated together conceptually is, at base, conflictual. At best, this inefficient conceptualization leads to suboptimal outcomes in the case of migration and belonging issues, which certain historical contexts exacerbate. At worst, her arguments could be stretched to imply that any attempt to articulate such apparently incongruent views of rights together in the absence of institutional mechanisms that define their different purviews clearly in a globalized, deterritorialized setting is doomed to protracted difficulties, if not complete failure. In view of the many human rights successes over the last sixty-five years, it would be prudent to resist such a stretch. It seems fairer to say, as I have in this chapter, that the paradox of rights underpins a series of conceptual, normative, legal, governmental, and international institutional voids into which large groups of people can potentially slide and eventually disappear.

The central conclusion to be drawn from this is that the lack of effective regional institutions protecting human rights is not the only, and not the primary, source of the trouble the North American partners have encountered in cooperating on migration and security issues. The most crucial step in future efforts to bridge the institutional voids needs to begin at the conceptual level, or we risk importing the very same conceptual and logical problems encoded in the Rights of Man and the UDHR into the institutional redesigns of today and tomorrow. Theoretical developments to find a better way to express and articulate them alongside national citizenship rights and state-bound conceptions of sovereignty are absolutely necessary, if not sufficient. Without them, it is not only possible that formal and normative institutional development in the future toward better protection of minimum rights will encounter repeated conflicts similar to the ones discussed in this chapter. If Arendt's arguments are correct—and there is much contemporary evidence to suggest that they might be—it is likely.

## NOTES

1. Acknowledgment: this chapter builds on and extends an argument applied to the femicides in Ciudad Juarez, Mexico, in Emma R. Norman, "Falling through the Cracks: Superfluous Women at the Fault Lines of Citizenship, Sovereignty, and Human Rights," in *Feminist (Im)Mobilities in Fortress North America: Identities, Citizenships, and Human Rights in Transnational Perspective*, ed. Anne Runyan et al. (Farnham, UK: Ashgate, 2013):

in press. I am grateful to Ashley Biser, Gaspare Genna, Julián Castro-Rea, Jane H. Bayes, and two anonymous reviewers whose discussions with me or thoughtful comments on earlier drafts added depth and focus to the chapter's arguments.

2. Jeffrey Ayres and Laura Macdonald, "Deep Integration and Shallow Governance: The Limits to Civil Society Engagement across North America," *Policy and Society* 25 (2006): 23–42; Isabel Studer and Carol Wise, eds., *Requiem or Revival? The Promise of North American Integration* (Washington DC: Brookings Institution, 2007); Christina Gabriel and Laura Macdonald, "Migration and Citizenship Rights in a North American Space," in *Requiem or Revival? The Promise of North American Integration*, ed. Isabel Studer and Carol Wise, (Washington, DC: Brookings Institution, 2007): 267–287; Gaspare Genna and David Mayer-Foulkes, eds., "Beyond Borders: Migration, Security, and Cooperation in North America," *Politics & Policy* 39 Special Issue (2011); Lucy Luccisano, "Comparing Public Social Provision and Citizenship in the U.S., Canada and Mexico: Are There Implications for a North American Space?" *Politics and Policy* 35 (2007): 716–751; Ann Capling and Kim Richard Nossal, "The Contradictions of Regionalism in North America," *Review of International Studies* 35, no. 1 (2009): 147–167; Claude Denis, "Canadians in Trouble Abroad: Citizenship, Personal Security and North American Regionalization," *Politics & Policy* 35, no. 4 (2007): 648–663. Accessed November 7, 2012, http://onlinelibrary.wiley.com/doi/10.1111/j.1747-1346.2007.00078.x/abstract.

3. For a fuller theoretical discussion of the connections between Arendt's arguments on rights, superfluousness, and state sovereignty than I can give here, see Emma R. Norman, "Violence and Deprivation: Arendt and the Pervasiveness of Superfluous Life" (paper presented at the annual meeting of the *Midwest Political Science Association*, Chicago, IL, April 2–5, 2009). For detailed theoretical treatments of her work on "the right to have rights" and political evil, see Richard J. Bernstein, "Are Arendt's Reflections on Evil Still Relevant?" *Review of Politics* 70 (2008): 64–76; Richard J. Bernstein, *Hannah Arendt and the Jewish Question* (Cambridge: MIT, 1996); Dana R. Villa, *Politics, Philosophy, Terror: Essays on the Thought of Hannah Arendt* (Princeton, NJ: Princeton University Press, 1999); Giorgio Agamben, *Homo Sacer: Sovereign Power and Bare Life* (Stanford, CA: Stanford University Press, 1998); Peg Birmingham, *Hannah Arendt and Human Rights: The Predicament of Common Responsibility* (Bloomington: Indiana University Press, 2006); James D. Ingram, "What Is a 'Right to Have Rights'?: Three Images of the Politics of Human Rights," *American Political Science Review* 102 (2008): 401–416. For more on applying Arendt's critique of human rights and superfluousness to contemporary practical political issues see Emma R. Norman, "Superfluousness, Human Rights and the State: Applying Arendt to Questions of Femicide, Narco Violence and Illegal Immigration in a Globalized World" (paper presented at the annual meeting of the Midwest Political Science Association, Chicago, IL, March 31–April 3, 2011).

4. Hannah Arendt, *The Origins of Totalitarianism* (1951; New York: Harcourt Brace, 1966), 300.

5. Arendt, *Origins*, 291.

6. Ibid.

7. Arendt, *Origins*, 298.

8. Arendt, *Origins*, 285.

9. Bridget Cotter, "Hannah Arendt and the 'Right' to Have Rights," in *Hannah Arendt and International Relations: Readings Across the Lines*, ed. Anthony F. Lang and John Williams (New York: Palgrave Macmillan, 2005): 97.

70   *Emma R. Norman*

10. Arendt, *Origins*, 294.
11. Arendt, *Origins*, 296.
12. Arendt, *Origins*, 283, citing R. Yewdall Jermings, "Some International Aspects of the Refugee Question," *British Yearbook of International Law*, 1939.
13. Agamben, *Homo Sacer*, 126.
14. UDHR, Article 15: "(1) Everyone has the right to a nationality. (2) No one shall be arbitrarily deprived of his nationality nor denied the right to change his nationality." United Nations, "Universal Declaration of Human Rights," 1948, accessed August 8, 2012, http://www.un.org/en/documents/udhr/index.shtml#a15.
15. See Julia Harrington, "African Arguments," African Arguments, 2009, accessed January 14, 2012, http://africanarguments.org/2009/10/the-right-to-citizenship-under-international-law/; Emma R. Norman, "Falling through the Cracks: Superfluous Women at the Fault Lines of Citizenship, Sovereignty, and Human Rights," in *Feminist (Im)Mobilities in Fortress North America: Identities, Citizenships, and Human Rights in Transnational Perspective*, ed. Anne Runyan et al. (Farnham, UK: Ashgate, 2013).
16. Arendt, *Origins*, 295–296.
17. Arendt, *Origins*, 296.
18. Including, to some extent, many nontotalitarian European states—particularly regarding the role of the police in dealing with stateless persons. Arendt, *Origins*, 283–288.
19. See George Friedman, "Germany and the Failure of Multiculturalism,"Stratfor, October 19, 2010, accessed March 9, 2011, http://www.stratfor.com/weekly/20101018_germany_and_failure_multiculturalism?utm_source=GWeekly&utm_medium=email&utm_campaign=101019&utm_content=readmore&elq=c02dbcc02ca74bf8b1cab74400f424ec; Laura Kuenssberg, "State Multiculturalism Has Failed, Says David Cameron," *BBC News*, February 5, 2011, accessed March 9, 2012, http://www.bbc.co.uk/news/uk-politics-12371994; Imran Awan, "'I'm a Muslim Not an Extremist': How the Prevent Strategy Has Constructed a 'Suspect' Community," *Politics & Policy* 40, 6 (2012): 1158–1185; Euronews, "Europeans: Nationalist Rhetoric Rubs Off," YouTube, June 16, 2007, accessed September 20, 2012, http://www.youtube.com/watch?v=PuX1aWKCJYU; Charles Clover, "Putin Turns Up Nationalist Rhetoric," *Financial Times*, February 23, 2012; cf. Bhikhu Parekh, "The Future of Multi-ethnic Britain," Runnymede Trust, 2000, accessed September 12, 2012, http://www.runnymedetrust.org/projects/meb/report.html.
20. Arendt, *Origins*, 294–295.
21. Arendt, *Origins*, 447–455.
22. Arendt, *Origins*, 287–288.
23. Administrative detention of refugees and asylum seekers is widespread in Europe, the United States, and Australasia in restrictive detention centers and frequently in prisons. For example, from 2001 to 2008 the Australian government shipped asylum seekers to offshore camps on Nauru and Manus Islands, Papua New Guinea. Both camps were shut in 2008, but the Christmas Island detention center remains to deal with Australia's policy of mandatory detention for unauthorized aliens. See Cotter, "Hannah Arendt," 95–112. See also Stephanie J. Silverman, "'Regrettable but Necessary'? A Historical and Theoretical Study of the Rise of the UK Immigration Detention Estate and Its Opposition," *Politics & Policy* 40, 6 (2012): 1131–1157, for a detailed analysis of the "rise of the UK immigration detention state."
24. See Arendt, *Origins*, 447–455.
25. Arendt, *Origins*, 445.

## Immigration and Institutional Voids 71

26. Arendt, *Origins*, 295–296.
27. Arendt, *Origins*, 443.
28. She later contrasted this with the terrifyingly increased potential for super-fluousness brought about by technological advances like the A-bomb. "The frightening coincidence of the modern population explosion with the discovery of technical devices that, through automation, will make large sections of the population 'superfluous' even in terms of labor, and that, through nuclear energy, make it possible to deal with this twofold threat by the use of instruments beside which Hitler's gassing installations look like an evil child's fumbling toys, should be enough to make us tremble." Hannah Arendt, *Eichmann in Jerusalem: A Report on the Banality of Evil* (New York: Viking, 1963): 273.
29. Norman, "Falling."
30. Gabriel and Macdonald, "Migration," 271.
31. See L. Schuster and J. Solomos, "Rights and Wrongs across European Borders: Migrants, Minorities and Citizenship," *Citizenship Studies* 6 (2002): 37–54; Yasemin Soysal, "Citizenship and Identity: Living in Diasporas in Postwar Europe," in *The Postnational Self: Belonging and Identity*, ed. Ulf Hedetoft and Mette Hjort (Minneapolis: University of Minnesota Press, 2002): 137–151; Yasemin Soysal, *Limits of Citizenship: Migrants and Postnational Membership in Europe* (Chicago: University of Chicago Press, 1994); S. Benhabib and J. Resnick, "Introduction: Citizenship and Migration Theory Engendered," in *Migrations and Mobilities: Citizenship, Borders and Gender*, ed. S. Benhabib and J. Resnick (New York: New York University Press, 2009): 1–47; L. Bosniak, "Denationalizing Citizenship," in *Citizenship Today: Global Perspectives and Practices*, ed. T. A. Aleinikoff and D. B. Klusmeyer (Washington, DC: Carnegie Endowment for International Peace, 2001): 237–252.
32. Trade Compliance Center, "Chapter Sixteen of the North American Free Trade Agreement," Export.gov, accessed March 10, 2012, http://tcc.export.gov/Trade_Agreements/Exporters_Guides/List_All_Guides/NAFTA_chapter16_guide.asp.
33. Citizenship and Immigration Canada, "Canada Imposes a Visa on Mexico," July 13, 2009, accessed December 8, 2010, http://www.cic.gc.ca/english/department/media/releases/2009/2009–07–13.asp.
34. Canadian Council for Refugees, "Safe Third Country Decision Welcomed by Rights Organizations and John Doe," November 30, 2007, accessed March 9, 2012, http://ccrweb.ca/eng/media/pressreleases/30nov07.htm.
35. Steven E. Gunkel and Ana-María González Wahl, "Unauthorized Migrants and the (Il)Logic of 'Crime Control': A Human Rights Perspective on US Federal and Local State Immigration Policies," *Sociology Compass* 6 (2012): 26; cf. Gabriel and Macdonald, "Migration."
36. US Government Accountability Office (GAO), *U.S. Customs and Border Protection's Border Security Fencing, Infrastructure and Technology Fiscal Year 2011 Expenditure Plan*, November 17, 2011, accessed February 5, 2013, http://www.gao.gov/new.items/d12106r.pdf.
37. Roxanne L. Doty, "Bare Life: Border-Crossing Deaths and Spaces of Moral Alibi," *Environment and Planning D: Society and Space* 29 (2011): 599–612; cf. Wayne A. Cornelius, Scott Borger, Adam Sawyer, David Keyes, Clare Appleby, Kristen Parks, Gabriel Lozada, and Jonathan Hicken, "Controlling Unauthorized Immigration from Mexico: The Failure of 'Prevention through Deterrence' and the Need for Comprehensive Reform," Immigration Policy Center, June 10, 2008, accessed September 10, 2012, http://www.immigrationforum.org/images/uploads/CCISbriefing061008.pdf.
38. Arendt, *Origins*, 278.
39. Arendt, *Origins*, 279.

72  *Emma R. Norman*

40. Along the drug routes from Central America, throughout the border region, and due to many other factors unrelated to the narco wars.
41. Gunkel and González Wahl, "Unauthorized Migrants," 40.
42. Gunkel and González Wahl, "Unauthorized Migrants," 39.
43. Gunkel and González Wahl, "Unauthorized Migrants," 40.
44. Aimee Mayer, Jessica Lynd, Christopher Tansey, Molly Hofsommer, Misty Seemans, Kaitlin Brush, and Leah Chavla, "International Legal Updates," *Human Rights Brief* 18 (2010): 31.
45. Ibid.
46. Ibid.
47. Ibid.
48. See Agamben, *Homo Sacer*.
49. Adam Liptak, "Blocking Parts of Arizona Law, Justices Allow Its Centerpiece," *New York Times*, June 25, 2012.
50. European Parliament, "European Parliament Resolution of September 9, 2010 on the Situation of Roma and on Freedom of Movement within the European Union," 2010, accessed August 29, 2012, http://www.europarl.europa.eu/sides/getDoc.do?pubRef=-//EP//TEXT+TA+P7-TA-2010-0312+0+DOC+XML+V0//EN.
51. It should be noted that the French government complied only after claiming the expulsions of the Roma were based on questions of national security, not ethnicity (Mayer et al., "International Legal Updates," 36), an argument paralleled at the US subnational state level in the February 7, 2012, Arizona brief to the Supreme Court in defense of the four provisions it blocked of SB 1070 (Ben Winograd, "In Fight over SB 1070, Arizona Makes an All-Too Familiar Case to the Supreme Court," Immigration Impact, February 7, 2012, accessed February 16, 2012, http://immigrationimpact.com/2012/02/07/in-fight-over-sb-1070-arizona-makes-an-all-too-familiar-case-to-the-supreme-court/).
52. The bitter row over the Roma reignited in August 2012, when France again expelled from its soil 240 Roma and dismantled two other Roma encampments, leaving many Roma homeless (see Human Rights Watch, "France Renews Crackdown on Roma," August 10, 2012, accessed September 1, 2012, http://www.hrw.org/news/2012/08/10/france-renewed-crackdown-roma). While this has again evoked public outcry in Europe (see Timothy Spence, "Rights Groups Press Europe for Robust Response to Mass Roma Expulsions," *Interdependent*, September 21, 2012, United Nations Association, accessed September 30, 2012, http://www.theinterdependent.com/human-rights/article/rights-groups-press-europe-for-robust-response-to-mass-roma-expulsions), the reoccurrence casts doubt on the long-term effectiveness of EU institutional responses to member states' expressions of state sovereignty via deportation. It likewise questions the long-term ability of any existing or future regional institutions to effectively protect human rights even if their institutional powers are strong.
53. At the time of writing, the EU has not responded with a formal resolution to the ongoing 2012 French Roma expulsions and Roma camp dismantlement, or similar discrimination policies against the Roma in Italy and several other member states (see Amnesty International, "Op-Ed: Europe's Roma Discrimination Shame," October 25, 2012, accessed February 5, 2013, http://www.amnesty.org/en/news/op-ed-don-t-forget-past-abuses-fix-current-attitudes-towards-europe-s-roma-2012-10-25).
54. Mary Bauer, "Testimony before Congressional Ad Hoc HB 56 Hearing," Southern Poverty Law Center, November 21, 2011, accessed June 3, 2012, http://www.splcenter.org/get-informed/news/testimony-before-congressional-ad-hoc-hb56-hearing.

*Immigration and Institutional Voids* 73

55. Ibid.
56. Michele Waslin, "Discrediting 'Self-Deportation' as Immigration Policy," American Immigration Council, February 6, 2012, accessed September 2, 2012, http://www.immigrationpolicy.org/special-reports/discrediting-"self-deportation"-immigration-policy; Campbell Robertson and Julia Preston, "Appeals Court Draws Boundaries on Alabama's Immigration Law," *New York Times*, August 21, 2012.
57. Robertson and Preston, "Appeals Court."
58. Michele Waslin, "New Report Examines Dire Consequences of 'Attrition through Enforcement Immigration Strategy,' " Immigration Impact, February 6, 2012, accessed February 15, 2012, http://immigrationimpact.com/2012/02/06/new-report-examines-dire-consequences-of-attrition-through-enforcement-immigration-strategy/.
59. Ibid.
60. Bob Moser, "Samaritans in the Desert." *Nation* 20 (2003): 13, cited by Gunkel and González Wahl, "Unauthorized Migrants," 39.
61. Winograd, "Arizona Makes an All-Too Familiar Case."
62. Arendt, *Origins*, 279.
63. Gunkel and González Wahl, "Unauthorized Migrants," 40; Silverman, " 'Regrettable," 1134.
64. See Soysal, *Limits of Citizenship*; Soysal, "Citizenship and Identity."
65. See Norman, "Falling."
66. Arendt, *Eichmann*; see also Judith Butler, "Hannah Arendt's Challenge to Adolf Eichmann," *Guardian*, August 29, 2011.
67. Randall Amster, "Arizona Bans Ethnic Studies and, Along with It, Reason and Justice," *Truthout*, December 28, 2010, accessed January 15, 2012, http://www.truth-out.org/arizona-bans-ethnic-studies-and-along-with-it-reason-and-justice66340.
68. State of Arizona. HB 2281, Section 1, Chapter 15, Article 1, 15–111. House of Representatives. [0]2010. Accessed Jan. 14, 2011, http://www.azleg.gov/legtext/49leg/2r/bills/hb2281s.pdf.
69. In Alabama, a new law that became effective on April 1, 2012, required all employers to hire only verified employees in return for immunity from liability for employing an unauthorized alien. First violations of the new law require the termination of employment of the unauthorized alien and a sworn affidavit on the part of the employer never to hire one again. Second violations incur a revocation of all an employer's business licenses in the county. Subsequent violations extend this statewide. Mississippi, South Carolina, North Carolina, and Arizona already require all or most employers to participate in the program. Many states, most notably Colorado, Georgia, South Carolina, and Virginia laws require its use for certain sectors: public employers, state agencies, or government contractors.
70. Pete Kasperowicz, "House Passes Bill Extending E-Verify, Other Immigration Programs," *The Hill: Floor Action Blog*, September 13, 2012, accessed September 29, http://thehill.com/blogs/floor-action/house/249455-house-passes-bill-extending-e-verify-other-immigration-programs.
71. Anthony Burke, "Recovering Humanity from Man: Hannah Arendt's Troubled Cosmopolitanism," *International Politics* 45 (2008): 514–521.
72. Birmingham, *Hannah Arendt*, 7.
73. Arendt, *Origins*, 236.
74. E.g., H. L. A. Hart, "Positivism and the Separation of Law and Morals," *Harvard Law Review* 7 (1958): 593. H. L. A. Hart, *Essays on Jurisprudence and Philosophy* (Oxford: Clarendon, 1983); Hans Kelsen, *General Theory of Law and State*, trans. A. Wedberg (New York: Russell and Russell, 1945).
75. E.g., Ronald Dworkin, *Taking Rights Seriously* (Cambridge MA: Harvard University Press, 1978).

## 74  Emma R. Norman

76. Birmingham, *Hannah Arendt*, 7.
77. Hannah Arendt, *Essays in Understanding*, ed. Jerome Kohn (New York: Harcourt Brace, 1994), 445.
78. André Duarte, "Biopolitics and the Dissemination of Violence: The Arendtian Critique of the Present," April 27, 2005, HannahArendt.net, accessed March 8, 2009, accessed February 5, 2013, http://www.hannaharendt.net/index.php/han/article/view/69/102; see also Agamben, *Homo Sacer*.
79. Arendt, *Eichmann*.
80. Arendt, *Origins*.
81. Hannah Arendt, *On Violence* (San Diego, CA: Harvest Books, 1970).
82. Hannah Arendt, *The Life of the Mind* (New York: Harcourt Brace Jovanovich, 1978).
83. Hannah Arendt, *The Human Condition* (Chicago: University of Chicago Press, 1958).

## REFERENCES

Agamben, Giorgio. 1998. *Homo Sacer: Sovereign Power and Bare Life*. Stanford, CA: Stanford University Press.
Amnesty International. "Op-Ed: Europe's Roma Discrimination Shame." 2012. Accessed October 26, 2012. http://www.amnesty.org/en/news/op-ed-don-t-forget-past-abuses-fix-current-attitudes-towards-europe-s-roma-2012-10-25.
Amster, Randall. "Arizona Bans Ethnic Studies and, Along with It, Reason and Justice." *Truthout*. December 28, 2010. Accessed January 15, 2012. http://www.truth-out.org/arizona-bans-ethnic-studies-and-along-with-it-reason-and-justice66340.
Arendt, Hannah. *Eichmann in Jerusalem: A Report on the Banality of Evil*. New York: Viking, 1963.
———. *Essays in Understanding*. Edited by Jerome Kohn. New York: Harcourt Brace, 1994.
———. *The Human Condition*. Chicago: University of Chicago Press, 1958.
———. *The Life of the Mind*. New York: Harcourt Brace Jovanovich, 1978.
———. *On Violence*. San Diego: Harvest Books, 1970.
———. *The Origins of Totalitarianism*. 1951. New York: Harcourt Brace, 1966.
Awan, Imran. "'I'm a Muslim Not an Extremist': How the Prevent Strategy Has Constructed a 'Suspect' Community." *Politics & Policy* 40, no. 6 (2012): 1158–1185.
Ayres, Jeffrey, and Laura Macdonald. "Deep Integration and Shallow Governance: The Limits to Civil Society Engagement across North America." *Policy and Society* 25, no. 3 (2006): 23–42.
Bauer, Mary. "Testimony before Congressional Ad Hoc HB 56 Hearing." Southern Poverty Law Center. November 21, 2011. Accessed June 3, 2012. http://www.splcenter.org/get-informed/news/testimony-before-congressional-ad-hoc-hb56-hearing.
*BBC News*. "State Multiculturalism Has Failed, Says David Cameron." 2011. Accessed September 12, 2012. http://www.bbc.co.uk/news/uk-politics-12371994.
Benhabib, S., and J. Resnick. "Introduction: Citizenship and Migration Theory Engendered." In *Migrations and Mobilities: Citizenship, Borders and Gender*, edited by S. Benhabib and J. Resnick, 1–46. New York: New York University Press, 2009.
Bernstein, Richard J. "Are Arendt's Reflections on Evil Still Relevant?" *Review of Politics* 70 (2008): 64–76.
———. *Hannah Arendt and the Jewish Question*. Cambridge: MIT, 1996.
Birmingham, Peg. *Hannah Arendt and Human Rights: The Predicament of Common Responsibility*. Bloomington: Indiana University Press, 2006.

Bosniak, L. "Denationalizing Citizenship." In *Citizenship Today: Global Perspectives and Practices*, edited by T. A. Aleinikoff and D. B. Klusmeyer, 237–252. Washington, DC: Carnegie Endowment for International Peace, 2001.

Burke, Anthony. "Recovering Humanity from Man: Hannah Arendt's Troubled Cosmopolitanism." *International Politics* 45 (2008): 514–521.

Butler, Judith. "Hannah Arendt's Challenge to Adolf Eichmann." *Guardian*. August 29, 2011. Accessed October 25, 2012. http://www.guardian.co.uk/commentisfree/2011/aug/29/hannah-arendt-adolf-eichmann-banality-of-evil.

Canadian Council for Refugees. "Safe Third Country Decision Welcomed by Rights Organizations and John Doe." November 30, 2007. Accessed March 9, 2012. http://ccrweb.ca/eng/media/pressreleases/30nov07.htm.

Citizenship and Immigration Canada. "Canada Imposes a Visa on Mexico." July 13, 2009. Accessed December 8, 2010. http://www.cic.gc.ca/english/department/media/releases/2009/2009–07–13.asp.

Clover, Charles. "Putin Turns Up Nationalist Rhetoric." *Financial Times*. February 23, 2012. Accessed March 20, 2012. http://www.ft.com/cms/s/0/bc48785c-5e17–11e1–8c87–00144feabdc0.html#axzz28Qk7xt2V.

Cornelius, Wayne A., Scott Borger, Adam Sawyer, David Keyes, Clare Appleby, Kristen Parks, Gabriel Lozada, and Jonathan Hicken. "Controlling Unauthorized Immigration from Mexico: The Failure of 'Prevention through Deterrence' and the Need for Comprehensive Reform." Immigration Policy Center. June 10, 2008. Accessed September 10, 2012. http://www.immigrationforum.org/images/uploads/CCISbriefing061008.pdf.

Cotter, Bridget. "Hannah Arendt and the 'Right' to Have Rights." In *Hannah Arendt and International Relations: Readings across the Lines*, edited by Anthony F. Lang and John Williams, 95–112. New York: Palgrave Macmillan, 2005.

Doty, Roxanne L. "Bare Life: Border-Crossing Deaths and Spaces of Moral Alibi." *Environment and Planning D: Society and Space* 29, no. 4 (2011): 599–612. Accessed September 10, 2012. http://www.envplan.com/abstract.cgi?id=d3110.

Duarte, André. "Biopolitics and the Dissemination of Violence: The Arendtian Critique of the Present." HannahArendt.net. April 27, 2005. Accessed March 8, 2009. http://www.hannaharendt.net/index.php/han/article/view/69/102.

Dworkin, Ronald. *Taking Rights Seriously*. Cambridge, MA: Harvard University Press, 1978.

Euronews. "EN—Europeans: Nationalist Rhetoric Rubs Off." YouTube. June 16, 2007. Accessed September 20, 2012. http://www.youtube.com/watch?v=PuX1aWKCJYU.

European Parliament. "European Parliament Resolution of September 9 2010 on the Situation of Roma and on Freedom of Movement within the European Union." 2010. Accessed August 29, 2012. http://www.europarl.europa.eu/sides/getDoc.do?pubRef=-//EP//TEXT+TA+P7-TA-2010-0312+0+DOC+XML+V0//EN.

Friedman, George. "Germany and the Failure of Multiculturalism." Stratfor. October 19, 2010. Accessed March 9, 2011. http://www.stratfor.com/weekly/20101018_germany_and_failure_multiculturalism?utm_source=GWeekly&utm_medium=email&utm_campaign=101019&utm_content=readmore&elq=c02dbc c02ca74bf8b1cab74400f424ec.

Gabriel, Christina, and Laura Macdonald. "Migration and Citizenship Rights in a North American Space." In *Requiem or Revival? The Promise of North American Integration*, edited by Isabel Studer and Carol Wise, 267–287. Washington DC: Brookings Institution, 2007.

Genna, Gaspare, and David Mayer-Foulkes, eds. "Beyond Borders: Migration, Security, and Cooperation in North America." *Politics & Policy Special Issue* 39, no. 1 (2011). Accessed February 27, 2012. http://onlinelibrary.wiley.com/doi/10.1111/polp.2011.39.issue-1/issuetoc.

76 *Emma R. Norman*

Gunkel, Steven E., and Ana-María González Wahl. "Unauthorized Migrants and the (Il)Logic of 'Crime Control': A Human Rights Perspective on US Federal and Local State Immigration Policies." *Sociology Compass* 6, no. 1 (2012): 26–45.

Harrington, Julia. "African Arguments." African Arguments. 2009. Accessed January 14, 2012. http://africanarguments.org/2009/10/the-right-to-citizenship-under-international-law/.

Hart, H. L. A. *Essays on Jurisprudence and Philosophy*. Oxford: Clarendon, 1983.

———. "Positivism and the Separation of Law and Morals." *Harvard Law Review* 71, no. 4 (1958): 593–629.

Human Rights Watch. "France Renews Crackdown on Roma." August 10, 2012. Accessed September 1, 2012. http://www.hrw.org/news/2012/08/10/france-renewed-crackdown-roma.

Ingram, James D. "What Is a 'Right to Have Rights'?: Three Images of the Politics of Human Rights." *American Political Science Review* 102, no. 4 (2008): 401–416.

Jermings, R. Yewdall. "Some International Aspects of the Refugee Question." *British Yearbook of International Law*. 1939.

Kasperowicz, Pete. "House Passes Bill Extending E-Verify, Other Immigration Programs." *The Hill: Floor Action Blog*. September 13, 2012. Accessed September 29. http://thehill.com/blogs/floor-action/house/249455-house-passes-bill-extending-e-verify-other-immigration-programs.

Kelsen, Hans. *General Theory of Law and State*. Translated by A. Wedberg. New York: Russell and Russell, 1945.

Kuenssberg, Laura. "State Multiculturalism Has Failed, Says David Cameron." *BBC News*. February 5, 2011. Accessed March 9, 2012. http://www.bbc.co.uk/news/uk-politics-12371994.

Liptak, Adam. "Blocking Parts of Arizona Law, Justices Allow Its Centerpiece." *New York Times*. June 25, 2012. Accessed July 1, 2012. http://www.nytimes.com/2012/06/26/us/supreme-court-rejects-part-of-arizona-immigration-law.html.

Luccisano, Lucy. "Comparing Public Social Provision and Citizenship in the U.S., Canada and Mexico: Are There Implications for a North American Space?" *Politics and Policy* 35, no. 4 (2007): 716–751.

Mayer, Aimee, Jessica Lynd, Christopher Tansey, Molly Hofsommer, Misty Seemans, Kaitlin Brush, and Leah Chavla. "International Legal Updates." *Human Rights Brief* 18, no. 1 (2010): 31–41.

Moser, Bob. "Samaritans in the Desert." *Nation* 276, no. 20 (2003): 13–18.

Norman, Emma R. "Falling through the Cracks: Superfluous Women at the Fault Lines of Citizenship, Sovereignty, and Human Rights." In *Feminist (Im)Mobilities in Fortress North America: Identities, Citizenships, and Human Rights in Transnational Perspective*, edited by Anne Runyan et al. Farnham, UK: Ashgate, forthcoming.

———. "Superfluousness, Human Rights and the State: Applying Arendt to Questions of Femicide, Narco Violence and Illegal Immigration in a Globalized World." Paper presented at the annual meeting of the Midwest Political Science Association, Chicago, IL, March 31–April 3, 2011.

———. "Violence and Deprivation: Arendt and the Pervasiveness of Superfluous Life." Paper presented at the annual meeting of the Midwest Political Science Association, Chicago, IL, April 2–5, 2009.

Parekh, Bhikhu. *The Future of Multi-ethnic Britain*. Runnymede Trust. 2000. Accessed September 12, 2012. http://www.runnymedetrust.org/projects/meb/report.html.

Robertson, Campbell, and Julia Preston. "Appeals Court Draws Boundaries on Alabama's Immigration Law." *New York Times*. August 21, 2012. Accessed

September 1, 2012. http://www.nytimes.com/2012/08/22/us/appeals-court-limits-alabamas-immigration-law.html?_r=0

Schuster, L., and J. Solomos. "Rights and Wrongs across European Borders: Migrants, Minorities and Citizenship." *Citizenship Studies* 6, no. 1 (2002): 37–54.

Silverman, Stephanie J. " 'Regrettable but Necessary'? A Historical and Theoretical Study of the Rise of the UK Immigration Detention Estate and Its Opposition." *Politics & Policy* 40, no. 6 (2012): 1131–1157.

Soysal, Yasemin. "Citizenship and Identity: Living in Diasporas in Postwar Europe," in *The Postnational Self: Belonging and Identity*, edited by Ulf Hedetoft and Mette Hjort, 137–151. Minneapolis: University of Minnesota Press, 2002.

———. *Limits of Citizenship: Migrants and Postnational Membership in Europe.* Chicago: University of Chicago Press, 1994.

Spence, Timothy. "Rights Groups Press Europe for Robust Response to Mass Roma Expulsions." *Interdependent*. United Nations Association. September 21, 2012. Accessed September 30, 2012. http://www.theinterdependent.com/human-rights/article/rights-groups-press-europe-for-robust-response-to-mass-roma-expulsions.

State of Arizona. HB 2281, Section 1, Chapter 15, Article 1, 15–111. House of Representatives. 2010. Accessed Jan. 14, 2011. http://www.azleg.gov/legtext/49leg/2r/bills/hb2281s.pdf.

Studer, Isabel, and Carol Wise, eds. *Requiem or Revival? The Promise of North American Integration*. Washington DC: Brookings Institution, 2007.

Trade Compliance Center. "Chapter 16 of the North American Free Trade Agreement." Export.gov. Accessed March 10, 2012. http://tcc.export.gov/Trade_Agreements/Exporters_Guides/List_All_Guides/NAFTA_chapter16_guide.asp.

United Nations. "Universal Declaration of Human Rights." 1948. Accessed August 8, 2012. http://www.un.org/en/documents/udhr/index.shtml#a15.

US Government Accountability Office (GAO). *U.S. Customs and Border Protection's Border Security Fencing, Infrastructure and Technology Fiscal Year 2011 Expenditure Plan*. November 17, 2011. http://www.gao.gov/new.items/d12106r.pdf.

Villa, Dana R. *Politics, Philosophy, Terror: Essays on the Thought of Hannah Arendt.* Princeton, NJ: Princeton University Press, 1999.

Waslin, Michele. "Discrediting "Self-Deportation" as Immigration Policy." American Immigration Council. February 6, 2012. Accessed September 2, 2012. http://www.immigrationpolicy.org/special-reports/discrediting-"self-deportation"-immigration-policy.

———. "New Report Examines Dire Consequences of 'Attrition through Enforcement Immigration Strategy.' " Immigration Impact. February 6, 2012. Accessed February 15, 2012. http://immigrationimpact.com/2012/02/06/new-report-examines-dire-consequences-of-attrition-through-enforcement-immigration-strategy/.

Winograd, Ben. "In Fight over SB 1070, Arizona Makes an All-Too Familiar Case to the Supreme Court." Immigration Impact. February 7, 2012. Accessed February 16, 2012. http://immigrationimpact.com/2012/02/07/in-fight-over-sb-1070-arizona-makes-an-all-too-familiar-case-to-the-supreme-court/.

# 5 Democracy and Development for Mexico

*David A. Mayer-Foulkes*
*and Raúl García-Barrios*

## INTRODUCTION

In the last two decades Mexico has lived through two fundamental transformations of its social and economic life. First, it adopted as its central strategy for economic growth a program of economic liberalization, and opened its markets to global international trade. Second, its decades-long transformation towards democracy finally overcame seventy years of uninterrupted rule by the Institutional Revolutionary Party (PRI) that emerged from the Mexican Revolution. Each of these sets of deep changes had promised to bring with it long-sought solutions to the problems of poverty, inequality and a deficient state of rights and rule of law. Instead, the country has experienced low rates of economic growth, continued poverty and unemployment, and twelve years of deadlock in Congress, and now faces a painful and costly war on drugs.

The situation has reached such a level of difficulty and pessimism that simply stating "peace, democracy and development for Mexico" seems naive. The need to reevaluate the economic and political thought that orients Mexico's development arises naturally. Even without the drug war, the wide spectrum of social classes in Mexico gives rise to conflicting views and aims on development that are enough to block political, and even academic, dialogue on our economic and social reality.

At the same time, these problems now concur with a global economic crisis that itself brings up internationally the need for a paradigmatic shift in thinking. Both developed and underdeveloped countries now need to make their own "local" policies work in a global context. In particular, the United States has been hard hit by the economic crisis and is under the impact of economic forces, of which it is at the same time one of the main actors and yet hardly aware of their functioning and consequences. While the United States puts its eyes mainly on Asia, Europe and the Middle East, for Mexico its own development is intimately tied to the United States, in economic terms, in a cross-cultural dialogue of economic and political ideas, and in the never ending impacts of power. Mexico's problems are not isolated, but instead occur in a context of globalization that is now common across the world.

Democracy and Development for Mexico    79

It is thus inevitable that, while our purpose is to develop an economic and political synthesis of ideas that can contribute to a common-good consensus for economic and political development in Mexico, we at the same time must address some of the fundamental dilemmas faced by the United States and globalization, trying to contribute to a basis for cross-country dialogue.

Even today, a decade into the twenty-first century, economic thinking is still based on a series of paradigms that represent beliefs and convictions rather than well-established social fact. There are still schools in economics: neoclassical, Keynesian, Marxist and the modern theory of economic growth can hardly be thought of as belonging to the same discipline. Historical context and political preferences continue to be strong determinants of the predominant modes of economic thinking used to formulate policy. The mix of these determinants is considerably different in Mexico and the United States. Nevertheless, the seminal ideas from which they draw, running along schools or strands of thought, have the same origins. Our purpose is to conduct an objective discussion of these various political economy paradigms and to contribute to a synthesis that can serve to evaluate and formulate policy.

A necessary feature that emerges in this synthesis is an ethical content and a search for true humanity. Justice, equality, freedom and community matter to our science, which must illuminate policy making that is ethical, vibrantly human and sustainable.

In what follows we successively discuss the contributions of different schools in economics, put them in a critical perspective under the light of historical and economic realities, and find how they fit together to make a single body of economic thought.

In an epilogue, we then explore what our synthesis has to say on North American integration.

## A SINGLE BODY OF ECONOMIC THOUGHT

### Neoclassical Economics

In neoclassical economics, the mathematical jewel is the theory of general equilibrium. This theory shows how, when many small agents each produce and consume so as to maximize their own production profits and consumption utilities, free market exchange can lead to a certain kind of optimum and efficiency: that no economic improvement exists making anyone better off that does not make someone else worse off.[1]

This result has an ethical level in that given an initial distribution of assets, market exchange produces for its participants the best possible result for cooperating through exchange of goods and services. In that sense, participation is free and voluntary. It is unnecessary for a government to intervene for this result to be obtained. This result is very attractive, because if a society is characterized by a broadly equal distribution of wealth, then the market

## 80   David A. Mayer-Foulkes and Raúl García-Barrios

mechanism is a means to coordinate the economic actions and desires of a multitude of people, without the need for government. Combined with property rights, it also rewards individual initiative with the fruits of its efforts. However, market exchange as such will leave inequality and poverty untouched.

The idea that government should not interfere with economic life but instead restrict itself to the provision of public goods and the maintenance of market institutions is supported by these optimal properties of market exchange.

Government itself, when it fails and is characterized by the abuse of power, does not have the ethical level of markets. Thus, for the purpose of clarity, we define four ethical levels:

E0. No ethical level—abuse of power
E1. Individual rights, Pareto efficiency
E2. Individual rights and pursuit of equality
E3. E2 plus extensive human rights and community values

At ethical level E0, the rich and powerful can force a transfer from the poor. At level E1, individuals live according to their assets and wealth, billionaires and homeless side by side. At level E2, while there are property rights, there are also economic obligations from the rich towards the poor, and society continually restores equality. At this point, ethical level E2 could be perceived by many as an external imposition. Ethical level E3 represents a wider, non-economicist, integrated conception of equality, humanity and community.

Economists acknowledge that the perfect markets result holds only under stringent conditions: a) production has diminishing returns, consumption diminishing marginal utility; b) all agents are perfectly informed about the relevant present and future actions of all other agents; and c) all agents are too small to engage in strategic economic behavior affecting any market.

If any of these conditions does not hold, the attractive properties of market exchange are lost, and their ethical level tends to move, from E1 towards E0: a) if there are increasing returns to scale, theory predicts monopolies and oligopolies will form, with the result that market exchange tends to concentrate resources into a few wealthy hands; b) when there are large agents, strategic behavior including credible threats can again allow large agents to take advantage of small agents; and c) problems of information will also allow some people to take advantage of others, or will result in coordination problems, leading to difficulties in the formation of equilibrium.

The evident scientific question arises: to what extent is the theory of general perfect market equilibrium an approximate representation of actual market exchange?

First, let it be stated that there is no textbook, well-accepted answer to this question. Some people believe that the economy behaves approximately as if markets were perfect. Another position is that each market has to be thought of and tested separately.

One might think that there might be some academic consensus as to how closely the main economic theory, as currently taught in the United States, matches up to reality—there isn't. Instead there are strong convictions, and these have a strong impact on policy.

A straightforward look at the facts, though, shows that most markets are concentrated and therefore do not consist of small agents. In the United States, from 1935 to 1992, on average the four largest firms in 459 industries produced 38.4% of all shipments. Similarly, from 1992 to 2002, the two hundred largest manufacturing companies accounted for 40% of manufacturing value added. In 2007, the fifty largest US firms by value added produced about 25% of US value added, with only about a 17% and decreasing participation of payroll and employees, reflecting both technology and market power levels. The ratio of value added to payroll rose from 2.05 to 2.58 over this period, probably as an impact of globalization.[2]

Since markets usually have many consumers but only a few producers, the consensus in the profession is that market structure depends on the characteristics of production. For example, when there are increasing returns to scale, as in the presence of fixed costs in automated production, production tends to concentrate. In the history of the United States, large-scale enterprise began to characterize production in the last decade of the nineteenth century. During that decade the banking sectors of Boston and Providence became concentrated,[3] and the first wave of mergers and acquisitions recognized by economic historians took place from 1893 to 1904, giving birth to the main steel, telephone, oil, mining, railroad and other giants of the basic manufacturing and transportation industries.[4]

The theory of technological change is based on markets not being competitive. Instead technological innovation yields market power for the provision of certain goods in certain locations. In fact the same holds for automated production, since it involves fixed costs and is therefore subject to increasing returns. Perhaps, therefore, the consensus would be that a good part of the market equilibrium approximates monopolistic competition, with market power obtaining returns. This is consistent with Hall's (1988) study investigating whether US industry pricing is competitive, which finds that marginal cost is often well below price.

The next evident scientific question is: to what extent is there stability *to the dynamics of competition*? Given the actual dynamics of competition, is the competitive or monopolistic structure of the market equilibrium stable? Again, the question of stability of the overall structure and estimates of its overall market efficiency are for all intents and purposes absent from economic literature. Even so, the same data we looked at before points instead to the stability of market concentration. Between 1947 and 1987 the average proportion of shipments of the four largest firms across industrial manufacturing codes fluctuated only between 36.6% and 38.9%. However, in surprisingly unknown work, Blatt[5] shows that general equilibrium is unstable. See Keen[6] for a concise summary of this.

We also ask the following scientific questions. To what extent are financial markets compatible with competition? Is the process of achieving general equilibrium stable in itself? These have to be complemented by the following ethical question: To what extent is the ethical level E1, associated with market efficiency, compatible with the ethical level E2, which values equality?

One way of examining the relation between financial markets and competition in production is to look at the history of merger waves in the United States. The fourth, fifth and sixth merger waves described by Lipton[7] were financed through hostile takeover bids, junk bond financing, leveraged buyouts, megadeals and derivative assets. Mayer-Foulkes[8] shows that even production markets subject to diminishing returns and sunk costs, which can sustain a competitive equilibrium, can be converted into monopolies by a well-developed financial system. The essential mechanism is a change in the ownership structure of production, brought about by the financial system by borrowing from small agents to finance large agents.

In addition we note that in the two historical episodes of extreme liberalization that the United States has experienced, in the 1920s and from 1982 to the present, income concentration rose and the financial system finally became unstable, leading to the stock market crashes of 1929 and 2008. For example, from 1982 to the present the income share of the top US decile rose from 35%, the approximate level since 1942, to 50%, a figure unparalleled since 1929 (Figure 5.1[9]).

Indeed, the tulip mania, often considered the first speculative bubble, took place in 1637, not too long after the Dutch stock markets first came into existence in 1602.

Thus, we can generally conclude with the following stylized facts about market production and exchange. Competitive market production has not been the norm in the United States or Europe at least since the 1890s. Instead, there has been a high level of market concentration. Concentration levels have been approximately stable during most of that time, which was mostly regulated. During periods of high liberalization, income became more concentrated and financial markets played a very significant role in generating merger waves in production, further destabilizing competition. Those periods ended with full-scale crashes of the financial markets.

In fact, under the recent wave of globalization a great amount of concentration took place. In 2007 89.3% of global Foreign Direct Investment FDI inflows consisted of mergers and acquisitions. By 2008, the world's top one hundred nonfinancial transnational corporations produced 14.1% of global output, rising but still below US levels of concentration.[10]

How does market concentration affect its ethical impact? The answer has two parts. First, market power is well known not to be Pareto efficient. In addition it introduces a tendency for income to concentrate, therefore producing more and more unequal endowments as time proceeds. Hence market concentration tends to reduce ethical levels from E1 towards E0.

Second, it is not too difficult to show the following. Market exchange under perfect competition is equivalent to maximizing a social utility function that weights wealthier individuals more strongly (Negishi's theorem). There is nothing mysterious about this statement: wealthier people can purchase more than poorer people, and production is oriented to these levels of purchasing. The welfare theorem states that this is the best result that can be obtained subject to the initial allocation of wealth. Now suppose that we consider the social utility function that results from market exchange in the same way under an equal allocation of wealth, and consider maximization of this function to represent an ethical level of E2, concerned with equality as well as individual rights. Under this ethical objective function, the welfare theorems for the actual distribution of wealth represent a second best that is not obtained because of the Pareto restriction—no transfer of wealth.

The fact that people value transferring wealth from the wealthy to the poor can be evidenced in various ways. For example, the existence of progressive taxation: from the 1940s through to the 1970s "social transfers" were considered one of the roles of government in the entire developed world—particularly in Europe. In the United States the existence in December 2011 of 1.6 million nonprofit organizations with a $1.9 trillion revenue and $6.3 trillion assets is witness to the same concern.[11] By comparison in 2007 there were 7.2 million employer firms with $28.8 trillion in shipments.[12]

To summarize, while competitive markets are E1-ethical, they are E2-unethical. Concentrated markets tend to be E1-unethical as well.

Finally, is the macroeconomic process of achieving supply and demand equilibrium stable in itself? This takes us to another school of thought.

## Keynes

Keynes and a series of other authors[13] are concerned with macroeconomic disequilibrium to explain the business cycle and the Great Depression. Keynes' explanation is that investment forms an essential part of demand. In other words, production is used for consumption and for investment. However, investment decisions are inherently somewhat erratic, because they look towards the future, which is uncertain and even radically unknowable. Aggregate demand can change erratically, and producers are therefore uncertain about how much to produce. Because a considerable proportion of the product is destined to the investment (an average of 16.1% from 1950 to 2008), this introduces instability in the formation of macroeconomic equilibrium.

Keynes proposed that the government could mitigate the business cycle by spending to raise aggregate demand when investment was low, and reduce spending at the high end of the cycle. These policies were not successful during the stagflation of the 1970s, and led to the neoclassical counterrevolution. One of the failings of Keynesian policies was government overspending through growth and boom periods, an ethical failure. In these circumstances,

## 84    David A. Mayer-Foulkes and Raúl García-Barrios

a series of papers showed that if agents had rational expectations, there would be no disequilibrium, and only unexpected government spending would have an impact. While with regard to government spending and inflation, there may be enough informed agents, particularly large financial agents, for this to be true, the necessary hypotheses to rule out disequilibrium—perfect foresight—are again too strong to be realistic. It thus follows that the study of macroeconomic disequilibrium and the role of aggregate demand is a necessary part of economics and economic management.

Investment is not the only origin of macroeconomic instability. The financial system and its role in creating money through banking as well as the changing creditworthiness criteria that are used across the business cycle also play a role in creating medium- and long-term instability (Minsky Financial Instability Hypothesis—see Keen, cited in note 6).

Neoclassical economics does not have a good theory of finance and its interaction with the real economy. The compatibility of the financial system with a competitive market is never even questioned, though the financial system can change the ownership structure of production, as noted earlier. Nevertheless the "conviction," powered by strong economic interests,[14] that markets should be left alone to do their work led to the deregularization of financial markets in the United States. The result is that financial markets are now an oligopoly with a few main players that can profit from global volatility, and that Americans have entrusted their savings to the largest casino ever.

What is most disturbing is that fashion has played a substantial role in determining the content of mainstream economics in the United States. But, in fact, when a few academics prove a theorem,[15] is that enough to shift policy or is the underlying causal logic instead that market deregulation becomes attractive to big economic players?

To whom are free markets, lower taxes and therefore lower government spending more attractive than to those with market power?

That is how a few theorems shelve the study of macroeconomic disequilibrium.

There are even further sources of macroeconomic instability, presented in full modelistic style by Flaschel.[16] Among them is Goodwin's cycle[17] involving the negotiation of real wages, which originates with ideas in Marx, to whom we turn next.

## Marx

Up to this point, we have gotten away without the use of the word "capital." In neoclassical economics and even Keynes, capital and labor are simply factors of production. But for Marx the heart of the matter is people, and how their role as labor or capital transforms them. What seems just the normal state of affairs—a factory worker and a factory owner—for Marx represents the categories of labor and capital taking over people's lives in alienation. The laborer cannot create his work and is alienated from his own product. The owner so easily becomes unethical.

## Democracy and Development for Mexico    85

The influence of demand and supply on the formation of social classes—for example, the middle class based on human capital—is undeniable. So is the impact of the economy weakening family life and atomizing society into individuals, at the detriment of community. Even character traits and personalities respond to job descriptions. Recently it was corporate psychopaths who implemented the strategies that caused the global financial crisis.[18]

For our purposes we can extract from Marx his central motivations: to achieve an egalitarian society characterized by aggregate, ethical rationality, humanity and well-being. For Marx the human endeavor is subsumed in the aggregate to the dance imposed by capital's search for profit. In fact, when market power dominates markets—financial or productive—at a global scale, and the greedy pursuit of unfettered self-interest threatens global sustainability and even human survival, is this view too far amiss? Marx's view is consistent with today's monopolistic competition, represented by global financial and nonfinancial transnationals.

Indeed, given an egalitarian distribution of assets, the neoclassical ideal of perfectly competitive markets with many small producers working with shared technology levels is much closer to the socialist ideal than it is to the current reality of laissez-faire global capitalism. Remove elements of the inadvertent assumption that perfect competition is stable, and the contradictions between the classicals and Marx are less than they would have at first appeared.

For Marx, capital is not just about men and machines. It is calculating its returns without any other consideration; shaping technology to reduce the participation of labor; influencing politics to reduce worker's rights, regulations, taxes and so on; shaping competition to gain market power. There is a pie to be cut and playing fair might just lose the race. Not only will market power be endogenous, but also there is conflict between labor and capital for participation in the benefits of production. From the neoclassical point of view, competition solves all these problems, making capital and labor each obtain its marginal return. But this holds only under very special conditions, for this marginal rate is itself endogenous,[19] which nevertheless seem attractive from a technocratic point of view. In general, labor participation is strongly influenced by aggregate negotiation at the workplace.

Assume that some combination between negotiation and demand and supply determines equilibrium wages. The result is that there need not be full employment, and that wages rise with employment. When wages rise, investment may diminish, causing a reduction in wages and then again a rise in investment. This gives rise to cyclical economic growth in what is known as Goodwin's model.[20] This model can be combined with Solow's growth model[21] and is conspicuously absent in mainstream textbooks. If there are important heterogeneities between different types of agents under capitalism, surely the one between workers and capital is one of the main ones.

The logic of qualitative change—dialectical logic—is central to Marx's thought. Technological change creates new classes of people and drives historical change through such logic. For example, increased technological change drove the emergence of human capital, which has been central to developed societies, as well as the demographic transition. Modern mathematics can model these qualitative changes through changes in steady states.[22] Similarly economic thought transcends the frameworks set by its founders. Marx was not able to see the demographic transition because it occurred after his time, just as Adam Smith did not consider today's industrial concentration the norm. Finally, there is one transformation that can now define a new economics: it is to fully include the ethical dimension.

The American and French Revolutions inspired a wave of democratic and nationalist revolutions in Europe in 1848. This is known in some countries as the Spring of Nations or Springtime of the Peoples.[23] A parallel can be drawn with the modern day Arab Spring, highlighting the violence with which tyrants defend their status quo. At that time Marx and Engels wrote the *Communist Manifesto*, underscoring the issues of capitalist injustice and proposing a further, economic dimension to democratic revolution.

Marx's ideals inspired social movements in many countries through the twentieth century and the emergence of socialist regimes. These did not achieve the level of egalitarianism and well-being that had been hoped for. The main reasons were that democracy was rejected and that the main proposed tool for solving the problems of capitalism was government, whose ethical level was therefore E0.

While capitalism can produce excesses of greed, this is a human failing that occurs in other circumstances as well. For a government to perform at a higher ethical level, it is necessary for the many to be able to put limits on the powerful, an essentially democratic function.

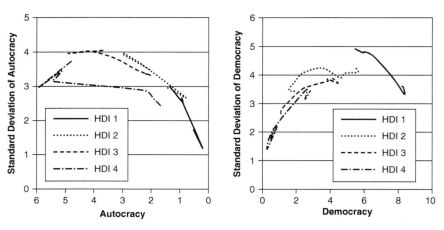

*Figure 5.1* Evolution of mean and standard deviation of autocracy and democracy across human development country groups, 1970–2010.

Note: HD1 is the group of twenty-eight countries with the highest human development index (HDI) in 1970; HD2 the next highest twenty-eight countries, and so on. Each trajectory is plotted every five years from 1970 to 2010.

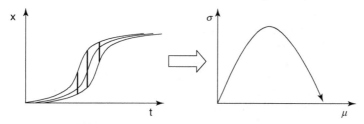

*Figure 5.2* When a group of countries undergoes a transition in *x* through time, this can be observed in the (µ,σ) plane.

Democratic revolution eventually consolidated in Western Europe, the United States, Canada and other neo-European countries, with an ethical level between E0 and E1. These institutional arrangements constitute a steady state in which concentrated economic and political power cannot join forces to produce an autocracy, but instead the majorities can put a limit to the abuse of power. The majorities can organize their collective action by means of the rule of law, a series of grassroots organizations, property rights and enough economic power. Such a democratic balance of power moving beyond an ethical level E0 remains to be achieved in most countries of the world. Nevertheless, Figure 5.1 shows that there is a global transition away from autocracy and towards democracy. This can be viewed as an integral part of human development.[24] Figure 5.2 shows how a transition maps onto the (µ,σ) plane (mean and standard deviation) as in Figure 5.1.

Capitalism itself is consistent with and can strengthen both autocracy and democracy. Moreover, democracy in itself is not a guarantee of equity, and can therefore remain at an ethical level of E1 or worse. Even so, once democracy is present, the road is open to an increased ethical level of governance.

Let us define Marxian revolution as putting capital and technology to the service of humanity and its extended rights. There is nothing in dialectic logic to imply that such a transformation has to be violent. Instead, what is clearly necessary is to develop governance with an ethical level of at least E2, and perhaps as a step towards higher ethical levels. Democracy, which is quintessentially a tool for qualitative transformation through dialogue, can provide a means for such ethical governance and transformation. In fact, democratic transformation is essential to economic growth and development.

## Modern Economic Growth

The emergence of the Industrial Revolution in the second half of the eighteenth century sparked development and underdevelopment across the globe. By 1820 Great Britain had become the workshop of the world, trading industrial goods for raw materials, and had outcompeted India's textile production at the international level. This later extended to the domestic market. India became underdeveloped until the present time.

Some countries, such as the United States and Germany, unburdened by sunk industrial investments, were able to catch up and overtake Great Britain through the second industrial revolution, involving the chemical and electric industries. Most Western and other countries that eventually attained development experienced several decades of "miracle" rapid growth. Examples include Denmark, Sweden, Italy, Japan, South Korea, Taiwan, Hong Kong, Singapore, Ireland and Germany in the nineteenth century, Western Germany after WWII, and Cyprus, Iceland, Spain, Malta, Portugal and Israel in the second half of the twentieth century. Most other countries in Asia, Africa and Latin America remained underdeveloped, with Latin America characterized by less trade, a middle level of average income and high inequality.

Development theory, studying this panorama of unequal development, proposed the existence of virtuous and vicious circles capable of retarding economic development in the long term. The neoclassical counterrevolution simply threw these theories out. The argument was that they were not valid in the globalized world of trade and foreign direct investment being created in the 1980s. As the Washington Consensus (a term coined in 1989) imposed liberalization throughout the world, it was as if the US mainstream academia produced a theory on order, since market power thrives on free market policies. As Stiglitz[25] later stated, it was as if these theories had been designed to promote the interests of western nations and their large corporations. At first, economic growth was theorized simply as intertemporal equilibrium in capital accumulation. Again, armed with a couple of theorems, the brand-new, untried, research predicted that liberalization would bring economic growth to all. When Barro first ran his regressions, his prediction of convergence was met with the reality of divergence.[26] He therefore created the concept of conditional convergence, which only implies countries remain in an equilibrium path (convergent or not) but was nevertheless trumpeted as "convergence" by the profession. In fact, the first period of globalization saw the Great Divergence, separating out countries into developed and underdeveloped countries. Divergence continued through the second half of the twentieth century, and through the wave of globalization starting in the 1980s.

As the new theory of economic growth continued to develop, the concepts of human capital and technology were introduced to be able to explain the facts, and econometric estimates concluded that technological differences are the main explanatory fact for income differences. The demographic transition was also highlighted as a fundamental fact and motor of human development, itself driven by the returns to human capital. Urbanization is also a fundamental aspect of modernization, as are institutional arrangements. However, institutions have been highlighted particularly as a prerequisite for the functioning of markets,[27] rather than as an endogenous component in multiple equilibria, the reason being that the presence of multiple equilibria in human development, technology and institutions demands policy action for the poor, while the idea that markets will work on their

*Democracy and Development for Mexico*    89

own removes this emphasis and presses for some type of laissez-faire. In fact, few theories explain the possible coexistence of development, under-development and miracle growth under globalization, representing different equilibria that can subsist under and be strengthened by trade and foreign direct investment.[28] Indeed, globalization policy is conducted under a competitive understanding of trade and investment, when we have seen that production is concentrated instead. In fact, most of FDI has represented a process of market concentration. It is little understood how innovation itself is oligopolized in advanced countries (e.g., Microsoft-Apple), market power being obtained *for* innovation in mature industries rather than *from* innovation. This process might itself be at the heart of underdevelopment, which faces the obstacle of overcoming this level of market power so as to carry out high levels of innovation.

Most theories of the 2008 financial crisis still consider it an isolated phenomenon of the developed world, give ad hoc explanations for the emergence of the savings boom that led to the meltdown,[29] concentrate on the regulatory aspects of financial markets and turn a blind eye to their oligopolization. Such is the nature of neoclassical blindness, for which the special features and interests of corporate economics need not be considered for an economic diagnosis, much less antitrust action against the financial giants.

We now consider how the theory of modern economic growth stands in relation to neoclassical theory, Keynes and Marx. First, technology is the main driver of differences in income per capita between countries. Another fundamental process is the demographic transition, in which people's preferences change towards having fewer and better educated children. In turn, this depends on the returns to human capital and therefore on the extent to which countries are involved in the process of technological change and adoption. Urbanization and institutional change are also critical processes of development. None of these fundamental processes of development—technological change, human development, urbanization, demographic transition and institutional change—can be understood by means of the neoclassical paradigm. Technological change occurs through market power; human capital involves market failures; urbanization is driven by externalities and optimized through government regulation; the demographic transition involves all of these, and institutions are the framework in which politics and economics merge. Thus, in effect research on long-term development has found the neoclassical paradigm to be an insufficient basis for long-term policy. Added to this, while economists with a more pronounced neoclassical conviction tend to believe in a homogenous description of developed and underdeveloped economies, described by a single equilibrium that varies quantitatively according to exogenous determinants, a wider approach more concerned with obstacles to development and qualitative transformation considers multiple equilibria that endogenize these fundamental processes. This again implies that, on their own, market policies do not necessarily lead to development.

90   David A. Mayer-Foulkes and Raúl García-Barrios

The recent extremes in economic liberalization have weakened democracy by increasing the power of the elites and by weakening the social and community cohesion that lends strength to majorities and protects minorities. Policies continually improving income distribution are essential for maintaining equity and stable democracies.

Now, as far as economic instability is concerned, globalization faces the huge challenge of how to deal with global business cycles, which first synchronized when the information technology bubble burst in 2000. In fact, globalization faces huge challenges in generating governance on a whole series of fronts including economic stability, economic development, health and sustainability.

Because capital now stands at a global level, with white- and blue-collar workers competing across nations, it is now also essential to understand how technological change, human capital, institutional development, the rule of law (including the control of transnationals), sustainability and community must work together to achieve viable, acceptable, propoor economic and human development.

## Synthesis

The different strands of economic thought we have examined can be viewed as a single body of knowledge from the following perspective.

Competition in the market economy reaches a balance at a considerable level of concentration of production, which increases as regulation decreases. While mainstream economics provides a methodological point of departure, perfect competition does not provide an adequate paradigm for policy, including trade and development policy. Financial markets in particular can function as instruments of economic concentration. The neoclassical understanding of markets is invalid because it is inconsistent with the full reality of imperfect competition. Economic liberalization strengthens market power and therefore tends to weaken democracy by worsening the income distribution and reducing social cohesion. Instead, policies counteracting the impact of market power are needed.

With regard to Keynesian economics, instability is an essential concern for economic policy that cannot be assumed away, particularly in a context of global, international synchronization of the business cycle.

With regard to Marxist economics, the determinants of worker and human capital participation in income, including conflicts of interest, cannot be assumed away either. It is also necessary to understand and fully consider determinants in political economy, community, family and quality of life, in order to truly put economic and social arrangements at the service of humanity.

Even at their theoretical best, the ethical level of markets is insufficient for achieving an egalitarian society. This implies that it is indispensable to develop a sufficiently ethical level of governance, at the local, national, regional and global levels, so as to adequately regulate economic activity and distribute its benefits. This is particularly important in the presence of poverty and development traps, and of the global sustainability challenge. An objective and ethical economics is essential.

## CONCLUSION: A DEMOCRATIC, ETHICAL AND EGALITARIAN COMMITMENT

What does this perspective for a single body of economic thought say for Mexico?

First, economic liberalization is not enough to promote economic growth and development. It needs to be complemented with government policies making technological change, human capital accumulation, urbanization and economic equality accessible for all.

Second, democracy is essential for effective economic policy, but difficult to achieve. This is especially so when emerging from an authoritarian status quo. The basic lines of power that have run from the top to bottom need to run instead from the bottom to the top.

Ethical governance, based on a strengthened, participative democracy, is essential for an egalitarian Mexico, and essential for its economic development.

## EPILOGUE: NORTH AMERICAN INTEGRATION

What light do our discussion and synthesis throw on North American integration?

The first thing that stands out is that the vision and policy instruments underlying North American integration are based on a defective theory. This theory proposes that the market mechanism is a sufficient means to coordinate the economic integration and optimal development of the three North American countries, with only a minimal need for government intervention. This position naturally gives rise to the institutional void that is explored in this book. This void implies that the fundamental processes of development are left unattended by policy: technological change, human development, urbanization, demographic transition, migration and institutional change.

Various aspects of this institutional void are explored in the book. These include labor and rights issues, discussed in the chapters by Norman, Nolan, and Gabriel and Macdonald; health issues discussed by Barnes, and the deep need for organization felt by the Mexican population in the United States, documented by Bayes and Gonzalez. Moreover, the systematic, long-term impact of institutional differences on economic integration is documented and quantified by Genna. Finally, the incorrectness of the neoclassical theory implies that, as a political current, it is an ideology. Its defense has a political tint and supports specific interests, with consequences explored in Castro-Rea's chapter on the negative impact of the conservative ideology on North America.

92  *David A. Mayer-Foulkes and Raúl García-Barrios*

It is amazing that, as discussed earlier, the economic understanding that has shaped the policies of North American integration in fact ignores the main processes of development. One measure of the differences in development that it fails to address with adequate policies is the wage differential faced by Mexican migrants. This is documented by Aguayo-Téllez, Acharya and Rivera-Mendoza in their chapter on migration. In fact, migration is to be expected at this stage of Mexico's development, as part of its transition to the urban way of life. Without adequate policies for development in Mexico, it is natural for a good proportion of rural migration to head towards the United States. Moreover, even Mexico's cities do not develop well enough to retain their population.

The second thing that stands out is that the simplistic vision of free trade as a win-win policy ignores not only the long, global history of development and underdevelopment that occurred in the context of trade, but also the fact that North American integration can be understood only in the full global context. As stated in the introduction, the rise of US trade and investment in China was hardly predicted when NAFTA was signed, and deeply impacted the interaction between Mexico and the United States. It also deeply affects the interaction between the United States and Canada, as noted in Snodgrass and Gessner's chapter. In addition, US security concerns carry a global stamp that is documented in Snodgrass and Gessner's and Dominguez and Velazquez's chapters.

One of the blind spots of neoclassical economic theory, particularly with regards to trade, is to ignore the possibility of virtuous and vicious economic circles. However, it is precisely this possibility that can make economic differences persist between countries in the context of globalization. The economic relation between the United States and Canada is characteristic of the relation between developed countries under globalization, that is, complementary specialization, and the one between the United States and Mexico is instead characteristic of the relation between developed and underdeveloped countries, namely factor exchange.[30] This is what brings about a state of integration in North America characterized by the coexistence of a close relation of approximate equals between the United States and Canada and an arm's length relation of unequals between the United States/Canada and Mexico, as pointed out in the Dominguez and Velazquez chapter with regards to security, which has led, among other negative consequences, to the infamous war on drugs, whose impact is partly documented in Arceo-Gómez's chapter.

What North American integration truly requires is an effective development policy for Mexico. The economic reasons we have discussed provide enough justification for this conclusion. However, incorporating a more ethical basis for policy, ranging from citizen and community rights, through self-sustaining social programs, to endogenous technological innovation, would also make a big difference. A positive US role in supporting effective development would

Democracy and Development for Mexico    93

be welcome both at the North American and at the global levels. Indeed, this is the only rational policy for global cooperation and sustainability. Nevertheless, Mexico's development is ultimately Mexico's responsibility.

## NOTES

1. This is the concept of Pareto efficiency.
2. Data from the US Census Bureau: Economic Census 1992, "Concentration Ratios for the U.S.," http://www.census.gov/epcd/www/concentration92-47.xls; and Economic Censuses 1997, 2002, 2007.
3. Naomi R. Lamoreaux, "Bank Mergers in Late Nineteenth-Century New England: The Contingent Nature of Structural Change," *Journal of Economic History* 51 (1991): 537–557.
4. Martin Lipton, "Merger Waves in the 19th, 20th and 21st Centuries" (Davies Lecture, Osgoode Hall Law School, York University, September 14, 2006), http://osgoode.yorku.ca/.
5. J.M. Blatt, *Dynamic Economic Systems: A Post Keynesian Approach* (Armonk, NY: M. E. Sharpe, 1983).
6. Steve Keen, "A Monetary Minsky Model of the Great Moderation and the Great Recession," *Journal of Economic Behavior and Organization* (2011), doi: 10.1016/j.jebo.2011.01.010 (2011) 183.
7. M. Lipton, "Merger Waves in the 19th, 20th and 21st Centuries," Davies Lecture, Osgoode Hall Law School. York University. September 14, 2006, http://osgoode.yorku.ca/.
8. D. Mayer-Foulkes, "Vulnerable Markets," Centro de Investigación y Docencia Económicas (CIDE), July 4, 2011, http://ssrn.com/abstract=1878683.
9. Anthony B. Atkinson, Thomas Piketty and Emmanuel Saez, "Top Incomes in the Long Run of History," *Journal of Economic Literature* 49 (2011): 1.
10. Data from UNCTAD (2008).
11. Data from the National Center for Charitable Statistics: http://nccsdataweb.urban.org/tablewiz/tw_bmf.php.
12. Data from the US Census Bureau, Statistical Abstract of the United States, 2012, http://www.census.gov/compendia/statab/cats/business_enterprise/establishments_employees_payroll.html.
13. See, for example, Peter Flaschel, *The Macrodynamics of Capitalism: Elements for a Synthesis of Marx, Keynes and Schumpeter*, 2nd ed. (Berlin: Springer-Verlag, 2009).
14. Robert Weissman and James Donahue, *Sold Out: How Wall Street and Washington Betrayed America* (2009), http://www.wallstreetwatch.org/reports/sold_out.pdf.
15. R. E. Lucas, Jr., "Expectations and the Neutrality of Money," *Journal of Economic Theory* 4 (1972): 103–124.
16. Flaschel, *The Macrodynamics of Capitalism*.
17. R. Goodwin, "A Growth Cycle," in *Socialism, Capitalism and Economic Growth*, ed. C.H. Feinstein (Cambridge: Cambridge University Press, 1967) pp 54–58.
18. Clive R. Boddy, "The Corporate Psychopaths Theory of the Global Financial Crisis," *Journal of Business Ethics* 102 (2011): 2, doi: 10.1007/s10551–011–0810–4.
19. See, for example, Daron Acemoglu, "Directed Technical Change," *Review of Economic Studies* 69 (2002): 4.

20. Goodwin, "A Growth Cycle."
21. R. Solow, "A Contribution to the Theory of Economic Growth," *Quarterly Journal of Economics* 70 (1956): 65–94.
22. See, for example, O. Galor and David N. Weil, "Population, Technology, and Growth: From Malthusian Stagnation to the Demographic Transition and Beyond," *American Economic Review* 90 (2000): 4.
23. J. Merriman, *A History of Modern Europe: From the French Revolution to the Present* (New York: Norton, 1996).
24. Figure 5.1 is based on Polity IV data; see the discussion in Mayer-Foulkes, "Vulnerable Markets."
25. Joseph E. Stiglitz, *Globalization and Its Discontents* (New York: Norton, 2002).
26. R. Barro, "Economic Growth in a Cross Section of Countries," *Quarterly Journal of Economics* 196, no. 2 (1991): 407–443.
27. See, for example, Dani Rodrik, Arvind Subramanian and Francesco Trebbi, "Institutions Rule: The Primacy of Institutions over Geography and Integration in Economic Development" (NBER Working Paper 9305, National Bureau of Economic Research, 2002).
28. D. Mayer-Foulkes, "Long-Term Fundamentals of the 2008 Economic Crisis," Centro de Investigación y Docencia Económicas (CIDE), March 24, 2009, http://ssrn.com/abstract=1367918 or http://dx.doi.org/10.2139/ssrn.1367918, gives such a model also explaining the long-term antecedents of the 2008 crisis, and proposing a harmonization of global taxes that can fund local and global governance and development, reduce the tensions of globalization, and continue to promote integration.
29. D. Mayer-Foulkes, "Vulnerable Markets," available at http://ssrn.com/abstract=1878683 (2011).
30. Ibid.

## REFERENCES

Acemoglu, D. "Directed Technical Change." *Review of Economic Studies* 69, no. 4 (2002): 781–809.
Atkinson, A. B., T. Piketty and E. Saez. "Top Incomes in the Long Run of History." *Journal of Economic Literature* 49, no. 1 (2011): 3–71.
Barro, R. "Economic Growth in a Cross Section of Countries." *Quarterly Journal of Economics* 196, no. 2 (1991): 407–443.
Blatt, J. M. *Dynamic Economic Systems: A Post Keynesian Approach*. Armonk, NY: M. E. Sharpe, 1983.
Boddy, C. R. "The Corporate Psychopaths Theory of the Global Financial Crisis." *Journal of Business Ethics* 102, no. 2 (2011): 255–259. doi: 10.1007/s10551-011-0810-4.
Flaschel, P. *The Macrodynamics of Capitalism: Elements for a Synthesis of Marx, Keynes and Schumpeter*. 2nd ed. Berlin: Springer-Verlag, 2009.
Galor, O., and David N. Weil. "Population, Technology, and Growth: From Malthusian Stagnation to the Demographic Transition and Beyond." *American Economic Review* 90, no. 4 (2000): 806–828.
Goodwin, R. "A Growth Cycle." In *Socialism, Capitalism and Economic Growth*, edited by C. H. Feinstein, 54–58. Cambridge: Cambridge University Press, 1967.
Keen, S. "A Monetary Minsky Model of the Great Moderation and the Great Recession." *Journal of Economic Behavior and Organization* (2011). doi: 10.1016/j.jebo.2011.01.010.

Lamoreaux, N. R. "Bank Mergers in Late Nineteenth-Century New England: The Contingent Nature of Structural Change." *Journal of Economic History* 51 (1991): 537–557.

Lipton, M. "Merger Waves in the 19th, 20th and 21st Centuries." Davies Lecture, Osgoode Hall Law School. York University. September 14, 2006. http://osgoode.yorku.ca/.

Lucas, R. E., Jr. "Expectations and the Neutrality of Money." *Journal of Economic Theory* 4 (1972): 103–124.

Mayer-Foulkes, D. "Long-Term Fundamentals of the 2008 Economic Crisis." Centro de Investigación y Docencia Económicas (CIDE). March 24, 2009. http://ssrn.com/abstract=1367918 or http://dx.doi.org/10.2139/ssrn.1367918.

———. "Vulnerable Markets." Centro de Investigación y Docencia Económicas (CIDE). July 4, 2011. http://ssrn.com/abstract=1878683.

Merriman, J. *A History of Modern Europe: From the French Revolution to the Present*. New York: Norton, 1996.

Rodrik, D., A. Subramanian and F. Trebbi. "Institutions Rule: The Primacy of Institutions over Geography and Integration in Economic Development." NBER Working Paper 9305. National Bureau of Economic Research. 2002.

Solow, R. "A Contribution to the Theory of Economic Growth." *The Quarterly Journal of Economics* 70 (1956): 65–94.

Stiglitz, J. E. *Globalization and Its Discontents*. New York: Norton, 2002.

Weissman, R., and J. Donahue. *Sold Out: How Wall Street and Washington Betrayed America*. 2009. http://www.wallstreetwatch.org/reports/sold_out.pdf.

# Part II

# Examples of Institutional Building in North America

# 6 The Evolution of US-Mexico Labor Cooperation and the NAALC Institutions

## Kimberly A. Nolan García

Mexican-US relations in the area of labor cooperation have become an important aspect of the binational agenda, mostly due to the effect that the North American Free Trade Agreement (NAFTA) has had on strengthening US-Mexico relations in general. Labor cooperation has also become more important over time as the relationship has been channeled through the NAFTA institutions that were set up to promote labor issues. However, in recent years, formal channels of labor cooperation—conceptualized here as meetings between the representatives of these respective governments—have broken down considerably.

In this chapter, I offer an account of how the formal channels for labor cooperation between the United States and Mexico have evolved, and offer a panorama of the scope and content of US-Mexico labor cooperation since 1994, based principally on a review of the North American Agreement on Labor Cooperation (NAALC), NAFTA's parallel accord on labor.[1] Unlike in other areas of cooperation in North America, labor can potentially benefit from a range of new institutions established by NAFTA to open channels of communication at all levels of government between the NAFTA countries. A unique labor dispute resolution mechanism allows these states to pinpoint common labor violations, encouraging them to collaborate to strengthen labor protections for the workers of North America. Yet I argue that while the NAFTA labor side accord features strong institutions created to reinforce trilateral cooperation on labor issues, the weak resolutions across NAALC cases and the breakdown of labor cooperation across these and other channels show that institutional frameworks are not enough to sustain labor cooperation in North America. Rather, the absence of a genuine commitment to labor rights enforcement on the part of the governments involved has meant that the framework of the NAALC agreement has been adapted by member states to avoid labor cooperation, leading to the breakdown of these channels of collaboration in recent years. As such, this contribution to the edited volume shows that institutions are necessary, but not a sufficient condition for promoting cooperation among the states in North America.

## EARLY EFFORTS AT COOPERATION ON US-MEXICO LABOR ISSUES

As late as the early 1980s, Mexican-US relations were strained, but labor issues by themselves were not normally part of these frictions.[2] During that decade, Mexican-US relations in general were strengthened through the advent of the Mexico-United States Binational Commission in 1981. Composed at first of the Mexican Secretary and Deputy Secretaries of Foreign Relations, the US Secretary and Undersecretary of State, the US Trade Representative, and his Mexican counterparts in Economía and Hacienda, the idea behind the commission was to set forth a schedule of bilateral talks about issues important to both states, in order to open high-level channels of communication on specific issue areas. As such, the Binational Commission served then, as now, as at the most important forum for high-level dialogue between the executives of both states.[3] By 1986, this group was expanded to include the Attorneys General, and by 1989, as the areas of US-Mexico cooperation themselves expanded, the Binational Commission included all cabinet members from both states, including the two secretaries for labor.[4]

The first formal channel of US-Mexico cooperation on labor issues dates from the first meetings of the full Binational Commission. However, the discussion at the bilateral meeting revolves around those issues most pressing to either country, which in recent years has meant that those perennial issues like an immigration deal for Mexico[5] and trade and security issues remain at the top of the agenda, and labor issues are not necessarily at the forefront of the conversation.[6] Labor issues would become more salient as the Mexicans approached the US delegation at the 1990 World Economic Forum and asked them to consider a trade deal.[7] Once Canada asked to be included, and all three states publicly declared an intention to negotiate what would eventually become NAFTA, labor issues took on a new importance in North America.

Trilateral cooperation around labor issues became an important aspect of North American integration for a number of reasons. First, initial discussions on the trade deal imagined labor mobility within North America, an idea quickly scrapped, but since taken up again in recent discussions on reopening the NAFTA agreements.[8] Even without EU-style integrated labor markets, it is clear that migrant Mexican labor is an important part of the labor force in both Canada and the United States, especially in agriculture.[9] As such, labor is no longer a bordered phenomenon in some productive sectors in North America, while access to labor arbitration remains largely rooted in domestic processes. With a set of supranational standards and institutions, migrant workers who experienced violations of their rights could apply for redress regardless of where the violations took place, and without regard to their national status.[10] Second, the United States and Canada both had mature industrial relations systems and efficient labor law enforcement mechanisms, while Mexico's labor laws may have been the most progressive, but enforcement was and remains problematic. Given these asymmetries, US policy makers

## The Evolution of US-Mexico Labor Cooperation 101

worried that a trade agreement may draw US business to Mexico, where labor costs were cheaper and workers' rights less well enforced.

Meanwhile, a groundswell of opposition to the trade accord formed.[11] In the United States, the very idea of a trade agreement with Mexico threw the biggest fears that unions in the United States had about industrial relocation into high relief. Organized labor believed that NAFTA represented an extension of the 1968 Border Industrialization Program into the Mexican interior, bringing with it the attendant social and political problems that were associated with the *maquila* sector at the border, and feared that NAFTA would draw US manufacturing jobs to Mexico.[12] A network emerged, led by labor, and joined by environmental advocates, human rights groups and faith-based organizations to lead opposition to NAFTA in the United States.[13]

It quickly became clear that the trade accord would have to address labor issues in order to pass Congressional ratification. Democratic legislators, responding to unions' concerns that trade integration would pull jobs from the United States to Mexico, and worried that weaker labor regulations in Mexico would then create pressures to weaken regulations in the United States, lobbied for the inclusion of some labor guarantees to the negotiation agenda.[14] Even prior to the vote on fast-track that would give President George H.W. Bush Congressional authority to negotiate the agreement, Dan Rostenkowski (D-IL), the chairman of the House Ways and Means Committee, and Lloyd Bentsen (D-TX), chair of the Senate Finance Committee, sent a letter to Bush to make it clear that without labor and environmental guarantees, they could not guarantee Democrats would ratify an end agreement.[15] As such, the Democrats tied fast-track authority to the inclusion of labor protections in the text of the trade accord. The Bush administration accepted an "action plan" that promised that any final agreement would include worker adjustment and retraining programs.[16] Democrat votes in favor thus secured, fast-track authority passed in May of 1991, and the negotiations on the commercial aspects of the NAFTA accord began in 1992. As these drew to a close, the negotiation over the side agreements on labor and the environment began. After six rounds that threatened at times to upend the entire trade accord,[17] an agreement was reached in August of 1993, and the side accords were signed in September.

### THE NAALC INSTITUTIONS

Even though the national labor confederations in the United States, Canada and Mexico were invited to make presentations on what the labor side agreement should encompass at one point during the negotiations, the NAALC was less comprehensive than either US labor or the Congressional coalitions expected. For example, instead of developing new regional labor standards, the labor side agreement obliges the three nations only to "effectively enforce" their own national labor laws.[18]

102 *Kimberly A. Nolan García*

The text of the agreement underscores that the NAALC accord in spirit was meant to encourage cooperation in North America among states to further a mutually recognized interest in promoting labor protections.[19] As such, the NAALC agreement enumerates eleven labor rights principles, including freedom of association and the right to collective bargaining, health and occupational safety, protection from discrimination at work, technical labor standards (including wages and hours) and the rights of migrant workers,[20] which largely mirror the labor rights enumerated in the International Labor Organization's 1998 *Declaration on Fundamental Principles and Rights at Work.*

The agreement also lays out a series of new institutions dedicated to both cooperative consultations on labor rights issues and the arbitration and resolution of labor rights standards. For example, National Administrative Offices (NAO) were established in each state to manage the process of filing cases for dispute resolution.[21] The NAALC also established a Commission for Labor Cooperation (CLC), a trinational secretariat that assists the NAOs and the three labor ministers in administering the cooperative activities associated with the NAALC. Apart from the events that are mandated by the ministerial agreements at the end of NAALC dispute resolution, the CLC is charged with organizing workshops and other events that bring together experts and policy makers from all three states, to identify areas where cooperation on labor-related issues would be beneficial to North American workers.

The preamble to the NAALC text clearly states the intention of the NAFTA partners to strengthen cooperation on labor rights issues, and to protect basic workers' rights while respecting the constitution and laws of each party.[22] If the NAALC reflects a common interest in improving cooperation on labor issues in the NAFTA states, and a commitment to enforcing those rights, we should expect first that cooperation on labor issues would deepen over time, as officials charged with these institutions begin to forge the communication channels on which that cooperation rests. We should also see that as the dispute process takes shape, resolutions that favor cooperation might dominate, but also that case resolutions would tend to push for improvements in labor rights practices across all three states.

In effect, this is what we see in both areas of the NAALC, though there are inconsistencies over time. First, the NAALC institutions have served to strengthen and institutionalize contact between US and Mexican labor officials in a manner that has been constant, and at times, fruitful, for promoting labor rights protection in both countries. The work of the CLC in particular has been one of the major achievements of the NAALC in promoting trinational cooperation on labor issues. Since 1994, the commission has coordinated sixty-nine cooperative activities, fifty-four of which were held in Mexico. These activities have ranged widely, from seminars on health and safety issues, to conferences about Mexico's labor justice system, to worker outreach regarding the rights of women workers and agricultural workers. However, while cooperative activities were common in the first years of

The Evolution of US-Mexico Labor Cooperation    103

the agreement, they have tapered off considerably in more recent years, for reasons I detail ahead.

In terms of dispute resolution, the case resolutions most often end in recommendations to hold ministerial consultations, which are official talks between the labor ministers in the filing and target states. Though ministerial consultations are perhaps the least desirable resolutions because they are promises to talk about labor rights violations and not act on them, ministerial consultations remain the most important formal channels for dialogue about labor rights that NAFTA can offer. A number of positive resolutions favorable to labor have been possible under the NAALC, even within ministerial consultations rulings. For example, a range of activities mandated by the Ministerial Council have led to worker outreach initiatives, firm-level reversals of government policies or even policy change.[23] These positive resolutions were part of the consultations process, but went beyond the scope of the NAALC to promote case outcomes that in the end encouraged labor rights protections, especially in Mexico.[24] However, most critics of the NAALC have charged that case resolutions have been too limited to promote labor rights improvements, especially in Mexico. I describe the labor dispute panel and discuss some plausible reasons as to why improvements in labor protections have been generally limited under the agreement in the next section.

## NAALC LABOR ARBITRATION AND CASE RESOLUTIONS

In establishing channels for dispute resolution, NAFTA features a panel for labor issues that is unrelated to the dispute provisions for investment or commerce, and is unique in that it allows *individuals* to bring cases against states for labor rights violations under the terms of the agreement.[25] During the arbitration process, any citizen or group can file a complaint with a National Administrative Office regarding the targeted state's performance on labor law enforcement. Each state is bound to manage the complaints process according to the procedural guidelines established by the NAALC.[26] Once a petition is filed, the NAO where it is submitted has the option to review the complaint further. If a review is granted, the NAO then researches the allegations, attempts to verify them through discussions with the NAO in the state where the violation took place, and most importantly, assesses whether the violations are consistent with national labor law in the state in question, even if these contravene the NAALC's eleven labor principles. The NAO then makes a public report on how issues raised in the case should be addressed.

Because of a feature that allows for third-party participation in the monitoring and enforcement of the labor accord, the NAALC served as a focal point for groups to continue to work together, and gave them a new focus on where to build upon the relationships they had forged during the anti-NAFTA campaigns. The new dispute resolution mechanism provided them the political arena to test whether the side accord would adequately enforce

104 *Kimberly A. Nolan García*

the labor rights principles included in the agreement.[27] Once the NAALC came into force, the same groups that spearheaded the effort to stop NAFTA began to work together to file the first petitions on labor rights violations in Mexico, and, over time, groups not initially involved in the anti-NAFTA campaigns would also become involved in using the dispute resolution process, filing mostly cases against Mexico.[28]

Through 2012, forty-one petitions have been filed regarding labor rights violations in thirty-five separate cases.[29] Table 6.1 provides an overview of the types of labor rights violations that were presented in these cases, and which types of violations were reported in each of the three NAFTA states.[30]

As Table 6.1 shows, of the forty-one petitions have been filed over the life of the NAALC, the majority of the petitions, twenty-six, were filed against Mexico. Fourteen petitions were filed against the United States, and just two petitions have been filed against Canada. Table 6.1 also shows that the most pressing labor rights issue in all states, according to the filing patterns, is the right to freedom of association. The violation of the right to association and/ or collective bargaining is cited in nearly every petition filed on Mexico, while in the United States, freedom of association issues appear in nearly half of the petitions. What is also notable is that every petition on the rights of migrant workers has been filed against the United States. Finally, of the thirty-six cases submitted to the NAALC to date, twenty-four, or just over 66%, have been accepted for review.

Once cases are reviewed, NAO offices can suggest three types of redress. For health and safety violations, the full range of remedies is available, including the first level of ministerial consultations, and then later, the creation of a panel of experts for adjudication (the ECE), panel arbitration, fines and trade sanctions. Cases involving child labor or minimum wage disputes are subject to ministerial consultations, and fines and trade sanctions. Cases concerning "technical labor standards" such as forced labor, minimum employment standards, discrimination, workers' compensation or protection of migrants are limited to ministerial consultations and expert evaluation by

*Table 6.1* NAALC Petitions Filed 1994–2012

| Class of violation | Totals | US | MEX | CAN |
| --- | --- | --- | --- | --- |
| Freedom of association | 28 | 7 | 21 | 2 |
| Occupational health and safety | 17 | 5 | 12 | 0 |
| Rights of migrant workers | 7 | 8 | 0 | 0 |
| Child labor | 2 | 0 | 2 | 0 |
| Minimum standards of employment | 16 | 6 | 10 | 0 |
| Discrimination | 19 | 2 | 16 | 0 |
| Access to impartial labor tribunals | 7 | 5 | 2 | 1 |
| Total petitions filed | 41 | 14 | 26 | 2 |

## The Evolution of US-Mexico Labor Cooperation    105

the ECE.[31] Freedom of association, the right to organize, the right to strike and collective bargaining disputes are afforded the least redress—these cases are exempt from all redress except Ministerial Consultations, even though these violations are among the most common in the case set.

It is important to note that no case to date has moved to the panel of experts stage, or has gone to panel arbitration, much less moved to trade sanctions. Rather, the highest level of resolution for any case selected for review has been to conduct Ministerial Consultations.[32] These often result in ministerial agreements, formal pronouncements on what states might now do to resolve recurrent labor rights violations, which may include cooperative activities and public outreach programs that are then overseen by the CLC.

The fact that most cases (15, or 41%) have ended in meetings between government officials to talk about labor issues rather than resolve them at the plant level is within the spirit of the agreement, but also has been one of the points of contention for critics of the NAALC, who charge that the NAALC is "toothless" because it doesn't go far enough on punishing labor rights violations.[33] One reason may be that that the NAALC institutions were designed to not have strong regulatory power,[34] and therefore simply do not have the enforcement capacity that early challengers to NAFTA wanted. One example of this is that most of the petitions, twenty-eight of the total forty-one, include freedom of association issues as the main labor violation, but it is precisely these cases that are not eligible for resolution beyond Ministerial Consultations, including panel arbitration that would assess and apply trade sanctions.

The negotiation of the side accord suggests that concerns over state sovereignty trumped the importance of compliance assigned to this new mechanism. The United States imposed the clause and the environmental side accord onto the NAFTA text in order to satisfy the demands of domestic constituencies, and without this support, the commercial aspects of the accord would not have passed Congress.[35] Mexico and Canada were pressured to accept an agreement they did not want in order to gain preferential access to the US market.[36] As a result, the text of the agreement makes consistent references to respect for the domestic labor laws of each state, and the agreement does not create new labor standards, but is based on the enforcement of domestic labor laws—even when these are not consistent with accepted international labor standards. Nor does the NAALC include any area where agents of the NAFTA states can intervene in domestic labor policy or practices, and the trade sanctions that would serve as the point of leverage for motivating changes in labor practices within states come only at the end of a series of negotiations, and only for a small class of labor rights violations that are not the most common in any of the NAFTA states. Yet no state would have signed an agreement that had a stronger capacity to punish labor rights violations, because no state wanted any other state to interfere in their labor laws or practices. In particular, Mexico nearly withdrew from the entire agreement over issues of state sovereignty.[37]

## 106 *Kimberly A. Nolan García*

Finally, of all of the potential cases that could be brought to NAALC arbitration, only very few cases have been filed for dispute resolution over the course of the sixteen years that the panel has been in effect. While the Mexican NAO notes that the dearth of cases reflects that the Mexican system of labor justice is capable of handling disputes without resorting to supranational forms of adjudication,[38] an alternative explanation is that disappointment with NAALC arbitration has led to fewer cases being filed overall. Further, as the NAALC process has become politicized in recent years, some filing groups have determined that their resources are better spent on other labor-related activities, such as strengthening efforts at cross-border labor organizing.

## THE RECENT BREAKDOWN IN BINATIONAL LABOR COOPERATION

There has been a significant decline in the number of petitions filed each year at the NAALC since 2001. Whereas prior to 2006, the number of petitions filed each year varied (in 1998, ten petitions were filed, but for most years two to four petitions were submitted per year), from 2006 to 2009 not a single petition was filed, and just four new cases have been filed since the Obama administration took office.

The number of cooperative activities overseen by the CLC has also declined dramatically, and the CLC itself has fallen apart. Whereas in the first year of the NAALC sixteen cooperative activities were realized, and until 2001, six to nine activities were scheduled each year, in more recent years only one or two activities have been realized. Because of the steep decline in CLC activity, the CLC office was closed in August of 2010, and has not been reopened.

While critics of the NAALC contend that the weak enforcement mechanisms are part of the reason why few new cases have been filed,[39] this explanation ignores that while labor unions turned away from the NAALC after the earliest test cases,[40] nongovernmental organizations continued to file petitions through the early period (accounting for the ten petitions filed in 1998 alone), and labor unions returned to the process, partnering with nongovernmental organizations (NGOs) to file the current cases. It is more likely that the recent breakdown in US-Mexico cooperation over labor issues in general has contributed to the stagnation in the NAALC process.

## POLITICIZATION OF THE NAALC PROCESS

As administrations in the United States change with the presidential electoral cycle, governmental priorities also shift, but an alternation in political parties can have an important effect on the ways that US bureaucracies

## The Evolution of US-Mexico Labor Cooperation    107

function. In particular, a Democratic administration is more likely to take on a prolabor agenda given that the AFL-CIO is a major supporter of the Democratic Party, and as such, labor issues generally become more important in the overall domestic agenda during Democratic administrations. In turn, subsequent Republican administrations may then attempt to minimize any political influence unions may have gained during the previous administration. As such, after the 2000 election, the Bush administration moved to isolate the Department of Labor and reverse the initiatives begun under the relatively prolabor Clinton administration. The appointment of Republican officials that were hostile to labor into administrative positions in the Department of Labor,[41] the reorganization of the international wing where the NAO is housed (the Bureau International Labor Affairs, ILAB), and cuts in funding to international labor rights programs during the Bush administration all in turn affected the way that the US Department of Labor addressed labor issues, including international efforts like the NAALC.[42] In turn, during the Bush administration very few cases were accepted, and few cases moved forward through the process.[43]

With the US NAO tied up in the politicization of the Department of Labor, Mexico took the opportunity to step back from the NAALC, given that it was the United States that was constantly engaging Mexico on discussing labor violations, and pushing them to agree to various cooperative efforts. With the United States suddenly not interested in pursuing labor cooperation further, Mexico was then better able to reassert its own lack of interest in the NAALC, creating a new, more defensive position vis-à-vis the US NAO.[44] This in turn created new barriers to communication between the NAOs that caused friction in the relationship, and limited the ways that the US NAO could engage their Mexican counterparts.

Though the NAALC respects state sovereignty in its design, and therefore allows each state the right to interpret their NAALC obligations as they see fit, the overall impact that Mexico's defensive position has left in the United States is the perception that the Mexicans are no longer willing to cooperate on labor issues. The fact that the Mexican NAO has refused to participate in cooperative activities around even migrant labor issues, the *singular* labor issue that is important to them, only adds to the image that the Mexicans have become obstinate.[45]

The Obama administration came into office in 2009 with a prolabor agenda and a renewed commitment to international labor rights issues, and has appointed staff and administrators that are committed to enforcing labor rights protections in the United States and abroad. However, at the end of the term, it is clear that this administration is less interested in reinvigorating US-Mexican cooperation around labor rights than was initially expected. The first new NAALC petition under the administration was filed at the US NAO in late 2011. It concerns the requisition of the Luz y Fuerza del Centro power company in central Mexico, and the dissolution of the Mexican Electrician's union (SME) as a result of the takeover.[46] The US

108  *Kimberly A. Nolan García*

NAO has decided to review this case, as has the Canadian NAO with their version of the submission, and for the first time ever, both NAOs will complete the review process together. In accepting this case, the US Department of Labor could potentially usher in a new era of a more aggressive US NAO, and a stronger NAALC.

The preceding discussion of NAFTA's labor side agreement underlines that in comparison to other issues, labor cooperation is one area of North American integration that is highly legalized with a deep range of institutions, yet the institutionalization of labor cooperation is not enough to assure cooperation in North America, nor the protection of labor rights. The creation of new labor offices, a trinational commission, regular meetings between high-level officials, and continuous trilateral communication through the channels established by the side agreement have all largely failed to maintain and deepen cooperation on North American labor rights over time. While the NAALC institutions have promoted cooperation on labor issues much beyond the level of contact between these states pre-NAFTA, that cooperation has broken down considerably in recent years. Further, the case resolutions show overall that arbitration has not gone far enough to promote labor protections in North America, even if there have been small gains for workers along the way. In sum then, the NAALC institutions have pushed states in the general direction of improving communication and coordination around labor issues, even if dispute resolution has been limited in promoting labor protections for North American workers.

## CONCLUSIONS

While labor issues have always been overshadowed by more pressing concerns between Mexico, the United States and Canada, after NAFTA, labor became a consistent piece of bilateral cooperation. The NAALC established formal institutions and channels of communication for labor representatives, and the case process promoted cross-border mobilization between members of civil society in the United States, Mexico and Canada. In turn, these new channels of communication have formed the basis for better understanding of labor law and practice in the NAFTA states.[47]

While labor issues may never become as important to diplomatic relations as immigration or security issues, the path that labor cooperation has taken since NAFTA can provide some lessons on how the larger bilateral relationship could be nurtured and sustained. First, the structure of cooperation under the NAALC necessarily demanded constant contact between labor bureaucrats as the NAOs interacted to ask questions, solicit information and determine overall what should be done with each of the petitions that the offices received. In turn, staff members developed a rapport with their counterparts that reinforced the cooperative spirit of the agreement, and kept the NAALC process from becoming adversarial. In turn, the cooperative spirit

The Evolution of US-Mexico Labor Cooperation   109

of the agreement set the tone for the activities of the CLC, which in the end, remains a core achievement of the agreement.

Second, the fallout after the politicization of the Department of Labor under the leadership of Elaine Chao shows that the bilateral relationship between Mexico and the United States—the major players in the NAALC accord—needs to be actively supported, and that support for bilateral cooperation needs to come from both sides. When the US NAO was caught in the politicization of the Department of Labor, the Mexican NAO then also withdrew from the NAALC process, in part because the United States was no longer pushing them to participate. This in turn had an important effect on how the NAALC institutions functioned, as once they were neglected by the official channels, petition sponsors then turned away from the process as well. To date, the NAALC has not yet recovered from that neglect.

The danger here lies in the potential breakdown of cooperation when, for example, the United States loses focus on Mexico as policy priorities shift towards other regions of the world. US negligence towards issues important to the Mexicans could also reinforce the tendency towards indifference within Mexico, especially since Mexico also prefers to let the United States take the lead on how the bilateral relationship will evolve. Both sides need to take a more active role in promoting the bilateral relationship if US-Mexico cooperation, so important to both countries, is to prosper through changes in administrations and the attendant priority shifts.

Finally, the discussion shows that the institutionalization of trinational cooperation is not enough to deepen cooperation in North America. The attachment of the labor side agreement to the NAFTA text set the stage for labor cooperation by establishing new institutions and a dispute resolution process that was cooperative in spirit, leading to new channels of communication between states around labor issues. However, without strong guidance from the agreement itself on how the new NAALC regulations were to be interpreted and applied, each state used the cases filed for dispute resolution as an arena to test its partners, and avoided using the NAALC as a strong tool for labor rights enforcement. Once subject to political interests within states, the NAALC broke down considerably. In the absence of a genuine commitment to labor enforcement from any of the three states, efforts at labor cooperation will remain stagnant, even with a wide set of institutions available to promote that cooperation.

## NOTES

1. I focus on the US-Mexico political dynamics of the NAALC, to the exclusion of Canadian participation, for a number of reasons. First, while the NAALC is a trilateral agreement, in structure and implementation it is essentially a game between the United States and Mexico. Canada participates much less in the NAALC process because labor law is reserved for the provinces, and therefore the NAALC has the force of treaty only in the provinces that have ratified the

110  *Kimberly A. Nolan García*

agreement: Manitoba, Prince Edward Island and Alberta. As a result, Canadian participation is generally circumscribed to receiving and hearing cases about the United States and Mexico. In practice, very few petitions involving labor rights violations in Canada are filed at the NAALC, and the Canadian NAO has been used mostly as part of a secondary filing strategy, with sponsors filing concurrent petitions in Canada in the event that the United States declines to review a case about Mexico. (Maquila Solidarity Network Coordinator), in discussion with the author, June 28, 2005.

2. Robert A. Pastor and Jorge G. Castañeda, *Limits to Friendship: The United States and Mexico*, 2nd ed. (New York: Vintage, 1989).

3. Secretaria de Relaciones Exteriores (SRE), "Comisión Binacional Mexico-Estados Unidos [Mexico-United States Binational Commission]," news release, SRE, Mexico City, n.d., on file with the author.

4. Alejandro Becerra Gelover, "Mecanismos de Comunicación Intergubermental entre Mexico y Estados Unidos," *El Cotidiano* 20, no. 127 (2004): 101–108. In Mexico, the counterpart to the US Department of Labor is the Ministry of Work and Social Welfare, STPS by its Spanish acronym.

5. *BBC News*, "Mexico/EEUU: La clave es Migración," accessed March 1, 2009, http://news.bbc.co.uk/hi/spanish/latin_america/newsid_2517000/2517113.stm.

6. *El Siglo de Torreón*, "Inicia la reunión binacional Mexico-EU [The Mexico-US Binational Meeting Begins]," November 12, 2003, accessed on November 11, 2010, http://www.elsiglodetorreon.com.mx/noticia/59700.inicia-reunion-binacional-mexico-eu.html.

7. Maxwell A. Cameron and Brian W. Tomlin, *The Making of NAFTA: How the Deal Was Done* (Ithaca: Cornell University Press, 2000).

8. Emilio C. Viano, "An American Dilemma: The Flow of Trade versus the Flow of People in NAFTA," *Denning Law Journal* 22 (2010): 87–115.

9. See Gabriel and MacDonald in this volume.

10. The most recent NAALC cases on the violations of migrants' rights make clear that access to labor tribunals in the state where the violations took place is nearly impossible once workers return to their home countries, making it easy for employers to exploit already vulnerable migrant workers.

11. I provide a much more detailed treatment of the emergence of the anti-NAFTA network in the United States, Canada and Mexico in Kimberly Nolan García, "The Evolution of Mexico-US Labor Cooperation (1994–2009): Achievements and Challenges," *Politics and Policy* 39, no. 1 (2011): 91–117.

12. Frederick Mayer, *Interpreting NAFTA: The Science and Art of Political Analysis* (New York: Colombia University Press, 1998).

13. The International Labor Education and Research Fund, Greenpeace, the United Auto Workers, the AFL-CIO, the Natural Resources Defense Council and the Family Farm Coalition were joined by an additional sixty-two advocacy groups to form the Mobilization on Development, Trade, Labor and the Environment—the MODTLE Crew (see Mayer, *Interpreting NAFTA*).

14. See Emilie M. Hafner-Burton, *Forced to Be Good: Why Trade Agreements Boost Human Rights* (Ithaca: Cornell University Press, 2009); Mayer, *Interpreting NAFTA*; Cameron and Tomlin, *Making of NAFTA*.

15. Frederick Mayer, "Negotiating the NAFTA: Political Lessons for the FTAA," in *Greening the Americas: NAFTA's Lessons for Hemispheric Trade*, ed. C. L. Deere and D. Esty (Cambridge: MIT, 2002), 97–118.

16. The administration committed to "expanded US-Mexico labor cooperation" and "an expanded program of environmental cooperation" as part of the negotiations. Mayer, *Interpreting NAFTA*, 90.

17. Cameron and Tomlin, *Making of NAFTA*.

# The Evolution of US-Mexico Labor Cooperation   111

18. Lance Compa, "NAFTA's Side Labor Agreement and International Labor Solidarity," *Antipode* 33, no. 3 (2001): 451–467; International Labor Rights Fund, *North American Free Trade Agreement and Labor Rights*, 1995, on file with the author.

19. NAALC, *North American Agreement on Labor Cooperation (NAALC): Between the Government of the United States of America, the Government of Canada, and the Government of the United Mexican States*, 1993, accessed February 1, 2013, http://www.dol.gov/ilab/regs/naalc/naalc.htm.

20. NAALC, *North American Agreement*.

21. In the United States, the NAO is now known as the Office of Trade and Labor Affairs (OTLA). I will refer to it as the US NAO to stay consistent with the parallel institutions in Mexico and Canada.

22. NAALC, *North American Agreement*.

23. Kimberly A. Nolan García, "Persuasion, Coercion and the Domestic Costs of Compliance: Evaluating the NAALC Resolutions against Mexico" (DT 231, CIDE Serie de *Documentos de Trabajo* de la División de Estudios Internacionales, Mexico City, 2012).

24. Nolan García, "Persuasion."

25. Dispute resolution is more formally one of the steps towards the adjudication of labor issues in the NAALC process. However, I refer to the entire process as dispute resolution, though there are important differences between dispute resolution in the NAALC and the commercial, dumping and investor disputes in the NAFTA.

26. NAALC, *North American Agreement*.

27. See Tamara Kay, "Labor Transnationalism and Global Governance: The Impact of NAFTA on Transnational Labor Relationships in North America," *American Journal of Sociology* 111, no. 3 (2005): 715–756; Joel Stillerman, "Transnational Activist Networks and the Emergence of Labor Internationalism in the NAFTA Countries," *Social Science History* 27, no. 4 (2003): 577–601.

28. Kimberly Nolan García, "Transnational Actors and Labor Rights Enforcement in the North American Free Trade Agreement," *Latin American Politics and Society* 53, no. 2 (2011): 29–60.

29. Petitions must be filed in states other than those where the violations take place. As such, five petitions against Mexico have been double-filed in both the United States and Canada. I count the petitions that were filed at more than one NAO as separate cases, as they are reviewed separately by the different NAOs if accepted, and feature separate resolutions that may or may not come to similar conclusions. More than one petition may be filed about a specific case. I treat these as separate petitions in the accounting of petitions and cases. All data collected here is coded from the original petitions filed at any NAO (known as public communications), and the NAO reports (known as public reports of review), collected from all three NAOs in the US NAO Reading Room in Washington, DC. A full accounting of the petitions—the years they were filed, the NAOs that received them, and their outcomes—is included in Nolan García, "Evolution."

30. Since labor rights petitions can list violations of more than one of the eleven NAALC principles (here categorized by a collapsed seven-point class of violation), Table 6.1 does not add to forty-one.

31. NAALC, *North American Agreement*.

32. An additional five cases are pending resolutions. Four cases were resolved outside of the formal channels of NAALC dispute resolution once petitions were filed, and are not included here.

33. Terry Collingsworth, "International Worker Rights Enforcement: Proposals Following a Test Case," in *Human Rights, Labor Rights and International*

112 *Kimberly A. Nolan García*

*Trade,* ed. L. Compa and S. F. Diamond (Philadelphia: University of Pennsylvania Press, 1996), 227–250; Graciela Bensusán, "NAFTA and Labor: Impacts and Outlooks," in *NAFTA in the New Millennium,* ed. E. J. Chambers and P. J. Smith (San Diego: Center for US-Mexican Studies, 2002), 243–264; Parbudyal Singh, "NAFTA and Labor: A Canadian Perspective," *Journal of Labor Research* 23, no. 3 (2002): 433–447; Parbudyal Singh and Roy J. Adams, "Neither a Gem nor a Scam: The Progress of the North American Agreement on Labor Cooperation," *Labor Studies Journal* 26, no. 1 (2001): 1–15.

34. Marley S. Weiss, "Two Steps Forward, One Step Back or Vice Versa: Labor Rights under Free Trade Agreements from NAFTA through Jordan via Chile to Latin America and Beyond," *University of San Francisco Law Review* 37 (2003): 689–755; Ruth Buchanan and Rusby Chaparro, "International Institutions and Transnational Advocacy: The Case of the North American Agreement on Labor Cooperation," *UCLA Journal of International Law and Foreign Affairs* 13, no. 129 (2008): 129–159.

35. Hafner-Burton, *Forced to Be Good.*

36. Cameron and Tomlin, *Making of NAFTA.*

37. Cameron and Tomlin, *Making of NAFTA.*

38. Subcoordinator for Hemispheric Labor Policy, Secretariat for Labor and Social Security, Mexico City, Mexico in discussion with the author, July 26, 2006.

39. Singh and Adams, "Neither a Gem nor a Scam."

40. John H. Hovis, "Re: Submission No 940004," letter to Irasema Garza, January 19, 1994, on file with the author.

41. For reference, Mark Wilson, who was appointed deputy assistant secretary in charge of workplace standards, was Chao's colleague at the Heritage Center, where he once published a report entitled *How to Close Down the Department of Labor.* Steven Law, the deputy secretary, was once the chief legal officer at the US Chamber of Commerce.

42. I detail the appointment of anti-labor officials, the cuts in funding and the reorganization of the ILAB, and the effects these changes had on the operation of international programs in Nolan García, "Evolution."

43. For example, the North Carolina Public Employees and H2B Visa cases have been on hold since 2004.

44. Mexico took on a highly legalistic interpretation of its responsibilities under the NAALC, refusing to participate with the US NAO except for those activities and communication channels that were explicitly noted in the text of the NAALC agreement.

45. Acting Director, Committee for Labor Cooperation, Washington, DC, in discussion with the author, June 13, 2007.

46. Luz y Fuerza was dissolved by presidential decree, and its responsibilities were transferred to the National Electricity Commission, the CFE. Since Luz y Fuerza no longer legally exists, neither does the SME. The petition casts the disbanding of Luz y Fuerza as a freedom of association issue, as it charges that the requisition of the company was motivated by the ongoing hostilities between the Calderon government and the SME. Sindicato Mexicano de Electricistas, public communication to the US Office of Trade Agreement Implementation (OTLA), Washington, DC, 2011.

47. In the United States, for example, the basic structure of Mexican industrial relations, the labor board system and the challenges of union registration are now well known, whereas only ten years ago this sort of information was solidly the province of serious observers and policy makers close to labor. Program Coordinator, AFL-CIO Solidarity Center-Mexico, in discussion with the author, July 25, 2006.

## REFERENCES

*BBC News.* "Mexico/EEUU: La clave es Migración." 2002. Accessed March 1, 2009. http://news.bbc.co.uk/hi/spanish/latin_america/newsid_2517000/2517113.stm.

Becerra Gelover, Alejandro. "Mecanismos de comunicación intergubermental entre Mexico y Estados Unidos." *El Cotidiano* 20, no. 127 (2004): 101–108.

Bensusán, Graciela. "NAFTA and Labor: Impacts and Outlooks." In *NAFTA in the New Millennium*, edited by E.J. Chambers and P.J. Smith, 243–264. San Diego: Center for US-Mexican Studies, 2002.

Buchanan, Ruth, and Rusby Chaparro. "International Institutions and Transnational Advocacy: The Case of the North American Agreement on Labor Cooperation." *UCLA Journal of International Law and Foreign Affairs* 13, no. 129 (2008): 129–159.

Cameron, Maxwell A., and Brian W. Tomlin. *The Making of NAFTA: How the Deal Was Done*. Ithaca: Cornell University Press, 2000.

Collingsworth, Terry. "International Worker Rights Enforcement: Proposals Following a Test Case." In *Human Rights, Labor Rights and International Trade*, edited by L. Compa and S.F. Diamond, 227–250. Philadelphia: University of Pennsylvania Press, 1996.

Compa, Lance. "NAFTA's Side Labor Agreement and International Labor Solidarity." *Antipode* 33, no. 3 (2001): 451–467.

Hafner-Burton, Emilie M. *Forced to Be Good: Why Trade Agreements Boost Human Rights*. Ithaca: Cornell University Press, 2009.

Hovis, John H. "Re: Submission No 940004." Letter to Irasema Garza. January 19, 1994. On file with the author.

International Labor Rights Fund. *North American Free Trade Agreement and Labor Rights*. 1995. On file with the author.

Kay, Tamara. "Labor Transnationalism and Global Governance: The Impact of NAFTA on Transnational Labor Relationships in North America." *American Journal of Sociology* 111, no. 3 (2005): 715–756.

Mayer, Frederick. *Interpreting NAFTA: The Science and Art of Political Analysis*. New York: Colombia University Press, 1998.

———. "Negotiating the NAFTA: Political Lessons for the FTAA." In *Greening the Americas: NAFTA's Lessons for Hemispheric Trade*, edited by C.L. Deere and D. Esty, 97–118. Cambridge: MIT, 2002.

NAALC. *North American Agreement on Labor Cooperation (NAALC): Between the Government of the United States of America, the Government of Canada, and the Government of the United Mexican States*. 1993. Available at http://www.dol. gov/ilab/regs/naalc/naalc.htm, last accessed 02/01/2013.

Nolan García, Kimberly A. "The Evolution of Mexico-US Labor Cooperation (1994–2009): Achievements and Challenges," *Politics and Policy* 39, no. 1 (2011): 91–117.

———. "Persuasion, Coercion and the Domestic Costs of Compliance: Evaluating the NAALC Resolutions against Mexico." DT 231. CIDE Serie de *Documentos de Trabajo* de la División de Estudios Internacionales. Mexico City. 2012.

———. "Transnational Actors and Labor Rights Enforcement in the North American Free Trade Agreement," *Latin American Politics and Society* 53, no. 2 (2011): 29–60.

Pastor, Robert A., and Jorge G. Castañeda. *Limits to Friendship: The United States and Mexico*. 2nd ed. New York: Vintage, 1989.

Secretaria de Relaciones Exteriores (SRE). "Comisión Binacional Mexico-Estados Unidos [Mexico-United States Binational Commission]." News release. SRE. Mexico City. n.d. On file with the author.

## 114 *Kimberly A. Nolan García*

*El Siglo de Torreón.* "Inicia la reunión binacional Mexico-EU [The Mexico-US Binational Meeting Begins]." November 12, 2003. Accessed November 11, 2010. http://www.elsiglodetorreon.com.mx/noticia/59700.inicia-reunion-binacional-mexico-eu.html.

Sindicato Mexicano de Electricistas. Public communication to the US Office of Trade Agreement Implementation (OTLA), Washington, DC, 2011.

Singh, Parbudyal. "NAFTA and Labor: A Canadian Perspective." *Journal of Labor Research* 23, no. 3 (2002): 433–447.

Singh, Parbudyal, and Roy J. Adams. "Neither a Gem nor a Scam: The Progress of the North American Agreement on Labor Cooperation." *Labor Studies Journal* 26, no. 1 (2001): 1–15.

Stillerman, Joel. "Transnational Activist Networks and the Emergence of Labor Internationalism in the NAFTA Countries." *Social Science History* 27, no. 4 (2003): 577–601.

Viano, Emilio C. "An American Dilemma: The Flow of Trade versus the Flow of People in NAFTA," *Denning Law Journal* 22 (2010): 87–115.

Weiss, Marley S. "Two Steps Forward, One Step Back or Vice Versa: Labor Rights Under Free Trade Agreements from NAFTA through Jordan via Chile to Latin America and Beyond." *University of San Francisco Law Review* 37 (2003): 689–755.

# 7 Citizenship at the Margins
## The Canadian Seasonal Agricultural Worker Program and Civil Society Advocacy[1]

*Christina Gabriel and Laura Macdonald*

Migration and citizenship issues continue to plague the North American "partnership." Labor mobility was a pressing issue that was largely ignored during the North American Free Trade Agreement (NAFTA) negotiations, apart from the NAFTA visa that was introduced in chapter 16 of the agreement. In the United States, efforts at comprehensive immigration reform remain mired in Congress, although advocates hope that President Obama will fulfill his promise to carry out such reform during his second term. Meanwhile, some US states continue to adopt increasingly punitive and restrictive measures to restrict the rights of migrants (such as the recent legislation passed in the Arizona legislature). The high proportion of undocumented migrants who come to the United States from Mexico make this a truly North American problem, and the bad will it has created between the two countries threatens to stall deeper integration.

In this context, Canadian programs and the Canadian immigration model are sometimes held up as "best practices," particularly the long-standing, low-wage, sector-specific, temporary Seasonal Agricultural Workers Program (SAWP). Under this program, agricultural workers are brought to Canada from Mexico and the Caribbean. Workers are selected by their respective governments. And states also play a critical role in the administration of the program and overseeing workers' rights.

Issues related to migration and citizenship are usually conceptualized as part of the mandate of the nation-state. In real life, however, actors from multiple scales, both governmental and nongovernmental, play important roles in the lives and the citizenship struggles of migrants. As argued by Kerry Preibisch, civil society actors, as they engage with state policies, represent a form of "globalization from below."[2] This article describes how these nonstate actors attempt to intervene in the way in which noncitizen migrant workers are positioned in relation to changing practices of social citizenship in Canada. Our attention in this study is on social rights, rather than political rights, which are often the main focus of analysis in discussions of citizenship and migration in North America. We draw on a case study of Mexican agricultural migrant workers in Ontario to argue that while pro-migrant advocacy operates at a variety of scales from the local

## 116   *Christina Gabriel and Laura Macdonald*

to the national to the international and extraterritorial, local struggles are particularly important in advancing the interests of migrant workers. We also argue that despite the attention to migrant rights within the SAWP program, the formal recognition of rights by state actors is insufficient because of the vulnerable status of these workers, necessitating intervention by civil society actors.

This article is organized in three sections. First we briefly review some aspects of the changing nature of governance and citizenship that inform our case study. The second section highlights some of the broad parameters of the SAWP program "from above" and how it acts to circumscribe the rights of migrant workers. Lastly, using examples from primary fieldwork in Leamington, Toronto and Ottawa, we map the ways in which these parameters are contested, challenged and in some cases reinforced by civil society actors representing migrant workers.

## CITIZENSHIP AND RIGHTS FOR
## TEMPORARY AGRICULTURAL WORKERS

T. H. Marshall's tripartite formulation of citizenship as rights—political, civil and social—is still referenced as a starting point in many interrogations of citizenship more than 50 years after it was written. In particular, his understanding of social rights attached to the welfare state remains influential. He referred to this element as encompassing "[t]he whole range from the right to a modicum of economic welfare and security to the right to share to the full in the social heritage and to live the life of a civilized being according to the standards prevailing in the society."[3] Marshall emphasized social rights because of his insistence that individuals are unable to really enjoy full political and civil rights without access to a broad range of social rights that allow them to "live the life of a civilized being."[4] In our study of Mexican migrant agricultural workers in Canada, the right to access health care, safe working conditions, employment insurance, parental leave, pensions, and the right to organize are among the social rights highlighted as particularly relevant to workers' situation and to which they do not have complete access, even if they are legally entitled to them. Although scholars have criticized Marshall's work on a number of grounds, many groups have used a conceptualization of substantive social rights as a way to advance a social justice agenda that demands greater equality for those citizen subjects who are excluded from the political community. Even aliens/noncitizens who are positioned on the margins of the nation are also "workers, taxpayers, consumers, neighbors, they are persons who constitute part of the life of the (nationally bounded) political community." And they are not completely without rights.[5]

In this chapter we build on Grugel and Piper's insight regarding the importance of international agencies and migrant-centered nongovernmental

*Citizenship at the Margins* 117

organizations that "struggle to reframe a states-led agenda in the direction of rights and to transform the governance regime into one that acts to mitigate the human suffering migration entails."[6] While self-organization is desirable, it is often very difficult because of legal status, types of jobs and "the lack of democratic space and recognition of associational rights in destination countries." For these reasons nonstate actors, whether unions, community organizations or faith groups, can play roles both in the delivery of social rights including language training and education and in advocating on behalf of migrants.[7] As we see in the case of Mexican agricultural workers in Canada, nonstate actors help migrants to access social rights to which they are legally entitled,[8] as well as pushing for the extension of these rights beyond the narrow constraints within which they currently operate. In doing so, we argue, they are expanding conventional understandings of citizenship.

## THE CANADA-MEXICO SEASONAL AGRICULTURAL WORKERS PROGRAM

The Mexican migrant population in Canada is very small compared to the large numbers of Mexicans who reside in the United States. Mexican nationals in the United States numbered 12.7 million individuals or about 32 percent of the total foreign-born population in 2008; of these, about seven million are estimated to be undocumented, representing 59 percent of the total irregular population in the United States.[9] While the Mexican immigrant population in Canada is small—fifty thousand in 2006,[10] Mexico is an important sending country for temporary workers. In 2008, 20,900 Mexican entered Canada as temporary foreign workers, placing Mexico second to the United States as a source country.[11] Moreover, there has been rapid growth of the numbers of Mexicans in Canada between the 1991 and 2001 census, "making it the largest group of immigrants from Spanish Latin America and among the fastest growing from any country."[12]

The Commonwealth and Mexican Seasonal Agricultural Workers Program (SAWP) is one of Canada's oldest and long-standing temporary worker programs. In the late 1950s growers complained of labor shortages in Canada's agricultural sector. In 1966, the Canadian government signed a bilateral agreement with Jamaica initially and then several other Caribbean countries to recruit temporary workers to address what was ostensibly a short-term labor shortage. Mexico subsequently entered the program in 1974 when it signed a memorandum of understanding (MOU) with Canada. It has been suggested that this expansion is related, in part, to an attempt to discipline the Caribbean workers and their representatives' calls for better working conditions and wages.[13] Today, more than forty years later, the program has grown enormously—from 264 Jamaicans workers in 1966 to more than 21,000 in 2008.[14] This said, the SAWP accounts for only a small portion of all temporary workers in Canada.[15]

118   *Christina Gabriel and Laura Macdonald*

Recent figures indicate Mexican workers dominate in the SAWP, accounting for 11,798 workers, as compared to 5,916 from Jamaica in 2008.[16] The vast majority of workers employed under this program are men—in 2005, Mexican women numbered only 356 workers.[17] For the most part SAWP workers are found in fruits, vegetables and horticulture. Analysts have underscored how the very viability and competiveness of these sectors are dependent on a labor force that is flexible, disciplined, unfree and reliable.[18] With the exceptions of New Brunswick and Newfoundland and Labrador, all Canadian provinces are participants in SAWP. However, the majority of workers—nearly eighteen thousand—are concentrated in the province of Ontario.[19] In 2005 the average length of stay for Mexican workers in Ontario was 20.7 weeks.[20]

Under the terms of the program, workers are selected by the Mexican government through 139 State Employment Service Offices, but workers are required to travel to Mexico City to complete the process, which includes health checks and the issuing of a visa. At this time they are also advised regarding rights and obligations under the Canada-Mexico agreement. Employers assume travel expenses, including airfare, and then deduct these costs from workers' wages.[21] Workers are employed for a specified period anywhere from four to eight months. They "work 10–12 hour days, six days a week for four to eight months."[22] The employer must: provide free housing (except in British Columbia) that meets a provincially acceptable standard; provide kitchen utensils or meals, and ensure that workers are entered into a provincial health insurance plan and workers' compensation.[23] Employers provide evaluations of each worker at the end of the season, and these assessments play a critical role in determining whether the worker will be allowed to return in subsequent years.[24] Once their contract expires, workers in the SAWP program must return home.

On the one hand, a number of the SAWP's features have been lauded, and it is hailed as a "best practice model"[25] for a number of reasons. These include the participation of employers in program design and administration as well as the critical role of the sending state, Mexico, in recruiting and overseeing the welfare of its citizens in Canada.[26] Others emphasize that local communities benefit through the growth of the agricultural sector and the increased demand for local services and goods, in addition to the provision of a needed labor force.[27] Equally important is the fact that the majority of SAWP workers return home at the end of their contract. A World Bank 2006 estimate places the overstay rate among SAWP workers as 1.5 percent.[28] In some ways the program requirements ensure this outcome:

> Recruitment policies for low skill workers coming to work on farms give preference to individuals with dependents, while visa restrictions require them to leave their families behind. These policies are principally designed to deter visa overstay or permanent settlement by choosing workers with more reasons to return home than to stay.[29]

Additionally, other research has found that most temporary workers arrive in debt. This situation gives them incentives to be good workers and adhere to SAWP rules so that they can return in subsequent years in order to eliminate their debts and save earnings. This usually happens in the second or third year.[30]

On the other hand, the design of SAWP circumscribes key citizenship rights of temporary workers and renders them vulnerable to workplace abuse. Under the program's terms, workers are tied to one employer, live on-site in employer-provided accommodation and are not permitted to apply for permanent status.[31] The fact that SAWP workers are limited to one employer, that it is very difficult to transfer from one employer to another and that losing a job means immediate deportation gives employers significant power over workers. "Since a migrant's presence in Canada is dependent on a sole employer, most comply with all nature of employer requests and are reticent to raise issues around working and living conditions."[32] It has been argued that these workers can be considered under "servile status" according to the terms of the 1957 UN Supplementary Convention on the Abolition of Slavery, the Slave Trade, and Institutions and Practices Similar to Slavery.[33] Others simply refer to the inability of SAWP workers to circulate freely in the labor market as a form of unfree labor.[34]

Control is also evident in the fact that SAWP allows employers to request workers by name to return in subsequent years. This is rationalized on the basis that nominated workers constitute a pool of experienced labor. One study outlined the effects that flow from this process. Firstly, the process provides a measure of security of employment for named workers and as a result reduces pressures for the growth of undocumented workers. Secondly, it engenders a paternalistic relationship between workers and employers. But, thirdly, "the imbalance in the power relationship between employer and employee is exacerbated when the employer has the ability to determine the worker's future participation in the [SAWP] through the 'naming process.'"[35]

A key criticism of the SAWP is that it offers no path to permanent status and by extension Canadian citizenship, despite what may be significant labor market and social attachment. For example, Basok[36] notes that some workers have returned to the same region in Ontario for the last twenty years. Nevertheless, SAWP workers are unable to participate in the political process and thereby have no influence in changing the terms and conditions of their employment through electoral channels.[37] The SAWP stands in contrast to Canada's other "low-skilled program," the Live-in-Caregiver Program (LCP), which allows temporary foreign domestic workers to change their status once they meet certain conditions. In this respect, the SAWP is similar to the comparable H-2A Temporary Agricultural Worker visa in the United States, and both differ from programs aimed at high-skill workers. These latter programs, such as the US H-1B and L-I visas and the Canadian Experience Class, often permit workers to eventually apply for permanent residence.

120  *Christina Gabriel and Laura Macdonald*

This said, Mexican workers contracted under the SAWP are theoretically entitled to many of the same obligations and social rights that permanent residents and Canadian citizens receive. For example, they are responsible for Canadian Employment Insurance premiums and Canada Pension Plan payments, as well as Canadian income tax. They are entitled to free health care under the health care system of the province in which they are working and workers' compensation insurance to cover on-the-job injury and illness.[38] The rights provided to workers under this program thus seem to go well beyond those available even to Mexican workers who obtain an H-2A Temporary Agricultural Worker visa in the United States (a program that is in many respects similar to the SAWP), let alone the minimal rights available to undocumented workers in the United States and Canada.[39] In practice, however, the line between authorized and unauthorized worker is often blurred since workers may not be aware of their rights and governments often need to be pushed to deliver these rights in a timely and appropriate fashion.[40]

As noted earlier, a key feature of the Canada-Mexico SAWP, in contrast with other forms of temporary worker recruitment, is the involvement of the Mexican government, through the Mexican consulates in Canada, in overseeing workers' conditions and ensuring that their rights are respected, as well as in advertising the program and recruiting workers in Mexico. Also, workers in the SAWP may be repatriated if their employer is unsatisfied with their work, without recourse to appeal. The fact that the Mexican consulates are responsible not only for the rights of their citizens, but also for the overall success of the program, sometimes places them in a contradictory position. Critics argue that the consulate is not always sufficiently active in protecting workers' rights.[41] As critics have argued, the program is not necessarily "best practice" in terms of workers' rights and in fact frequently places them in precarious conditions. It is precisely these conditions that civil society actors are contesting, in their efforts to secure migrant social rights.

## CIVIL SOCIETY ACTORS AND MIGRANT
## SOCIAL RIGHTS IN ONTARIO[42]

Civil society organizations, as Grugel and Piper[43] point out, play a fundamental role in making the connection between formal and substantive citizenship rights, as well as in highlighting the inequities that result from workers' marginal status. Our research revealed the critical role played by civil society organizations in helping migrant workers access the social rights to which they are entitled, educating them about the fact that they do have social rights in Canada, and lobbying governments to extend the social rights provided to migrant agricultural workers. Table 7.1 summarizes the organizations interviewed, their location, constituency, scale of operation, main activities and the social rights each organization addresses.

## Citizenship at the Margins    121

*Table 7.1*   Profile of Civil Society Organizations Interviewed

| Organization / Location | Sector | Scale of operation | Main activities | Social rights addressed |
| --- | --- | --- | --- | --- |
| KAIROS – Toronto | Churches | Transnational, national | Advocacy, education | Broad range |
| Canadian Labour Congress – Ottawa | Labor | National | Advocacy (Transitional Worker Advocacy Group, TWAG), education | Right to organize, other broad social rights |
| United Food and Commercial Workers (UFCW) and Agricultural Worker Alliance (AWA) – Toronto/ Leamington | Labor | Transnational, national, provincial, local | Advocacy, legal struggles, worker support | Broad range, focusing on labor rights |
| Frontier College – Leamington | Education | Local | Literacy, language training | Literacy |
| Migrant Workers Community Program (MWCP) – Leamington | Community | Local | Migrant integration, language | Cultural rights |

Our interviews displayed some tensions among community groups' different conceptions of migrants' rights. They also revealed, however, the way in which civil society actors can challenge prevailing notions of citizenship and belonging, and can work across sectors, and even across borders, to promote the expansion of social rights. The migrant workers' lack of access to formal citizenship status means they are denied many fundamental social rights that Canadian citizens take for granted, and they lack the basic security to advocate for even those rights to which they are legally entitled. Factors such as lack of knowledge of their rights, lack of language skills, dependence on employers and lack of access to transportation and physical isolation play important roles in limiting workers' access to these rights.

Because of the much smaller size of the Mexican population in Canada compared to the United States, Mexican SAWP workers are often deeply

## 122 Christina Gabriel and Laura Macdonald

isolated and cannot draw upon the dense array of civil society organizations (like hometown associations) and informal networks that exist in many US communities. Nevertheless, in recent years a variety of Canadian civil society organizations have begun to organize to defend and expand the range of rights available to these workers. From the labor sector, representatives from three organizations were interviewed: the national office of the United Food and Commercial Workers' Union (UFCW), the Agricultural Workers Alliance (AWA), established in 2008 by the UFCW to assist migrant workers, and the Ottawa-based Canadian Labour Congress (CLC).[44] Both the CLC and UFCW are active at the national and international level, while the AWA works at the grassroots level, in a series of nine agriculture workers support centers across Canada, including the Leamington center we visited, which was the first one established (in 2002).[45] Among the nonlabor civil society organizations, two of them are national organizations. KAIROS, based in Toronto, is a faith-based organization, formed in 2001 by the major Christian denominations in Canada. It was established to promote peace and social justice in Canada and around the world.[46] We also interviewed the representative of the Leamington office of Frontier College, which has perhaps the longest history of involvement with migrant workers.[47] Frontier College began in 1899 as the Canadian Reading Camp Movement, offering basic education and literacy training to laborers in remote rural locations. Today it provides literacy training in both urban and rural areas. The Leamington office provides "laborer-teacher" volunteers to promote literacy and English-speaking skills among workers on local farms. While Frontier College is a national organization, its involvement is primarily at the local level, and it does not engage in extensive advocacy around migrant rights. Finally, we also visited the office of the community-based Migrant Worker Community Program (MWCP). The MWCP is funded by the South Essex Community Council, Frontier College, some local churches, the town of Kingsville and Municipality of Leamington, the local hospitals, Mexican consulate, the police and the growers' association. It is not explicitly "rights-oriented," but promotes community integration and communication through fiestas, fairs, bicycle safety activities and a weekly radio show.

## INTERNATIONAL/TRANSNATIONAL ACTIVITIES

Despite the fact that migrant workers occupy a transnational social space, most of the work of CSOs in support of migrant workers is national, provincial or local in scope, as a result of the absence of strong mechanisms at the North American or international levels for promoting migrant workers' rights. Three of the organizations in our sample—KAIROS, UFCW and the CLC—are active at the international level, although other groups may make reference to the human rights standards established in international bodies like the United Nations or the International Labor Organization (ILO). The

## Citizenship at the Margins 123

institutional weakness of NAFTA discussed in this volume is reflected in the lack of attention to the rights of migrant workers. As a result, there is little coordination across North American borders among migrants' rights organizations.

Nevertheless, some of the agencies we studied do include international work as one aspect of their multidimensional activities. The work of UFCW Canada (which is itself part of a cross-border union based in the United States) is the most multiscalar of all of these agencies, and multiscalar engagement is a conscious element of the union's strategies. Stan Raper, national coordinator of the Agricultural Workers Alliance for UFCW Canada, expressed frustration with ILO conventions as a tool for advocacy:

> I used to wave them around, I don't anymore. I've kind of lost hope that our Canadian government will ever acknowledge the conventions that have been signed, which I find tragic. We use them in our legal challenges, we use them to educate people about the hypocrisy of our Canadian government and the fact that they sign conventions that they have no ability to enforce because labor standards are provincial jurisdiction and the provinces aren't prepared to sign on to something that the feds agreed to.[48]

Karl Flecker, the national director of the CLC's Human Rights and Anti-racism Department, also expressed skepticism about the value of such mechanisms as the ILO conventions as well as the NAFTA side accord on labor rights, because of its lack of mechanisms for monitoring and enforcement of provisions:

> So these side agreements . . . are negotiated with eyes wide shut to what the consequences are for labor market planning, development, immigration and integration policy issues. Because as you bring in large numbers of migrant workers who are put in precarious and vulnerable situations, then a number of consequences happen–xenophobia, discrimination, human trafficking, and a contributing factor to the downward social pressure on wages and public policy issues because the population starts to spiral.[49]

In the absence of enforceable international standards in the area of migrant rights, the UFCW has focused its international efforts on lobbying governments of the sender states, including Mexico, Thailand, Guatemala, Jamaica and the eastern Caribbean countries. According to Raper, the UFCW has worked with the Mexican Senate's committees on migration, as well as with campesino organizations and sending states in Mexico. Raper notes that the UFCW has tried to counter some of the "basic propaganda" about the SAWP program in Mexico:

> when we started showing them the number of workers that were sent home in a box and how many had lost their limbs and how many were

124 *Christina Gabriel and Laura Macdonald*

being repatriated and how many went AWOL or became undocumented workers, it was a bit of a shock, I think, because most of them had bought into the concept that this was a great program.[50]

Raper also says that the Mexican consulate in Leamington and the embassy in Ottawa have recognized the need for greater education of consular officials on provincial labor laws and employment standards. Nonstate actors can thus play an important role at a transnational scale, educating sending states about the perils that their citizens may face when working abroad, and helping them facilitate access to social rights to which their citizens are entitled.

One of the other organizations interviewed for this study, KAIROS, also has an international mandate and perspective that stems from its faith-based perspective. The coordinator of KAIROS's Refugee and Migration Program, Alfredo Barahona, has participated in a new international coalition, the International Assembly of Migrants and Refugees. This group was created by migrants' organizations in response to the government-led Global Forum on Migration and Development. Despite KAIROS's clear commitment to international work and to linking global and local struggles, the organization's work in this area has been facing pressures due to government cutbacks.[51]

## National and Provincial Engagement

While international engagement may be recognized as strategically important for some organizations, the existing mechanisms for global governance of migration are relatively weak. As a result, considerable attention is devoted by migrant-support organizations to lobbying national and provincial governments. As noted earlier, responsibility for migrant workers' rights in Canada is split between the federal and provincial jurisdictions, which often makes it difficult for migrant rights groups to determine where to focus their efforts. At the federal level, the CLC, the national confederation of Canadian trade unions, has taken the lead in coordinating responses to the expansion of the temporary foreign worker category in Canada among unions and migrants' rights organizations. Flecker reflects on the fact that Canadian unions have a less than stellar record on immigration issues: "Well I think, very candidly, labor has not had a noble history on the issue of immigration into Canada. There are well-documented parts of the labor movement where they were antagonistic, hostile, xenophobic, discriminatory, racist and exclusionary."[52] Flecker notes that over time, primarily because of the work within unions of racialized and aboriginal workers, "parts of the labor movement have evolved and changed and matured and recognized that there's a fundamental need to have solidarity among all workers."[53] Nonetheless, tensions remain, which came out in the first meetings of the group established by the CLC, the Temporary Worker Advocacy Group (TWAG):

## Citizenship at the Margins   125

[T]here were points in this meeting when there was xenophobia and racism that was disheartening put on the table, coming from some individuals. At the same time, also what was coming out was a level of sharing of the emerging growth of the [temporary worker] program across much more than just the agricultural sector.[54]

TWAG, initially composed of civil society organizations, began inviting government representatives from Citizenship and Immigration and the HRSDC branch responsible for the Temporary Foreign Worker program to the TWAG meetings. Despite improvements in the federal government's infrastructure for managing the program, and higher levels of dialogue, Flecker expresses frustration about the lack of government response to the substantive critiques raised by civil society groups.[55]

While the CLC has had to struggle with legacies of racism and exclusionary attitudes in the labor movement, organizations that began from a pro-migrant, human rights perspective bring a different approach. KAIROS representative Alfredo Barahona argues that their focus has been to bring a faith-based perspective and a human rights framework to the table in promoting national coalitions advocating rights of migrant workers. KAIROS worked with the UFCW and others to establish a Migrant Justice Network, bringing together cross-sectoral groups representing academics, unions, grassroots organizations and churches, to speak out on issues related to migrant workers and lobby governments for policy changes. While KAIROS may reject state-based conceptions of citizenship, this perspective might create tensions with other groups involved in the same coalition:

So different organizations are at different levels. While one organization might be ready to say, no one is illegal; to use some specific example, no one is illegal on planet Earth. Other organizations are not ready to say that, because other organizations are still restricted by legalistic, legislative aspects . . . A migrant worker from Mexico who comes here to work and spends 8 to 9 months of the year for 25 years, of course he's going to be thinking, what is illegal about me? From a human being perspective, what is illegal about me? Why is it that I cannot become a citizen in this country? Why is it that I cannot bring my family to this country?[56]

Barahona expressed frustration with the division of powers between federal and provincial jurisdictions:

Even though the migrant workers fall within the TFWP, which is a federal jurisdiction, the labor standards and the monitoring fall at the provincial level. So [different levels of governments are] passing the buck to one another, and trying to say, well that's not our responsibility or that's not our jurisdiction. I say, that is your jurisdiction, you need to work together.[57]

126   *Christina Gabriel and Laura Macdonald*

Barahona also confessed to frustration with the apparent lack of response by the federal and provincial governments to their lobbying efforts.

In addition to lobbying tactics, civil society actors also engage in a series of legal challenges to promote respect for migrants' rights, particularly social rights. The UFCW has played a leading role in this regard. Stan Raper of the UFCW says that the union adopted this form of struggle because they felt they had to "force governments to govern. We could be waiting for twenty, thirty years before a government realizes they've signed international conventions."[58] "We're saying, 'time's up. Legal challenges are going to force you to do some of this stuff.'"[59] The legal challenges brought by or involving the UFCW have focused on employment insurance, occupational health and safety, employee association and collective bargaining.

For example, with respect to occupational health and safety coverage in Ontario, the UFCW has been successful in fighting for farm workers, both migrant and nonmigrant. In 2003, the union brought a challenge against the Occupational Health and Safety Act (OHSA), which at the time did not cover farm workers. The challenge was successful, and the Ontario government extended OHSA coverage to all agricultural workers, effective June 30, 2006.

## Local Engagements

Finally, it appears that some of the most important progress in delivering concrete social benefits to workers has occurred at the local community level. As stated by Kerry Preibisch, local agencies supporting migrant agricultural workers are "part of the rural local landscape."[60] For the purpose of this chapter, we are focusing on the case of Leamington, Ontario, an area receiving large numbers of SAWP workers.

Leamington, Ontario, a town of some twenty-nine thousand people, has for decades served as host of thousands of temporary migrant workers, particularly from Mexico, who work in the area's thriving greenhouse sector. The large size of the migrant agricultural workforce may mean that workers are less isolated and receive more services than workers in smaller communities. Nevertheless, Mexican workers have faced considerable challenges in accessing the social benefits to which they are entitled. Because of the large size of the local Mexican population (estimated at around 4,200 workers in the fall of 2009), the Mexican government opened a consulate in Leamington in November 2007. The consulate serves as an important interlocutor for Mexican migrants.[61]

Two types of nonstate actors working to improve the situation of migrant agricultural workers are present in Leamington. On the one hand, there are two agencies that have an apolitical approach focused on providing services to workers; the other is the AWA, linked to the UFCW, which takes a more adversarial and rights-based approach to its work. In the first category, the Migrant Worker Community Program (MWCP) began in 2001, and took over some programs that had been run by the South Essex Arts Centre, including a bike safety program[62] and cultural festivals. The MWCP receives support from local governments (the towns of Kingsville and Leamington), the police and the growers' association. Much of the effort of the association is focused on making the Leamington environment more welcoming for workers. The MWCP also provides Spanish classes for the community, English classes for migrants through partnership with Frontier College and a Spanish-language radio program. The Ontario Greenhouse Growers Association newsletter advocates support for this community association in the following terms: "Having a stable and contented workforce within the greenhouse sector is essential to the economic well-being of the community."[63]

Somewhat similar in orientation is the work of Frontier College. From its Leamington office, Frontier College runs Spanish classes for local residents and English classes for immigrants, including temporary foreign workers. They also run the Laborer-Teacher program, in which university and college students are recruited to live and work on the farms alongside migrant workers, and to provide English classes in the evenings or on weekends. The growers pay their wages and the students are recruited by and volunteer with Frontier College. In 2008, ten or eleven growers were part of the program in Southwestern Ontario, with a volunteer force of sixteen laborer-teachers. Since Frontier College works directly with growers, it has to be very sensitive to farmers' concerns. The Frontier College representative we interviewed refused to answer some of our questions related to human rights, since he said that these were not relevant to the work of his organization. He commented on tensions within the community that affect his organization's work:

> It's been a little difficult in this area to find growers. There's been a real—"we don't want any outsiders". They're really concerned about unionization. This is what we hear from them and what we have a sense of, what has happened. *El Contrato*, the movie which was filmed down here, certainly did not help the situation at all. So I've spoken to some former growers that had LTs [Laborer-Teachers] and they've said they had some great experiences and the last time was not a great experience. As they say, they're busy enough trying to make a living, let alone trying to worry about somebody coming onto the farm and trying to stir up the guys.[64]

When asked how laborer-teachers are instructed to navigate these issues, he replied, We tell them they have to tread a very, very fine line. If we're asked to leave, we've just defeated what our goal is. Our goal is literacy, our goal is not to try to unionize, our goal is not trying to make life on the farm better for the worker. But maybe through literacy, they can strive to try to improve it on their own, through education, through literacy.[65]

128   *Christina Gabriel and Laura Macdonald*

The Frontier College staff occasionally receives requests to assist with other issues faced by migrants, like providing Spanish interpretation at the hospital, or immigration issues. Frontier College refuses to get involved in certain types of immigration issues that might create friction with government funders or farmers: "We've had phone calls when there have been, let's say, visits, raids to farms by Immigration, and we just say, we can't help you. That's not in our realm or scheme of things. We're here to help with literacy but we can't get into that. From a humanitarian point, some people would say—we have to follow what our guidelines are, and what our scope is. Getting into that is beyond our scope."[66]

In contrast to the MCWP and Frontier College, the Agricultural Workers Alliance (AWA) approaches the situation in Leamington from a much more political perspective. The AWA is made up of a series of worker support centers launched by the UFCW in 2002 to provide a number of support and advocacy services at no cost to domestic as well as migrant agricultural workers. The Leamington worker support center has been in place for almost nine years, again reflecting the large numbers of migrant workers in the community. The center is staffed by a man-and-wife team, who work year round despite the fact that they are paid only six months out of the year.[67] René Vidal, the AWA coordinator, has worked in the office for all of these years, and summarizes the work of the center:

> We're trying to advocate for the workers, for what they need—worker's compensation, CPP, unemployment insurance, immigration, hospitals, lawyers, whatever they feel they need. We even try to work with the [Mexican] consulate who's supposed to represent the workers . . . So what we do here is try to help the workers know what they need, with respect to filling out forms, especially for parental benefits. Probably parental benefits is one of the biggest jobs we have in here, representing these workers when they're allowed that.[68]

As Vidal notes, migrant workers' access to parental benefits (either for themselves or for their spouses at home) has been a major victory in the struggle of the UFCW and the AWA to promote workers' access to social citizenship rights. Across the country, AWA centers have helped file more than $23 million in accumulated parental benefit claims on behalf of SAWP workers who have been paying EI premiums.[69] Center staff also help workers with delays in receiving Ontario Health cards, with receiving reimbursements for medical care, and with concerns about accommodations, working conditions, hours of work, rest periods, inadequate training and knowledge, costs of transportation and food and overtime pay.[70] Vidal reflects on the problems workers face in accessing social rights:

> One of the things we see is that most workers, they don't have a voice. They've been forced to do some kind of job they're not supposed to be

Citizenship at the Margins   129

doing. One of the things they do is spray chemicals. They do it without training and no protection. That's one of the things we're facing a lot here. The consulate allows them to do it, and we don't agree with that, because we've been having problems here in the hospital with workers. We could prevent it if they knew what to do when there's an accident. There's been fatalities here, there's been people die because there's an accident, and that accident couldn't happen if there had been training. If there's a spill, if he wants to go to the hospital, and what happens to that poor fellow with that accident, the foreman tells him, no no no, you have to finish your job. When he gets to the corner, he faints. And this is a long story, but this is one of the problems we have, the chemicals inside the greenhouses.[71]

Vidal also underlines the issue of the importance of workers' inability to claim EI benefits other than parental benefits:

When they get laid off, they go home, and they don't collect unemployment. The government says, no, you're out of the country, you don't collect. We already fought for this, and we lost. The only thing we got is the parental benefits, and that's peanuts. I'm sorry to say it, but that's nothing for all the money [workers pay into the plan]. It's a lot of money.[72]

Vidal commented on the tensions within the Leamington community, and the lack of government support for AWA work, stating that the local government refuses to provide support for the AWA because it claims it is already supporting another organization (the MWCP). He described the work of that group as ineffectual in addressing workers' real needs.[73]

Vidal stated that the local Catholic church had been trying to get the MWCP and AWA to work together: "we've been trying to get relationships, but when we get together, it's like this, we can't, it's like water and oil, we can't mix."[74] The Catholic church also used to rent a large house to the AWA, and gave them three-year contract, but after two years they said they were going to sell it and they would have to leave. The UFCW offered to buy the house, but the church refused to sell it to them, and tore it down for parking: "I feel bad because we see that money is too powerful, it can buy churches. The church made that move, so that's why we had to move here, because of the pressure from the farmers."[75] The small size of the Leamington community intensifies the social pressures on local activists: "So the people from that cultural program and from the church, they don't want us. So we are the ones who have persisted because we have been strong. The only strength we have is the trust from the workers, that's the only thing we have."[76] These tensions between groups within this small community reflect the complexity of issues facing migrant workers, and the lack of homogeneity of the civil society sector.

## 130 *Christina Gabriel and Laura Macdonald*

## CONCLUSION

As we have seen, Mexican migrant agricultural workers occupy a precarious position within the Canadian community. Workers' lack of formal citizenship status, their isolation, lack of English language skills, and the vulnerability to employer demands, which is a condition of the structure of the SAWP program, heighten their lack of access to social citizenship rights. In this situation, nonstate actors from diverse sectors play a critical role at the local, provincial, national and extraterritorial levels, in advocating for the expansion of workers' legal rights, and their access to existing rights. As Grugel and Piper argue, these nonstate actors are reframing a "states-led agenda" and challenging the citizen/noncitizen dichotomy. Different nonstate agencies engage at different levels, in an often complementary, but sometimes conflictual, fashion.

As this chapter demonstrates, this sphere of civil society engagement is not homogeneous and unproblematic. Tensions exist within and between types of actors, and organizations like unions are engaged in an internal struggle to combat decades of racism and discrimination against noncitizen migrants. Organizations adopt different strategies and tactics, depending on their historical trajectory, mandates and conceptions of rights. It is important to note that the organizations we examined are led by Canadian citizens (some of whom are former migrants). Noncitizen migrant workers, who are only temporary residents of Canada (although they may return year after year), thus far have limited capacity to form and run their own organizations. Canadian civil society actors do not necessarily reflect the priorities or perspectives of the migrants themselves, and are an inadequate substitute for migrant-led agencies, even though they do provide valuable services.[77] The expanding reliance of Canadian producers on the import of vulnerable noncitizen foreign workers, both within the SAWP or through other mechanisms, means the tasks faced by these agencies continue to grow. Nevertheless, the last several years have seen increased cross-sectoral cooperation by civil society agencies to contest prevailing legal frameworks and to promote new rights for migrant agricultural workers.

## NOTES

1. We thank the Social Sciences and Humanities Research Council of Canada for funding that supported this research, and especially thank Christine Hughes and Thomas Collombat for their research assistance, and Jane Bayes and Christine Hughes and two anonymous reviewers for their comments on earlier drafts. This article is a slightly revised version of Christina Gabriel and Laura Macdonald, "Citizenship at the Margins: The Canadian Seasonal Agricultural Worker Program and Civil Society Advocacy," Politics and Policy, Vol. 39, issue 1, 2011, pp 45–67. Reprinted with permission.
2. Kerry Preibisch, "Globalizing Work, Globalizing Citizenship, Community-Migrant Worker Alliances in Southwestern Ontario," in *Organizing the*

## Citizenship at the Margins  131

*Transnational*, ed. Luin Goldring and Sailaja Krishnaumurti (Vancouver: UBC, 2007), 111. Preibisch provides a useful classification of different types of civil society actors active in advocating for migrant workers' rights in rural Ontario.

3. T. H. Marshall and Tom Bottomore, *Citizenship and Social Class: Forty Years On* (London: Pluto, 1992), 8.
4. Ibid., 8.
5. L. Bosniak, "Universal Citizenship and the Problem of Alienage," *North Western Law Review* 94, no. 3 (2000): 975.
6. Jean Grugel and Nicola Piper, *Critical Perspectives on Global Governance* (Abingdon, UK: Routledge, 2007), 21.
7. Ibid., 61.
8. See Tanya Basok, "Post-National Citizenship, Social Exclusion and Migrants Rights: Mexican Seasonal Workers in Canada," *Citizenship Studies* 8, no. 1 (2004), 47–64.
9. Pew Hispanic Center, "Mexican Immigrants in the United States, 2008," April 15, 2009, 1–2, accessed August 8, 2010, www.pewhispanic.org. See also Jennifer Van Hook, Frank D. Bean and Jeffrey Passel, "Unauthorized Migrants Living in the United States: A Mid-decade Portrait," *Migration Information Source* (2005), accessed August 6, 2010, http://www.migrationinformation.org/Feature/display.cfm?ID=329.
10. Francisco Alba, "Mexico: A Crucial Crossroads," *Migration Information Source*, February 2010, accessed December 20, 2010, http://www.migrationinformation.org/feature/print.cfm?ID=772.
11. Citizenship and Immigration Canada, *Facts and Figures: Immigrant Overview of Permanent and Temporary Residents 2008*, C&I-1035-06-09E (Ottawa: Minister of Public Works and Government Services, 2009), 57, accessed October 26, 2010, http://www.cic.gc.ca/english/pdf/research-stats/facts2008.pdf.
12. Richard E. Mueller, "Mexican Immigrants and Temporary Residents in Canada: Current Knowledge and Future Research," *Migraciones Internacionales* 3, no. 1 (2005): 33. The Canadian government's 2010 imposition of a visa requirement on Mexican visitors may act as an impediment to the growth of migrant flows.
13. Vic Satzewich, "Business or Bureaucratic Dominance in Immigration Policymaking in Canada: Why Was Mexico Included in the Caribbean Seasonal Agricultural Workers Program in 1974?" *International Migration and Integration* 8 (2007): 273.
14. UFCW Canada, *The Status of Migrant Farm Workers in Canada 2008–2009* (Toronto: UFCW, 2009), 8, accessed November 22, 2012, http://www.ufcw.ca/Theme/UFCW/files/PDF%202009/2009ReportEN.pdf.
15. Meyer Siemiatycki, "Marginalizing Migrants: Canada's Rising Reliance on Temporary Foreign Workers," *Canadian Issues* Spring (2010): 61.
16. UFCW, *Status of Migrant Farm Workers*, 8.
17. Ricardo Trumper and Lloyd Wong, "Temporary Workers in Canada: A National Perspective," *Canadian Issues* Spring (2010): 86.
18. Ibid. See also Basok, "Post-National Citizenship," and Austina Reed, "Canada's Experience with Managed Migration: The Strategic Use of Temporary Foreign Worker Programs," *International Journal* 63, no. 2 (2008): 469–484. As Veena Verma puts it: "Reliable in this context means no threat of leaving the job during critical harvest periods despite low wages and difficult working conditions." *The Regulatory and Policy Framework of the Caribbean Seasonal Agricultural Workers Program* (Ottawa: North-South Institute, 2007), 8.
19. UFCW, *Status of Migrant Farm Workers*, 8.

## 132 *Christina Gabriel and Laura Macdonald*

20. Verma, *Regulatory and Policy Framework*, 9.
21. Philip Martin, Manola Abella and Christiane Kuptsch, *Managing Labor Migration in the Twenty-First Century* (New Haven: Yale Press, 2006), 12–13.
22. Mueller, "Mexican Immigrants," 44.
23. Citizenship and Immigration Canada, "Seasonal Agricultural Worker Program," 2009, accessed November 22, 2012, http:www.hrsdc.gc.ca./eng/workplaceskills/foreign_workers/ei_tfw/sawp_tfw.shtml.
24. Philip Martin, "Global Forum on Migration and Development: Roundtable 2.1 Fostering More Opportunities of Legal Migration in North America," 2008, Archives.migrationanddevelopment.net/fostering-more. . .legal-migration-in-north-america/. . ./file-Cached
25. See Tanya Basok, "Canada's Temporary Migration Program: A Model Despite Flaws," *Migration Information Source* 12 (2007); Jenna Hennebry and Kerry Preibisch, "A Model for Managed Migration? Re-examining Best Practices in Canada's Seasonal Agricultural Worker Program," *International Migration* 50, no. s1 (2010); Martin, Abella and Kuptsch, *Managing Labor Migration*, pages e19–e40.
26. Martin, Abella and Kuptsch, *Managing Labor Migration*, 113.
27. Basok, "Post-National Citizenship."
28. Basok, "Canada's Temporary Migration Program."
29. Hennebry and Preibisch, "Model," 10.
30. Martin, "Global Forum," 17–18.
31. Eugénie Depatie-Pelletier, "Restrictions on Rights and Freedoms of Low-Skilled Temporary Foreign Workers," *Canadian Issues*, Spring 2010, 64.
32. Hennebry and Preibisch, "Model," 10.
33. Depatie-Pelletier, "Restrictions," 64.
34. Trumper and Wong, "Temporary Workers," 151.
35. Verma, *Regulatory and Policy Framework*, 10.
36. Basok, "Post-National Citizenship," 54.
37. Verma, *Regulatory and Policy Framework*, 14.
38. Human Resources and Skills Development Canada (HRSDC), "Seasonal Agricultural Worker Program," n.d., accessed August 8, 2010, http://www.hrsdc.gc.ca/eng/workplaceskills/foreign_workers/ei_tfw/sawp_tfw.shtml.
39. See Christina Gabriel and Laura Macdonald, "Debates on Temporary Agricultural Worker Migration in the North American Context," in *Legislated Inequality: Temporary Labour Migration in Canada*, ed. Patti Tamara Lenard and Christine Straehle (Montreal-Kingston: McGill-Queens, 2012), 95–116.
40. Basok, "Post-National Citizenship."
41. Karl Flecker (Canadian Labour Congress), in discussion with the author, October 23, 2009.
42. The primary research for this project is based on interviews with civil society organizations working with Mexican temporary agricultural workers in Ontario and Quebec. We conducted interviews with eight organizations based in the following communities: Montreal, Quebec; Toronto, Ontario; Ottawa, Ontario; and Leamington, Ontario (where a large number of the Mexican workers are based). These organizations were selected to represent a range of different groups working in this sector: community-based, union and faith-based, and also to represent groups working at different levels: local, national and international. Each interview lasted about one hour and was based on a preestablished research schedule. All participants were given the option of anonymity.
43. Grugel and Piper, *Critical Perspectives*.
44. The CLC is the main umbrella group of Canadian trade unions, which brings together Canada's national and international unions, the provincial and territorial federations of labor and 130 district labor councils.

## Citizenship at the Margins 133

45. See also Basok, "Post-National Citizenship" for a discussion of the work of the AWA in Leamington.
46. KAIROS brought together a number of preexisting interchurch coalitions working on issues of human rights and social justice, and in Africa, Asia and Latin America. Note that KAIROS's federal government funding was recently cut, and the future of the organization's work in this sector is in doubt. See http://kairoscanada.org/en/.
47. Preibisch, "Globalizing Work."
48. Stan Raper (national coordinator of the Agricultural Workers Alliance), in discussion with the author, October 30, 2009.
49. Flecker, discussion.
50. Raper, discussion.
51. KAIROS was "defunded" by the Canadian International Development Agency (CIDA) in 2009 after it had steadily received CIDA funding since 1973. The government's decision not to renew KAIROS funding was strongly protested by a wide range of Canadian individuals and civil society organizations. See http://www.kairoscanada.org/en/who-we-are/cida-funding-cuts/.
52. Flecker, discussion.
53. This shift towards a more positive attitude towards immigration occurred earlier in Canada than in the United States, where the labor movement has been slow to embrace a pro-immigration stance. It was not until 2000 when the AFL-CIO reversed its earlier policy stance, which advocated government sanctions against employers who knowingly hired undocumented workers, and which was silent on the issue of amnesty for undocumented migrants. Earlier leadership had been complacent about the effects of migration on the organization's capacity to organize the unorganized, but this position shifted rapidly beginning in the late 1990s. Julie R. Watts, *Immigration Policy and the Challenge of Globalization: Unions and Employers in Unlikely Alliance* (Ithaca: ILR Press, 2002), 145–146.
54. Flecker, discussion.
55. Ibid.
56. Alfredo Barahona (KAIROS representative), in discussion with the author, October 30, 2009.
57. Ibid.
58. Kerry Preibisch, "Forcing Governments to Govern in Defence of Noncitizen Workers: A Story about the Canadian Labour Movement's Alliance with Agricultural Migrants. Interview with Stan Raper," in *Organizing the Transnational*, ed. Luin Goldring and Sailaja Krishnamurti (Vancouver: UBC Press, 2007), 119.
59. Ibid., 124.
60. Preibisch, "Globalizing Work," 103.
61. The Mexican foreign ministry did not grant us permission to interview the Leamington consul.
62. Bicycles are the most common form of transportation for migrant workers in rural communities.
63. *Greenhouse Canada*, "OGVG Supports Migrant Worker Programs," March 13, 2008, accessed November 22, 2012, http://www.greenhousecanada.com/content/view/1095/38/.
64. Representative, Frontier College, in discussion with author, October 29, 2009. This movie was produced by the UFCW and is highly critical of the treatment of Mexican agricultural workers in Ontario.
65. Ibid.
66. Ibid.
67. The couple's two-week-old baby was with them in the office during the interview.

## 134 Christina Gabriel and Laura Macdonald

68. René Vidal (coordinator, AWA, Leamington), in discussion with the author, October 29, 2009.
69. UFCW, *Status of Migrant Farm Workers*, 9.
70. UFCW, *Status of Migrant Farm Workers*, 10.
71. Vidal, discussion.
72. Ibid.
73. Ibid.
74. Ibid.
75. Ibid.
76. Vidal, discussion.
77. The perspectives of migrant workers themselves were beyond the scope of this study.

## REFERENCES

Alba, Francisco. "Mexico: A Crucial Crossroads." *Migration Information Source.* February 2010.
Basok, Tanya. "Canada's Temporary Migration Program: A Model Despite Flaws." *Migration Information Source*, November 12, 2007.
———. "Post-National Citizenship, Social Exclusion and Migrants Rights: Mexican Seasonal Workers in Canada." *Citizenship Studies* 8, no. 1 (2004): 47–64.
Bosniak, L. "Universal Citizenship and the Problem of Alienage." *North Western Law Review* 94, no. 3 (2000): 963–984.
Citizenship and Immigration Canada. *Facts and Figures: Immigrant Overview of Permanent and Temporary Residents 2008*. C&I-1035–06–09E. Ottawa: Minister of Public Works and Government Services, 2009.
———. "Seasonal Agricultural Worker Program." 2009. http:www.hrsdc.gc.ca./eng/workplaceskills/foreign_workers/ei_tfw/sawp_tfw.shtml.
Depatie-Pelletier, Eugénie. "Restrictions on Rights and Freedoms of Low-Skilled Temporary Foreign Workers." *Canadian Issues* Spring (2010): 64–67.
Grugel, Jean, and Nicola Piper. *Critical Perspectives on Global Governance*. UK: Routledge, 2007.
Hennebry, Jenna, and Kerry Preibisch. "A Model for Managed Migration? Re-examining Best Practices in Canada's Seasonal Agricultural Worker Program." *International Migration* (2010): 1–33. Early View, February 8, 2010 doi:10.1111/j.1468 2435.2009.00598.x.
Human Resources and Skills Development Canada (HRSDC). "Seasonal Agricultural Worker Program." n.d. Accessed August 8, 2010. http://www.hrsdc.gc.ca/eng/workplaceskills/foreign_workers/ei_tfw/sawp_tfw.shtml.
Marshall, T.H. "Citizenship and Social Class." Reprinted in *Citizenship and Social Class*, by T.H. Marshall and Tom Bottomore, 1950. London: Pluto Press, 1992.
Martin, Philip. "Global Forum on Migration and Development: Roundtable 2.1 Fostering More Opportunities of Legal Migration in North America." August 20, 2008. Archives.migrationanddevelopment.net/fostering-more. . .legal-migration-in-north-america/. . ./file-Cached.
Martin, P., Manola Abella and Christiane Kuptsch. *Managing Labor Migration in the Twenty-First Century*. New Haven: Yale Press, 2006.
Mueller, Richard E. "Mexican Immigrants and Temporary Residents in Canada: Current Knowledge and Future Research." *Migraciones Internacionales* 3, no. 1 (2005): 32–56.
Pew Hispanic Center. "Mexican Immigrants in the United States." April 15, 2009. Accessed August 8, 2010. www.pewhispanic.org.

Preibisch, K. "Migrant Agricultural Workers and Processes of Social Inclusion in Rural Canada: Encuentros and Desencuentros." *Canadian Journal of Latin American and Caribbean Studies* 29, no. 57 (2004): 203–239.

Preibisch, K. "Forcing Governments to Govern in Defence of Noncitizen Workers: A Story about the Canadian Labour Movement's Alliance with Agricultural Migrants. Interview with Stan Raper." In *Organizing the Transnational*, edited by Luin Goldring and Sailaja Krishnamurti. Vancouver: UBC Press, 2007, 115–128.

———. "Globalizing Work, Globalizing Citizenship, Community-Migrant Worker Alliances in Southwestern Ontario." In *Organizing the Transnational*, edited by Luin Goldring and Sailaja Krishnaumurti. Vancouver: UBC Press, 2007, 97–114.

Reed, Austina. "Canada's Experience with Managed Migration: The Strategic Use of Temporary Foreign Worker Programs." *International Journal* 63, no. 2 (2008): 469–484.

Satzewich, Vic. "Business or Bureaucratic Dominance in Immigration Policymaking in Canada: Why Was Mexico Included in the Caribbean Seasonal Agricultural Workers Program in 1974?" *International Migration and Integration* 8 (2007): 255–275.

Siemiatycki, Meyer. "Marginalizing Migrants: Canada's Rising Reliance on Temporary Foreign Workers." *Canadian Issues* Spring (2010): 60–63.

Trumper, Ricardo, and Lloyd Wong. "Canada's Guest Workers: Racialized, Gendered and Flexible." In *Race and Racism in 21st Century Canada*, edited by Sean Hier and B. Singh Bolaria, 150–170. Peterborough: Broadview, 2007, 150–170.

———. "Temporary Workers in Canada: A National Perspective." *Canadian Issues* Spring (2010): 83–89.

UFCW Canada. *The Status of Migrant Farm Workers in Canada 2008–2009*. Toronto: UFCW, 2009. Accessed November 22, 2012. http://www.ufcw.ca/Theme/UFCW/files/PDF%202009/2009ReportEN.pdf.

Van Hook, Jennifer, Frank D. Bean and Jeffrey Passel. "Unauthorized Migrants Living in the United States: A Mid-decade Portrait." *Migration Information Source* (2005). Accessed August 6, 2010. http://www.migrationinformation.org/Feature/display.cfm?ID=329.

Verma, Veena. *The Regulatory and Policy Framework of the Caribbean Seasonal Agricultural Workers Program*. Ottawa: North-South Institute, 2007.

Watts, Julie R. *Immigration Policy and the Challenge of Globalization: Unions and Employers in Unlikely Alliance*. Ithaca: ILR Press, 2002.

# 8 Organizing the Mexican Diaspora
## Can It Strengthen North American Integration?

*Jane H. Bayes and Laura Gonzalez*[1]

In this book concerned with furthering the integration of North America, especially with regard to immigration and security, the question posed by this chapter is whether and to what extent an unusual trinational organization, *Consejo Consultivo del Instituto de los Mexicanos en el Exterior* (CC-IME), created by the Mexican government in response to demands from the Mexican diaspora, contributes to building institutions that can advance this integration process.

For those who envisioned the North American Free Trade Agreement (NAFTA) to be something like the European Union, a region integrated by a free flow of capital, goods and people across national borders, a region with a common currency and with executive, legislative and judicial governing institutions, NAFTA has not made much progress. The reasons for this situation are legion. NAFTA was never intended to do more than encourage trade and investment within the region and perhaps to create jobs in Mexico to staunch the flow of Mexican migrants to the United States and Canada. For the first fifteen years of NAFTA's existence, trade and investment did occur, but even after 9/11, the flow of Mexicans north did not abate significantly. The movement of US manufacturing plants to Mexico created job dislocation in the United States, while US and Canadian investment and marketing undermined many indigenous Mexican products and businesses. With the 2008 recession, hostile attitudes and repressive laws directed towards Mexican migrants have increased in the United States and Canada. The violence generated by the Calderón government's unsuccessful attempts to eliminate Mexican drug cartels has been another factor discouraging integration. From the Mexican point of view, other barriers to further integration with the North include the fear by Mexico that it will be overwhelmed and colonized once again by the United States and Canada and that further integration with the North will jeopardize Mexico's integration with its southern neighbors. All three nations have engaged in multiple trade agreements with other countries since 1994.

In this environment, what forces are pushing for increased integration from the Mexican perspective? Aside from the prospect of encouraging more foreign investment and trade and the creation of more jobs in Mexico,

*Organizing the Mexican Diaspora* 137

the Mexican government has three major reasons to seek further integration. First, Mexican immigrants in the United States and Canada send remittances back to Mexico that rival Mexico's petroleum exports in value. Mexico wants to encourage remittance flows. Servicing Mexican migrants in the United States and Canada by establishing trinational organizations such as the CC-IME is one way to do this. A second reason for Mexico to further integration is that the Mexican diaspora in the United States exerts considerable influence in Mexican elections, partly because of the wealth and political activity of Mexicans living in the United States and partly because those who have migrated have considerable political influence among their families and hometowns in Mexico. Mexican politicians actively campaign in the United States and seek to maintain their ties with Mexican communities in the United States and Canada. A third reason that Mexico seeks further integration is that Mexicans living in the United States and Canada can and do engage in politics in the United States. As their numbers grow, US citizens of Mexican origin are becoming increasingly powerful in US state, local and national politics in ways that are both similar to and different from other diasporas in the United States, such as those from Cuba or Israel. This connection can give Mexico a voice—albeit an indirect voice—in US and Canadian policy making.

The reasons for the US and Canadian governments to seek further integration with Mexico are less apparent, especially in a time of recession. US and Canadian businesses in the United States and Canada need Mexican labor, yet the cultural presence of growing numbers of Mexicans in Alabama, Georgia, North Carolina and even Arizona and Utah is igniting nativist movements and punitive legislation at the state and local levels.

The Mexican communities in the United States and Mexican immigrants themselves are a major impetus for the further integration of Mexico and the United States. Mexican communities in the Southwest have long maintained ties to hometowns and home states in Mexico. Because of chain migration, those who come first to the United States or Canada tend to encourage others from their home locales to come and settle in the same cities or towns in the United States or Canada. Many of these, especially first- and second-generation migrants, maintain a dual identity if not dual citizenship. Some go back and forth regularly and/or communicate regularly with relatives in Mexico. Many of these migrants have economic interests in both countries. Some are involved in politics in both countries. They read the Spanish press about events in both the United States and Mexico or Canada and Mexico. While some may identify more with Mexico and others with the United States or Canada, many yearn to belong to both their home and host countries. This group of people provides a grassroots base for building institutions to integrate the three NAFTA countries. The Mexican government has sought to provide an institutional structure for integrating these migrants into the societies, polities and economies of the United States and Canada in the form of the CC-IME, the topic of inquiry for this chapter. While the

## 138   Jane H. Bayes and Laura Gonzalez

activities of migrants do not build the kind of institutional integration that the cooperation of all three countries' government ministries could generate, they can further integration by: 1) protecting Mexican migrants in the United States and Canada; 2) helping to integrate Mexican migrants into the societies, polities and economies of the United States and Canada, including access to education, health care and citizenship and encouraging political and civic participation; 3) building and strengthening cross border economic, social and political relationships and networks wherever possible; 4) building the capacity to lobby in all three countries; 5) educating and building awareness among the peoples of all three countries about the countries of the region.

## METHODOLOGY

The information for this chapter is derived from nine years of research using political science and anthropological methodologies such as participant observation, participatory research, open-ended interviews with CC-IME advisors in all three cohorts and with IME staff, attendance and participation at meetings as well as access to internal documents and decision making. One of us, Laura Gonzalez, was an elected member of the first cohort. She has attended meetings of all three cohorts. Jane Bayes has attended meetings of the third cohort. We use both the emic (the views of those being studied) and the etic (the views of the observer) points of view. We have engaged in conversations with CC-IME advisors and staff in a multitude of venues, in official meetings and interviews, but also in their homes, over meals, on buses and at receptions. For this chapter, we sent an e-mail to the first three generations of CC-IME advisors (over 300 people serving from 2003 to 2011) asking them to identify any organizations that had grown out of the CC-IME or existing organizations that had been helped by the CC-IME. The results of that inquiry are a part of this chapter. The organizations discussed in this chapter are a sample of the most well-known of the organizations involved with the CC-IME in the United States, but they are not the only ones. Others that deserve further investigation include the *Instituto de los Mexicanos en Canadá, El Consejo Binacional por un México Mejor* and *Organización Espejo*, which were created in Michoacán, Mexico by CC-IME advisors.[2]

## MEXICO'S EFFORTS AT ORGANIZING ITS DIASPORA

In the 1980s, many groups concerned with issues of integration were in existence in the United States, including the Mutualistas, *el Congreso Mexicanista*, the GI Forum, *Alianza Hispano-Americano, La Liga Protectora*

*Latina*, the League of United Latin American Citizens (LULAC), the National Council of La Raza (NCLR), the Mexican American Youth Organization (MAYO) and the Mexican American Student Organization (MASA), as well as hometown associations or *Clubes de Oriundos*. From the end of the Bracero Program in 1964, the attitude of the Mexican government towards Mexican emigrants in the United States was largely one of avoidance. This changed in the 1990s as the increased flows of emigrants and remittances across the US/Mexico border, along with a recognition that Mexican politics were taking place in the United States as well as in Mexico, caused the Mexican government to respond to demands for help and recognition from relatively well-established and wealthy Mexican migrant groups in the United States. Some Mexican states with large numbers of migrants, like Guanajuato and Zacatecas, recognized the importance of immigrant remittances and established programs like "Dos por Uno" and "Tres por Uno" that double or triple every dollar that a migrant sends back home with state, local and sometimes federal money to be used in a local Mexican project. Another impetus was the recognition by Mexico that its exponentially growing diaspora in the United States is a potential economic and perhaps political resource for Mexico if political alliances and ties are maintained. In the early 1990s, President Carlos Salinas de Gortari (1988–1994) strengthened and expanded Mexican consular offices in the United States and created the *Programa para las Comunidades Mexicanas en el Extranjero* (PCME) within the Ministry of Foreign Relations (SRE). PCME is a forerunner of the Instituto de los Mexicanos en el Exterior (IME).[3]

PCME worked directly with consulates and hometown associations to encourage Mexican migrants to maintain their ties with their Mexican communities of origin and initiated a variety of programs directed at K-12 education, sports, health, culture, business and tourism activities that continue to be central to the CC-IME today. Perhaps the most interesting and novel idea pursued by the Mexican government in the 1990s to retain the allegiance and support of the Mexican diaspora during this period was to create a dual nationality status for migrants. The Nationality Act of 1998 distinguished between nationality and citizenship and allowed Mexican-born citizens to keep their status as Mexican nationals when they became the citizens of another country, such as the United States. It stated that a Mexican-born citizen who chose to become a citizen of another country would lose his/her political rights but could maintain her/his Mexican nationality, thereby having dual nationality. Mexican nationality carried with it the rights to certain social benefits and the right to own property in Mexico. Furthermore, it was another way to retain the ties of Mexican migrants to Mexico. Not only could Mexican-born citizens retain their Mexican nationality when they became citizens of another country, but their foreign-born children could be Mexican nationals as well.

140  *Jane H. Bayes and Laura Gonzalez*

## THE CREATION OF THE *INSTITUTO DE LOS MEXICANOS EN EL EXTERIOR* (IME) AND THE *CONSEJO CONSULTIVO DEL INSTITUTO DE LOS MEXICANOS EN EL EXTERIOR* (CC-IME)

The election of Vicente Fox in 2000 brought a dramatic change in Mexican state policy towards its emigrants. The first evidence of this new approach began when Fox created the *Oficina Presidencial para Mexicanos en el Extranjero* (OPME). This office provided emigrants and their descendants with privileged access to the president and encouraged them to participate in the transformation of Mexico, albeit in very neoliberal ways. The priority issues for the OPME were remittances, the promotion of business centers, the distribution of Mexican products in the United States and the encouragement of investment, especially in regions with large numbers of emigrants.[4] In 2003, President Fox created a new structure and a new policy. This bureaucratic reorganization combined the PCME of the 1990s with the OPME of 2000 to create a new governmental hierarchy. This was the birth of the CC-IME.

## THE COMPOSITION OF THE CC-IME

The CC-IME is a remarkable and unique transnational organization of community leaders of Mexican origin or descent, organized by the IME in the *Secretaría de Relaciones Exteriores* or Ministry of Foreign Relations and charged with providing the Mexican government with advice and suggestions concerning Mexico's policies towards its diaspora. The forty-six (now fifty-five) Mexican consulates in the United States and Canada were charged with forming an elected body of around 120 advisors from the diaspora in North America to compose the CC-IME. Drawing on their lists of contacts in the Mexican and Mexican American communities in the United States, the Mexican consulates solicited nominations and self-nominations to be on the CC-IME. The positions on the CC-IME were proportioned according to the relative size of the diasporic population in the area (for example, Los Angeles had eleven spots and Dallas had four). In each consulate's jurisdiction, candidates were elected (or sometimes appointed) by those who attended the meetings held by the consulates. The advisors created six commissions on distinct issues: political, legal, health, education, culture and the border. In addition, twelve major Mexican American organizations were asked to send representatives. This process identified well-known community leaders from all parts of the United States active in a variety of different fields to come together to advise the Mexican government. To be eligible for election, a candidate had to be of Mexican origin or Mexican descent and speak Spanish fluently. The stated purpose of this council was to advise the Mexican government about the needs of Mexicans living abroad. The IME, in turn, was to solicit and listen to advice from the CC-IME, to make policies, coordinate Mexican governmental agencies charged with emigrant

*Organizing the Mexican Diaspora* 141

affairs and implement the policies once decisions had been made. The IME had the support of President Fox in that Fox gave a radio address to Mexicans living abroad every week and gave this effort priority with regard to funding and attention. Members of the CC-IME were elected for three-year terms and were invited to travel, with travel expenses paid, twice a year to Mexico or other places in the United States to advise Mexican governmental officials. Not only did the advisors meet with their commissions on the national level, but they also had state or regional meetings where they met all the leaders in their own states or region and learned about the work and issues that the other commissions were addressing.

## WHAT ARE SOME OF THE ORGANIZATIONAL CONSEQUENCES OF THE CC-IME?

The activities of the CC-IME and its predecessors, PCME and OPME, have kept the Mexican government in contact with its diaspora, but they have also served to stimulate the independent organization of the Mexican diaspora in the United States and Canada. By having advisors chosen (often elected) locally, the 300-plus advisors of the three cohorts since 2003 all are leaders in their local communities with specific interests, institutional affiliations and experience in dealing with migrant problems. They are all connected by a common CC-IME experience and have developed friendships and a readily available list of e-mail addresses. For three years, the IME brings these migrant leaders together from all parts of the United States and Canada (two times in Mexico, but sometimes in the United States) to discuss issues and problems and possible solutions. They network with one another, communicate constantly by e-mail and telephone, strategize and inform one another about migrant issues in all parts of the United States and Canada. From the beginning, tensions have existed with regard to their exact role *vis à vis* the Mexican government. Many advisors assume an independent agency with regard to rules, agenda setting and procedures, while the Mexican government officials that fund, staff and organize the meetings perceive advisors to be advisors and not decision makers.

The bulk of the work that CC-IME advisors perform takes place within the context of the substantive and regional commissions. The Mexican state, through the IME, its consulates and the CC-IME, establishes the framework and support for these activities, but the initiative and the accomplishments of these commissions are the product of CC-IME advisors. Some of the commissions are focused more on events and activities in Mexico (the Business and Development and the Political Commissions). Others sponsor activities directed primarily at diasporian communities in the United States (the Health, Education, Legal, Border, Media and Regional Commissions). For some of the advisors, the exposure to the deliberative processes and decision

142   *Jane H. Bayes and Laura Gonzalez*

making that takes place in the commissions is extremely educational. Those who are primarily oriented towards the United States learn much about issue areas and conditions in Mexico as well as other parts of the United States and Canada. They not only learn how to contribute to the CC-IME's commission policy work, but also gain skills and contacts that they take back with them to their own communities. In this sense, the CC-IME is an organization that is building institutional infrastructure among the diaspora in the United States and Canada, an infrastructure that is not necessarily identifiable as one cohesive disciplined and unified organization but one that recruits leaders and potential leaders from the diverse communities that the Mexican diaspora represents in the United States and Canada, and gives them opportunities to develop knowledge, skills, contacts and ways to "make a difference" while serving for three years as an advisor. They are then in a position to return to their own communities to continue to organize them in ways that are appropriate to the locality.[5] Their lobbying work can also generate an impact on the Mexican legislation that benefits Mexicans abroad, such as the recently approved bill that provides Mexican citizenship for third-generation descendants and eliminate burdens such as the residency time requirement for Mexicans who have just returned to Mexico, a project embraced by the Political Commission from the third cohort.[6]

## ORGANIZATIONAL STRUCTURES AND THE ROLE OF THE CC-IME

Within the United States and Canada are myriads of community nongovernmental organizations that are committed to working for immigrant rights and/or migrant welfare. For example, the website for one umbrella group, Reform Immigration 4 America, lists 816 groups as affiliates in forty-four states—including Puerto Rico. Most are in California (132), New York (55), Washington DC (50), Florida (47), Illinois (45) and Texas (42). In the next tier are: North Carolina (39), Pennsylvania (32) and New Jersey (31); and finally, in the last tier are Colorado (27), Georgia (26), Massachusetts (24), Michigan (24), Arizona (21) and Maryland (20). These are not all immigrant organizations, but they are all organizations concerned about immigrant affairs and immigrant welfare (Reform Immigration for America website). Many CC-IME advisors are members of groups such as these as well as a variety of groups related to their own occupations and interests in the United States. Many also participate in groups or organizations related to their Mexican state or place of origin. CC-IME advisors because of their extensive local and national connections are often able to facilitate, expand and leverage existing programs. The Health Initiative of the Americas is a prime example of this kind of integrative process. Some are responses to ideas and initiatives of Mexican consulate officials or CC-IME staff, such as *Asociación de Jóvenes Unidos en Acción (AJUA)*, the *Red de Mujeres Mexicanas en el Exterior*

Organizing the Mexican Diaspora 143

(REMEX) and 100 Amigos Working for Mexico and California (Cien Amigos). Still others are initiated by CC-IME advisors who start new initiatives using their own groups or organizations. Examples of these are the American Mexican Anti-discrimination Alliance (AMADA) 2007–2009, *Fundación* MEX-I-CAN, started in 2009, *Congreso del Pueblo*, begun in 2010, and the Mexican American Coalition (MXAC), which came into being in 2010.

## LEVERAGING EXISTING PROGRAMS

### The Health Initiative of the Americas

The Health Initiative of the Americas is associated with the School of Public Health at the University of California, Berkeley. A member of the first cohort of the CC-IME 2003–2005 is employed by UC Berkeley and was able to bring together the Berkeley School of Public Health with local, state and national government agencies, community-based organizations and volunteers to enhance and expand three health programs that had begun under the *Programa para las Comunidades Mexicanas en el Exterior* (PCME). One of these is the Bi-national Health Week. A second is *Ventanas de Salud*, which provides a place in the Mexican consulates for immigrants to get health advice. A third is the Binational Policy Forum, which holds an annual conference of representatives from federal, state and community organizations to examine and promote immigrant health issues as a policy priority in the United States, Mexico, Canada and South and Central American countries. Using the resources of the University of California, local foundations and Mexican consulates, these programs were enhanced and expanded first locally in California. Then CC-IME advisors from other parts the United States and Canada and other Mexican consulates served as "godfathers" and "godmothers" to institute the programs throughout all three nations.[7]

## MEXICAN GOVERNMENT-INITIATED ORGANIZATIONS

### Asociación de Jóvenes Unidos en Acción (AJUA)

Because Ambassador Carlos García de Alba, the Mexican governmental official in charge of CC-IME in 2009, was concerned about the lack of youth among CC-IME advisors, he invited three of the CC-IME advisors who were under thirty years of age to meet with about forty Mexican American youth gathered at the World Youth Forum that was meeting in Aguascalientes, Mexico, in 2010 to encourage them to apply to become CC-IME advisors. Several problems have plagued this group. At the end of the first year, only twelve of the original forty remained. The second year, the IME organized a second group, but this time many were from other countries: England, Argentina, Mexico and Belgium. Not only was language

144 *Jane H. Bayes and Laura Gonzalez*

a problem, but the interests of the participants were very different. Some of the youth leaders tried to bring the two groups together but found that their own time limitations, the diversity of the groups and schedule availability (with a nine-hour time difference) were significant obstacles. One success is that some of these youth are now members of the new CC-IME cohort for 2012–2015.[8]

## *Red de Mujeres Mexicanas en el Exterior*: A Nascent Mexican Government-Encouraged Initiative

After several meetings of CC-IME advisors with members of the *Instituto de la Mujer* in Mexico, in 2010 at a CC-IME meeting in Mexico City, IME's staff suggested that CC-IME members form a women's network. A group of twenty-one women met and formed a *Red de Mujers Mexicanas en el Exterior*, elected officers and made some plans for communication and a future meeting. The IME and the SRE are willing to host a space on their website, Redes Mexico. Meetings are planned for this year. The purpose of this group is to improve the well-being of migrant women and their families. This includes working on issues such as: domestic violence, self-esteem, staying in school, scholarships, college opportunities, internships, birth control, HIV, bank accounts, financial information, health, mammograms, cancer, diabetes, mental health, nutrition, how to read the labels of food products, legal issues, immigration law and criminal justice. With some support from the IME, the executive committee of this group has been meeting, obtaining resources and gathering information in preparation for the years ahead.

## 100 Amigos Working for California and Mexico (*Cien Amigos*)

The idea for *Cien Amigos* came from the Mexican consul in the Sacramento, California, Ambassador Carlos González Gutierrez; however, the organization itself is separate from the Mexican consulate. The organization began in 2010 as a part of the centennial celebration of the Mexican Revolution by five friends. Drawing on lessons learned from the CC-IME experience, *Cien Amigos* differed in three important ways. The first is that *Cien Amigos* requires all one hundred members to pay $500 a year to be a member. While this limits the organization to those who can afford this fee, the practice means that *Cien Amigos* can be financially and politically independent with an annual budget of around $50,000. Second, membership in *Cien Amigos* is by invitation only. Many of those who had been CC-IME advisors in the past were well aware of the political difficulties and time-consuming frustrations that have accompanied the CC-IME's elections around the country and wished to avoid the loss of energy, resources and effectiveness that they associate with these election or selection processes. A third important difference

*Organizing the Mexican Diaspora* 145

is that *Cien Amigos* is a 501(c)(4) corporation instead of a 501(c)(3) corporation. As a result, it is not tax-exempt and it can engage in political activities.

Most *Cien Amigos* members are well-established community leaders with many local, state and national connections and with extensive backgrounds in education, business, law or other professions. The agenda for the group includes a variety of cultural, economic, political and educational projects headed by different members. One political effort involves building relations with all local elected officials with a Mexican background. Another effort concerns inviting Mexican officials to speak and/or visit northern California. Political advocacy and the education of the Mexican diaspora in northern California are other extremely important projects. To take advantage of grants for education provided by the Mexican government, Mexican consuls must raise matching funds. The Mexican government gives almost $1 million for education to its fifty-two consul and embassy offices in the United States and Canada. This amounts to about $35,000 per consulate. *Cien Amigos* has established a nonprofit 501(c)(4) corporation to raise scholarship monies and has provided that its members may give as much as $250 of their $500 *Cien Amigo* annual dues to this fund for scholarships for Mexican American students at the high school, college and university levels.[9] *Cien Amigos* then chooses those students who will receive the scholarships. Community outreach including fundraising events for scholarships and education are other important activities. One-day events, such as Advocacy Day, Education Fair Day or Women's Leadership Day, bring people from the community together to acquire new skills and to learn about opportunities, about their rights, about each other and about what they can do for their communities.[10]

## CC-IME–INITIATED ORGANIZATIONS

### American Mexican Anti-discrimination Alliance (AMADA)

AMADA is a very interesting example of CC-IME members using their own initiative, resources and connections to create a new organization separate from the Mexican government. Founded in 2008, the organization grew out of discussions in the CC-IME Media Commission as a means of preventing hate, defamation, xenophobia, bigotry and discrimination against individuals of Mexican ancestry. Although the organization lasted only two years due to lack of funds, one of its important activities involved a two-day training session of its members sponsored by the American Jewish Committee, the Jewish Anti-defamation League, the Mexican Embassy and the IME. One of AMADA's members was able to arrange this training, which involved learning how to lobby in Washington and how to mobilize as an interest group in United States politics.[11]

# 146 *Jane H. Bayes and Laura Gonzalez*

## The Mexican American Coalition (MXAC)

This organization was created formally in 2009 by a group of CC-IME advisors from all three cohorts who were concerned about informing, organizing and advocating to advance the interests of the Mexican American community, such as building support for immigration reform, monitoring respect for migrant rights and promoting the economic and social contributions of migrants in the United States. It was also intended to be an outlet to express the opinions of the Mexican American leaders and to serve as a tool to educate the community. Another goal was to unify the diverse voices of the Mexican diaspora in the United States and Canada. A major first task was to help launch the Reform Immigration for America Campaign (RIFA) in Washington, DC, in June 2010. Some of the actions involved in this effort included the organization of "house parties" to connect hundreds of Mexican leaders in an informative session to learn about the immigration reform bill introduced in Congress by Congressman Luis Gutiérrez (D-IL). During the most active months around the possible introduction of the immigration reform bill, the Mexican American Coalition was responsible for the translation into English and Spanish of dozens of press release documents, informative flyers, letters and public service announcements. This was the beginning of the MX-Coalition, which drew on the institutional resources and community-organizing knowledge of groups like the Illinois Coalition for Immigrant and Refugee Rights (ICIRR) and the technical and administrative skills of one of the CC-IME's younger members to organize a major immigration reform march in Washington, DC, in March of 2010. The electronic network that resulted from this effort includes all the members of the three CC-IME cohorts from around the country, plus a host of Spanish newspapers, radio stations, immigration organizations and other community leaders, which continues to function, creating a loose organization or network of 634 well-placed and well-connected leaders that can be used for a multitude of issues. This organization was incorporated in Florida in 2010 and continues to function with fourteen national representatives from different regions in the United States and Canada, who meet either in person, via conference call or online as needed. Certain members specialize in particular topics depending on the information they receive. All members post news from the press in their respective regions. One member sends everything related to Immigration Reform for America. Several send news, information and reports gleaned from the White House, think tanks, universities, hometown associations, new books and other government networks, news from Mexico from senators working on the Mexican immigration law, political action alerts, lobbying efforts, legal information, notices of webinars, workshops and other training that can help immigrants. A volunteer group of seven CC-IME members manages the flow of information on this electronic network.[12]

## *Fundación* MEX-I-CAN

Started by one CC-IME advisor with a career and connections in the TV production world, the *Fundación* MEX-I-CAN exists to promote the pride and dignity of Mexican and Latin identity in the United States. As a project of the CC-IME Media Commission, the group plays on the *"Si Se Puede"* phrase of the American Farmworkers Union to proclaim its mission of empowering Mexicans and Latino/as in the United States. The group promotes special events, concerts, ballets, conferences and fundraisers to publicize and promote pride in Mexican culture.[13]

## *Congreso del Pueblo*

The *Congreso del Pueblo* was created in 2010 by CC-IME advisors to provide a place for Mexican American leaders to study and endorse candidates running for office in Mexico and the United States. CC-IME advisors have an interest in Mexican as well as United States or Canadian politics. The CC-IME, however, is not a political organization. The *Congreso del Pueblo* attempts to satisfy this need to participate in the political process both in Mexico and the United States. Many members of this group have been interested in running for public office in Mexico and/or in endorsing candidates for office in Mexico. Because Mexicans living abroad can now vote and even more because those living in the United States and Canada often strongly influence the votes of their relatives still living in Mexico, Mexican politicians have for many years campaigned in the United States. The *Congreso del Pueblo* is a diverse, inclusive and nonpartisan organization interested in advancing candidates who advocate for migrants' interests. It provides a space for those in the Mexican diaspora to discuss and endorse candidates. They would like to be able to raise funds to support candidates as well as endorse them, but do not have the resources for that at present. This group uses conference calls and e-mails for much of their business. With presidential elections in both countries this year, the *Congreso del Pueblo* has scheduled a number of events leading up to a special day on June 15, when all three Mexican parties will be presenting their platforms to the group. With regard to US politics, the *Congreso del Pueblo* supported Jerry Brown for California governor and plans to support President Obama in his reelection bid. They also endorse candidates in US congressional and local elections.[14]

## CIVIL SOCIETY GROUPS THAT HAVE BEEN HELPED BY THE CC-IME

Responses to an e-mail questionnaire sent to all CC-IME cohorts indicate that the CC-IME has been important in strengthening and enhancing the operations of many groups concerned with immigrants and immigration that

# 148  *Jane H. Bayes and Laura Gonzalez*

were already in existence in the United States and in Mexico. Established groups in the United States such as League for United Latin American Citizens (LULAC), National Council of La Raza (NCLR), Reform Immigration 4 America (RI4A), Center for Community Change (CCC) and many unions such as the State Employees International Union (SEIU) were reported to have benefited from the CC-IME. The Tennessee Immigrant Rights Coalition, the *Red Mexicana de Líderes y Organizaciones Migrantes* (Mexican Network of Migrant Leaders and Organizations) and the *Centro de Orientación de los Derechos de los Migrantes* (Center of Orientation for the Rights of Migrants ) in Canada, *La Federación de Clubes Michoacanos en California Lázaro Cárdenas del Río* and the language school at the University of Texas Center for Hispanic Achievement (LUCHA) were other organizations cited as having been strengthened by the CC-IME. Some respondents also mentioned organizations in Mexico such as *El Consejo Binacional por un Mexico Mejor* (The Bi-national Council for a Better Mexico) and *Organización Espejo* (Mirror Organization), which were created in Morelia, Michoacán, by CC-IME advisors.

## THE IMPORTANCE OF INSTITUTIONALIZATION FOR FURTHERING INTEGRATION

A major problem that most of the organizational efforts started by CC-IME advisors face is the problem of sustained funding and continuity in leadership. One of the reasons that the Health Initiative of the Americas programs have been so successful is that they have been linked with existing institutions in the United States and Canada as well as with the Mexican consulates. The Health Initiative in the Americas project has been successful largely because of its ties with the University of California, Berkeley, and because of the support it receives from the Mexican consulates. The Mexican American Coalition was most successful when it was linked with the ICIRR. AMADA was most effective when it joined with the American Jewish Committee and other organizations. These are situations in which CC-IME advisors with their contacts have acted as bridges or catalysts to further leverage existing programs or create new ones. Where this sort of linking together of existing institutions with CC-IME initiatives does not exist, CC-IME initiatives tend to be short-lived.

## WHAT KINDS OF INSTITUTIONS ARE NEEDED TO FURTHER INTEGRATE NORTH AMERICA?

The question of whether Mexico, the United States and Canada should increase the cooperative relationship they began by signing NAFTA in 1994 is anything but settled. In 2005, US president George Bush, Mexican president Vicente Fox and Canadian prime minister Paul Martin met in Texas, where

## Organizing the Mexican Diaspora   149

they agreed to create a Security and Prosperity Partnership (SPP) among the three countries. While this partnership established in 2006 was not at the level of a treaty, the three countries did agree to work on a ministerial level to try to implement smart border security measures, to develop a common approach to emergencies and disasters including health epidemics, to make improvements in aviation and maritime security and to promote collaboration in energy, transportation, financial services, technology and other areas to facilitate business and reduce the costs of trade. In addition, the SPP created "working groups" in each country, with a mandate of overseeing "harmonization," or "integration," in over 300 policy areas. The SPP created a North American Competitiveness Council, composed of top corporate executives of global firms, to provide advice. A major priority in 2008 concerned harmonizing regulatory policies among the three countries.[15] Perhaps because the tone of these integrative activities was neoliberal in nature, seeking to reduce regulations, and promote free trade rather than addressing other problems such as the environment or labor, the SPP did not last beyond 2008 when Barack Obama came into the presidency.

What the SPP experience demonstrates when compared to that of the CC-IME as a trinational institution is that the activities of the CC-IME, while extremely novel and innovative with regard to having a governmental ministry organize its diaspora to engage in community organizing, cannot compare to the power of having all three governments employing a variety of ministries in the integration enterprise from the top down to address a host of issues. Yet the political obstacles to top-down integration are so great at this point and so likely to lead to further painful economic dislocations, that the CC-IME model of grassroots democratic trilateral involvement may represent one of the most positive kinds of North American integration possible at this time. Other ways to create or reinforce socioeconomic integration among the peoples who live and work in Canada, the United States and Mexico may be through the strengthening of ties between regions in the three countries. Patterns of chain migration allow those in the Mexican diaspora to build and maintain ties between receiving regions in the United States and Canada and sending regions in Mexico. To the extent that groups of entrepreneurs, elected officials and governors from different states or regions in the United States and Canada can organize and cooperate with their counterparts in regions or states in Mexico to help improve communication, services, the flow of goods and investment and perhaps even labor, a decentralized and regional form of integration may provide a promising model of integration for the future.

## NOTES

1. The authors are most grateful to Lorena Colin and Leni González, former CC-IME advisors, for their help and advice in obtaining information for this chapter.
2. Another group administered by the IME is Red de Talentos Mexicanos (Network of Talented Mexicans), which began as a partnership between Advanced Micro

## 150  *Jane H. Bayes and Laura Gonzalez*

Devices (AMD) and the United States-Mexico Foundation for Science (FUMEC) with the support of the National Council of Science and Technology—*Consejo Nacional de Ciencia y Tecnología (CONACYT)*—and the Ministry of Economy (SE). While this group is similar to the CC-IME in that it consists of members of the Mexican diaspora, it differs in that its outreach is to the Mexican diaspora in all parts of the world, not just the Mexican diaspora spread throughout the United States and Canada. It also is different in that it seeks to harness the support of highly skilled Mexican migrants to help advance Mexico's knowledge industries. Its mission and activities contribute to the organization of the Mexican diaspora; however, it is separate and distinct from the CC-IME, whose activities are more oriented towards migrants and their well-being.

3. Carlos González Gutiérrez, "Fostering Identities: Mexico's Relations with Its Diaspora," *Journal of American History* 86 (1999): 545; Laura Gonzalez, "El Consejo Consultivo, ¿Apéndice o Pilar Central del Instituto de los Mexicanos en el Exterior?" in *Mexicanos en el Exterior, Trayectoria y Perspectivas (1990–2010)*, 181 (Mexico City: Secretaría de Relaciones Exteriores (SRE) and Instituto Matías Romero, 2010): 181; Alexandra Delano, *Mexico and Its Diaspora in the United States: Policies of Emigration Since 1848* (Cambridge: Cambridge University Press, 2011).

4. Instituto de los Mexicanos en el Exterior, *Report de Actividades 2003–2004* [*Activities Report 2003–2004*] (Mexico City: Secretaría de Relaciones Exteriores/IME, 2004).

5. Jane H. Bayes and Laura Gonzalez, "Globalization, Transnationalism and Intersecting Geographies of Power: The Case of the *Consejo Consultivo del Instituto de los Mexicanos en el Exterior* (CC-IME): A Study in Progress," *Politics & Policy* 39 (2011): 11.

6. Lorena Colin, CC-IME advisor 2009–2011, in discussion with the authors, February 25, 2012.

7. Xochitl Castañeda, CC-IME advisor 2003–2005 and 2009–2011, in discussion with the authors, February 23, 2012; Health Initiative for the Americas, accessed February 24, 2012, http://hia.berkeley.edu/index.php?page=access-to-health-care.

8. Colin, email message to the author, February 25, 2012.

9. Maricela Gallegos, CC-IME advisor 2003–2005, in discussion with the authors, April 15, 2012.

10. Carlos González Gutiérrez, IME's Excecutive Director 2003–2009, in discussion with the authors, February 28, 2012; Gallegos, discussion.

11. Leni González, CC-IME advisor 2003–2005, in discussion with the authors, February 17, 2012.

12. Lorena Colin, in discussion with the authors, February 23, 2012.

13. *Fundación* MEX-I-CAN 2012,[2] http://mexicopuede.com/mic/en-us/english.aspx#.URP1tqXhrHg.

14. Jerry Dominguez, CC-IME advisor 2009–2011, in discussion with the authors, April 16, 2012.

15. Government of Canada, "Initial Work Plan: Regulatory Cooperative Work Plan," in *Mexican Talent Network: The Institutional Perspective of Mexico* (Mexico City: Secretaría de Relaciones Exteriores/IME, 2007).

## REFERENCES

Bayes, Jane H., and Laura Gonzalez. "Globalization, Transnationalism and Intersecting Geographies of Power: The Case of the *Consejo Consultivo del Instituto*

## Organizing the Mexican Diaspora   151

*de los Mexicanos en el Exterior* (CC-IME): A Study in Progress." *Politics & Policy* 39, no. 1 (2011): 11–14.

Delano, Alexandra. *Mexico and Its Diaspora in the United States: Policies of Emigration Since 1848*. Cambridge: Cambridge University Press, 2011.

Fundación MEX-I-CAN. "Organización de los Mexicanos a favor de los Hispanos." 2012. Accessed April 13, 2012. http://mexicopuede.com/mic/en-us/english.aspx#.URP1tqXhrHg.

Gonzalez, Laura. "El Consejo Consultivo, ¿Apéndice o Pilar Central del Instituto de los Mexicanos en el Exterior?" In *Mexicanos en el Exterior, Trayectoria y Perspectivas (1990–2010)*, 181–190. Mexico City: Secretaría de Relaciones Exteriores (SRE) and Instituto Matías Romero, 2010.

González Gutiérrez, Carlos. "Fostering Identities: Mexico's Relations with Its Diaspora." *Journal of American History* 86, no. 2 (1999): 545–567.

———. "Viente Años de Tejer Redes." In *Mexicanos en el Exterior, Trayectoria y Perspectivas (1990–2010)*. 41–57. Mexico City: Secretaría de Relaciones Exteriores (SRE) and Instituto Matías Romero, 2012.

Government of Canada. "Initial Work Plan: Regulatory Cooperative Work Plan." In *Mexican Talent Network: The Institutional Perspective of Mexico*. Mexico City: Secretaría de Relaciones Exteriores/IME, 2007. Accessed February 24, 2012. http://spp-psp.gc.ca/eic/site/spp-psp.nsf/eng/0096.html.

Health Initiatives of the Americas. Accessed February 24, 2012. http://hia.berkeley.edu/index.php?page=access-to-health-care.

Instituto de los Mexicanos en el Exterior (IME). *Report de Actividades 2003–2004 [Activities Report 2003–2004]*. Mexico City: Secretaría de Relaciones Exteriores/IME, 2004.

Secretaría de Relaciones Exteriores (SRE). *Mexicanos en el Exterior: Trayectoria y Perspectivas (1990–2010)*. Mexico City: Secretaria de Relaciones Exteriores and Instituto Matías Romero, 2010.

# 9 What Does the 2010 Affordable Care Act Mean for Securing Immigrant Health in North America?

*Nielan Barnes*

This chapter addresses the problem of institutional void(s) in relation to securing adequate access to health and health care for immigrants in North America. Within the post–North American Free Trade Agreement (NAFTA) context, North America has increasingly relied on temporary migrant and immigrant labor from the global South (particularly Mexico) as the United States and Canada have expanded temporary labor programs to meet the need for agricultural and low-skilled workers. Arguably, because migrants and immigrants are not citizens, the nation-state is not responsible for meeting their legal, health and human service or advocacy needs. Yet in an increasingly globalized world, South-to-North labor mobility and immigration and migration patterns mean that a significant number of individuals from the global South (Africa, Latin America, most of Asia) live outside their home nation. Who (and what institutions) is responsible for ensuring the labor, health and human rights of these global workers?

The primary policy and institution-building mechanisms in North America—NAFTA (1994), Security and Prosperity Partnership (SSP) (2005), Merida Initiative (2007)—have largely neglected questions of labor mobility and immigration, and by extension immigrant labor's health and human rights. In fact, US and Canadian immigration policies generally have become stricter (especially in regard to Mexican nationals) as part of the post-9/11 emphasis on security. Both NAFTA and the SSP are primarily a set of trilateral trade agreements, whereas agreements on coordinating environmental, social and public health policy and programs have occurred primarily on the side, and as "binational" (versus trilateral) efforts.

As stated in the introduction to the volume, the lack of effective North American leadership and institutions is not due to the lack of common problems facing the three countries but rather that the continent has addressed its problems uni- or bilaterally, leaving trilateral solutions the least utilized tools. This chapter argues that a human rights framework can generate effective trilateral approaches to building institutions (policies and programs) that meet labor, health and human needs of immigrant and migrant populations in North America.

## Securing Immigrant Health in North America    153

The geopolitical position of the US-Mexico border as one of the largest and busiest land borders in the world generated the growth of a "binational" and/or "border" health institutional framework that addresses environmental health and infectious disease (TB, HIV, SARS) from the early 1900s to present.[1] Another place to look for more recent examples of effective multilateral approaches to immigrant and migrant health is the European Union (EU). Admittedly, EU migration trends do not match North American trends; however, much can be learned from the challenges faced by countries such as Spain, Portugal,[2] France, the Netherlands[3] and Sweden,[4] which establish migrant health as a human right, even for the undocumented. Given the diverse nature of EU members and migration patterns, many challenges exist to providing health care for mobile populations. Even in EU and North American nations where health care is universal the policy framework is only a point of reference from which practices emerge at the local and regional levels. Looking at the local and regional levels of practice in both the EU and North America, it "appears that in different contexts different strategies have developed to manage the paradox of health care"[5] for immigrants, migrants and the undocumented. In contexts with no or partial access, strategies for service provision to immigrants are variable yet can be characterized as "functional ignorance" (services provided on a "don't ask, don't tell" basis) or "partial acceptance" (systematic partial access to services).[6]

The 2010 US Affordable Care Act (ACA) marks a positive shift towards establishing a national health care system and provides an opening for asking many questions: Is it possible for the United States to move from a market to a universal health care model that provides care to the 45 million uninsured? Is it possible to use a human rights framework to leverage the debates about the ACA to develop more democratic health care systems? More specifically, what does the ACA mean for the health of immigrants and migrants in the United States?

The 2010 ACA intersects with a long history of binational health policy and programming directed towards (im)migrants along the US-Mexico border. As well, more recent multi/binational EU policies and programs provide a series of newer examples for developing regional and multisector trilateral agreements in North America, yet problems exist at two levels. Without a unified human rights–driven approach, moving from policy to action in a way that involves all three North American nations in an equal and meaningful manner, from national to local levels, presents many challenges; and second, the provision of health and social services is still based on differential access to labor, citizenship and/or economic—not full access to human—rights.[7]

While others[8] have set forth the general prospects of the US health care reform plans from a human rights perspective, this chapter uses a human rights framework to assess what the 2010 ACA means for immigrant health in the United States (and North America in general). To that end the chapter

## 154   *Nielan Barnes*

briefly sets forth the historical precedents of human rights theories and approaches to public health; outlines a human rights framework for public health; then uses this framework to assess how the ACA and civil society responses will affect immigrant access to health in the United States.

## HISTORICAL PRECEDENTS FOR HEALTH AS A HUMAN RIGHT

A large amount of scholarship, activism and institution building indicates there is an important relationship between human rights and health.[9] The adoption of the Universal Declaration of Human Rights (UDHR) in 1948 marks the international recognition of the "right to health" as a set of basic human rights by most nation-states.[10] Historically, it was the nation-state's responsibility to guarantee the health and human rights of citizens and workers, and most nation-states acknowledge this fact in the constitution and via health care and taxation systems. Yet, based on a 2008 study of 194 countries,[11] only fifty-six governments formerly recognize the "right to health" in the country constitution. Mexico and Canada are included in that group, yet both countries have deep problems with delivering adequate health care for all citizens.

The applied link between human rights and health exists in public health theory and practice. The 1948 UDHR generated a significant force of international public health organizations such as the World Health Organization (WHO), the Pan American Health Organization (PAHO), Oxfam, Medecins san Frontieres, UNAIDS, Center for Disease Control (CDS), etc. Much of the work of these organizations occurs in the developing world, where nation-states have struggled to provide basic population needs. At its core, international public health theory and action are informed by the idea that health is a right justified by membership in a nation-state and/or workplace. The right to health has a strong legal basis in international law; the real problem is "whether institutional safety nets enforce the legal articulation of these rights."[12] Ultimately, there are two problems at hand: Should health be viewed as a right or commodity? And does either model generate institutions that effectively achieve public health goals and meet population health needs? A human rights perspective says market models of health care delivery are not effective; universal health care is a better option, yet it also is problematic, particularly for noncitizens and "stateless" groups.[13]

Given that human rights are guaranteed by a state, the lack of transnational or supranational institutions dealing with labor mobility in North America leaves undocumented immigrants as "stateless people" whose rights become superfluous, as Norman states in her chapter in this volume. Because they lack a state to enforce their rights, they have become meaningless and nonexistent. I argue, however, that social movements based on "health as a human right" and other forms of civil society action indicate that at local, regional and supranational levels it is the relationship between citizenship status and access to rights that is superfluous (i.e., "don't ask, don't tell" strategies, sanctuary cities, etc.). When states fail to provide for their populations' health, contentious social movements can occur, such as the 1970s' women's health movement, but most notably the HIV/AIDS movement of the 1980s to the present. In the field of HIV public health, policy makers and practitioners have been challenged to integrate human rights into public health and rethink approaches based on social categories that produce inequalities and exclusion.[14] That health equals a human right versus a commodity is the framework required to drive the institutionalization process. In order to make the idea of health as a human right a reality, civil society action and input must be integral to the institutionalization process; it is this participation of civil society that removes the superfluousness of human rights.

## RESEARCH DESIGN AND METHODOLOGY

This chapter utilizes a human rights framework to analyze the impact of the 2010 ACA on immigrant health in the United States. The primary questions driving the analysis are: What human rights principles can be applied to immigrant health policy in the United States? What does the ACA mean for the health of immigrants and migrants in the United States? To answer the first question requires a review of the health and human rights literature (both theoretical and applied policy documents) to produce a framework—a set of principles and themes (knowledge domains). The primary concepts and themes identified include "coresponsibility," "poverty initiatives," "mobilized civil society," "regionalism" and "intersectorality." These principles and themes are then organized into a framework used to organize a qualitative investigation of the second question about the 2010 ACA and its effect on immigrants.

I use a combination of qualitative methods (including participant observation, in-depth semistructured interviews, archival research and policy analysis) to collect and compare data across the knowledge domains of the framework. In-depth interviews were conducted with health policy makers, health service providers, representatives from community-based organizations and other key actors (such as researchers, foundations, development agencies and international nongovernmental organizations (NGOs)). Participant observation took place at numerous events, including applied health forums, conferences, health policy planning meetings and civil society events from 2005 to 2012. Finally, a historical comparative analysis of health policy documents, conference and workshop proceedings and organizational literature (including brochures, websites, annual reports and internal documents) was conducted. Data from interviews, participant observation and archival documents were transcribed and triangulated to verify the patterns and explanations discussed in the results.

## 156  *Nielan Barnes*

### HEALTH AS A HUMAN RIGHT: CONCEPTS AND
### PRINCIPLES FOR HUMAN RIGHTS FRAMEWORKS

What does a human rights approach to health in North America look like? The applied and theoretical literature suggests diverse ways of operationalizing human rights frameworks; the following is a synthesis of the common core aspects of most approaches. First and foremost, any framework must "systematically question whether proposed policies and actions create a principle of justice."[15] Is "health" (or its converse, illness and disease) distributed evenly among populations? If not, why and how can it be remedied? According to world-renowned medical doctor and anthropologist Paul Farmer, the answer is relatively simple: There is a strong and well-documented correlation between poverty and poor health that exists at the structural level of society. From a human rights perspective we can link structural social conditions to "entire populations that find themselves socially vulnerable and in need of social protection based on human and social rights, rather than circumstantial protection against particular or conceptually isolated risk factors."[16] The strategy assumes there is a deep causal relationship between poverty and illness and that a human rights–informed political approach will focus on realizing rights by satisfying basic needs. In the United States and North America in general, those who are poor often also claim status in other "minority" groups (women, LGBTQ individuals, elderly, minority ethnic, immigrant, etc.); in this chapter the focus is (im) migrants. But, ultimately, the key to ensuring a baseline of adequate human health is addressing poverty and providing basic human security needs.

As stated in the chapter by García-Barrios and Mayer-Foulkes, economic liberalization is not enough to promote economic growth and development but must be complemented with government policies that link health to technological change, human capital accumulation, urbanization and economic equality. Rooting health within a broader commitment to "human and social rights and the development of the social environment" is referred to by Filho as generating "spaces of humanization."[17] The development of such spaces as part of a health care system must focus on the most disadvantaged people while aiming to address the needs of all. It is necessary to put forward a meaningful interpretation of universal access; for access to be truly universal it must be affordable, equitable and comprehensive.[18] Such a system does not restrict care at the expense of good health in order to cut costs or gain profit; it contains costs by preventing disease and ill health, not by denying care to those who need it.

In North America there is a dearth of policy and programming (as evidenced by NAFTA, the Security and Prosperity Partnership, etc.) that considers preventative health care provision and/or poverty reduction. As stated in the introduction to this volume, the problem of institutionalization is tied to the process of creating values and cognitive frames. Institutionalization requires a foundation of shared values between actors. If institutions are lacking

# Securing Immigrant Health in North America    157

or inefficient, the simple remedy is to generate shared values—easier said than done. The United States must overcome what Rudiger calls a "characteristically American hostility toward any shared public obligations beyond the physical safety of individuals and their property."[19] Rudiger also states that appropriating core aspects of American identity (specifically that the precept of unalienable rights be applied to health) could help to bolster human rights arguments and develop a human rights–based political culture.

In addressing poverty and applying a human rights framework, the concept of "coresponsibility" is important. Coresponsibility refers to the duty of the state to act as guarantor of the rights of society while the citizenry engages in "building a reality where this is actually possible."[20] In the case at hand, coresponsibility occurs when the nation-state and civil society share responsibility for poverty reduction and health care provision. "Coresponsibility" between government and civil society NGOs and Community Based Organizations is a strategy that is also widely used in Canada and Mexico, and in international development,[21] and it is a concept that informs the operation of many federally funded public health centers and poverty initiatives that serve the poor and uninsured.

In the 2008 US presidential election, "shared responsibility" emerged as a bipartisan rhetorical device and signaled a discursive opening for discussing health care as a common good.[22] At its best policy and programming informed by shared or coresponsibility can generate democratic civil society development and social movements as well as intraregional and intersectoral dynamism and innovation. However, the "dark side" of coresponsibility emerges when it does not address "persisting tensions and blind spots in health care reform proposals, notably around issues of universality and equity in health care."[23] These problems are linked to the limited accountability of the private sector and the government and the lack of incentive for either to prioritize health. Also, the "unsavory practice of substituting government obligations with NGO or community action"[24] tends to miscast human rights approaches by "shifting the burden of redress . . . onto populations already marginalized."[25] Finally, the shared responsibility model still puts the primary burden on the individual, because public health is allocated based on protective and punitive functions and health care remains a private matter and is not valued as a public good.[26]

Regardless of its dark side, shared responsibility approaches recognize the importance of fomenting a strong civil society for strong democratic governance. According to Filho "the right to health can be a driving force for political action that builds democracy on the foundation of social justice . . . Human rights principles offer a normative framework than enables activist and policy makers to develop analytical and advocacy tools for assessing and changing policy and practice."[27] At the organizational level, such a rights-based response integrates three concepts—universality, equality and comprehensiveness.[28] Operationally, organizations tend to use ethics to guide action and leverage theoretical and empirical findings to make

## 158 *Nielan Barnes*

a case for health care as a right and public good; and "analysis" replaces "messaging." Institutionalizing these practices within organizations can inform more powerful methods for establishing accountability for meeting basic human needs.[29] In particular, London argues that civil society mobilization must underlie all the different modalities of human rights approaches to health and that "without an active civil society, paper commitments to rights mean very little."[30] Rudiger agrees that a successful human rights approach must support the grassroots and give agency and voice to those who are vulnerable.[31]

## REGIONALISM AND DEMOCRACY

A wide range of academic and applied fields, including human rights, public health, international relations and political science, recognize that the power of the nation-state has weakened under the contemporary global capitalist system and that entities such as NAFTA, the EU and other trade bloc regions have major economic powers in their own right. The role of subregions formed by nonstate actors and supranational institutions (including hometown associations, transnational social movements and networks, migration flows and borders) has also become increasingly important to both local and global governance. There are many advantages to subregions and regional agreements, particularly in the areas of immigration and public health.

For example, Filho emphasizes the importance of "understanding social territories," which are living spaces such as cities and rural areas where social determinants and exposures—and health inequities—are produced.[32] Operating from an understanding of social territories would require decentralization of government administration and forming subregions to promote local capacity building and intersector coordination. Such an approach fosters the design of new institutionality that is closely linked with the existing situation and therefore capable of building social alternatives in response to complexity, which creates democratic governability. Fundamental to that approach is rooting health within a broader commitment to human and social rights and the development of the social environment to create "spaces of humanization."

The research suggests a strong civil society pursuing change at the state and local levels is the best approach. For example, the Human Right to Health Program pursues practical changes at the state level by fostering a participatory process that includes the involvement of those who are denied their rights. This program is "exploring the feasibility of establishing local universal health care zones, possibly through expanding community health centers—which provide care regardless of an individual's ability to pay."[33]

Some problems with human rights approaches to health include lack of a unifying framework that links human rights organizations operating

# Securing Immigrant Health in North America 159

under different principles (such as quality of care, cultural appropriateness, nondiscrimination, etc.). Participation and accountability receive little attention. Additionally, many activists see consumer rights as the best way to achieve health care reform, thus reinforcing the private industry,[34] such as the US-Mexico market in binational health care insurance.[35] Regardless of the underlying model, "with the right tactics, incremental reforms [at the state level] might have strategic value far beyond any substantive change that they may achieve. This requires engaging in practical reform efforts with a firm normative framework in place."[36]

To summarize the framework, most human rights approaches acknowledge that poverty reduction and improved human health are linked and that poverty reduction initiatives should be at the foundation of public health programs. "Coresponsibility" between government and civil society to solve poverty and health problems is integral to human rights and public health approaches; in particular the fomenting of civil society leads to more democratic and effective institutions. The nitty gritty of policy and programming (and institution building) involves multilateral and multisectoral actors working to maintain a key set of organizational and policy/programming principles (i.e., that access to resources be universal, equal and comprehensive; action and information be driven by ethics, empirical data and analysis) within specific geopolitical regions.

## APPLYING THE FRAMEWORK

To apply the framework already outlined, we have to investigate the following specific questions: How does health policy (specifically, the ACA) provide for minorities and the poor (poverty reduction)? Is "coresponsibility" (both rhetoric and practice) part of the discussion and process between actors? Is civil society involved? Does the policy promote democratic, intersector and/or regional collaboration? Are actors working to ensure that access to resources be universal, equal and comprehensive; and that action and information be driven by ethics, empirical data and analysis?

First it is important to acknowledge the ACA is a step towards Canadian and Mexican universal models of health care. Even so, Mexico's and Canada's health systems have severe resource constraints, and both countries deny care on the basis of legal citizenship status (i.e., Canada's Bill C-31 Refugee Exclusion Act that cuts refugees' benefits to the Interim Federal Health Program; the 2011 Canadian Federal Court of Appeal's decision in *Toussaint v. Attorney General* to exclude illegal immigrants from the federal health insurance program). After all, "universal health care" does not guarantee equitable access for all—only citizens and documented residents.

The United States has a long and embattled history of unsuccessful attempts to institute universal health care and is one of last industrial democracies to nationalize its health care system. From 1939, when the first

160 *Nielan Barnes*

health insurance plan was created in Baylor, Texas, until 2010, the US government—both Republican and Democrat—allowed the health care "system" to run largely on market principles. From the 1980s onward the United States avoided health care reform, and both the numbers of uninsured and the profits of the health care insurance industry skyrocketed. Ultimately, the US health care system is a conglomerate of options: the majority is private (employer-based or self-purchased) insurance (approximately 65 percent), and the rest government programs (Medicare, Medicaid, military). Over time, the percent of people receiving health care via employment has declined, placing an increasing burden on individuals (and explaining the rise in the numbers of uninsured) to either purchase their own insurance and/or increasingly rely on civil society and community services.

Being a US citizen does not guarantee access to health care—by 2010 approximately 47 million people were uninsured (11 million of whom are undocumented residents).[37] According to WHO reports,[38] the US health care system has consistently ranked #37 in quality and #1 in cost because it is based on a market model. The health care industry profits are into the billions of dollars due to gouging clients and denying care. Market-based medicine ensures that those most in need of health care receive the least amount of care and pay more for it, even when insured. Markets and economic incentives of actors do not address questions of health because the incentives work in the wrong direction.

As Castro-Rea argues in this volume, the uneven actions regarding North American integration are mostly due to the inherent contradictions of conservatism, an ideology that combines market goals with nonnegotiable social concerns, hypernationalism and xenophobia. This is true for health care in the United States: "failure to develop a health care system that guarantees equal access to care for everyone can be directly attributed to successive US governments' resistance to recognizing the human right to health and health care. . . . The crisis in health care is linked to the disregard of social and economic rights in the United States more generally. Caught in a political paradigm that designates human needs as personal, market-driven choices, health care has been excluded from the shrinking domain of public goods."[39]

## How Does the ACA Provide for the Marginal and Poor? Assessing Health Policy Reform's Effect on Immigrants

The ability of North American health care systems to provide adequate services is deeply conditioned by differences in: 1) the geopolitical nature of US-Canada and US-Mexico borders; 2) national health care systems; and 3) national, state and local-level immigration and health policies and programs,[40] by which a nation or region provides a set of health, labor and human rights to immigrants, migrants and stateless or undocumented individuals. Another important condition is how histories of nation building, globalization of the economy and patterns of human migration in North

America have led to the rapid growth of Latino immigrant populations (largely from Mexico and Central America) in Canada and the United States, as well as Mexico. One important and controversial result has been an ever-increasing number of undocumented or nonstatus individuals. Although the population by its very nature is hard to measure, estimates range from 20,000 to 200,000 in Canada,[41] 11.6 million in the United States[42] and 240,000 in Mexico.[43] The United States clearly has the larger undocumented population, whereas the population is smaller in Canada, largely because it is geographically more difficult to reach. In the United States (and the rest of North America), the health of undocumented immigrants and migrants is extremely important because they make up a large segment of the uninsured (25 percent in the United States) and have historically been excluded from most health care benefits due to lack of citizenship and/or inability to pay for care (see Table 9.1).

The different national health care models of the United States, Canada and Mexico also shape views about extending the right to health care to noncitizens and nonstatus individuals. Even though Mexico and Canada both instituted national health plans (in 1943 and 1984, respectively) it is on the basis of citizenship (or legal residence) that one has legal access to benefits. All three countries offer some basic public benefits to immigrants at the poverty level, and yet research shows that immigrants under-use benefits due to lack of knowledge, language barriers, lack of transportation, etc.[44] Regardless, there exists much negative political debate and media controversy about "illegal immigrant" abuse of medical services in the United States and Canada.

Generally speaking, migrants and immigrants with and without status experience both high rates of labor abuses and low rates of health and human service utilization, even in the EU and Canada, where universal health care exists and immigration policies are historically more open and inclusive. According to numerous studies,[45] immigrants in the United States use health care services much less (55 percent) than native-born Americans. Per capita health expenditures average $1,139 for immigrants versus $2,564 for nonimmigrants, and 30 percent of immigrants used no health care at all in the course of a year. Even immigrants with health insurance used 52 percent less health care than nonimmigrants, and Latino immigrants who did use health services had the lowest expenditures—$962 per person versus $1,870 per person for US-born Latinos and $3,117 for US-born whites. It is ironic that many immigrants actually subsidize health care for the rest of us and, at the same time, the future economic success of the United States and North America depends on having a healthy immigrant workforce.

Prior to 2010 two federal acts were passed that affect immigrant access to health care. The first was the 1996 the Personal Responsibility and Work Opportunity Reconciliation Act (PRWORA), which barred legal immigrants from Medicaid and the State Children's Health Insurance Program (SCHIP) for five years after entry into the United States, excluding emergency

## 162  *Nielan Barnes*

*Table 9.1*  Im(migrant) Access to Health Care: Policies, Programs and Services Pre- and Post-2010 ACA

|  | Pre-ACA | Post-ACA |
| --- | --- | --- |
| Number and type of uninsured | • "45 million uninsured" (includes 11 million undocumented and foreign-born)<br><br>• Latinos make up 32 percent of the uninsured (COFEM) | • Undocumented are excluded<br>• Increase coverage for 60 percent of uninsured Latinos<br>• 23 million would remain uninsured by 2019; 33 percent would be undocumented |
| Immigration policy | • Ongoing lack of comprehensive immigration reform in all three North American countries; left to each state to regulate | |
| Health policy | | |
| Federal level | • 1996 Personal Responsibility and Work Opportunity Reconciliation Act (legal immigrants barred from Medicaid – and in 1997 SCHIP – for five years excluding emergency)<br>• 2005 Deficit Reduction Act required Medicaid agencies to obtain proof of citizenship; implemented in 2006 | • Undocumented are denied<br>• Limited access to some federal programs remains for undocumented (funded via states): Title V of the Social Security Act (Maternal and Child Health Services Block Grant); Title X of the Public Health Service Act (family planning); Federally Qualified Health Centers (FQCHC), health care for the homeless, and migrant health clinics; emergency Medicaid; SCHIP |
| State level | • States pass laws both restricting/improving access:<br>• Prop 187 in California (1994)<br>• Prop 200 (2004) and SB 1070 in Arizona (2010) | • Path to coverage for undocumented is state-level reform, state-only funded programs and services, and the private market<br>• Little support exists for including undocumented immigrants in state health care reform[i] |

| | Pre-PPACA | Post-PPACA |
|---|---|---|
| Health services | | |
| Immigrant/ migrant access to health care insurance and services | • Sanctuary cities<br>• "Don't ask, don't tell" public service provision (Alta Med in Los Angeles)<br>• Community health centers, migrant clinics<br>• Private health insurance (e.g., Blue Cross in California) | • Increasing reliance on "FQCHC" and community-based services and providers |

Increasing reliance on external/private sector to meet needs of immigrants and undocumented

- Multinational and multisectoral health initiatives (Health Initiative of the Americas)
- Mexican consulate programs ("Ventanillas de Salud," and place-of-origin immigrant and migrant health programs)
- Private "multinational" health insurance exchanges (foreign-born and immigrants historically pay more out of pocket)
- Medical professionals required to be "health literate" with immigrant/migrant health programs in all three (CA-US-MX) health care systems
- Labor unions as key actors in policy convergence

[i] Sanchez, Gabriel R, Shannon Sanchez-Youngman, Amelia A.R. Murphy, Amy Sue Goodin, Richard Santos, and R. Burciaga Valdez. "Explaining Public Support (or Lack Therof) for Extending Health Coverage to Undocumented Migrants." *Journal of Health Care for the Poor and Underserved* 22 (2011): 683–699.

care. The second was the 2005 Deficit Reduction Act, which required that Medicaid providers obtain proof of citizenship. Both of these policies had the effect of shifting responsibility for immigrant health care from the federal to the state and local levels and generating regional "politics of scale"[46] based on anti-/pro-immigrant health activism. In response to these policies, some states and counties implemented programs expanding health coverage to immigrants (Illinois, New York and California); other states (Arizona, Colorado, Georgia and Virginia) passed laws that restrict immigrant and non-citizen access to health care. The specific sociohistorical nature of regional "immigration politics" will shape access to health care for immigrants as different US states adopt the ACA policies.

US states' responses to the ACA are mixed, but in general the 2010 ACA has a positive effect on immigrants while leaving out the undocumented. The positive effects include: 1) requiring employers to buy health insurance, extending it to (7.3 million) previously uninsured (Californian) individuals, many of whom are Latinos; 2) state-based health insurance exchanges will offer subsidies to those with incomes 133–400 percent above poverty level

164   *Nielan Barnes*

and many Latino immigrants will be newly eligible; 3) Medicaid will be expanded to cover more individuals below the poverty line (Latino immigrants are more likely to live in poverty than native-born); however, recent immigrants face a five-year waiting period; 4) the law provides $11 billion annually over five years in funding to community health centers (CHCs) where Latino immigrants and undocumented immigrants are more likely to seek care (33 percent of CHC users are Latino); and 5) everyone, including Latinos, will benefit from laws banning underwriting (banning insurance based on previous medical history).

Latinos are both the largest minority group and the largest immigrant group in the United States; within that Mexicans represent the largest percentage of immigrants, with the majority living in California.[47] According to a recent report by UCLA and UC Berkeley Labor Institutes,[48] the majority (66 percent) of the remaining uninsured in California will be Latinos (particularly those with limited English proficiency) residing in Los Angeles and other Southern California counties. And 57 percent of those Californians who remain uninsured will have household incomes at or below 200 percent of the federal poverty level.

Ultimately, even though Latinos make up 32 percent of the uninsured (the largest uninsured ethnic group in the United States) the reform will increase coverage for only 60 percent in that group. According to the Health Initiative of the Americas "long-stay documented Latino immigrant families with low incomes will be better off but many others within the Latino community will be excluded. The law may serve to exacerbate health disparities by immigration status, potentially undermining the many ways in which the law can otherwise benefit California's Latino community."[49] Additionally, the exclusion of some legal immigrants and all undocumented immigrants from health care "creates a class system in health care based largely on immigration status—of the 23 million people who would remain uninsured by 2019, 33 percent would be undocumented (im)migrants."[50]

While the ACA stipulates undocumented immigrants do not qualify for health care, it does markedly increase funding for federally qualified public health programs available to segments of the undocumented population through Title V of the Social Security Act (Maternal and Child Health Services Block Grant) and Title X of the Public Health Service Act (Family Planning). As well, the ACA increases funding for Federally Qualified Community Health Centers (FQCHCs), health care for the homeless and migrant health clinics, which provide comprehensive primary care including prenatal care, without regard to immigration status.[51] Because these programs will be one of the few ways many undocumented and poor immigrants receive health benefits, FQCHCs and migrant/homeless health clinics will experience a rise in service usage over time. Historically, FQCHCs in immigrant-dense communities have met gaps in social services for immigrants by partnering with civil society organizations and actors (community-based, nonprofit service providers and activists) and providing services on a "don't

## Securing Immigrant Health in North America 165

ask, don't tell" basis. Given the growing importance of FQCHCs, continuing to partner with civil society organizations to provide care regardless of immigration status is an important strategy.

Still not ideal from a human rights perspective, the 2010 ACA marks a partial shift in the US position on health care as an economic versus human right. Even though access to health care is still primarily tied to employment, the expansion of care to the underserved (students, elderly, poor) funded by the state (via taxes) signifies a shift to a more communitarian (social welfare) state. One of the central issues is that the ACA does not actually provide universal care. Some of the groups that may have limited or no access to health care under the new policies are immigrants, migrants, refugees and other non-US citizens. In particular, those without documents represent close to 11 million (25 percent) of the uninsured and will still remain without health insurance under the ACA.

### Is "Coresponsibility" (Both Rhetoric and Practice) Part of the Discussion and Process between Actors?

To begin to answer this question we can examine the "coresponsibility" as rhetoric and action in a number of arenas: the 2008 and 2012 presidential elections; legal challenges of the ACA in the US court system; anti- and pro-immigrant policies passed in US states, cities and counties; and civil society action ranging from the May Day Immigrant Labor marches to local migrant health outreach events.

The debates, messages and political platforms of the 2008 and 2012 presidential elections provide a window to view political rhetoric about immigration and health. Specifically, how does the political climate from which the ACA emerged resonate with the concept of "shared (or co-) responsibility"? Rudiger's analysis of the 2008 election states that the notion of shared responsibility "emerged as a normative frame in the 2008 Democratic primaries . . . signaling a discursive opening for conceiving health care as a common good"[52] but did little to address issues of universality and equity. The health care debates of the 2012 election were similar, with a Democratic vision of a country that emphasizes community and shared responsibility pushing back against a Republican vision of self-reliance and individual responsibility, but with little emphasis on universal equity.

Obama's win in the 2012 presidential election means that the ACA will go into full effect in 2014. Meanwhile some US states (California, Colorado, Nevada, Utah, Oregon and Washington) are already setting up health insurance exchanges in anticipation of the ACA, while others (Texas, Florida, Wisconsin, Louisiana and South Carolina) are opting out. One of the major points of contention against the ACA is whether it is constitutional to mandate a person purchase health insurance; at present, twenty-five lawsuits challenging this and other aspects of the act are making their way through the US court system. For states that contain a large number of undocumented

## 166  *Nielan Barnes*

immigrants—such as California, Texas Florida and New York[53]—the way in which health care reform plays out will have a direct effect on immigrant health outcomes.

Indeed, in all US states, partisan politics will directly shape immigrant access to health and social services of all types. Unfortunately, a rising number of US states and municipalities are proposing and passing anti-immigrant legislation[54] that negatively affects immigrant health care access. According to the January 2012 report of the National Conference of State Legislators (NCSL) Immigrant Policy Project, "in 2011, state legislators introduced 1,607 bills and resolutions relating to immigrants and refugees in all 50 states and Puerto Rico. This is a significant increase compared with 2010, when 46 states considered more than 1,400 bills and resolutions pertaining to immigrants."[55] The NCSL Project notes that even though more legislation was proposed in 2011, about 11 percent fewer bills were passed than in previous years. Much of the proposed and passed legislation focused on restrictions in the areas of employment, health, identification, drivers and other licenses, law enforcement, public benefits and human trafficking. As a result of the climate of fear produced by anti-immigrant policies in specific states and counties, many immigrants have stopped shopping or going to church and have closed bank accounts,[56] and may also limit use of social and health services.[57] According to a 2010 report from COFEM,[58] 85 percent of immigrants live in mixed-status households; new identification requirements will mean that eligible members of immigrant status–discordant families may avoid seeking preventative care. Another result of anti-immigrant policies is increasing internal migration away from anti-immigrant areas (such as Oklahoma and Arizona) to more immigrant friendly regions in the United States.[59]

## Is Civil Society Involved? Does the Policy Promote Democratic Intersector and/or Regional Collaboration?

Even before the ACA, public health and civil society sectors in US states that have large numbers of immigrants and undocumented individuals were working to legislate access to health and social services—some, like California, increasing access to care and others, such as Arizona, eliminating care.[60] Without a doubt, the involvement of nonstate actors such as civil society organizations and the private sector in developing multisector immigrant health initiatives has been pivotal to providing health care to immigrants, yet the degree to which such initiatives result in health care that is universal, equal and comprehensive per a human rights framework is questionable.

In Mexico, the United States and Canada, access to health and human services for (im)migrant workers is viewed by public health and civil society actors as a human and labor right. All three nations have signed international documents supporting protection of the human rights of migrants,[61] but policy implementation and enforcement at the local level is difficult, particularly in southern Mexico and along the US-Mexico border. As a result of the trilateral institutional void created by decreasing access to care,

## Securing Immigrant Health in North America   167

civil society organizations emerged and/or expanded to meet gaps in care for certain constituencies (e.g., those with HIV/AIDS and/or TB, migrants and immigrants, etc.) within the US-Mexico border region.[62] Of particular note is the Health Initiative of the Americas (HIA), a program of the University of California that emerged in 2001 from networks forged among agencies and organizations working on migrant and immigrant health issues. Originally named the California-Mexico Health Initiative (CMHI), the HIA was the first statewide, multisector, collaborative effort in California to address "border" and immigrant health issues. The California HealthCare Foundation (CHCF) and the California Endowment joined with the University of California (UC) system, the governments of California and Mexico and a wide range of researchers and nonprofits on both sides of the border to create the HIA. The main partners include the Secretariats of Health and Foreign Affairs of Mexico, El Salvador and Guatemala, the Institute for Mexicans Abroad, the Mexican Social Security Institute, California's Department of Health Services, the California Endowment, the California HealthCare Foundation (CHCF) and the Robert Wood Johnson Foundation.

The HIA is based at UC Berkeley and is funded by grants from CHCF, the California Endowment and the State of California. The HIA addresses four areas: health education and disease prevention, including management of chronic diseases and emergent health conditions; public and private health insurance coverage and eligibility for immigrant and migrant workers and their families; access to and use of health care systems; and occupational health and safety. Since its inception, the HIA has worked closely with FQCHCs such as AltaMed and the San Yisdro Health Center in California to innovate service provision to accommodate local circumstances (i.e., provide services on a "don't ask, don't tell" basis; develop memorandums of understanding (MOUs) with community organizations). The discordance between public health practices and immigration policy opens up space for such local-level innovation at the political and technical levels of the policy assessment framework.[63]

Under the ACA, FQCHCs—despite their increased funding—will bear the brunt of the policies' exclusionary mechanisms against immigrants. In fact, expanded FQCHC capacity is the only real improvement marginalized immigrants will see, and FQCHCs generally provide only primary (not acute or specialty) care. Additionally, the reform carries an amendment (the Hyde Amendment) that bans federal funding of abortion procedures, meaning low-income women of all immigration statuses will have fewer family planning options. These limits in the ACA coverage of immigrants clearly go against a human rights health policy framework because the ACA mandates against providing universal, equal, comprehensive care.

Local innovation aside, federal and state political pressures to control (and reform) the (im)migration process, as well as limit social and health services to (im)migrants, mean that the burdens of service provision and immigration enforcement have shifted heavily to local and regional police, doctors, educators, employers and community-based organizations. Arguably,

168  *Nielan Barnes*

the increasing involvement of regional and local Canadian, US and Mexican civil society organizations in responding to (im)migrant health and human rights issues is a product of global trends towards a form of inclusive neoliberalism in which North American countries have moved away from reliance on the federal government toward greater reliance on subnational governments and civil society.[64] The problem has been that much of the work—and institutions—of both governments and civil society have been based on a market model, not a model of universal access. Given the limits of the market model for providing universal access to health care, civil society has been and will continue to be involved in meeting immigrant health needs before and after the ACA, yet in an uneven and unequal manner. Intersector and/ or regional health initiatives (such as the HIA in California) and FQCHCs provide many innovative solutions but will continue to carry the brunt of the immigrant health care burden.

A number of other factors (see Table 9.1) are also important to meeting the health gap for immigrants in North America, including Mexican (and now Central American) consulate programs (such as "Ventanillas de Salud," and place-of-origin immigrant and migrant health programs); the growth of "multinational" health insurance exchanges; increasing numbers of medical professionals required to be "health literate" with immigrant/migrant health programs in all three (CA-US-MX) health care systems; and the growing importance of labor unions as key actors in policy convergence.

## CONCLUSION

This chapter explores fundamental questions regarding cooperation in the region on health and population mobility. The ACA provides an opportunity for North America to consider human health from a human rights perspective, and build more effective and democratic health care and social service institutions from the local to international levels. According to the chapter in this volume by Mayer-Foulkes and García-Barrios, democratic transformation is essential for successful economic growth and development. Economic liberalization has weakened democracy in North America by increasing the power of economic and political elites and by weakening the social cohesion that protects minorities such as immigrants. Policies like the ACA, although not ideal from a human rights perspective, are essential for developing and maintaining healthy and stable democracies. To move beyond partial democratic practices, strategies for service provision to immigrants must transform strategies of "functional ignorance" (services provided on a "don't ask, don't tell" basis) and "partial acceptance" (systematic partial access to services) towards universal, equal and comprehensive access not just for immigrants, but all individuals residing in the North American region.

Securing Immigrant Health in North America   169

Additionally, equitable practices and strategies for providing health care require institutionalization via regulation and harmonization by either a specific treaty or through the establishment of multilateral health care agencies. Either way, there must be a multilateral settlement regarding the health of immigrants and migrants in the North American region in order to negotiate new (post–9/11) obstacles to economic growth and political harmony. Issues such as security, migration and health require long-term perspectives and solutions, which require political leadership through effective institutions. The destinies of Canada, Mexico and the United States are irrevocably linked, and it is in the best interest of all three nations to find a balance between their respective interests, instead of yielding to the priorities of the politically and economically dominant partner, or to economic interests that compromise human health and quality of life.

## NOTES

1. See Nielan Barnes, "Paradoxes and Asymmetries of Transnational Networks: A Comparative Case Study of Mexico's Community-Based AIDS Organizations," *Social Science and Medicine* 66, no. 4 (2008): 933–944; Nielan Barnes, "Canada-US-Mexico Integration: Assessing (Im)migrant Health Policy Convergence," *International Journal of Canadian Studies* 44 (2011): 83–104; Nielan Barnes, "North American Integration? Civil Society and Immigrant Health Policy Convergence," *Politics and Policy* 39, no. 1 (2011): 69–89; Julie Collins-Dogrul, "Governing Transnational Social Problems: Public Health Politics on the US–Mexico Border," *Global Networks* 12, no.1 (2012): 109–128.
2. Maria-Jose Peiro and Benedict Roumyana, "Migrant Health Policy: The Portuguese and Spanish EU Presidencies," *Eurohealth* 16, no. 1 (2010): 1–4.
3. Ursula Karl-Trummer, Sonja Novak-Zezula and Birgit Metzler, "Access to Health Care for Undocumented Migrants in the EU: A First Landscape of NowHereland," *Eurohealth* 16 (2010): 13–16.
4. *The Local*, "Sweden to Give Illegal Immigrants Healthcare," June 28, 2012, http://www.thelocal.se/41702/20120628/.
5. Ursula Karl-Trummer, Sonja Novak-Zezula and Birgit Metzler, "Access to Health Care for Undocumented Migrants in the EU," *Eurohealth* 16, no. 1 (2010): 13–16.
6. Ibid.
7. See Anita Davies, Anna Basten and Chiear Frattini, "Migration: A Social Determinant of Migrants' Health," *Eurohealth* 16 (2010): 10–12; Anja Rudiger, "From Market Competition to Solidarity? Assessing the Prospects of US Health Care Reform Plans from a Human Rights Perspective," *Health and Human Rights* 10 (2008): 123–136.
8. Ibid.
9. See Rudiger, "From Market Competition to Solidarity?," 123–136; Armando de Negri Filho, "A Human Rights Approach to Quality of Life and Health: Applications to Public Health Programming," *Health and Human Rights* 10 (2008): 93–101; G. Backman et al., "Health Systems and the Right to Health: An Assessment of 194 Countries," *Lancet* 372, no. 9655 (2008): 2047–2085; Lindsey Kingston, Elizabeth Cohen and Christopher Morley, "Debate: Limitations on Universality: The "Right to Health" and the Necessity of Legal Nationality," *BMC International Health and Human Rights* 10, no. 11 (2010):

170   *Nielan Barnes*

1–12; Leslie London, "What Is a Human Rights-Based Approach to Health and Does It Matter?" *Health and Human Rights* 10, no. 1 (2008): 65–80; Paul Farmer, *Pathologies of Power: Health, Human Rights, and the New War on the Poor* (Berkeley: University of California Press, 2003); Paola Pace, "What Can Be Done in EU Member States to Better Protect the Health of Migrants?" *Eurohealth* 16, no. 1 (2010): 5–10; Tanya Basok and Emily Carasco, "Advancing the Rights of Non-citizens in Canada: A Human Rights Approach to Migrant Rights," *Human Rights Quarterly* 32 (2010): 342–366.

10. Kingston, Cohen and Morley, "Debate: Limitations," 1–12.
11. Backman et al., "Health Systems," 2047–2085.
12. Kingston, Cohen and Morley, "Debate: Limitations," p. 3.
13. Ibid.
14. London, "Human Rights-Based Approach," 65–80.
15. Filho, "Human Rights Approach," p. 95.
16. Ibid p. 97.
17. Filho, "Human Rights Approach."
18. Rudiger, "Market Competition," 123–136.
19. See Rudiger, "From Market Competition to Solidarity?," p. 123.
20. Filho, "Human Rights Approach," p. 98.
21. Alan Fowler, "Partnerships: Negotiating Relationships—A Source for Non-Governmental Development Organisations," Occasional Papers Series No: 32, International NGO Training and Research Centre (INTRAC), 2009.
22. Rudiger, "Market Competition," 123–136.
23. Ibid, p. 124.
24. London, "Human Rights-Based Approach," p. 4.
25. Ibid, p. 4.
26. Rudiger, "Market Competition," 123–136.
27. Ibid, p.123.
28. Ibid, p. 123.
29. London, "Human Rights-Based Approach," 65–80.
30. Leslie London, "What Is a Human Rights-Based Approach to Health and Does It Matter?" *Health and Human Rights* 10, no. 1 (2008): p. 67.
31. See Rudiger, "From Market Competition to Solidarity?," 123–136.
32. Filho, "Human Rights Approach."
33. Rudiger, "Market Competition," p. 133.
34. Ibid.
35. Barnes, "Assessing," 83–104.
36. Rudiger, "Market Competition," p. 133.
37. Ibid.
38. Karen Davis, Cathy Schoen and Kristof Stremikis. *Mirror, Mirror on the Wall: How the Performance of the U.S. Health Care System Compares Internationally, 2010 Update* (New York: World Health Organization, Commonwealth Fund, 2010).
39. Rudiger, "Market Competition," p. 123.
40. For extended explanation of the intersection between North American health and immigration polices and services, see Barnes, "Canada-US-Mexico Integration," and "North American Integration."
41. Lilian Magalhaes, Christine Carrasco and Denise Gastaldo, "Undocumented Migrants in Canada: A Scope Literature Review on Health, Access to Services and Working Conditions," *Journal Immigrant and Minority Health* 12, no. 1 (2010): 132–151.
42. Jeffrey Passel, D'Vera Cohn and Ana Gonzalez-Barrera, "Net Migration from Mexico Falls to Zero—and Perhaps Less" (Pew Research Center, Pew Hispanic Center, 2012).

## Securing Immigrant Health in North America   171

43. Barnes, "Civil Society," 69–89.
44. Raul Hinojosa-Ojeda, Max Hadler and Paule Cruz-Takash, "What Health Care Reform Means for Immigrants" (white paper, COFEM, UCLA, Los Angeles, 2010).
45. See Hinojosa-Ojeda, Hadler and Cruz-Takash, "Health Care Reform"; Kaiser Commission on Medicaid and the Uninsured, *Connecting Eligible Immigrant Families to Health Coverage and Care: Key Lessons from Outreach and Enrollment Workers* (Washington, DC: Kaiser, 2011); Alan Waxman and Raymond Cox, *Health Care for Undocumented Immigrants, ACOG Committee Opinion*, no. 425 (2009): 251–254; Michael Gusmano, *Undocumented Immigrants in the United States: Use of Health Care* (Garrison, NY: Hastings Center, 2012); Patrick Glen, "Health Care and the Illegal Immigrant" (Georgetown Public Law and Legal Theory Research Paper no. 12–024, Georgetown University, 2012).
46. Monica Varsanyi, "Liberalism and Nativism: Local Anti-Immigrant Policy Activism and an Emerging Politics of Scale," *International Journal of Urban and Regional Research* 35, no. 2 (2011): 295–311.
47. Kate Brick, A. E. Challinor and Marc R. Rosenblum, *Mexican and Central American Immigrants in the US*, (Washington D.C.:Migration Policy Institute, 2011); Seth Motel and Eileen Patten, *The 10 Largest Hispanic Origin Groups: Characteristics, Rankings, Top Counties* (Washington, DC: Pew Hispanic Center, 2012).
48. Laurel Lucia, Ken Jacobs, Miranda Dietz, Dave Graham-Squire and Nadereh Pourat, *After Millions of Californians Gain Health Coverage under the Health Care Act Who Will Remain Uninsured?* (Berkeley: UCLA Center for Health Policy Research and UC Berkeley Center for Labor Research and Education, 2012).
49. Health Initiative of the Americas, *Health Reform and California's Latino Immigrant Community* (Berkeley: University of California, Health Initiative of the Americas, 2011), p. 1.
50. Hinojosa-Ojeda, Hadler and Cruz-Takash, "Health Care Reform," p. 7.
51. Waxman and Cox, "Health Care for Undocumented," 251–254.
52. See Rudiger, "From Market Competition to Solidarity?," p. 124.
53. Pew Center, "Illegal Immigrants Dispersing," Stateline Daily Newservice of the Pew Center, April 14, 2009, http://www.pewstates.org/projects/stateline/headlines/illegal-immigrants-dispersing-85899384679.
54. NCSL, *2006 State Legislation Related to Immigration: Enacted, Vetoed, and Pending Gubernatorial Action* (Washington D.C.: NCSL Immigrant Policy Project, 2006); NCSL, *2007 Enacted State Legislation Related to Immigrants and Immigration* (Washington D.C.: NCSL Immigrant Policy Project, 2008).
55. NCSL, *Immigrant Policy Project* (Washington D.C.: NCSL, 2011), http://www.ncsl.org/issues-research/immig/state-laws-related-to-immigration-and-immigrants.aspx.
56. Pamela Constable, "Immigrants Feel Less Welcome in Frederick," *Washington Post*, May 6, 2008; Southern Poverty Law Center, *Climate of Fear: Latino Immigrants in Suffolk County NY* (Montgomery, AL: Southern Poverty Law Center, 2009); Southern Poverty Law Center, *Close to Slavery: Guestworker Programs in the United States* (Montgomery, AL: Southern Poverty Law Center, 2007).
57. Julia Field Costich, "Legislating a Public Health Nightmare: The Anti-immigrant Provisions of the 'Contract with America,'" *Kentucky Law Journal* 90 (2001–2002): 1043–1070.
58. See Hinojosa-Ojeda, Hadler and Cruz-Takash, "Health Care Reform."

## 172   Nielan Barnes

59. Randal Archibold, "Arizona Seeing Signs of Flight by Immigrants," *New York Times*, February 12, 2008; James Pinkerton, "Immigrants Flock to Texas amid Crackdowns," *Houston Chronicle*, Feburary 4, 2008.
60. NCSL, *Immigrant Policy Project* (Washington D.C.: NCSL, 2011).
61. Francois Crepeau and Delphine Nakache, "Controlling Irregular Migration in Canada: Reconciling Security Concerns with Human Rights Protection," *IRPP Choices* 12, no.1 (2006): 1–42.
62. Margaret Laws, "Foundation Approaches to US-Mexico Border and Binational Health Funding," *Health Affairs* 21 no. 4 (2002): 271–277.
63. Barnes, "Assessing," 83–104.
64. Rianne Mahon and Laura Macdonald, "Poverty Policy and Politics in Canada and Mexico: 'Inclusive' Liberalism?" (paper presented at the International Studies Association Meeting, Chicago, March 2007).

## REFERENCES

Archibold, Randal. "Arizona Seeing Signs of Flight by Immigrants." *New York Times*. February 12, 2008.

Backman, Gunilla., P. Hunt, R. Khosla, C. Jaramillo-Strouss, B. M. Fikre, C. Rumble, D. Pevalin, et al. "Health Systems and the Right to Health: And Assessment of 194 Countries." *Lancet* 372, no. 9655 (2008): 2047–2085.

Barnes, Nielan. "Canada-US-Mexico Integration: Assessing (Im)migrant Health Policy Convergence." *International Journal of Canadian Studies*, no. 44 (2011): 83-104.

———. "North American Integration? Civil Society and Immigrant Health Policy Convergence." *Politics and Policy* 39, no. 1 (2011): 69–89.

———. "Paradoxes and Asymmetries of Transnational Networks: A Comparative Case Study of Mexico's Community-Based AIDS Organizations." *Social Science and Medicine* 66, no. 4 (2008): 933–944.

Basok, Tanya, and Emily Carasco. "Advancing the Rights of Non-citizens in Canada: A Human Rights Approach to Migrant Rights." *Human Rights Quarterly* 32 (2010): 342–366.

Brick, Kate, A. E. Challinor and Marc R. Rosenblum. *Mexican and Central American Immigrants in the US*. Washington D.C.: Migration Policy Institute, 2011.

Collins-Dogrul, Julie. "Governing Transnational Social Problems: Public Health Politics on the US–Mexico Border." *Global Networks* 12, no. 1 (2012): 109–128.

Constable, Pamela. "Immigrants Feel Less Welcome in Frederick." *Washington Post*. May 6, 2008.

Costich, Julia Field. "Legislating a Public Health Nightmare: The Anti-immigrant Provisions of the "Contract with America." *Kentucky Law Journal* 90 (2001–2002): 1043–1070.

Crepeau, Francois, and Delphine Nakache. "Controlling Irregular Migration in Canada: Reconciling Security Concerns with Human Rights Protection." *IRPP Choices* 12, no. 1 (2006): 1-42.

Davies, Anita, Anna Basten and Chiear Frattini. "Migration: A Social Determinant of Migrants' Health." *Eurohealth* 16, no. 1 (2010): 10–12.

Davis, Karen, Cathy Schoen and Kristof Stremikis. *Mirror, Mirror on the Wall: How the Performance of the U.S. Health Care System Compares Internationally, 2010 Update*. New York: World Health Organization, Commonwealth Fund, 2010.

Farmer, Paul. *Pathologies of Power: Health, Human Rights, and the New War on the Poor*. Berkeley: University of California Press, 2003.

## Securing Immigrant Health in North America    173

Filho, Armando de Negri. "A Human Rights Approach to Quality of Life and Health: Applications to Public Health Programming." *Health and Human Rights* 10, no. 1 (2008): 93–101.

Fowler, Alan. "Partnerships: Negotiating Relationships—A Source for Non-governmental Development Organisations." Occasional Papers Series No: 32. International NGO Training and Research Centre (INTRAC). 2009.

Glen, Patrick. "Health Care and the Illegal Immigrant." Georgetown Public Law and Legal Theory Research Paper no. 12–024. Georgetown University. 2012.

Gusmano, Michael. *Undocumented Immigrants in the United States: Use of Health Care.* Garrison, NY: Hastings Center, 2012.

Health Initiative of the Americas. *Health Reform and California's Latino Immigrant Community.* Berkeley: University of California, Health Initiative of the Americas, 2011.

Hinojosa-Ojeda, Raul, Max Hadler and Paule Cruz-Takash. "What Health Care Reform Means for Immigrants." COFEM, UCLA. Los Angeles. 2010.

Kaiser Commission on Medicaid and the Uninsured. *Connecting Eligible Immigrant Families to Health Coverage and Care: Key Lessons from Outreach and Enrollment Workers.* Washington, DC: Kaiser, 2011.

Karl-Trummer, Ursula, Sonja Novak-Zezula and Birgit Metzler. "Access to Health Care for Undocumented Migrants in the EU: A First Landscape of Now Hereland." *Eurohealth* 16, no. 1 (2010): 13–16.

Kingston, Lindsey, Elizabeth Cohen and Christopher Morley. "Debate: Limitations on Universality: The 'Right to Health' and the Necessity of Legal Nationality." *BMC International Health and Human Rights* 10, no. 11 (2010): 1–12.

Laws, Margaret. *Foundation Approaches to US-Mexico Border and Binational Health Funding. Health Affairs* 21, no.4 (2002): 271–277.

*The Local.* "Sweden to Give Illegal Immigrants Healthcare." June 28, 2012, http://www.thelocal.se/41702/20120628/.

London, Leslie. "What Is a Human Rights-Based Approach to Health and Does It Matter?" *Health and Human Rights* 10, no. 1 (2008): 65–80.

Lucia, Laurel, Ken Jacobs, Miranda Dietz, Dave Graham-Squire and Nadereh Pourat. *After Millions of Californians Gain Health Coverage under the Health Care Act Who Will Remain Uninsured?* Berkeley: UCLA Center for Health Policy Research and UC Berkeley Center for Labor Research and Education, 2012.

Magalhaes, Lilian, Christine Carrasco and Denise Gastaldo. "Undocumented Migrants in Canada: A Scope Literature Review on Health, Access to Services and Working Conditions." *Journal Immigrant and Minority Health* 12, no. 1 (2010): 132–151.

Mahon, Rianne, and Laura Macdonald. "Poverty Policy and Politics in Canada and Mexico: 'Inclusive' Liberalism?" Paper presented at the International Studies Association Meeting, Chicago, Feb 28–Mar 3, 2007.

Motel, Seth, and Eileen Patten. *The 10 Largest Hispanic Origin Groups: Characteristics, Rankings, Top Counties.* Washington, DC: Pew Hispanic Center, 2012.

National Conference of State Legislatures (NCSL). *2006 State Legislation Related to Immigration: Enacted, Vetoed, and Pending Gubernatorial Action.* Washington D.C.: NCSL Immigrant Policy Project, 2006.

———. *2007 Enacted State Legislation Related to Immigrants and Immigration.* Washington D.C.: NCSL Immigrant Policy Project, 2008.

———. *Immigrant Policy Project.* Washington D.C.: NCSL, 2011.

Pace, Paola. "What Can Be Done in EU Member States to Better Protect the Health of Migrants?" *Eurohealth* 16, no. 1 (2010): 5–10.

Passel, Jeffrey, D'Vera Cohn and Ana Gonzalez-Barrera. *Net Migration from Mexico Falls to Zero—and Perhaps Less.* Washington D.C.: Pew Research Center, Pew Hispanic Center, 2012.

## 174 Nielan Barnes

Peiro, Maria-Jose, and Benedict Roumyana. "Migrant Health Policy: The Portuguese and Spanish EU Presidencies." *Eurohealth* 16, no. 1 (2010): 1–4.

Pew Center. "Illegal Immigrants Dispersing." Stateline Daily Newservice of the Pew Center. April 14, 2009, http://www.pewstates.org/projects/stateline/headlines/illegal-immigrants-dispersing-85899384679.

Pinkerton, James. "Immigrants Flock to Texas amid Crackdowns." *Houston Chronicle*. February 4, 2008.

Rudiger, Anja. "From Market Competition to Solidarity? Assessing the Prospects of US Health Care Reform Plans from a Human Rights perspective." *Health and Human Rights* 10, no. 1 (2008): 123–136.Southern Poverty Law Center. *Climate of Fear: Latino Immigrants in Suffolk County NY*. Montgomery, AL: Southern Poverty Law Center, 2009.

———. *Close to Slavery: Guestworker Programs in the United States*. Montgomery, AL: Southern Poverty Law Center, 2007.

Varsanyi, Monica. "Liberalism and Nativism: Local Anti-immigrant Policy Activism and an Emerging Politics of Scale." *International Journal of Urban and Regional Research* 35, no. 2 (2011): 295–311.

Waxman, Alan, and Raymond Cox. "Health Care for Undocumented Immigrants." *ACOG Committee Opinion*, no. 425 (2009): 251–254.

# Part III

# Economic and Security Issues in Integration

# 10 Obstacles to Security Cooperation in North America

*Roberto Domínguez and Rafael Velázquez*

## INTRODUCTION

The literature on international relations has largely considered North America as a region formed by Canada and the United States, despite the fact that from a geographical perspective Mexico is also part of the region. The inclusion of Mexico as part of North America in the academic debates is mostly derived from the implementation of the North American Free Trade Agreement (NAFTA) and the attempts by scholars and decision makers to create regional arrangements to deal collectively with common challenges. The expectations of developing a North American community[1] was based on the assumptions that increasing economic interdependence would encourage the establishment of regional institutions and eventually deeper integration in the economic area would spill over to other sectors of the trilateral agenda. Contrary to such expectations, North America has been facing an institutional void since NAFTA came into effect almost two decades ago. While lip service was paid to the ideas of greater regional cooperation between the three countries, tangible steps for further economic integration remain at the lowest level of the Balassian[2] integration stages (free trade), and the spillover effects have not taken place. Security cooperation is not an exception to the overarching milieu of the relationship among the three countries. In fact, threats to stability such as those of terrorism or organized crime have produced and reinforced the bilateralization rather than the trilateralization of cooperation. In order to explain the dominant trends in regional security in the area, this chapter aims to explore the reasons why the North American partners are facing obstacles for developing deeper cooperation in the area of security from a regional perspective. By adopting a Wendtian[3] approach, this chapter argues that in the area of security, a cooperative system has emerged in the US-Canadian relationship while the US-Mexican relationship remains anchored in the logic of an individualistic system. The chapter starts with an overview of the theoretical approach to studying security in North America, followed by the analysis of ideas, perceptions, principles and policies regarding the security of North America.

## THE FRAGMENTED REGION: INDIVIDUALISTIC AND COOPERATIVE SYSTEMS

The study of contemporary security in North America has been explored from different theoretical perspectives based on security research focused on Europe and the transatlantic community. Against this background, North America has been defined as a pluralistic security community[4] in the sense that currently in North America there are no prospects of conflicts that would result in the use of force among the three countries. From a different angle, Bow[5] has argued that, to some extent, North America has developed some features of a security complex as envisioned by Buzan and Weaver[6]—namely, a cluster of states that must take one another into account when thinking about their national security. While these studies have contributed to the understanding of security in North America, they have provided a limited explanatory power due to the characteristics of the region: unlike the European Union or the North Atlantic Treaty Organization (NATO), the three countries in North America have opted for bilateral strategies to deal with specific threats and have avoided trilateral institutions with collective decision-making power. This trend has been identified as dual-bilateralism.[7]

Dual-bilateralism is a reflection of the institutional void in North America. As indicated in the introduction of this book, the regional institutional void is not due to the lack of common problems among the three countries, but to the inadequate or, in some cases, lack of overriding constructive policy agendas that move beyond the simplistic outline of liberalization or intergovernmental common lowest denominator.[8] The risk is that as interdependence grows and hence some challenges become common to the region, the societies in North America will produce suboptimal outcomes due to the lack of or the insufficient development of regional institutions. From the perspective of this chapter, as Feng and Genna[9] argue, regional integration and homogeneity of domestic institutions mutually promote each other. Lack of institutional homogeneity among the countries in North America when applied within this framework explains the lack of institutional cooperation at a regional level. Based on this premise, transformations of domestic institutions will pave the way to develop trust as a mechanism to overcome the traditional security dilemma and to increase cooperation to deal more effectively with regional threats. In this regard, the levels of accountability, transparency and effective implementation of policies in the three countries of North America have facilitated the cooperation between the United States and Canada, while Mexico still faces problems, preventing it from being seen as an effective reliable partner in the region. Table 10.1 indicates the general trend in the convergence/divergence and insufficient homogeneity among the three countries in the areas of democracy, corruption perceptions and government effectiveness; it is salient that the gap between Mexico and Canada/United States has not decreased in the past few years.

### Obstacles to Security Cooperation in North America 179

*Table 10.1* Comparison of the Three North American Countries

|  | Democracy index | | Corruption perceptions | | Government effectiveness | |
|---|---|---|---|---|---|---|
|  | 2011 | 2006 | 2011 | 2000 | 2010 | 2000 |
| Canada | 9.08 | 9.07 | 8.70 | 9.20 | 1.87 | 1.96 |
| United States | 8.11 | 8.22 | 7.10 | 7.80 | 1.44 | 1.86 |
| Mexico | 6.93 | 6.67 | 3.00 | 3.30 | 0.17 | 0.23 |

*Sources*: Democracy index developed by Economist Intelligence Unit (Index between 1 and 10); corruption perception index developed by Transparency International (index between 0 and 10); and government effectiveness developed by the World Bank (index between –2.5 and 2.5).

The initial assumption of the lack of homogeneity of domestic institutions helps to build the main argument of this chapter, in which there is a sequence between perceptions and principles, on the one hand, and the security policies implemented by the three countries in North America, on the other. Nonetheless, following Alexander Wendt, actors or agents have the "creative capacity" to transform regional structures if two conditions are met: there must be a reason to think of oneself in novel terms and the expected costs of intentional role change cannot be greater than its rewards.[10] Thus, if both conditions are met and following Wendt's reasoning, countries can change and produce a security system when a transformative process occurs on three different levels: breakdown of consensus, critical examination and new practices. In the case of the end of the Cold War, the first stage of intentional transformation was the breakdown of consensus about the identity commitment centered on the Leninist theory of imperialism. The breakdown of consensus made possible a second stage of critical examination of old ideas about self and other and, by extension, of the structures of interaction by which the ideas have been sustained. The result of such a critique was the identification of new "possible selves" and aspirations and hence new forms of interaction with the region and the world.[11] The emerging regional systems can take three different forms: a) competitive security systems, which are sustained by practices that create insecurity and distrust; b) individualistic systems states in which states are self-regarding about their security but are concerned primarily with absolute gains rather than relative; and c) "cooperative" security systems, in which states identify positively with one another so that the security of each is perceived as the responsibility of all.

In North America, there is no evidence of a regional system nor a breakdown of the consensus of the *status quo* of the two security systems in the region, which are the coexistence of a cooperative system (US and Canada) and an individualistic system (US/Canada and Mexico). In other words, when one adopts the model developed by Wendt, two out of the three systems prevail in North America: individualistic and cooperative. The cooperation

180    *Roberto Domínguez and Rafael Velázquez*

between the United States and Canada resembles the cooperative security system in which states identify themselves positively with one another and the parties are able to share and build common institutions, and the security of each is perceived as the responsibility of all. Conversely, the security relationships between the United States and Mexico as well as between Canada and Mexico are guided by the rationale of an individualist security system, in which states are ambiguous in the identification with one another, cooperation is limited as a result of distrust and security is perceived as an individual responsibility based on the rationale of absolute gains. The remainder of this chapter will address why these three countries have prioritized bilateral cooperation rather than trilateral cooperation by looking at perceptions, principles and policies in the area of security cooperation.

## IDEAS AND PERCEPTIONS

Several scholars have argued that ideas are central elements to changing the orientation of security institutions.[12] The wave of creating a security community in North America lasted from the late 1990s to the mid-2000s among scholars of regional and security governance. While think tanks and scholars embraced the viability of the regional community, the governments and elites responded cautiously and unenthusiastically. This wave, however, paved the way for dialogues between two different schools of ideas on the scope of a North American regional community: from a minimalist approach, the proposal was a superficial adaptation of NAFTA limited to the United States and Canada; from a maximalist view, a European Union–like entity was suggested, or a combination of both.[13]

## IDEAS FOR A NORTH AMERICAN COMMUNITY

In Mexico, for many years, the idea of a North American community was rejected due to the economic disparities between Mexico and the United States and the nationalistic approach of Mexican foreign policy. The idea of deeper economic interdependence with the United States was shaped by the financial crisis of the early 1980s, followed by the liberalization of the Mexican economy. The Salinas administration (1988–1994) then promoted the idea of economic integration with North America and signed NAFTA in 1992. Mexico and the United States understood that the North American community was limited to trade and investment and that security matters were not considered due to the historical record of US interference in Mexican affairs, the consequential reactive nationalistic approach of Mexican foreign policy and the Mexican government's distrust of US authorities. Even in the case of the North American Common Market, the consensus was to include free movement of goods, investments and services,[14] leaving migration or

*Obstacles to Security Cooperation in North America* 181

free movement of people off the negotiating table due to the opposition of most of the political spectrum in the United States.

President Vicente Fox (2000–2006) advocated deepening the North American integration process to include free movement of people and the creation of development funds, as it had been done in the European Union.[15] In particular, the Fox administration put forward an immigration agreement between Mexico and the United States to regulate the legal status of Mexican migrants. This proposal was known as NAFTA-Plus. However, the idea did not reverberate in the United States and Canada. After the 9/11 attacks in the United States, President Fox was ready to cooperate with the United States in the war against international terrorism, but he did not support President Bush's initiative to launch an attack on Iraq in 2003. This in turn cooled down the bilateral enthusiasm for further cooperation in the area of security. While day-to-day cooperation regarding security at lower government levels continued, it not was until 2005 when Mexico, the United States and Canada resumed cooperation in the area of security with the signing of the Security and Prosperity Partnership (SPP). However, this has produced very limited results. Neither President Barack Obama after 2008 nor his counterpart President Felipe Calderon showed much interest in continuing to strengthening the SPP. The political capital of President Obama was focused on ending the war in Iraq, while that of President Calderon was focused on the war against drug trafficking and organized crime. As a result, both countries preferred to continue working on the bilateral approach through the Merida Initiative, which has been one of the most visible mechanisms for cooperation between Mexico and the United States to combat drug trafficking. Thus far, the implementation of NAFTA has not furthered the development of security trilateral institutions, while a thematic regional agenda has failed to materialize in recent years.

Despite the lack of progress in the regionalization of security in North America, the role of Canada as a member of the North American region is often the subject of debate in Canadian academic and business circles. The discussion on the future of North America was triggered by the Big Idea, proposed by Wendy Dobson.[16] She argues that Canada and Mexico should facilitate US security goals, and in return the United States should commit to maintaining open borders even in the aftermath of an attack. Specifically, she recommends the consideration of a "strategic bargain," a "pragmatic mix of customs-union-like and common market-like proposals plus Canadian initiatives" in areas of strength that are of particular interest for Americans. In the case of the US-Canadian security relationship, Dobson proposes the following: a) investing in the border in order to make it more secure with fewer obstacles; b) mutual recognition of the security of immigration from third countries; c) energy as part of bilateral security; and d) a more active role for Canada with bilateral military defense. Likewise, she suggests that Canadians should proceed bilaterally, but be open to including Mexico

# 182    *Roberto Domínguez and Rafael Velázquez*

when it makes sense. Barnett and Williams[17] reject the Big Idea approach. They suggest that engaging in high-profile bilateral negotiations may well be a disadvantage for the weaker state, Canada. They urge a bilateral process in which the issues are addressed in an incremental and pragmatic manner. In this regard, they summarize their approach by focusing on the following areas: a) expanding successful approaches, such as the Smart Border Declaration; b) encouraging security cooperation; c) working towards a common external tariff; and d) identifying mutual interests in international trade negotiations. Along the same lines, in 2003 the Canadian Council of Chief Executives (CCCE) presented a strategy for advancing the Canadian-United States relationship. This strategy, entitled "Security and Prosperity: The Dynamics of a New Canada-United States Partnership in North America," or the "Treaty of North America," is based on five interlocking pillars: reinventing the border; maximizing economic efficiencies; building on resource security; sharing in continental and global security; and developing new institutions for managing the bilateral relationship.[18]

In a very comprehensive proposal and contrary to minimalist approaches to integration in North America, Robert Pastor presents his project of the North American community. Considering the pros and cons of European integration, he proposes the North American community that would emphasize institutional development at the regional level as well as with the creation of compensatory mechanisms to reduce the gap between Mexico and its two NAFTA partners.[19] In this regard, three institutions could be created. Unlike the European Commission, a North American Commission should be "lean and advisory, made up of just 15 distinguished individuals, five from each country."[20] Likewise, a single North American Inter-Parliamentary Group would merge the bilateral interparliamentary groups with a problem-solving approach. The third institution would be a Permanent Court on Trade and Investment, which would "permit the accumulation of precedent." Along with these institutions, a North American Customs Union and a North American Customs and Immigration Force would contribute to enhance trade exchanges and security. Perhaps one of the most important features of this proposal is that of the North American Investment Fund, which would invest US$200 billion in infrastructure over the next decade on the condition that Mexico would increase its tax revenue from 11 to 16 percent of its GDP.

## PERCEPTIONS OF THREATS

The information available from the public opinion surveys of the Chicago Council on Global Affairs from 2004 to 2010 indicates that two threats have been permanently ranked among the five top priorities within the United States: international terrorism and the possibility of unfriendly countries becoming nuclear powers. The US dependence on foreign oil, or disruption of

## Obstacles to Security Cooperation in North America 183

energy supply, was ranked among the top five priorities in 2006, 2008 and 2010, while violent Islamist groups in Pakistan and Afghanistan were salient in 2008 and 2010, and Iran's nuclear program was included as the third threat in 2010. While the main perceptions of threats in the United States stem from global sources and hence reflect the global role of the United States, two critical threats related to the North American region and more precisely to Mexico have also been included in this survey: drug-related violence and instability in Mexico were ranked eleventh in 2010, and the large numbers of immigrants and refugees coming into the United States were ranked fifth in 2004, fourth in 2006 and sixth in 2008.

In the case of Mexico, according to the "Mexico, the Americas, and the World 2010" survey, the main threat for national security is drug trafficking/ organized crime, which was ranked as the number one threat in 2010, with 82 percent of respondents identifying them as a "grave threat."[21] This perception has been consistent over the four editions of the survey (2004, 2006, 2008 and 2010), which reiterate that, unlike the United States, the main source of threat in Mexico is domestic. Other high-ranked threats in the 2010 survey are weapons trafficking (ranked fifth), nuclear weapons (ranked seventh) and international terrorism (ranked eighth) as an intermediate threat. In a regional context, Mexicans are less worried about border conflicts (ranked tenth), territorial disputes (ranked eleventh) and instability in neighboring countries (ranked twelfth).

Canada also perceives threats in a different way based on two public opinion polls. In the view of the Environics Institute,[22] the ranking of threats was the following in 2010: environment (16 percent); starvation (16 percent); war (14 percent); economy (14 percent); and terrorism (6 percent). According to the Canadian Defence and Foreign Affairs Institute, public perceptions have changed greatly regarding threats to the vital interests of Canada. Climate change dominates the agenda, while terrorism and potential epidemics have almost disappeared from Canadians' radar screens.[23] Roughly, 50 percent of Canadians deems that climate change is a critical threat to the vital interests of the country in the next ten years (49 percent in 2010 versus 52 percent in 2004). On the other hand, almost a quarter of the Canadian public (28 percent in 2010 versus 49 percent in 2004) considers international terrorism as a vital threat, which represents a figure below the one registered in 2004. In the case of migration, the concern over the number of immigrants and refugees has grown since 2004 (27 percent in 2010 versus 21 percent in 2004).

There is thus a significant difference in perceptions among the three countries in North America: Mexico perceives organized crime as the main threat, the United States reflects its threats as a result of its global role and Canada is focused on more soft security issues, such as climate change. While these different perceptions do not preclude security cooperation, they produce some obstacles for reaching significant consensus at the trilateral level.

## PRINCIPLES OF ACTION

The perceptions of security priorities in the three countries are one of the main influences on shaping the principles enacted in the guiding documents of security policies. In the case of the United States, the evaluation of the US strategies towards Mexico and Canada entails two distinct approaches. The 2010 *National Security Strategy* (NSS) identifies weapons of mass destruction and far-reaching networks of hatred and violence, and hence terrorism, as the main threats for the United States. While the NSS identifies North America as a region and advocates to "change the way we think about our shared borders, in order to secure and expedite the lawful and legitimate flow of people and goods while interdicting transnational threat[s] that threaten our open societies,"[24] the document continues and differentiates the approach of security to both neighboring countries:

> With Canada, our security cooperation includes our defense of North America and our efforts through NATO overseas . . . With Mexico, in addition to trade cooperation, we are working together to identify and interdict threats at the earliest opportunity, even before they reach North America. Stability and security in Mexico are indispensable to building a strong economic partnership, fighting the illicit drug and arms trade, and promoting sound immigration policy.[25]

Another essential document that enshrines the differentiated US perceptions of Mexico and Canada is the 2011 *Strategy to Combat Transnational Organized Crime*.[26] While there are no specific references to North America as a region, Canada is mentioned within the actions of sharing criminal intelligence and enhancing cooperation with groups such as the "Quintet of Attorneys-General" and the "Strategic Alliance Group," this last one being established with the United Kingdom, Canada, New Zealand and Australia. On the other hand, threats are emphasized when Mexico is mentioned. Initially, the document underscored the historic campaign of the Mexican government against transnational crime organizations. Later, the 2011 *Strategy* acknowledges that the demand for illicit drugs, both in the United States and abroad, fuels the power, impunity and violence of criminal organizations around the globe and that Mexican drug-trafficking organizations (DTOs) are escalating their violence to consolidate their market share within the Western Hemisphere, protect their operations in Mexico and expand their reach into the United States. It also describes the links between criminal networks and illicit arms dealers and the fact that the US federal law enforcement agencies have intercepted large numbers of weapons or other related items being smuggled into China, Russia, Mexico, the Philippines, Somalia, Turkmenistan and Yemen. Finally, the document states that transnational organized crime (TOC) in Mexico makes the US border more vulnerable because it creates and maintains illicit corridors for border crossings

## Obstacles to Security Cooperation in North America   185

that can be employed by other secondary criminal or terrorist actors or organizations.

Two official documents are significant in the review of Mexican national security principles: the National Development Plan (NDP)[27] and the National Program of Public Security 2008–2012 (NPPS).[28] Both documents indicate that Mexican officials focus on domestic issues rather than regional or global matters. The NPPS does not even mention the region of North America, nor the United States or Canada. According to this document, Mexico's national security policy is based on the following goals: to prevent criminal activities, to openly combat crime, to consolidate the rule of law, to improve technology to fight against organized crime, to professionalize police corporations and to reform the institutions in charge of combating crime. The NDP, similarly, while emphasizing the same goals, asserts that the Mexican government has to promote international cooperation to face organized crime, but this has to be carried out under the principles of "defense of sovereignty, territorial integrity and legal equality of States."[29] The NDP does not refer to North America as a region, nor does it establish particular strategies towards Canada or the United States. It mentions the northern neighbor only when it sets goals and strategies on border matters, particularly in the exchange of information for border security. In this regard, Mexico's policy against potential threats is based on a local vision and does not emphasize regional cooperation.

In the case of Canada, a report titled *Securing an Open Society: Canada's National Security Policy* was released in 2004 and served as the "first-ever policy of its kind"[30] to outline Canada's core national security interests and to design a plan to face the security threats deemed most serious. The report was reassessed in 2005 through the publishing of *Securing an Open Society: One Year Later*, in which the government of Canada reinforces the notion that the country's security policy revolves around three core interests: protecting Canada and the safety and security of Canadians; ensuring Canada is not a base for threats to its allies; and contributing to international security.[31] The report, which enshrines Canada's national security policy, focuses on six key areas: intelligence, emergency planning, public health emergencies, transportation security, border security and international security. While four of these priorities are mostly of a domestic nature, border security and international security are priorities that relate to Canada's role in the regional and international arena. With regard to border security, the Canadian government highlights the importance of Canada-US border programs, such as the Smart Border Declaration and the Free and Secure Trade (FAST) program. The report expresses the country's interest in developing the next generation of the border agenda with both Mexico and the United States, building on the success of the Smart Border Declaration. At the same time, Canada highlights its participation in UN and NATO operations. Regarding international security, the highest priority is placed on three key points: international terrorism; proliferation of weapons of mass destruction; and

## 186 *Roberto Domínguez and Rafael Velázquez*

failed and failing states and intra- and interstate conflict. In its 2005 update report, Canada lists as one of its priorities the revitalization of its North American partnership with Mexico and the United States "by enhancing security and promoting prosperity."[32] It sets out to work together to establish "a common approach to security to protect North America from external threats, prevent and respond to threats within North America, and further streamline the secure and efficient movement of legitimate, low-risk traffic across our shared borders."[33]

## POLICIES

Perceptions and principles aim to be transformed into policies in order to ameliorate challenges to stability. From the perspective of regional cooperation, the United States and Canada have developed more security policy instruments than the United States and Mexico. While the mutual trust is deeper in the former and both countries have traditionally cooperated in military and border management, in the latter there is a mutual distrust that has hampered further security cooperation.

## United States-Canada

Security military cooperation between the United States and Canada can be traced back to the North American Aerospace Defense Command (NORAD) in 1957. The NORAD commander, located in Colorado Springs, is responsible to the Canadian prime minister and the US president. As a result of the 9/11 attacks, NORAD was incorporated in the US Northern Command (NORTHCOM) mission to dissuade, prevent and confront threats directed towards the United States. The cooperation between NORAD and NORTH-COM has in fact provided the incentives for closer military cooperation between both countries to protect not only the air, but also the coastal and territorial space.[34] While some differences persist with regard to the global war on terror, Canada has deployed a military presence in Afghanistan alongside US and other NATO troops.

With regard to border cooperation, after the events of 9/11, the United States and Canada negotiated and signed the 32-point Smart Border Declaration in December 2001, a mechanism to simultaneously maintain the intensive trade exchange and protect the border. Bilateral cooperation has evolved in a more constructive way ever since, creating several instruments such as the Integrated Border Enforcement Team (IBET), which consists of the Royal Canadian Mounted Police, the Canada Border Services Agency, the US Border Patrol, the US Immigration and Customs Enforcement and the US Coast Guard. As of February 2012, there were 24 IBET units playing a critical role in maintaining the integrity and security of bilateral borders by assisting in national security investigations and combating organized crime and other

*Obstacles to Security Cooperation in North America* 187

criminal activities. On several occasions, the Royal Canadian Mounted Police (RCMP) and the US Coast Guard have collaborated on a special marine security project known as "Ship Rider," targeting cross-border criminal activity on our shared waters.[35]

## United States-Mexico

The distrust between Mexico and the United States operates in two directions. On the one hand, in light of the structural weaknesses of the Mexican state as a security provider, the United States is inclined to adopt unilateral policies; on the other, as a result of the history of US interventionism in Mexico and the disparity of power between the two countries, Mexico has been reluctant to cooperate in the area of security. Against this background, drug trafficking has been one of the main sources of threat in the bilateral relationship. The power amassed by drug-trafficking organizations (DTOs) has challenged the ability of the Mexican government to curb corruption in the forces fighting the phenomenon.[36] Due to its illegal nature, the magnitude of the economic power of drug-trafficking organizations is unclear and the estimates vary depending on the sources and the calculation method: the US Justice Department estimates that the profit of Mexican and Colombian cartels could reach between US\$18 and 39 billion from drug sales in the United States each year; the RAND Corporation calculates that all Mexican cartels generate close to US\$7 billion; and the Mexican Secretariat of Public Security speculated that the cartels spend more than US\$1 billion each year just to bribe the municipal police.[37]

The inability of the Mexican government to deal with the power of DTOs has produced operations that either implicitly or explicitly illustrate the distrust of the US government of the Mexican government as a reliable partner. Such operations include Operation Intercept (1969), which consisted of exhaustive searches of vehicles entering the United States through the Mexican border; Second Operation Intercept (1985), which was implemented two weeks after Enrique Camarena, an agent of the Drug Enforcement Agency (DEA), was abducted in Guadalajara; and Operation Casablanca (1998), which was developed by the DEA and the Treasury Department to uncover banks engaged in money laundering without informing the Mexican government. Another sign of distrust came to light as a result of the assassination of a US Border Patrol agent in December of 2010 with guns connected to the Fast and Furious Operation. This operation consisted of 2,000 weapons that the Bureau of Alcohol, Tobacco, Firearms and Explosives purposefully did not seize between 2009 and 2011 and allowed to be imported into Mexico by illegal buyers known as "straw purchasers."[38] In this context, based on cables made available by Wikileaks in 2012, the US ambassador to Mexico, Carlos Pascual, put into question "the ability of the Mexican army to pursue drug-trafficking organizations, warned about poor coordination among local security forces, and complained about official corruption, among other statements."[39]

188 *Roberto Domínguez and Rafael Velázquez*

While US unilateral actions have produced tensions in the bilateral relationship, sequential post facto dialogues have been produced as remedies to alleviate distrust and eventually have paved the way for temporary cooperation. Some examples are the following: the creation of the bilateral High Level Contact Group (1996) after the unilateral Casablanca Operation; the establishment of Operation Falcon (1990) after the kidnap of Alvarez Machain; and Operations Cooperation and Condor after the unilateral Operation Intercept.[40] A turning point in the bilateral cooperation is the Merida Initiative (MI) because this is the first time the United States provided military and police assistance to Mexico. In qualitative terms, the MI implies a change in perception in the bilateral relationship. On the one hand, the US government acknowledges that the United States is corresponsive for the violence that has occurred in Mexico due to the high levels of drug consumption in the United States. On the other, the Mexican government also recognizes that the country needs the help of its northern neighbor to fight against organized crime. Thirty years ago, it would have been difficult for the Mexican government to resort to US help in security matters. In quantitative terms, however, the MI does not represent a significant amount of money because the US government contributes only $1.2 billion for three years (2007–2010). This amount is insufficient compared to the Mexican challenge of drug trafficking. More precisely, the following elements are included in the MI: a) nonintrusive inspection equipment, b) software to improve communications, c) training for investigators and prosecutors, d) introduction of a witness protection program, e) thirteen Bell 412 EP utility helicopters and eight much larger UH-60 Black Hawk transport helicopters, f) four Spanish-built CASA CN-235 planes and g) antigang equipment.[41]

While the progress made by the MI is modest, it has paved the way for further cooperation. The most graphic example of the widening US support for President Calderon's strategy was the confirmation in March 2011 that the US Predator and Global Hawk drones were flying over Mexican territory in an effort to locate suspected drug traffickers and track their movements.[42] Likewise, the Department of Defense (DoD) increased its counternarcotics support to Mexico by 17-fold from funding levels of US$3 million per year before 2009 to US$51 million in fiscal year 2011, according to a top Pentagon official.[43]

In the case of border cooperation between the United States and Mexico, both countries signed the Border Partnership in March 2002. In 2006, amid rising crime on the southwest border, the US Immigration and Customs Enforcement (ICE) and the US Customs Border Protection (CBP) worked with other federal, state, local and foreign partners to establish the Border Enforcement Security Task Force (BEST), designed to attack TOC networks that exploit the bilateral border. Since then, this initiative has grown to 21 BESTs arrayed along the southwest and northern borders as well as at major seaports. These BESTs have seized more than 36,000 pounds of cocaine, 550 pounds of heroin, 485,000 pounds of marijuana, 4,300 weapons and

Obstacles to Security Cooperation in North America    189

US\$68 million, and led to the arrests of 5,910 individuals. The US-Mexico 21st Century Border Action Plan is also under negotiation to strengthen bilateral cooperation in the area of security.

## Mexico-Canada

There are a few bilateral actions between Mexico and Canada in the area of security. Before NAFTA was implemented, trade and security relations between Mexico and Canada were even more marginal. Despite some intrinsic nationalistic views on foreign policy in both countries,[44] Canada and Mexico started widening their ties in several issues, including security, after NAFTA came into force. Following the events of 9/11, both countries cooperated with the United States in its efforts against international terrorism. However, Mexico and Canada opposed backing up the United States in 2003 at the UN Security Council when Washington was forming an international coalition to attack Iraq. The reluctance of Mexico and Canada during the invasion of Iraq distanced them from the Bush administration and undermined the prospects of developing a regional common view to deal with the use of force to combat international terrorism.

In light of the violence in Mexico, Canada has implemented programs to exchange information with the Mexican government on drug trafficking and to train Mexican police forces.[45] However, as the drug war in Mexico intensified, the number of Mexicans applying for refugee status in Canada increased from a steady 1,000 a year to a peak of 9,309 in 2008, according to Langton's calculation.[46] In his view, as the increasing number of applications came through British Columbia, this wave of migrants was correlated to an attempt to traffic BC Bud marijuana through the comparatively more relaxed Canadian border. As a result, in July 2009, the Canadian government required Mexican nationals to apply for visas to visit Canada, an action that was not welcomed by the Mexican government.

## Trilateral

At the trilateral level, the Security and Prosperity Partnership (SPP) was signed in 2005. Unfortunately, due to the lack of interest and incentive by the three countries to develop a broader scheme of security cooperation, observers agree that the SPP failed to deliver specific policies[47] and that the security relationship in North America remains focused on bilateral relations. While the SPP developed working groups in the area of prosperity, the activity in the area of security was practically absent. There was also strong criticism in the three countries against the SPP. In Canada, the New Democratic Party censured the SPP openly since it considered it a liberal initiative that attacked Canada's sovereignty.[48] In the United States, there were a variety of conservative movements that opposed further integration with Mexico at all levels. For example, they deem illegal migrants a threat

## 190 *Roberto Domínguez and Rafael Velázquez*

to US national security and reject deeper integration that includes the free movement of people in the region. In Mexico, there are also nationalistic and left-wing groups that are against a broader integration with the United States because they consider the United States to be violating Mexico's sovereignty regarding security issues.

The change in the presidential administrations of the United States and Mexico was also a factor that undermined the initial cooperative impetus of the SPP. When Barack Obama was sworn in as president, there was little interest in Washington to deepen the SPP due to the 2008 economic crisis as well as the redefinition of the strategies in Iraq and Afghanistan. In Mexico, President Felipe Calderon cautiously approached the relationship with the United States by readjusting the priorities of the bilateral agenda. Unlike his predecessor, Vicente Fox, President Calderon decided to confront DTOs, toned down issues of migration, canceled the Binational Commission, a high-level cabinet mechanism to address key issues in the bilateral agenda, and suggested removing the US ambassador to Mexico in 2011. Against this background, the MI came to be a more effective instrument of security cooperation in comparison to the trilateral SPP. The silver lining aspect of the SPP is the practice of annual summits, which are opportunities to sustain a regular dialogue in North America, but still with insufficient tangible outcomes. For instance, in the sixth North American Leaders Summit in 2012, President Calderon urged President Obama and Prime Minister Harper to continue and strengthen their efforts against weapons trafficking and to reduce the demand for drugs.[49]

## CONCLUSION

Several scholars have argued that there is no trilateral security relationship in North America,[50] but rather a gravitational center represented by the United States exerting pressure over Mexico and Canada to the point that US security interests dominate the regional agenda.[51] Due to different ideas, perceptions, principles of actions, and policies in the three countries, the prospects of building a security community in North America are still feeble. Today, two bilateral security communities are clearly delineated in the region: Canada-United States and Mexico-United States. The first one has been able to develop more institutions of cooperation, while the second one has found several obstacles to strengthening weak institutions. A third relationship, between Mexico and Canada, remains underdeveloped, but tends to align along the rationale of distrust in Mexican effectiveness to deal with security.

From the policy-making standpoint, the different perceptions of threats to individual security percolate to the entire region. While the expectation would be to develop regional security instruments, the three countries are skeptical of further trilateral cooperation. While the range of cooperation goes from cyber-security to combating terrorism, one of the central threats

## Obstacles to Security Cooperation in North America    191

in the region emerges from drug-trafficking activities, particularly in Mexico due to the more than 50,000 deaths since 2006. In this regard, as an example of the complexity of policy coordination in the region, mechanisms to improve regional cooperation demand the active engagement of national and regional actors. For instance, in order to improve the effectiveness of the MI and the policies against drug trafficking, based on the experience of Plan Colombia and the analyses of Kenny and Serrano,[52] Felbab-Brown[53] and Felbab-Brown and Olson,[54] it would be pertinent to consider the adoption of the following elements in the case of Mexico: first, focusing on violent but common crime such as kidnapping, extortion and homicide; second, developing the political strategies to galvanize political support around the MI; third, implementing a comprehensive police reform and expanding the public prosecutor office's investigative capacities; fourth, building up the capacity of police and prosecutors to target not only high-value targets, but also the middle layer of criminal organizations (the lawyers, accountants and lieutenants in waiting) that are the pillars of their operations; and fifth, developing socioeconomic policies parallel with the use of force.

From the bilateral/regional perspective, the actions of the Mexican government must be accompanied by US policies for reducing the domestic demand of drugs. It is calculated that there has been a 57 percent rise in the US national drug control budget for supply-suppression programs between 2002 and 2008, while the demand reduction grew only 2.7 percent in the same period.[55] The other area to effectively deter violence is that of the traffic of arms. As a point of comparison, the United States has 54,000 legal firearms dealers, Canada has about 520 and Mexico has only one, strictly controlled by the army.[56] Finally, the debate on decriminalization of some drugs must be coordinated by the three countries because "there is no way that Mexico could get away with unilaterally decriminalizing possession, commerce, and consumption of drugs in Mexico if the United States did not do the same thing."[57] In sum, as noted in the example of drug trafficking, trilateral cooperation must be perceived as a collective good and a win-win game in favor of the security of all of the citizens of North America.

## NOTES

1. Robert Pastor, *Toward a North American Community: Lessons from the Old Word to the New* (Washington, DC: Institute for International Economics, 2001); Robert Pastor, *The North American Idea: A Vision of a Continental Future* (New York: Oxford University Press, 2011).
2. Bela Balassa, *The Theory of Economic Integration* (Homewood, IL: Richard D. Irwin, 1961).
3. Alexander Wendt, "Anarchy Is What States Make of It: The Social Construction of Power Politics," *International Organization* 46, no. 2 (1992): 391–425.
4. Guadalupe González and Stephan Haggard, "The United States and Mexico: A Pluralistic Security Community," in *Security Communities*, ed. Emanuel Adler (Cambridge: Cambridge University Press, 1998), 295–332.

## 192  Roberto Domínguez and Rafael Velázquez

5. Brian Bow, "North America as an Emergent Regional Security Complex" (paper presented at the International Studies Association, New Orleans, February 19–20, 2010).
6. Barry Buzan and Ole Weaver, *Regions and Powers: The Structure of International Security* (Cambridge: Cambridge University Press, 2003).
7. Robert Pastor, "Beyond NAFTA: The Emergence and Future of North America," in *Politics of North America: Redefining Continental Relations*, ed. Yasmeen Abu-Laban, Radha Jhappan and Fancois Rocher (Peterborough: Broadview, 2008), 461–476.
8. See introduction to this book by Genna and Mayer-Foulkes.
9. Yi Feng and Gaspare M. Genna, "Regional Integration and Domestic Institutional Homogeneity: A Comparative Analysis of Regional Integration in the Americas, Pacific Asia and Western Europe," *Review of International Political Economy* 10, no. 2 (2003): 278–309.
10. Wendt, "Anarchy,"419.
11. Ibid., 419–421.
12. Richard Ned Lebow and Janice Gross Stein, *We All Lost the Cold War* (Princeton: Princeton University Press, 1994); see also Wendt, "Anarchy."
13. Roberto Domínguez, "NAFTA: Assessments and Institutional Development," in *The European Union and Regional Integration A Comparative Perspective and Lessons for the Americas*, ed. Joaquín Roy and Roberto Domínguez (Miami: Jean Monnet Chair University of Miami-European Commission, 2005) 23–36.
14. José Flores Salgado and Federico Novelo Urdanivia, "Hacia el mercado común norteamericano," *Análisis Económico* 25, no. 58 (2010): 185–207.
15. Isidro Morales, *Post-NAFTA North America: Reshaping the Economic and Political Governance of a Changing Region* (Basingstoke, UK: Palgrave Macmillan, 2008), 124.
16. Wendy Dobson, "Shaping the Future of the North American Economic Space: A Framework for Action," *Commentary: The Border Papers* 162 (2002), 1–32.
17. Charles Barnett and Hugh Williams, "Renewing the Relationship: Canada and the United States in the 21st Century" (Conference Board of Canada Briefing, Ottawa, February 2003).
18. Thomas D'Aquino, "Security and Prosperity: The Dynamics of a New Canada-United States Partnership in North America" (paper presented to the Annual General Meeting of the Canadian Council of Chief Executives, Toronto, January 14, 2003).
19. Pastor, *North American Idea*.
20. Ibid, 463.
21. Guadalupe González, Jorge A Schiavon, David Crow and Gerardo Maldonado, *Mexico, the Americas, and the World 2010, Foreign Policy: Public Opinion and Leaders* (Mexico City: Centro de Investigación y Docencia Económicas, 2011), accessed February 20, 2012, http://mexicoyelmundo. cide.edu/2010/reporteingles10.pdf.
22. Environics Institute, *Focus Canada 2010 Public Opinion Research on the Record: Serving the Public Interest* (Toronto: Environics Institute for Survey Research, 2010), accessed November 12, 2012, http://www.queensu.ca/cora/_files/fc2010report.pdf.
23. Canadian Defence and Foreign Affairs Institute, "Threat Perceptions in Canada," 2010, accessed June 1, 2012, http://www.cdfai.org/PDF/Poll%20on%20Threat%20Perceptions%20in%20Canada.pdf.
24. White House, *National Security Strategy* (Washington, DC: 2010), accessed February 23, 2012, http://www.whitehouse.gov/sites/default/files/rss_viewer/national_security_strategy.pdf, 42.

## Obstacles to Security Cooperation in North America 193

25. Ibid., 42–43.
26. White House, *Strategy to Combat Transnational Organized Crime: Addressing Converging Threats to National Security* (Washington, DC: 2011), accessed July 23, 2011, http://www.whitehouse.gov/sites/default/files/Strategy_to_Combat_Transnational_Organized_Crime_July_2011.pdf.
27. Presidencia de la República, "Plan Nacional de Desarrollo," 2006, accessed April 12, 2012, http://pnd.presidencia.gob.mx/.
28. Secretaría de Seguridad Pública, *Programa Nacional de Seguridad Pública 2008–2012* (Mexico City, 2008), accessed March 15, 2012, http://www.ssp.df.gob.mx/TransparenciaSSP/MAdmvoVarios/5Planes%20PNSP%202008_2012.pdf.
29. Presidencia de la República, "Plan Nacional."
30. Public Safety Canada, *Securing an Open Society: Canada's National Security Policy* (Ottawa, 2004), accessed July 2, 2012, http://www.publicsafety.gc.ca/pol/ns/secpol04-eng.aspx.
31. Government of Canada, *Securing an Open Society: One Year Later* (Privy Council Office, 2005), accessed June 25, 2012, http://www.pco-bcp.gc.ca/docs/information/publications/aarchives/secure/secure-eng.pdf.
32. Ibid., 48.
33. Ibid., 49.
34. Athanasios Hristoulas, "Whatever Happened to the North America Security Perimeter?" (paper presented at the International Studies Association, New Orleans, February 19–20, 2010).
35. Royal Canadian Mounted Police (RCMP), "Border Integrity," 2010, accessed January 20, 2012, http://www.rcmp-grc.gc.ca/bi-if/index-eng.htm.
36. Jorge Chabat, "Drug Trafficking and the United States-Mexico Relations," in *Mexico's Security Failure, Collapse into Criminal Violence*, ed. Paul Kenny and Monica Serrano (New York: Routledge, 2012), 143–160.
37. Patrick Radden Keefe, "Cocaine Incorporated," *New York Times*, June 15, 2012.
38. Ed O'Keefe, "Rep. Issa Says No Proof White House Withheld Information in 'Fast and Furious' Inquiry," *Washington Post*, June 25, 2012.
39. Economist Intelligence Unit, "Mexico/USA: Clouded Relationship," *Business Latin America*, April 11, 2011, 1–2.
40. Chabat, "Drug Trafficking."
41. Jerry Langton, *Gangland: The Rise of the Mexican Drug Cartels from El Paso to Vancouver* (Mississauga, ON: John Wiley & Son, 2012), 121.
42. Ted Galen Carpenter, "Mexico Sours on Drug War," *National Interest*, November 16, 2011, accessed December 2, 2012, http://nationalinterest.org/commentary/mexico-sours-drug-war-6160.
43. E. Mora, "DoD to Increase Counter-Narcotics Support for Mexico 17-Fold Despite Mexican Security Forces Committing Unlawful Killings," CNSNews.com, April 12, 2012, accessed June 4, 2012, http://cnsnews.com/news/article/dod-increase-counter-narcotics-support-mexico-17-fold-despite-mexican-security-forces.
44. Raul Benitez and Athanasios Hristoulas, "México y Canadá: El reto de enfrentarse al crimen organizado," in *Canadá y México: La Agenda Pendiente*, ed. Alex Bugailiskis and Andrés Rozental (Toronto: McGill-Queen's University Press, 2012), 227–238.
45. Reid Morden, "Seguridad hemisférica: El dilema Canadá-México," in *Canadá y México: La Agenda Pendiente*, ed. Alex Bugailiskis and Andrés Rozental (Toronto: McGill-Queen's University Press, 2012), 219–226.
46. Langton, *Gangland*, 176–177.
47. Hristoulas, "Whatever Happened."

48. New Democrats Party (NDP), "New Democrats Celebrates Victory over SPP," 2009, accessed January 24, 2012, http://www.ndp.ca/press/new-democrats-celebrates-victory-over-spp.
49. Dan Robinson, "North American Leaders' Summit Focuses on Economy, Drugs, Trade," Voice of America, April 1, 2012, accessed May 25, 2012, http://www.voanews.com/content/economy-security-lead-north-american-summit-agenda-145814975/179460.html.
50. Stephen Clarkson, *Does North America Exist?* (Toronto: University of Toronto Press, 2008); Christina Gabriel and Laura MacDonald, "From the 49th Parallel to the Río Grande: U.S. Homeland Security and North American Borders," in *North American Politics: Globalization and Culture*, ed. Yasmeen Abu-Laban, Radha Jhappan and Francois Rocher (Peterborough: Broadview, 2007), 353–370; Peter Andreas, "A Tale of Two Borders: The U.S.-Mexico and U.S.-Canada Lines after 9–11," in *The Rebordering of North America: Integration and Exclusion in a New Security Context*, ed. Peter Andreas and Thomas Biersteker (New York: Routledge, 2003), 1–23.
51. Athanasios Hristoulas and Stephane Roussel, "North America Security and Foreign Policy: Does a Trilateral Community Exist?" in *North American Politics: Globalization and Culture*, ed. Yasmeen Abu-Laban, Radha Jhappan and Francois Rocher (Peterborough: Broadview, 2007), 371–388.
52. Paul Kenny and Monica Serrano, eds., *Mexico's Security Failure, Collapse into Criminal Violence* (New York: Routledge, 2012).
53. Vanda Felbab-Brown, "Lessons from Colombia for Mexico?" *ReVista: Harvard Review of Latin America* 11, no. 2 (Winter 2012): 48–51.
54. Vanda Felbab-Brown and Eric Olson, "A Better Strategy to Combat Organized Crime in Mexico and Central America," *Brookings Up Front* (blog), April 13, 2012, accessed November 24, 2012, http://www.brookings.edu/blogs/up-front/posts/2012/04/13-crime-central-america-felbabbrown.
55. Woodrow Wilson Center, *The United States and Mexico: Towards a Strategic Partnership. A Report of Four Working Groups on US-Mexico Relations* (Washington, DC: Woodrow Wilson International Center for Scholars, Mexico Institute, 2009), 15.
56. Langton, *Gangland*.
57. Jorge Castaneda, "Mexico's Failed Drug War," *Economic Development Bulletin* 13 (2010): 3.


## REFERENCES

Andreas, P. "A Tale of Two Borders: The U.S.-Mexico and U.S.-Canada Lines After 9–11." In *The Rebordering of North America: Integration and Exclusion in a New Security Context*, edited by Peter Andreas and Thomas Biersteker, 1–23 (New York: Routledge, 2003).

Balassa, B. *The Theory of Economic Integration* (Homewood, IL: Richard D. Irwin, 1961).

Barnett, Ch., and Hugh Williams. "Renewing the Relationship: Canada and the United States in the 21st Century." Conference Board of Canada Briefing. Ottawa, February 2003.

Benitez, R., and Athanasios Hristoulas. "México y Canadá: El reto de enfrentarse al crimen organizado." In *Canadá y México: La Agenda Pendiente*, edited by Alex Bugailiskis and Andrés Rozental, 227–238. Toronto: McGill-Queen's University Press, 2012.

Bow, B. "North America as an Emergent Regional Security Complex." Paper presented at the International Studies Association, New Orleans, February 19–20, 2010.

## Obstacles to Security Cooperation in North America    195

Buzan, B., and Ole Weaver. *Regions and Powers: The Structure of International Security*. Cambridge: Cambridge University Press, 2003.

Canadian Defence and Foreign Affairs Institute. "Threat Perceptions in Canada." January 2010. Accessed June 1, 2012. http://www.cdfai.org/PDF/Poll%20on%20 Threat%20Perceptions%20in%20Canada.pdf.

Castaneda, J. "Mexico's Failed Drug War." *Economic Development Bulletin* 13, no. 3 (2010): 1–4.

Chabat, J. "Drug Trafficking and the United States-Mexico Relations." In *Mexico's Security Failure, Collapse into Criminal Violence*, edited by Paul Kenny and Monica Serrano, 143–160. New York: Routledge, 2012.

Clarkson, S. *Does North America Exist?* Toronto: University of Toronto Press, 2008.

D'Aquino, T. "Security and Prosperity: The Dynamics of a New Canada-United States Partnership in North America." Paper presented to the Annual General Meeting of the Canadian Council of Chief Executives, Toronto, January 14, 2003.

Dobson, W. "Shaping the Future of the North American Economic Space: A Framework for Action." *Commentary: The Border Papers* 162 (2002): 1–32.

Domínguez, R. "NAFTA: Assessments and Institutional Development." In *The European Union and Regional Integration A Comparative Perspective and Lessons for the Americas*, edited by Joaquín Roy and Roberto Domínguez, 23–26. Miami: Jean Monnet Chair University of Miami-European Commission, 2005.

Economist Intelligence Unit. "Mexico/USA: Clouded Relationship." *Business Latin America*, April 11, 2011.

Environics Institute. *Focus Canada 2010 Public Opinion Research on the Record: Serving the Public Interest*. Toronto: Environics Institute for Survey Research, 2010. Accessed November 12, 2012. http://www.queensu.ca/cora/_files/fc2010 report.pdf.

Feng, Y., and Gaspare M. Genna. "Regional Integration and Domestic Institutional Homogeneity: A Comparative Analysis of Regional Integration in the Americas, Pacific Asia and Western Europe." *Review of International Political Economy* 10, no. 2 (2003): 278–309.

Felbab-Brown, V. "Lessons from Colombia for Mexico?" *ReVista: Harvard Review of Latin America* 11, no. 2 (Winter 2012): 48–51.

Felbab-Brown, V., and Eric Olson. "A Better Strategy to Combat Organized Crime in Mexico and Central America." *Brookings Up Front* (blog), April 13, 2012. Accessed November 24, 2012, http://www.brookings.edu/blogs/up-front/posts/2012/04/13-crime-central-america-felbabbrown.

Flores Salgado, J., and Federico Novelo Urdanivia. "Hacia el mercado común norteamericano." *Análisis Económico* 25, no. 58 (2010): 185–207.

Gabriel, Ch., and Laura MacDonald. "From the 49th Parallel to the Río Grande: U.S. Homeland Security and North American Borders." In *North American Politics: Globalization and Culture*, edited by Yasmeen Abu-Laban, Radha Jhappan and Francois Rocher, 353–370. Peterborough: Broadview, 2007.

Galen Carpenter, T. "Mexico Sours on Drug War." *National Interest*, November 16, 2011. Accessed December 2, 2012. http://nationalinterest.org/commentary/mexico-sours-drug-war-6160.

González, G., and Stephan Haggard. "The United States and Mexico: A Pluralistic Security Community." In *Security Communities*, edited by Emanuel Adler, 295–332. Cambridge: Cambridge University Press, 1998.

González, G., Jorge A Schiavon, David Crow and Gerardo Maldonado. *Mexico, the Americas, and the World 2010, Foreign Policy: Public Opinion and Leaders*. Mexico City: Centro de Investigación y Docencia Económicas, 2011. Accessed February 20, 2012. http://mexicoyelmundo.cide.edu/2010/reportein gles10.pdf.

## 196   Roberto Domínguez and Rafael Velázquez

Government of Canada. *Securing an Open Society: One Year Later*. Ottawa: Privy Council Office, 2005. Accessed June 25, 2012. http://www.pco-bcp.gc.ca/docs/information/publications/aarchives/secure/secure-eng.pdf.

Hristoulas, A. "Whatever Happened to the North America Security Perimeter?" Paper presented at the International Studies Association, New Orleans, February 19–20, 2010.

Hristoulas, A., and Stephane Roussel. "North America Security and Foreign Policy. Does a Trilateral Community Exist?" In *North American Politics: Globalization and Culture*, edited by Yasmeen Abu-Laban, Radha Jhappan and Francois Rocher, 371–388. Peterborough: Broadview, 2007.

Kenny, P., and Monica Serrano, eds. *Mexico's Security Failure, Collapse into Criminal Violence*. New York: Routledge, 2012.

Langton, J. *Gangland: The Rise of the Mexican Drug Cartels from El Paso to Vancouver*. Mississauga, ON: John Wiley & Son, 2012.

Mora, E. "DoD to Increase Counter-Narcotics Support for Mexico 17-Fold Despite Mexican Security Forces Committing Unlawful Killings." CNSNews.com. April 12, 2012. Accessed June 4, 2012. http://cnsnews.com/news/article/dod-increase-counter-narcotics-support-mexico-17-fold-despite-mexican-security-forces.

Morales, I. *Post-NAFTA North America: Reshaping the Economic and Political Governance of a Changing Region*. Basingstoke, UK: Palgrave Macmillan, 2008.

Morden, R. "Seguridad hemisférica: El dilema Canadá-México." In *Canadá y México: La Agenda Pendiente*, edited by Alex Bugailiskis and Andrés Rozental, 219–226. Toronto: McGill-Queen's University Press, 2012.

Ned Lebow, R., and Janice Gross Stein. *We All Lost the Cold War*. Princeton: Princeton University Press, 1994.

New Democrats Party (NDP). "New Democrats Celebrates Victory over SPP." 2009. Accessed January 24, 2012. http://www.ndp.ca/press/new-democrats-celebrates-victory-over-spp.

O'Keefe, E. "Rep. Issa Says No Proof White House Withheld Information in 'Fast and Furious' Inquiry." *Washington Post*. June 25, 2012.

Pastor, R. "Beyond NAFTA: The Emergence and Future of North America." In *Politics of North America: Redefining Continental Relations*, edited by Yasmeen Abu-Laban, Radha Jhappan and Fancois Rocher, 461–476. Peterborough: Broadview, 2008.

———. *The North American Idea: A Vision of a Continental Future*. New York: Oxford University Press, 2011.

———. *Toward a North American Community: Lessons from the Old Word to the New*. Washington, DC: Institute for International Economics, 2001.

Presidencia de la República. "Plan Nacional de Desarrollo." 2006. Accessed April 12, 2012. http://pnd.presidencia.gob.mx/.

Public Safety Canada. *Securing an Open Society: Canada's National Security Policy*. Ottawa, 2004. Accessed July 2, 2012. http://www.publicsafety.gc.ca/pol/ns/secpol04-eng.aspx.

Radden Keefe, P. "Cocaine Incorporated." *New York Times*, June 15, 2012.

Robinson, Dan. "North American Leaders' Summit Focuses on Economy, Drugs, Trade." Voice of America. April 1, 2012. Accessed May 25, 2012. http://www.voanews.com/content/economy-security-lead-north-american-summit-agenda-145814975/179460.html.

Royal Canadian Mounted Police (RCMP). "Border Integrity." 2010. Accessed January 20, 2012. http://www.rcmp-grc.gc.ca/bi-if/index-eng.htm.

Secretaría de Seguridad Pública. *Programa Nacional de Seguridad Pública 2008–2012*. 2008. Accessed March 15, 2012. http://www.ssp.df.gob.mx/TransparenciaSSP/MAdmvoVarios/5Planes%20PNSP%202008_2012.pdf.

Wendt, A. "Anarchy Is What States Make of It: The Social Construction of Power Politics." *International Organization* 46, no. 2 (1992): 391–425.

White House. *National Security Strategy*. Washington, DC: 2010. Accessed February 23, 2012. http://www.whitehouse.gov/sites/default/files/rss_viewer/national_security_strategy.pdf.

———. *Strategy to Combat Transnational Organized Crime: Addressing Converging Threats to National Security*. Washington, DC: 2011. Accessed July 23, 2011. http://www.whitehouse.gov/sites/default/files/Strategy_to_Combat_Transnational_Organized_Crime_July_2011.pdf.

Woodrow Wilson Center. *The United States and Mexico: Towards a Strategic Partnership. A Report of Four Working Groups on US-Mexico Relations*. Washington, DC: Woodrow Wilson International Center for Scholars, Mexico Institute, 2009.

# 11 Secure Borders and Uncertain Trade

*Coral R. Snodgrass and Guy H. Gessner*

## INTRODUCTION

The theme of this book is an examination of the institutions governing the interactions among the three nations of North America and the implications for these interactions in the absence of strong institutional governance mechanisms. Our project looks at one very specific set of interactions—namely, the functioning of supply chains across the Canada-US border. Unfortunately, this has been an area of continuing managerial challenges where borders have thickened and, until recently, there has been little meaningful cooperation. This state of affairs represents a 180-degree shift in thinking about the Canada-US border and the importance of its smooth functioning to the economies of these two partners in what is still the largest bilateral trade relationship in the world. This change in perspective, especially on the part of US policy makers, can be viewed primarily as the result of the terrorist attacks of September 11, 2001, and continued threats of terrorism.

Our project examines the decision making of managers who make the day-to-day decisions supporting this cross border trade relationship. Prior to 9/11, the governments of Canada and the United States had a long history of trade cooperation that allowed an atmosphere of interdependency to develop between companies on both sides of the border. Consequently, the cross border supply chains developed by managers were used to move subcomponents and finished goods across the border as though it were invisible. There has been much research done on the institutional level of broad national policies and gross trade figures to describe the health of the relationship between Canada and the United States in general since 9/11. It is certainly the case that immediately following the events of 9/11, the governments of Canada and the United States enacted the Smart Border Accord in order to ensure that the border, while perhaps no longer invisible, was at least manageable. Within the Accord were provisions for such programs as Customs-Trade Partnership Against Terrorism (C-TPAT) and Free and Secure Trade (FAST). However, these institutional frameworks function only so long as managers subscribe to them. This project is designed to examine the use of these frameworks by examining the decisions made by the buyers

Secure Borders and Uncertain Trade   199

and sellers in the links of the supply chains that support this massive movement of goods and, to a growing extent, services across what is commonly referred to as the longest undefended international border in the world. Our research question is: How have the institutions regulating border security impacted the decision making of the Canadian and US managers responsible for maintaining the functioning of the supply chains linking the two nations?

## OVERVIEW OF THE CANADA-US RELATIONSHIP

### Trade between Canada and the United States

This research project is designed to examine the functioning of supply chains across the Canada-US border. In order to begin, a few statistics about this trade will provide some context. First of all, it is important to note that the trade between Canada and the United States is massive. In 2010, C$645.7 billion in goods and services crossed the border. That breaks down to about $1.8 billion each day. The Canadian government estimates that one in seven Canadian jobs depends on the trade with the United States. On the US side, 8 million jobs depend on this trade. The trade figures for 2010, while slightly off the all-time highs seen in 2008, are on the rebound. There also seems to be a decline in the dependence of Canada on trade with the US, as the percentage of total Canadian imports and exports with the United States declined from 75% in 2005 to 68% in 2009 (all figures from www.statcan.gc.ca).[1]

The content of that trade is fairly stable. The United States sends Canada vehicles, machinery and electrical equipment. Excluding energy, Canada sends the United States the same. Much of that can be explained by the fact that approximately 45% of the trade is intrafirm—that is, subsidiaries of the same firms sending subcomponents back and forth across the border. This is very characteristic of global supply chains linking industries across the two countries, especially the highly integrated supply chains in the automotive industry, located primarily in Ontario, Michigan, Ohio and New York. These interdependent linkages have grown substantially since the Auto Pact went into effect in the 1960s. The sheer intensity of the interdependency of these supply chains can be understood by noting that some of the components in the assembly of an automobile can cross the border as many as seven times before final assembly.[2] This is clearly an area where managers might feel the need to make some changes in the design of these supply chains. The distance between many of the automotive shipping and delivery points is short relative to the geographic size of the two countries enabling rapid cross border movements in normal times. But the new border-crossing challenges create more uncertainty in meeting time-sensitive delivery schedules characteristic of the auto industry.

There are also examples of intrafirm trade in other industries, such as processed foods. From the manager's perspective, the degree to which the

## 200   Coral R. Snodgrass and Guy H. Gessner

links in their supply chains are part of the same corporate family may decrease the flexibility of their choices and impact the nature of the choices made. As an example, while the Ontario apple growers may choose to find new customers, an assembly plant in Windsor making subcomponents in the auto industry may not be able to choose to sell those subassemblies to a different "buyer." But the buyer might choose to impose some cost or delivery constraints. At that point the manager in Windsor might decide it is time to move to Michigan or at least to build a warehouse in Michigan.

Another aspect of the trade relationship that is often mentioned as a critical element is the fact that Canada is the largest provider of energy to the United States. Canada is the largest supplier of foreign oil, electricity, natural gas and nuclear fuel. This fact combined with the importance of the automotive industry helps to explain the variations in the value of Canada-US trade. It is thought that the year-to-year changes in the value of Canada-US trade can in large part be accounted for by noting the weakening of the automotive sector and volatile energy prices. Thus the changes would not reflect the results of strategic shifts in the design of the supply chains.

## The Political Institutions Governing Canada-US Trade

The history of the political relationship between Canada and the United States throughout the 20th century is one of close cooperation and integrated views of appropriate international involvement. As examples, Canada and the United States were early members of the United Nations and the North Atlantic Treaty Organization (NATO). Canada and the United States developed the North American Aerospace Defense Command (NORAD) in 1958 to provide for the security of North America. The political atmosphere of trust and mutual regard for the future set the stage for economic integration through the Canada-US Free Trade Agreement in 1988 and the North American Free Trade Agreement (NAFTA) in 1994. All signals from the political arena were that cozy economic and commercial networks were in no danger of being outlawed.

Unfortunately, the events of September 11, 2001, marked a change in the thinking of policy makers in the United States. Specifically as this thinking applied to Canada, the fears of the chance of any future attacks and the mistaken belief that the 9/11 terrorists had come from Canada led to a very dramatic change in how the US policy makers viewed the border and anything that crosses it. Statements such as the much-quoted one by then US ambassador Paul Cellucci that "Security will trump trade" seemed to sum up the US attitude about the border.[3] It appears that this was not just rhetoric. Under George W. Bush, the Department of Homeland Security was formed. The Department has undertaken a series of measures aimed at "thickening" the border around the United States.

In reaction to the need to provide for better security at the border while still facilitating cross border activity, a number of programs were established.

## Secure Borders and Uncertain Trade    201

The Smart Border Accord established a series of steps designed to keep the border working. It provided for programs such as FAST to certify truck drivers across the border and the NEXUS program for trusted travelers crossing by car, truck or train. Customs-Trade Partnership Against Terrorism (C-TPAT) would provide clearance for goods. These programs all came at substantial costs. The Atlantic Provinces Trucking Association estimates that the trucking industry in Canada is paying $1 billion per year to comply with these new programs. They estimate that C-TPAT compliance alone can cost a company as much as $300,000.[4] Balanced against this are estimates from the Canadian government that inefficiencies at the Canada-US border account for a 1% decline in Canadian gross domestic product (GDP) or $1.6 billion in 2010.

Although border security seems to dominate the discussion about Canada-US trade, there are other important political issues to consider. As an example, labeling laws continue to be a problem under the "rules of origin" requirements of NAFTA. The result of these rules is an onerous documentation requirement for all those goods crossing the border. This becomes exacerbated when one considers those automotive subcomponents that cross the border seven times. Similarly, the US Department of Agriculture requires country of origin labels for imported food products. This has resulted in a decrease in the exports of Canadian cattle and hogs to the United States. In this case, it is not because the meat is considered "unsafe," as it was during the "mad cow" scare. It is because US importers do not want to do the paperwork. For them, it is easier to find a domestic supplier.[5] This suggests some Canadian suppliers may find out they have no relative or absolute competitive advantage.

Another piece of legislation that has negatively impacted the relationship between Canada and the United States is the "Buy American" provision in the American Recovery and Reinvestment Act of 2009. Under the original language, Canadian goods were classified as "American." However, there were selected circumstances inserted into the language that allowed Canadian firms to be denied access. This is true in spite of any requirement for equal treatment under NAFTA. The legislation further allows for decisions on access to be made at the state level. Not all of the states have signed on. Confusion and uncertainty over the access Canadian firms have into the supply chains for public projects in the United States lead many Canadian firms to simply not try.

It is clear from these examples that there is no overarching institutional framework governing the smooth functioning of cross border commercial activities in North America. One possible reason for this is the fact that NAFTA was designed solely to facilitate trade and investment among the three nations of North America. Issues of national sovereignty and independence were not part of the equation. This is why in discussions of cross border security any mention of a perimeter strategy wherein the external borders of North America would be pushed out to the geographic limits of the three nations has not gone far. These are three independent nations pursuing their own national goals.

Consequently, such conflicting signals from multiple levels of government are not to be unexpected in North America and are not unusual in international trading relationships. While it is certainly true that most countries want to increase their level of international trading activity, as evidenced by the existence of many types of trade agreements between many countries around the globe, there is usually an unavoidable conflict of interest in the form of the trade that takes place. Governments usually want to increase exports of finished goods and thereby increase GDP, domestic employment and taxes. While they want an increase in exports, they have little incentive to see domestic companies expand internationally by direct investment in foreign countries. On the other hand most governments welcome direct investments by foreign companies that increase GDP, jobs and domestic tax revenues. Therefore most governments through their policies seek to encourage increased international trade and international market expansions but will support only a limited number of strategies and tactics. Many levels of both the US and Canadian governments have active programs that try to attract companies on the opposite side of the border to move more operations to their side of the border.

## The Socioeconomic Institutions Surrounding Canada-US Trade

Changes in cross border trade cannot be understood just in terms of increased border security. The good news is that a number of studies indicate that the changes in trade are not related to increased border security.[6] While it is not the intent of this project to provide an exhaustive discussion of all aspects of the external environment of decision makers in global supply chains, it is important to note two aspects of the socioeconomic environment that form an important backdrop. First of all, the United States is in a recession. According to a study sponsored by the Conference Board of Canada, the decline in US household spending has actually led to a contraction in global trade—the first in 60 years![7] As was noted, a vast majority of Canadian exports to the United States are in energy, automotive, food and wood products. These four sectors have been very negatively impacted by the decline in the US economy as well as regulatory complications.[8] One way this decline has shown up in consumption figures is a precipitous drop in household spending. As residents in the United States are cutting back, they are buying less expensive food, not buying new cars and not building new houses. Taking the drop in housing starts as an example, this has led to a drop in the demand for wood and wood products. Canada is a major supplier of these products when housing is being built. Canada supplies 25% of the softwood lumber used in the United States, so it suffers substantially when houses are not being built. As a matter of fact, the previously cited study by the Conference Board predicted that the declines in domestic demand coupled with the decrease in exports would lead to a 1.7% decrease in real GDP in 2009.

The second point concerns the strength of the Canadian dollar. The Canadian dollar has strengthened against the US dollar over the early part of the 21st century. Some preliminary economic research indicates that these changes have not had a negative impact on cross border trade.[9] However, managers often cite exchange rates as a major factor in their decisions concerning supply chain partners.[10] Consequently, the impact of the changes in the exchange rate should be kept in mind as behaviors of supply chain managers are studied.

## THE INSTITUTIONAL CONTEXT OF CROSS BORDER MANAGEMENT

Both the economic conditions and the exchange rate are outside the control of individual managers, and for many managers consideration of them is not part of their daily reality. Procurement and other internationally sensitive business functions are exceptions, and these managers may keep a close eye on changing economic conditions and exchange rates, looking for arbitrage situations. When arbitrage or absolute advantage conditions do not exist, then what is left is dealing with realities of international borders. Anyone who lives within a few miles of any of the important border crossings between Canada and the United States is very familiar with the headlines and stories about what is happening at the border. "Border Crossings Slide" declares *Buffalo Business First* in an article decrying the decline in US customers at Niagara Falls, Ontario hotels, casinos and theaters.[11] "New Rules Crimp Canada Ties" laments the *Buffalo News* in an article on the impact of the new border rules that have led to a drop in trips across the Peace Bridge—conceivably for the first time in its 82-year history.[12] The article does go on to say that the recession and lousy weather may also have had an impact. "Border Laws Taking Toll on Business, Groups Say" reports on the joint efforts of the Canadian and American Chambers of Commerce to influence US policy makers.[13]

But it is not just the owners of bed-and-breakfasts, restaurants and tourist attractions who are seeing the negative impact of border security. Supply chain managers are also feeling the impact. As mentioned before, the costs of compliance with the border management programs such as FAST and C-TPAT are significant. It is also necessary for shippers to be members of programs on both sides of the border. These requirements plus the costs of border delays can cost a company as much as $1 million per year. The costs of the border are also combined with the paperwork burden that comes from such requirements as the "rules of origin" under NAFTA. Some transportation companies such as Purolator Corporation publish white papers to try to help customers prepare for the challenges of dealing with the Canada-US border. Other transportation companies have added accessorial charges to cover the additional costs of crossing the border. A study by

# 204 Coral R. Snodgrass and Guy H. Gessner

the Canadian Chamber of Commerce cites the example of the automotive industry and its integrated supply chains in North America.[14] It compares the paperwork burden for a shipment of 4,000 fully assembled foreign cars into the United States. That shipment would require one customs clearance form. A shipment of 4,000 vehicles that are assembled in Canada and the United States—therefore crossing the Canada-US border as many as seven times until final assembly—would require as many as 28,000 customs and security clearance forms. And the cost burden of that does not even count the costs of border delays!

The point is that the core of the relationship between Canada and the United States seems to be defined now more than ever before in terms of the legal and political differences that become apparent when attempting to conduct business across the border that separates the two countries. Changes in that relationship are manifest in changes in the institutions that define border policy. Changes in cross border business result from these changes in border policy. These changes are critical for Canadian managers. As an example, in 2005 as much as 38% of Canadian GDP was exports and 34% of GDP was imports. Canada is an exporting nation and exports mean there is a border. But historically the United States is not really an export nation, and the value of its domestic economy is much larger than the value of its exports. So the decision variables of US managers in cross border supply chains are not necessarily the same as those of their Canadian partners.

This brief review of the Canada-US trade relationship indicates some of the complexity of the decision-making environment for the managers tasked with keeping the supply chains moving. However, it is also clearly the case that, given the sheer volume of trade and the criticality of that trade to key industries in both countries, these managers will do whatever it takes to keep the goods moving. The next part of this chapter will explore the US side of the supply chains.

## US Purchasing Manager Decision Making in the Institutional Context of Increased Border Security

In the supply chains that cross the Canada-US border, many of the decisions about managing the relationships are made by the US purchasing managers who represent the large customers assembling subcomponents from their Canadian suppliers. One of the issues for Canadian suppliers in their relationship with their US customers is the fear that increased border security would negatively impact their "attractiveness" as suppliers because the costs of compliance with border security programs are so high and the delays at the border would lead to volatility in their delivery schedules. Macrolevel research on variations of trade volumes as a function of increased border security indicates there has not been a negative impact on trade between Canada and the United States.[15]

Another study examines the question of whether the impact of heightened border security has just not shown up yet.[16] This study also indicates that there has not been a decrease in Canada-US trade related to increased border security. However, the report also indicates that the Canadian firms in the study saw increased costs related to the need to comply with new border security programs and they assumed those costs internally. Thus the US customers did not see an increase in their costs of supplying out of Canada and were therefore not motivated to change suppliers. However, the Canadian suppliers were realizing lower profit margins.

Our study examined the decision making of US purchasing managers regarding their Canadian suppliers.[17] Their responses indicate that exchange rates were their most important factor in deciding to use Canadian suppliers (45% of respondents). Clearly costs are paramount in their minds. Their second reason is the opportunity to develop new business (34% of respondents). These US purchasing managers view their supply chain partners as assets to be used for their long-term viability. Traffic problems (11%) and security issues (3%) were not viewed as problems for the US managers.

The US purchasing managers were also asked about their perceived impact of increased border security. Only 24% reported a noticeable impact and 3% a great impact on their cross border business. They were also asked about the cost impact of increased border security. Their responses show that 53% thought the impact was less than 1% or none, while another 18% of the respondents didn't know. When asked about specific problems related to the border, 59% of the respondents cited longer wait times as the number one problem. When asked what they planned to do to solve any problems related to the functioning of their cross border supply chains, 35% of the respondents indicated they would seek a domestic supplier. The triggers for their decisions indicate that 59% of the respondents were concerned that longer waiting times at the border would lead to difficulty in maintaining just-in-time schedules and would increase inventory costs.

The conclusions to be drawn from these studies for Canadian managers are not discouraging, but they do indicate the need for some strategic rethinking. Clearly, there has not been an immediate change in the supply chains across the Canada-US border related to the increased border security requirements. Trade between the two countries is still robust. Changes in the volume of trade seem to be related more to the wider economic forces related to the recession in the United States and the wider impact of that economic decline. Further, it is the case that much of the trade across the border is intrafirm trade supported by supply chains that are not expected to change quickly. However, there are concerns that even those supply chains may hit a "tipping point" at which changes would be made. Further, it seems that one of the reasons that US purchasing managers have not made changes is that their Canadian suppliers are bearing the costs of compliance with border security programs.

It would appear from this research that US purchasing managers are concerned about timely delivery as well as total delivered cost. Both of those variables are subject to negative impact from border issues in terms of both border delays and costly compliance. If those two variables become problems, it is clear that US purchasing managers will seek domestic suppliers. It also can be deduced from these studies that US purchasing managers believe it is the task of the Canadian suppliers to make this work.

The implications for Canadian firms are that they need to begin to develop strategies to secure their place in their supply chains. This might include actions designed to integrate them further into North American supply chains. Or it might require a rethinking.

## Canadian Suppliers Decision Making in the Institutional Context of Increased Border Security

In order to examine the reactions of Canadian managers, we undertook a small study to ask about their relationships with their US customers. The size of the data base does not allow for rigorous statistical testing. However, there are some interesting findings that are worth mentioning. First of all, the responses confirm the importance of total delivered costs to their success. All of the respondents indicated that total delivered costs were either critical (70%) or very important (30%) to their ability to maintain their customers. Timely deliveries across the border did not seem as important.

The second interesting result is that there does not seem to be much movement in the geographic makeup of these firms' supply chains. By and large, they are located and competing in Canada and the United States. There was very little indication that even Mexico was figuring into their decision making. The respondents did, however, find the threat of low-cost competition to be either critical (9%) or very important (64%) to their ability to compete globally.

The third interesting result is the fact that the respondents found Canadian government regulations—either the multiple jurisdictions within Canada or the differences between Canada and other countries—to be critical (45% and 36%) or very important (19% and 27% respectively).

It may be speculated that some of these results are a function of the facts that the respondents are firms dealing directly at the Canada-US border and they have a constrained market reach. Nonetheless, they provide some direction for future research.

## NAFTA and the Institutional Framework for Automotive Production in Canada, Mexico and the US

The present study was undertaken to examine the shifts in the institutional context of managerial decision makers in Canada and the United States. This topic is of particular interest since historically the governments of these

*Secure Borders and Uncertain Trade*  207

two countries have worked under an assumption of an almost invisible border. Our research indicates that this assumption no longer obtains. There are changes in the design and administration of the supply chains linking companies across this border.

However, it is important to put these changes into a context other than just the changes in security regimes at the border. This becomes very clear when examining automotive trade within North America. A significant development that affects automotive trade across the US-Canada border and the US-Mexico border as well as Canada-Mexico trade is the continued growth of the Texas-Mexico Automotive Supercluster (TMASC). The study by TIP Strategies (2012) displays data from the International Organization of Motor Vehicle Manufacturers that captures the extent of changes that are taking place by comparing production in 2009 to 2010.[18] Car production in the United States is down 51% and Canada is down 38%, but Mexico is up 9%. Commercial vehicle production is down 31% in the United States, down 22% in Canada, but up 45% in Mexico.

This report provides clear data indicating that the geographic trend is investment in new automotive production in the southern United States and in Mexico, while at the same time the largest consumer of transportation products is the United States. There is no reason to assume this geographic shift is a direct result of changes in the security regime at the US-Canada border. Rather, there is little doubt that governments at many levels, especially at the state level in the United States, are competing for these investments. The success of these investments is dependent upon the ability to move parts, products and people across US borders. This industry will help to drive increased integration of the NAFTA economies, starting with practical concerns such as border-crossing logistics and security. What is not clear is whether the institutional frameworks developed by the governments of the three countries will in fact facilitate this integration.

## ADDRESSING THE INSTITUTIONAL VOID

During the development of the background research for this project, a number of key events occurred. On February 4, 2011, Barack Obama and Stephen Harper issued a joint declaration on a "Shared Vision for Perimeter Security and Economic Competitiveness." The declaration affirmed the importance of trade to the Canadian and US economies and recognized the need to find ways to make the border work. On December 7, 2011, these same two gentlemen announced the agreement on two action plans: The Action Plan on Perimeter Security and Economic Competitiveness and the Action Plan on Regulatory Cooperation. The first action plan addresses key problems at the border and aims to facilitate legitimate border crossings while also increasing security. The first key element of this action plan designed to alleviate problems at the border is new screening procedures for international shipments at the first port of entry under the "Cleared once, accepted twice" concept. This would eliminate the present requirement to rescreen shipments. The second feature calls for expanded membership in such trusted traveler and trader programs as NEXUS and FAST. The third calls for infrastructure improvements to help make these programs work—such as an expanded number of NEXUS lanes. Action plans such as those proposed should take much of the burden off of the actual Canada-US border crossing and move the border out to the perimeter of North America. A key area to watch is the North American border-crossing solutions that will be driven by the global auto industry.

## CONCLUSION

Our study was undertaken to examine the decision making of US and Canadian managers concerning their global supply chains in the face of increased security at the Canada-US border. The results from the US managers indicate that they are shifting the burdens of security compliance to their Canadian suppliers. The problem for the Canadian suppliers is that there is no clear answer as to the best course of action they can take to maintain their positions in their existing supply chains or the ones they want to develop. So while policy makers on both sides of the border work out the details of border management institutions designed to facilitate trade, Canadian managers are going ahead with whatever they have to do to stay in business. Two articles from the *Buffalo News* tell of a logistics firm from Toronto opening a facility in Wheatfield, near Buffalo, New York, and of another machine tool company moving its factory from Cambridge, Ontario, to Wheatfield.[19] It is these operational-level decisions by the managers in the trenches of global supply chain management that will provide the best information on the shape these supply chains will take in the future.

## NOTES

1. Statistics Canada, 2012, http://www.statcan.gc.ca.
2. Canadian Chamber of Commerce, "Finding the Balance: Shared Border of the Future" (Ottawa, ON, 2009).
3. John Herd Thompson, "Playing by the New Washington Rules: The US-Canada Relationship, 1994–2003," *The American Review of Canadian Studies* 33–1 (2003): 5–26.
4. Rebecca Penty, "Border US Regulatory Barriers Mean Increased Costs for Canadian Industry and Its Customers," *Telegraph Journal*, April 14, 2009, http://telegraphjournal.canadaeast.com/rss/article/634386.
5. Michael Armstrong, "Label Laws Cut Exports to the Bone," TheStar.com, July 20, 2009, http://www.thestar.com/printArticle/668159.
6. Michael Burt, "Tighter Border Security and Its Effect on Canadian Exports," (Conference Board of Canada, Ottawa, ON, 2007); Danielle Goldfarb,

"Reaching a Tipping Point? Effects of Post-9/11 Border Security on Canada's Trade and Investment" (Conference Board of Canada, Ottawa, ON, 2007).

7. Pedro Antunes, "Canadian Outlook Executive Summary" (Conference Board of Canada, Ottawa, ON, 2009).

8. Andrea Woo, "Softwood-Lumber Victory Unlikely to Halt Conflict between Canada and U.S.," *Globe and Mail*, July 18, 2012, http://www.theglobeandmail.com/report-on-business/industry-news/energy-and-resources/softwood-lumber-victory-unlikely-to-halt-conflict-between-canada-and-us/article4425659/.

9. Paul Sundell and Mathew Shane, "Canada: A Macroeconomic Study of the United States' Most Important Trade Partner" (WRS-06-02, United States Department of Agriculture, Washington, DC, September 2006).

10. Guy Gessner and Coral R. Snodgrass, "Border Security and Cross Border Trade: Decisions by US Purchasing Managers regarding Canadian Suppliers," *Proceedings of the Northeast Decision Sciences Institute*, March 30–April 1, Philadelphia, PA, 2005.

11. James Fink, "Border Crossings Slide," *Buffalo Business First*, September 11–17, 2009.

12. Phil Fairbanks and Brian Hayden, "New Rules Crimp Canadian Ties," *Buffalo News*, July 19, 2009.

13. Jerry Zremski, "Border Laws Taking Toll on Business, Groups Say," *Buffalo News*, July 22, 2009.

14. Canadian Chamber of Commerce, "Finding the Balance."

15. Burt, "Tighter Border Security."

16. Goldfarb, "Tipping Point."

17. Gessner and Snodgrass, "Border Security."

18. TIP Strategies, *The Texas-Mexico Automotive Supercluster: Vehicle Manufacturing Overview and Prospects* (Austin, TX: 2012).

19. Matt Glynn, "Canadian Firm Expands into WNY," *Buffalo News*, November 19, 2010; Thomas Prohaska, "Machine Tool Company to Move Factory from Canada," *Buffalo News*, November 23, 2009.

## REFERENCES

Armstrong, Michael. "Label Laws Cut Exports to the Bone." TheStar.com. July 20, 2009. http://www.thestar.com/printArticle/668159.

Antunes, Pedro. "Canadian Outlook Executive Summary." Conference Board of Canada. Ottawa, ON. 2009.

Burt, Michael. "Tighter Border Security and Its Effect on Canadian Exports." Conference Board of Canada. Ottawa, ON. 2007.

Canadian Chamber of Commerce. "Finding the Balance: Shared Border of the Future." Ottawa, ON. 2009.

Fairbanks, Phil, and Brian Hayden. "New Rules Crimp Canadian Ties." *Buffalo News*. July 19, 2009.

Fink, James. "Border Crossings Slide." *Buffalo Business First*. September 11–17, 2009.

Gessner, Guy, and Coral R. Snodgrass. "Border Security and Cross Border Trade: Decisions by US Purchasing Managers regarding Canadian Suppliers." *Proceedings of the Northeast Decision Sciences Institute*, March 30–April 1, Philadelphia, PA, 2005.

Glynn, Matt. "Canadian Firm Expands into WNY." *Buffalo News*. November 19, 2010.

Goldfarb, Danielle. "Reaching a Tipping Point? Effects of Post-9/11 Border Security on Canada's Trade and Investment." Conference Board of Canada. Ottawa, ON. 2007.

Penty, Rebecca. "Border US Regulatory Barriers Mean Increased Costs for Canadian Industry and Its Customers." *Telegraph Journal*. April 14, 2009. http://telegraph journal.canadaeast.com/rss/article/634386.

Prohaska, Thomas. "Machine Tool Company to Move Factory from Canada." *Buffalo News*. November 23, 2009.

Statistics Canada. 2012. http://www.statcan.gc.ca.

Sundell, Paul, and Mathew Shane. "Canada: A Macroeconomic Study of the United States' Most Important Trade Partner." WRS-06–02. United States Department of Agriculture. Washington, DC. September 2006.

TIP Strategies. *The Texas-Mexico Automotive Supercluster: Vehicle Manufacturing Overview and Prospects*. Austin, TX: 2012.

Woo, Andrea. "Softwood-Lumber Victory Unlikely to Halt Conflict between Canada and U.S." *Globe and Mail*. July 18, 2012. http://www.theglobeandmail.com/report-on-business/industry-news/energy-and-resources/softwood-lumber-victory-unlikely-to-halt-conflict-between-canada-and-us/article4425659/.

Zremski, Jerry. "Border Laws Taking Toll on Business, Groups Say." *Buffalo News*. July 22, 2009.

# 12 Drug-Related Violence and Forced Migration from Mexico to the United States

*Eva Olimpia Arceo-Gómez*

## INTRODUCTION

It is a well-known fact that the drug-related violence in Mexico has seen an upsurge in recent years. This increase in violent crimes has been attributed to the so-called "war against drug trafficking," which was declared when President Felipe Calderón took office in 2006. According to a report from the *Procuraduría General de la República* (the attorney general of Mexico) from 2006 to September 2011 there have been around 47,515 drug-related deaths in Mexico—10 percent of which are considered civilian casualties.[1] As a result, Mexicans have been fleeing areas where the conflict between drug cartels, or between drug lords and the Mexican army, has been more intense. International migration is certainly an attractive option, especially for those living closer to the border. This chapter aims at documenting the effect of drug-related violence on Mexican immigration to the United States, as well as characterizing the violence-led immigrants.

The first issue that arises is whether the war on drugs caused an increase of violence in Mexico. Dell presents rigorous econometric evidence that those municipalities in which the National Action Party (the same as that in the federal government) won close elections are more likely to experience an increase in drug-related homicides.[2] She establishes that those municipalities are more likely to ask for federal or military forces to combat drug lords. This crackdown in turn debilitates the "incumbent drug lord" and generates incentives for rival cartels to fight for the turf. As a result, homicides between members of rival drug cartels increase. She thus concludes that the war on drugs spearheaded by President Calderón and the National Action Party has indeed led to an upsurge in drug-related murder rates.

Previous literature has shown that violence caused by civil conflicts forces people to migrate to safer locations. This review of the literature will focus on Latin American case studies. Morrison studied whether violence from politically motivated conflicts is a determinant of migration in addition to economic factors in neoclassical economic models of migration.[3] He found that between 1976 and 1981, violence had a positive effect on Guatemalan migration, and moreover that escalating violence increases the magnitude

## 212 Eva Olimpia Arceo-Gómez

of this effect: the more violence there is, the greater is the effect of violence on migration. Morrison and May also found a link between migration and political violence in Guatemala.[4] Lundquist and Massey found a strong relation between Nicaraguan out-migration to the United States and the Contra war.[5] Alvarado and Massey studied the relationship of violence and migration from the perspective of world systems theory, linking economic openness to a rise in criminality.[6] Using data from 1979 to 2003, they found a positive effect of violence on migration only in Nicaragua, but not in Mexico, Costa Rica and Guatemala. Finally, Wood et al. found evidence that crime victimization in Latin America induces people to seriously think about moving to the United States.[7]

The Colombian case is particularly interesting since it shares many characteristics with the Mexican experience, despite having its origins in political opposition. There is evidence that crime and violence forced Colombians to migrate to safer locations within Colombia.[8] On their part, Rodríguez and Villa found evidence that the risk of kidnapping induces households to send some of their members to an international destination.[9] They also found that wealthier households are at greater risk of becoming kidnap victims.

Therefore it is not surprising that Mexicans exposed to drug-related violence are fleeing the conflict zones and that they are finding a safe haven in the United States. This phenomenon has been publicized in the American news media: the US cities in the southern border have seen a relative increase of middle-class Mexican migration. These new migrants have established new businesses in the United States,[10] and are therefore different from the archetypical Mexican migrants.

To my knowledge there is no research documenting this forced migration all across the US-Mexico border. This chapter attempts to fill this gap in the literature. The objective of the chapter is twofold. First, it will provide evidence of the changes in demographics along the US-Mexican border. Using data from Mexican administrative records of death certificates and the American Community Survey from 2000 to 2010, I will document how the upsurge in violence, as measured by homicide rates, led to an increase of immigrants in the southern border states of the United States.

The border region will be the focus of this study because the war on drugs has affected the northern states in Mexico disproportionately, particularly the border cities. Another reason to focus on the border region is that migration into the border cities in the United States is facilitated by the fact that Mexicans holding a Border Crossing Card can cross the border and travel up to 25 miles into the United States—and 75 miles into Arizona—without the need of an I-94. This variation in the traveling limits will allow me to compare changes in the Mexican migrants' characteristics between cities close to Mexico to those cities that are apparently "off limits."

The chapter will also document if there are changes in the openings of businesses in the counties along the US border using data from self-employment in the American Community Survey and data from the County

Business Patterns. The working hypothesis in this case is that Mexican migrants transfer their businesses to the United States or that they simply open businesses in the United States to make a living.

Using both a descriptive analysis and econometric estimations, we find that the upsurge in violence in Mexico did produce an increase in college-educated immigrants to the states on the southern US border, and there is evidence of a correlation with business openings in the United States; hence, the immigrants' investments were not limited to the southern border states. These findings suggest that drug-related violence in Mexico did produce a change in the type of immigrants from Mexico to the United States. The results imply that the violence spurred by the drug war has increased the cost of living in Mexico relative to the cost of migrating to the United States, so that many more Mexicans have been induced to migrate. These findings have very important implications for Mexico and the United States. The fact that college-educated immigrants, who are willing to invest in businesses, are fleeing the country entails a loss of both human and physical capital. According to growth theories,[11] these two types of investments are the main inputs for economic development. Hence, if the strategy against drug trafficking continues on this violent path, Mexico's economic growth will eventually be hampered.

Despite the fact that the United States is the largest market for the drugs distributed by Mexico's drug cartels, efforts to eradicate drug trafficking from Mexico are the result of mounting American pressure on Mexican authorities.[12] Prior to President Calderón's period, cooperation between Mexico and the United States was marked by distrust due to the rampant corruption among Mexican officials.[13] However, in the 2008 Department of Justice National Drug Threat Assessment, the US government recognized that "Mexican drug trafficking organizations represent the greatest organized crime threat to the United States."[14] In 2008 a great advance in security cooperation was made when Presidents George W. Bush and Felipe Calderón Hinojosa signed the Merida Initiative, which authorized a transfer of $1.4 billion to Mexico mostly in military equipment and technology, and to a lesser degree for the strengthening of Mexico's law enforcement institutions.[15] President Barack Obama supported the Merida Initiative, but he emphasized the need to address economic and social ills in the fight against drug trafficking and violence.[16] Despite these efforts, security cooperation between Mexico and the United States is still lacking. Three security issues are relatively abandoned in security cooperation: the demand for drugs in the United States, arms trafficking and money laundering.[17] Those issues are crucial if the intentions to weaken the drug cartels and to address security concerns in both countries are serious.

The rest of the chapter is organized as follows. Section 2 describes the data sources used in the analysis as well as the construction of some key variables. Section 3 documents the upsurge in homicides in Mexico, as well as the changing dynamics of migration to the United States along the southern border. Section 4 presents the econometric analysis. Finally, section 5 discusses the results and concludes.

## DATA

In both the descriptive and econometric analysis we used data from many different sources. We used the causes of death in death certificates to tally the homicides in Mexico. Those administrative records have information on the exact date of death; municipality and state of residence of the deceased; cause of death, described using the tenth version of the International Classification of Diseases;[18] age, gender and other sociodemographic characteristics. Given the topic of interest we took into account only those deaths of people 15 or more years of age. We also estimated homicides for two age groups of interest: those between 15 and 24 years old, and those between 25 and 44 years old.

The homicides rates were estimated as the number of homicides in a municipality over 100,000 inhabitants in the group of interest of that municipality. The population tallies were estimated using the 2000 and 2010 Mexican Censuses of Population, and the 2005 Population Count. The population for the years between surveys was extrapolated using a constant population growth rate.

Given that our main interest is the drug-related violence close to the border, the homicide rates were geo-referenced.[19] The geographical data was obtained from Mexico's National Statistics Institute (INEGI is its Spanish acronym).[20] In order to estimate the degree of exposure of US counties to Mexican migrants fleeing violence, we constructed a weighted homicide rate, where the weights were given by the square root of the distance between US counties and Mexican municipalities. The geographical coordinates of US counties were obtained from the Census Bureau.[21] We assumed that those counties farther than 500 kilometers from a Mexican municipality were not exposed to this kind of Mexican migration.

The characterization of immigrants in the United States was done using the 2000 Census of Population and the 2005 to 2010 American Community Surveys.[22] These surveys have information on sociodemographic characteristics, work behavior and job characteristics, country of birth, year of immigration and other variables. The descriptive analysis will use recent migrants—that is, those who have been in the United States during the last five years or less. The econometric analysis will focus on immigrants who arrived in the last year. That way we will be better enabled to relate immigration to violence in the last year.

Finally, the data on businesses comes from the County Business Patterns series compiled by the Census Bureau.[23] These series have data on the number of business establishments in US counties since 1986. The data set has information on the industry of the establishment, total number of establishments and number of establishments by employment-size classes. Unfortunately, the data does not specify whether the business belongs to an immigrant.

## VIOLENCE AND CHANGES IN MEXICAN IMMIGRATION

We will first document the rise in homicide rates in Mexico. Figure 12.1 presents the trends in homicide rates since 2000. Each of the panels in the figure compares homicide rates according to how close they are to the border. Panel A compares the municipalities in the northern-border states (denoted with a 1) with those in nonborder states (denoted by 0). It is easily verifiable that there has been a marked increase in the homicide rates all over Mexico since 2008, but particularly in the northern-border states: by 2010 the mean homicide rate in the northern states was about 37 homicides per 100,000 people, whereas in the rest of the country it was around 21 homicides per 100,000 people.

Panel B, C and D in Figure 12.1 look more closely at the homicide rates in municipalities near the border. The trend observed in panel A is mostly dominated by the violence exerted in municipalities closer to the border. Panel B compares municipalities in a radius of 150 miles from the border, panel C in a radius of 75 miles and panel D in a radius of 25 miles. As we

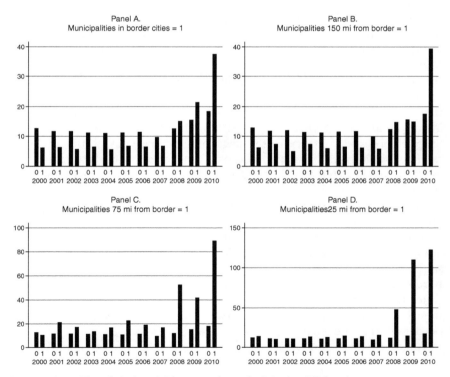

*Figure 12.1* Trends in homicide rates along the Mexico-US border.
Sources: Author's estimations using data from death certificates and the Mexican Census of Population for various years.

## 216   Eva Olimpia Arceo-Gómez

get closer to the border the homicide rates show an increasing pattern since 2008. For instance, panel D shows that municipalities within 25 miles of the border have a homicide rate of around 125 homicides per 100,000 people, while the rest of the municipalities in Mexico exhibit a homicide rate of less than 25. That is, the mean homicide rate in "border municipalities" is more than five times higher than the mean homicide rate in the rest of the country in 2010. Moreover, the mean homicide rate in these "border municipalities" has seen a tenfold increase since 2000.

Given these figures, it is not surprising that Mexicans are fleeing the border area. According to Mexico's Census of Population figures, in 2000 only about 9.5 percent of Mexicans migrating within the country came from border states: Baja California, Sonora, Chihuahua, Coahuila, Nuevo León and Tamaulipas. By 2010, almost 24 percent of Mexico's internal mobility was originated in the border states. Unfortunately, the census does not allow us to identify households that migrated to the United States. In order to characterize those immigrants, we will first present descriptive statistics of Mexican immigrants in the United States using data from the 2000 US Census of Population, and the 2005 and 2010 American Community Surveys.

Table 12.1 presents descriptive statistics of recent Mexican immigrants in the United States. Here recent immigrants are defined as those who migrated less than five years prior to the survey. The first trend that stands out is that Mexican migrants are older in 2000 than they were in 2010. Mexicans in the southern border states (California, Arizona, New Mexico and Texas) have a different age structure than those in the rest of the United States: they tend to be underage or between 36 and 64 with a higher proportion. We also find that a higher proportion of immigrants are females over time. Surprisingly, and contrary to the anecdotal evidence saying that wealthy *families* are the ones fleeing violence, over time fewer migrants were married in 2010 than in 2005, and the border exhibits only a slightly higher proportion of married immigrants.

One of the recurring arguments in the media is not only that wealthy families are migrating, but also that they are establishing businesses or otherwise investing in the United States. In order to find evidence of that, Table 12.1 also presents the proportion of self-employed immigrants. This proportion has increased since 2000, and it has always been higher in the border states. However, the proportion increased by more in nonborder states than in border states, suggesting that business people are in fact establishing their economic activities away from the border and not in the border cities as the media suggests.

Another way to find evidence of a wealthier-than-average immigrant is to look at the educational structure. The last three rows in Table 12.1 present the proportion of immigrants with secondary schooling, completed high school and whether they attended college or more. The statistics present evidence that immigrants are now better educated than in 2000, but also

## Drug-Related Violence and Forced Migration 217

*Table 12.1* Characteristics of Mexican Immigrants: Border versus Nonborder States

| | Nonborder states | | | Border states | | |
|---|---|---|---|---|---|---|
| | 2000 | 2005 | 2010 | 2000 | 2005 | 2010 |
| Age: 0 to 20 | 0.3742 | 0.2891 | 0.2613 | 0.4158 | 0.3552 | 0.3136 |
| Age: 21 to 35 | 0.4946 | 0.5350 | 0.5476 | 0.4388 | 0.4766 | 0.4362 |
| Age: 36 to 64 | 0.1035 | 0.1387 | 0.1535 | 0.1012 | 0.1264 | 0.1600 |
| Female | 0.3757 | 0.3870 | 0.4088 | 0.4468 | 0.4422 | 0.4734 |
| Married | 0.3836 | 0.4138 | 0.3534 | 0.3714 | 0.4093 | 0.3583 |
| Self-employed | 0.0272 | 0.0351 | 0.0499 | 0.0554 | 0.0786 | 0.0787 |
| Salaried | 0.9728 | 0.9649 | 0.9501 | 0.9446 | 0.9214 | 0.9213 |
| Secondary | 0.2457 | 0.3095 | 0.2992 | 0.1953 | 0.2277 | 0.2342 |
| High school | 0.0358 | 0.0412 | 0.0466 | 0.0337 | 0.0400 | 0.0638 |
| College | 0.0331 | 0.0357 | 0.0426 | 0.0268 | 0.0358 | 0.0589 |

*Sources*: Author's estimates using the 2000 US Census of Population, and the 2005 and 2010 American Community Surveys.

*Note*: All quantities represent proportions of the characteristic specified.

that there was a large influx of college-educated immigrants in the border states. So at least near the border, we do find some evidence of a changing face of Mexican immigrants.

Table 12.2 presents the same descriptive statistics for Mexicans living in the southern border states by distance to the border. We find that the population of Mexican migrants in those areas is getting older, but more so the closer they live to the border. A larger percentage of migrants are female as we move towards the border. These figures are strikingly different to those found in nonborder states: the percentage of female migrants in counties within 25 miles of the border is larger than 50 percent in 2010, whereas it is only around 40 percent in nonborder states that same year. The percentage of self-employed increased more in those counties within 75 miles of the border, but the increase is still lower than that observed in nonborder states. Finally, we find evidence that Mexican immigrants living closer to the border are much better educated, suggesting that wealthier-than-average Mexicans did migrate close to the border after 2005.

Table 12.3 estimates the growth rates in the number of business establishments and compares southern border states with the rest of the country. According to those figures, the growth rate of business establishments has indeed been higher in border states than the rest of the United States. The growth rate of businesses on the border has been more than 50 percentage points higher, despite the effects of the global recession of 2008. The businesses that exhibit the highest growth rates are those that employ between 10 and 19 workers, then those that employ between 20 to 49 people, and

218 *Eva Olimpia Arceo-Gómez*

*Table 12.2* Characteristics of Mexican Migrants Living in Border States by Distance to the Border

| Within | 150 mi. of border | | 75 mi. of border | | 25 mi. of border | |
|---|---|---|---|---|---|---|
| | 2005 | 2010 | 2005 | 2010 | 2005 | 2010 |
| Age: 0 to 20 | 0.3509 | 0.3299 | 0.3437 | 0.3084 | 0.3741 | 0.2953 |
| Age: 21 to 35 | 0.4760 | 0.4077 | 0.5270 | 0.4199 | 0.3815 | 0.3625 |
| Age: 36 to 64 | 0.1281 | 0.1545 | 0.1049 | 0.1703 | 0.1733 | 0.2160 |
| Female | 0.4571 | 0.4859 | 0.4027 | 0.4578 | 0.4940 | 0.5276 |
| Married | 0.3958 | 0.3304 | 0.4352 | 0.3861 | 0.4836 | 0.4112 |
| Self-employed | 0.0958 | 0.0921 | 0.0741 | 0.0962 | 0.1311 | 0.1307 |
| Salaried | 0.9042 | 0.9079 | 0.9259 | 0.9038 | 0.8689 | 0.8693 |
| Secondary | 0.2435 | 0.2325 | 0.2632 | 0.2442 | 0.2253 | 0.2009 |
| High school | 0.0404 | 0.0638 | 0.0355 | 0.0551 | 0.0586 | 0.0884 |
| College | 0.0307 | 0.0551 | 0.0232 | 0.0623 | 0.0668 | 0.1168 |

*Sources*: Author's estimates using the 2000 US Census of Population, and the 2005 and 2010 American Community Surveys.

*Note*: All quantities represent proportions of the characteristic specified.

*Table 12.3* Growth Rates in the Number of Establishments

| Growth rates (%) | Nonborder states | | Border states | |
|---|---|---|---|---|
| | 2005 | 2009 | 2005 | 2009 |
| Number of establishments | 1.5991 | −0.3453 | 1.9140 | 0.2776 |
| By employment size: | | | | |
| Establishments: 1 to 4 | 2.2106 | −0.4494 | 2.6715 | 0.1006 |
| Establishments: 5 to 9 | 0.8644 | −0.3075 | 1.2246 | 0.4493 |
| Establishments: 10 to 19 | 1.2393 | 0.1084 | 1.2209 | 0.9565 |
| Establishments: 20 to 49 | 0.7586 | −0.0753 | 0.8535 | 0.5629 |

*Source*: Author's estimates using County Business Patterns data series.

finally those that employ between 5 to 9 workers. So the businesses that are growing the most are not in the smallest employment-size category.

Finally, Table 12.4 compares the growth rates of number of establishments of counties that are closer to the border. According the table, the growth rate of the total number of establishments is the highest in the counties within 75 miles of the border. However, the establishments that employ between 20 and 49 workers grew more in the counties within 25 miles of the border. We conclude that the number of establishments in the border states in general, and those closer to the border in particular, grew more than in the rest of the country, even during the years of the global recession of 2008.

## Drug-Related Violence and Forced Migration   219

*Table 12.4*   Growth Rates in the Number of Establishment in Border States

| Growth rates (%) | Within: | | | | | |
| --- | --- | --- | --- | --- | --- | --- |
| | 150 mi. of border | | 75 mi. of border | | 25 mi. of border | |
| | 2005 | 2009 | 2005 | 2009 | 2005 | 2009 |
| Number of establishments | 2.7698 | −0.1066 | 3.6473 | 0.7176 | 2.6416 | 0.3315 |
| By employment size: | | | | | | |
| Establishments: 1 to 4 | 3.7894 | −0.1240 | 4.5158 | 0.8171 | 3.3226 | 0.1186 |
| Establishments: 5 to 9 | 1.7210 | 0.0751 | 2.4448 | 1.4668 | 1.8350 | 0.6419 |
| Establishments: 10 to 19 | 1.6851 | 0.4002 | 2.8767 | 0.6870 | 1.8876 | 1.2155 |
| Establishments: 20 to 49 | 1.2758 | −0.3625 | 2.5575 | 0.2742 | 2.3025 | 0.3148 |

*Source*: Author's estimates using County Business Patterns data series.

## ECONOMETRIC ANALYSIS

In order to strengthen the findings of the previous section, we estimated the following regression:

$$Y_{jt} = \alpha + \beta Homicide_{jt} + \gamma Urate_{jt} + \delta_j + \mu_t + \varepsilon_{jt,} \tag{1}$$

where $Y_{jt}$ is the logarithm of the outcome of interest in county $j$ and year $t$; *Homicide* is the logarithm of homicide rate weighted by distance to Mexican municipalities within 150 miles of the border; *Urate* is the logarithm of the unemployment rate; $\delta_j$ are county-fixed effects that control for county characteristics that are time-invariant; and $\mu_t$ are year-fixed effects that control for the overall health of the US economy. At this point it is worthwhile to remember that the weighted homicide rates are measuring the exposure to immigrants fleeing violence. The working hypothesis in this chapter is that immigrants tended to flee to places relatively close to the border, given that this type of migration is "facilitated" by Border Crossing Cards and Mexicans still have easy access to Mexico. The outcomes of interest will be the number of Mexicans who migrated in the year prior to the survey, and the number of business establishments. These outcomes will also be restricted to either migrants' characteristics or the employment size of the establishment.

Table 12.5 presents the estimates of equation (1) using the log of the number of Mexican immigrants. Our estimates suggest that the homicide rates caused an increase in the total Mexican immigrants in the United States. We find that a 1 percent increase in the weighted homicide rates is correlated with an increase of 0.57 percent of Mexican immigrants. Contrary to what we expected, homicide rates are negatively related to immigration of self-employed Mexicans: a 1 percent increase in the weighted homicide rates is correlated

## 220 *Eva Olimpia Arceo-Gómez*

*Table 12.5* Effect of Violence on Mexican Migration to the United States

| | Last year's Mexican immigrants | | | | |
| | Total | Self-employed | Education level | | |
| | | | College | High school | Secondary |
| Dependent variable: | (1) | (2) | (3) | (4) | (5) |
| Weighted homicide rate | 0.5730*** | −0.3939** | 0.1091 | -0.1406 | 0.0308 |
| | [0.1730] | [0.1677] | [0.1987] | [0.1802] | [0.2170] |
| Unemployment rate | −0.7951*** | 0.0054 | −0.2314* | −0.1619 | −0.4432** |
| | [0.2510] | [0.1155] | [0.1362] | [0.1300] | [0.1965] |
| Constant | 1.0284 | 0.5854* | 0.0059 | 0.2913 | 0.5492 |
| | [0.6969] | [0.3271] | [0.3966] | [0.3753] | [0.5526] |
| Observations | 2,254 | 2,254 | 2,254 | 2,254 | 2,254 |
| R-squared | 0.636 | 0.447 | 0.526 | 0.485 | 0.561 |
| Year FE | Y | Y | Y | Y | Y |
| County FE | Y | Y | Y | Y | Y |

*Note*: Dependent and explanatory variables are in logarithms. Robust standard errors in brackets. *** p<0.01, ** p<0.05, * p<0.1

with a decrease of 0.39 percent of self-employed Mexican immigrants. We do not find any significant effect of murder rates on immigration of Mexicans categorized by educational levels. The effect of county unemployment rates is negative as expected—that is, the higher the county unemployment rate, the lower is the influx of Mexican migrants to that country.

The foregoing results could be a consequence of spurious correlation between immigration and murder rates. We rule out this possibility by estimating equation (1) using the weighted death rates from internal causes (diseases) as an explanatory variable instead of weighted homicide rates. The results of this estimation are shown in column (1) of Table 12.6. As expected, death rates from internal causes are unrelated to Mexican immigrants in the United States.

The results found in Table 12.5 could also be a result of some counties having better economic conditions than others (where these conditions are somehow correlated to murder rates in Mexico and unmeasured by unemployment rates), and thus attracting immigrants from Mexico, Americans and immigrants from other countries. Columns (2) and (3) tackle this possibility. We do find a positive correlation between American immigrants and homicide rates in Mexico. Notwithstanding, we do not find any effect of homicide rates in Mexico on immigration from other countries. Finally, we estimate whether the murder rates by age groups of the victims have a

*Drug-Related Violence and Forced Migration* 221

*Table 12.6* Robustness Checks

| Dependent variable: | Mexican migrants | American migrants | Non-Mexican migrants | Mexican migrants | Mexican migrants |
|---|---|---|---|---|---|
| | (1) | (2) | (3) | (4) | (5) |
| Death rate (internal causes) | 1.4154 [2.2990] | | | | |
| Homicide rate | | 0.0281** [0.0124] | 0.1225 [0.1771] | | |
| Homicide rate: 15 to 24 | | | | 0.4618*** [0.1710] | |
| Homicide rate: 25 to 44 | | | | | 0.5043*** [0.1688] |
| Observations | 2,254 | 2,254 | 2,254 | 2,254 | 2,254 |

*Note:* Dependent and explanatory variables are in logarithms. Robust standard errors in brackets. The regression also controls for the log of the county unemployment rate, year- and county-fixed effects. *** p<0.01, ** p<0.05, * p<0.1

differential effect on immigration. We do not find such a differential effect, though both of the coefficients in columns (4) and (5) are smaller in magnitude than the effect of total murder rates.

Table 12.7 presents the effects of murder rates in Mexico on the number of business establishments in the United States. The results indicate that violence in Mexico has a small, but positive and significant, effect on business establishments: a 1 percent increase in weighted murder rates in Mexico leads to a 0.01 percent increase in the number of business establishments in the United States. We find a positive effect for establishments employing up to 19 workers. However, the results do not hold when we include internal death rates instead of homicide death rates (Table 12.8). There could be an omitted variable that is correlated to both the murder rates in Mexico and immigration in the United States, so those results should be taken with caution.

Since our working hypothesis establishes that immigrants mostly fled just across the border, we also estimated the following equation:

$$Y_{jt} = \alpha + \beta \, Homicide_{jt} + \pi Homicide_{jt} \times BorderSt_j + \gamma Urate_{jt} + \delta_j + \mu_t + \varepsilon_{jt}, \quad (2)$$

where all variables are defined as it was previously explained, and $BorderSt_j$ is an indicator variable that the county is in a southern border state. The parameter $\pi$ will identify the difference of the effect of homicides on border

222  *Eva Olimpia Arceo-Gómez*

*Table 12.7* Effect of Mexican Violence on the Number of Business Establishments in the United States

| | Total | Employment size | | | |
|---|---|---|---|---|---|
| | | 1 to 4 | 5 to 9 | 10 to 19 | 20 to 49 |
| Dependent variable | (1) | (2) | (3) | (4) | (5) |
| Homicide rate | 0.0109*** | 0.0091*** | 0.0138*** | 0.0136*** | 0.0089 |
| | [0.0023] | [0.0024] | [0.0041] | [0.0036] | [0.0068] |
| Unemployment rate | −0.0124*** | −0.0033 | −0.0088* | −0.0234*** | −0.0345*** |
| | [0.0032] | [0.0036] | [0.0047] | [0.0052] | [0.0059] |
| Constant | 10.6430*** | 10.0342*** | 9.0090*** | 8.5700*** | 8.1494*** |
| | [0.0090] | [0.0101] | [0.0128] | [0.0145] | [0.0164] |
| Observations | 1,880 | 1,880 | 1,880 | 1,880 | 1,880 |
| R-squared | 0.999 | 0.999 | 0.999 | 0.999 | 0.998 |
| Year FE | Y | Y | Y | Y | Y |
| County FE | Y | Y | Y | Y | Y |

*Note*: Dependent and explanatory variables are in logarithms. Robust standard errors in brackets. *** p<0.01, ** p<0.05, * p<0.1

states. Given our working hypothesis, we would expect that $\pi > 0$; hence, border states receive more immigrants and open more establishments as a consequence of violence in Mexico.

Table 12.9 presents the estimates of equation (2). As expected, the coefficient on the interaction term is positive (except for immigrants with high school education in column (4), where it is negative, though not statistically significant). In column (1) we find that an increase of 1 percent of the weighted homicide rate in Mexico produces an increase of 0.72 percent of the total immigration of Mexicans to the southern border of the United States. What is more interesting, however, is the effect of violence on college-educated immigrants: 1 percent of the weighted homicide rate in Mexico produces an increase of 2.03 percent of the immigration of college-educated Mexicans in the southern border states. This last finding is consistent with the hypothesis that wealthier-than-average Mexicans are the ones fleeing violence in Mexico. We do not find a positive effect on the number of immigrants with a high school diploma, but we find a positive effect on secondary-educated immigrants.

Table 12.10 presents the robustness checks for the estimation of equation (2). We do not find any evidence that the source of our results is merely spurious correlation. The results in Table 12.10 are more encouraging in the sense that we do not find an effect on the immigration of Americans anymore.

## Drug-Related Violence and Forced Migration    223

*Table 12.8*   Effect of Mexican Violence on the Number of Business Establishments on Southern US Border (fake experiment)

| Dependent variable | Total | Number of business establishments | | | |
|---|---|---|---|---|---|
| | | Employment size | | | |
| | | 1 to 4 | 5 to 9 | 10 to 19 | 20 to 49 |
| | (1) | (2) | (3) | (4) | (5) |
| Death rate (internal causes) | 0.1074*** | 0.0621** | 0.1709*** | 0.0904* | 0.1815*** |
| | [0.0341] | [0.0304] | [0.0488] | [0.0502] | [0.0594] |
| Unemployment rate | −0.0111*** | −0.0025 | −0.0067 | −0.0222*** | −0.0323*** |
| | [0.0033] | [0.0036] | [0.0047] | [0.0053] | [0.0060] |
| Constant | 10.5901*** | 10.0046*** | 8.9235*** | 8.5271*** | 8.0567*** |
| | [0.0208] | [0.0194] | [0.0295] | [0.0305] | [0.0345] |
| Observations | 1,880 | 1,880 | 1,880 | 1,880 | 1,880 |
| R-squared | 0.999 | 0.999 | 0.999 | 0.999 | 0.998 |
| Year FE | Y | Y | Y | Y | Y |
| County FE | Y | Y | Y | Y | Y |

*Note*: Dependent and explanatory variables are in logarithms. Robust standard errors in brackets. *** $p<0.01$, ** $p<0.05$, * $p<0.1$

However, we now find a positive effect on immigration from non-Mexican foreigners all over the United States, with no particular effect on the southern border states. The relative importance of murder rates by age groups continues to be smaller in magnitude than the effect of total murder rates in Mexico.

Finally, Table 12.11 shows the estimation of model (2) using the logarithm of number of business establishments as a dependent variable. We find that homicide rates have a smaller effect on businesses in border states than in the rest of the United States. These findings suggest that business openings are not exclusive of border states as the descriptive evidence suggests, but a general trend in the United States. However, we need to approach these results with caution. The robustness check using the death rate from internal causes is more encouraging (not shown), but it still does not allow us to rule out the presence of omitted variable bias in these estimations.

## DISCUSSION AND CONCLUDING REMARKS

Since President Felipe Calderón took office in 2006, Mexico has been waging a war against drug cartels. The war on drugs has been found to lead to an

## 224 *Eva Olimpia Arceo-Gómez*

*Table 12.9* Effect of Violence on Mexican Migration to US Southern Border States

| Dependent variable: | Last year's Mexican immigrants | | | | |
|---|---|---|---|---|---|
| | Total | Self-employed | Education level | | |
| | | | College | High school | Secondary |
| | (1) | (2) | (3) | (4) | (5) |
| Homicide rate | −0.1398 | −1.0227 | −1.8887 | −0.1099 | −0.4769** |
| | [0.2062] | [1.2021] | [1.1921] | [1.6735] | [0.1997] |
| Border dummy * Homicide | 0.7249*** | 0.6395 | 2.0315* | -0.0312 | 0.5162* |
| rate | [0.2548] | [1.2138] | [1.2072] | [1.6826] | [0.2859] |
| Unemployment rate | −0.7894*** | 0.0104 | −0.2154 | −0.1622 | −0.4391** |
| | [0.2516] | [0.1149] | [0.1362] | [0.1293] | [0.1969] |
| Constant | 1.0448 | 0.5999* | 0.0519 | 0.2906 | 0.5609 |
| | [0.6983] | [0.3255] | [0.3962] | [0.3738] | [0.5531] |
| Observations | 2,254 | 2,254 | 2,254 | 2,254 | 2,254 |
| R-squared | 0.636 | 0.447 | 0.527 | 0.485 | 0.561 |
| Year FE | Y | Y | Y | Y | Y |
| County FE | Y | Y | Y | Y | Y |

*Note*: Dependent and explanatory variables are in logarithms. Robust standard errors in brackets. *** $p<0.01$, ** $p<0.05$, * $p<0.1$

increase in murder rates. We find that there was a tenfold increase in murder rates all across the municipalities within 25 miles of the border between 2006 and 2010. This upsurge in violence has understandably become a powerful reason to flee those unsafe areas in search of a peaceful life. The American media has presented anecdotal evidence of the violence-led diaspora. According to the accounts, Mexicans who fled the war are wealthier than the prototypical Mexican immigrant. The new immigrants are opening businesses to make a living, or even making huge investments in order to apply for an E-2 visa.

Using both descriptive and econometric analyses, this chapter documents how violence on the border caused a spur in immigration to the United States, and particularly to the southern border states. According to our estimates, the Mexican immigration caused by violence is better educated than the economic Mexican migrants. We do not find, however, robust causal evidence on business openings or self-employed Mexican immigrants. Our evidence points to a positive correlation between murder rates in Mexico and the number of establishments all over the United States (not exclusively on the southern border).

*Drug-Related Violence and Forced Migration* 225

*Table 12.10* Robustness Checks of Model with Interactions

| Dependent variable: | Mexican migrants (1) | American migrants (2) | Non-Mexican migrants (3) | Mexican migrants (4) | Mexican migrants (5) |
|---|---|---|---|---|---|
| Death rate (internal causes) | −1.7031 | | | | |
| | [3.3064] | | | | |
| Border dummy * Death rate (internal causes) | 3.1398 [4.0206] | | | | |
| Homicide rate | | 0.0448 | 0.3908* | | |
| | | [0.0428] | [0.2068] | | |
| Border dummy * Homicide rate | | −0.0170 | −0.2728 | | |
| | | [0.0442] | [0.2648] | | |
| Homicide rate: 15 to 24 | | | | −0.1308 | |
| | | | | [0.1889] | |
| Border dummy * Homicide rate: 15 to 24 | | | | 0.6026** | |
| | | | | [0.2455] | |
| Homicide rate: 25 to 44 | | | | | −0.1780 |
| | | | | | [0.2447] |
| Border dummy * Homicide rate: 25 to 44 | | | | | 0.6899** |
| | | | | | [0.2818] |
| Observations | 2,254 | 2,254 | 2,254 | 2,254 | 2,254 |

*Note*: Dependent and explanatory variables are in logarithms. Robust standard errors in brackets. The regression also controls for the log of the county unemployment rate, year- and county-fixed effects. *** p<0.01, ** p<0.05, * p<0.1

## 226 Eva Olimpia Arceo-Gómez

*Table 12.11* Effect of Mexican Violence on the Number of Business Establishments on Southern US Border

| | | Number of business establishments | | | |
|---|---|---|---|---|---|
| | Total | Employment size | | | |
| | | 1 to 4 | 5 to 9 | 10 to 19 | 20 to 49 |
| Dependent variable | (1) | (2) | (3) | (4) | (5) |
| Homicide rate | 0.0223 | 0.0080 | 0.0545*** | 0.0513*** | 0.0296* |
| | [0.0143] | [0.0122] | [0.0187] | [0.0148] | [0.0165] |
| Border dummy × | −0.0117 | 0.0011 | −0.0416** | −0.0386** | −0.0212 |
| Homicide rate | [0.0145] | [0.0124] | [0.0191] | [0.0151] | [0.0178] |
| Unemployment rate | −0.0125*** | −0.0033 | −0.0091* | −0.0237*** | −0.0347*** |
| | [0.0033] | [0.0036] | [0.0047] | [0.0052] | [0.0059] |
| Constant | 10.6428*** | 10.0343*** | 9.0082*** | 8.5694*** | 8.1491*** |
| | [0.0090] | [0.0101] | [0.0128] | [0.0145] | [0.0165] |
| Observations | 1,880 | 1,880 | 1,880 | 1,880 | 1,880 |
| R-squared | 0.999 | 0.999 | 0.999 | 0.999 | 0.998 |
| Year FE | Y | Y | Y | Y | Y |
| County FE | Y | Y | Y | Y | Y |

*Note*: Dependent and explanatory variables are in logarithms. Robust standard errors in brackets. *** $p<0.01$, ** $p<0.05$, * $p<0.1$

These results have very important implications for both Mexico and the United States. First, we found college-educated people are fleeing violence in Mexico. This type of immigration amounts to a loss of human capital in Mexico, which is still relatively scarce as compared to developed nations. Second, we found that homicide rates are correlated with a boom of businesses and all over the United States. To Mexico, this result means that investment is flowing away from Mexico and into the United States. All in all, Mexico is losing both human and physical capital due to the upsurge in violence generated by the war on drugs. According to growth theories in economics, these losses will eventually hamper economic growth in Mexico. Mexico's loss is, however, the United States' gain.

Mexico is thus facing a large toll in human losses due to violence and migration. There have been great advances in US-Mexico security cooperation through the Merida Initiative and its current emphasis on community economic and social development. However, Mexico and the United States still have three important issues pending in their security agenda: US drug demand, arms trafficking and the transnational movement of drug money.

## Drug-Related Violence and Forced Migration 227

These issues need to be addressed if the war against drugs is indeed a serious effort.

## NOTES

1. Salvador Camarena, "La guerra contra el 'narco' en México ha causado 47,515 muertes violentas," *El País*, January 12, 2012. As of October 2011, the Drug Enforcement Administration estimated 43,000 casualties related to the Mexican drug war. Silvia Otero, "Van 43 mil muertos en la lucha a narco: DEA," *El Universal*, October 14, 2011. There have been several unofficial death tolls. According to a Tijuana newspaper, up to December 2011 there had been 60,420 deaths related to the drug war. Enrique Mendoza, "Quinto año de gobierno: 60 420 ejecuciones," *Zeta*, December 12, 2011.
2. Melissa Dell, "Trafficking Networks and the Mexican Drug War" (unpublished manuscript, 2011).
3. Andrew R. Morrison, "Violence or Economics: What Drives Internal Migration in Guatemala?" *Economic Development and Cultural Change* 41, no. 4 (1993): 817.
4. Andrew R. Morrison and Rachel A. May, "Escape from Terror: Violence and Migration in Post-Revolutionary Guatemala," *Latin American Research Review* 29, no. 2 (1994): 111.
5. Jennifer H. Lundquist and Douglas Massey, "Politics or Economics? International Migration during the Nicaraguan Contra War," *Journal of Latin American Studies* 37, no. 1 (2005): 29.
6. Steven E. Alvarado and Douglas S. Massey, "Search of Peace: Structural Adjustment, Violence, and International Migration," *Annals of the American Academy of Political and Social Science* 630, no. 1 (2010): 137.
7. Charles Wood, Chris Gibson, Ludmila Ribeiro and Paula Hamsho-Diaz, "Crime Victimization in Latin America and Intentions to Migrate to the United States," *International Migration Review* 44, no. 1 (2010): 3–24.
8. Stefanie Engel and Ana M. Ibáñez, "Displacement Due to Violence in Colombia: A Household-Level Analysis," *Economic Development and Cultural Change* 55, no. 2 (2007): 335; Ana M. Ibáñez and Carlos E. Vélez, "Civil Conflict and Forced Migration: The Micro Determinants and Welfare Losses of Displacement in Colombia," *World Development* 36, no. 4 (2008): 659; Nancy Lozano-Gracia, Gianfranco Piras, Ana M. Ibáñez and Geoffrey Hewings, "The Journey to Safety: Conflict-Driven Migration Flows in Colombia," *International Regional Science Review* 32, no. 2 (2010): 157.
9. Catherine Rodríguez and Edgar Villa, "Kidnap Risks and Migration: Evidence from Colombia," *Journal of Population Economics* 25, no. 3 (2012): 1139.
10. Andrew Becker, "New Migrant Class Flees Mexican Drug War," Center for Investigative Reporting, March 20, 2009, http://cironline.org/reports/new-migrant-class-flees-mexican-drug-war; Ana Campoy, "Mexicans Fleeing Violence Spur a Boom in El Paso," *Wall Street Journal*, October 26, 2009; Cecilia Garza, "New Refugees: Mexican Businesses Moving to Laredo" (unpublished manuscript, 2009); Mary B. Sheridan, "Drug War Sparks Exodus of Affluent Mexicans," *Washington Post*, August 26, 2011.
11. Gregory Mankiw, David Romer and David Weil, "A Contribution to the Empirics of Economic Growth," *Quarterly Journal of Economics* 107, no. 2 (1992): 407; Paul Roemer, "Endogenous Technological Change," *Journal of*

228  *Eva Olimpia Arceo-Gómez*

    *Political Economy* 98, no. 5 (1990): S71; Robert Solow, "A Contribution to the Theory of Economic Growth," *Quarterly Journal of Economics* 70, no. 1 (1956): 65.

12. Jorge Chabat, "Mexico's War on Drugs: No Margin for Maneuver," *Annals of the American Academy of Political and Social Science* 582 (2002): 134; Jorge Chabat, "La Iniciativa Mérida y la relación México-Estados Unidos: En busca de la confianza perdida" (Documento de Trabajo No. 195, Centro de Investigación y Docencia Económicas, División de Estudios Internacionales, 2010).

13. Luis Astorga and David A. Shirk, "Drug Trafficking Organizations and Counter-Drug Strategies in the U.S.-Mexican Context" (Evolving Democracy Series, Center for US-Mexican Studies, University of California, San Diego, 2010); Chabat, "La Iniciativa Mérida."

14. Cited by Shannon O'Neil, "Moving Beyond Merida in U.S.-Mexico Security Cooperation" (prepared statement for the United States House of Representatives, 111th Congress, 2010).

15. Chabat, "La Iniciativa Mérida"; O'Neil, "Moving Beyond Merida."

16. Obama's approach focuses on four pillars: "disrupting the ability of organized crime to operate, strengthening institutions to sustain the rule of law and human rights, building a 21st century border, and fostering strong and resilient communities." Eric L. Olson and Christopher E. Wilson, "Beyond Merida: The Evolving Approach to Security Cooperation" (Working Paper Series on U.S.-Mexico Security Cooperation, Woodrow Wilson Center for International Scholars, Trans-Border Institute, University of San Diego, 2010); O'Neil, "Moving beyond Merida." The ideas behind the first two pillars were already present in the Merida Initiative.

17. O'Neil, "Moving Beyond Merida."

18. In particular, homicides are classified using the X85 to Y09 codes, which describe assault inflicted with different objects, substances or actions.

19. I would like to thank Gabriel Parada for his help geo-referencing the data and estimating the distance to the border.

20. "Catálogo de claves de entidades federativas, municipios y localidades–consulta y descarga," INEGI, http://www.inegi.org.mx/geo/contenidos/geoestadistica/catalogoclaves.aspx.

21. http://www.census.gov/tiger/tms/gazetteer/county2k.txt.

22. Integrated Public Use Microdata Series, Version 5.0. http://usa.ipums.org/usa/.

23. "County Business Patterns (CBP), ZIP Code Business Patterns (ZBP)," United States Census Bureau, http://www.census.gov/econ/cbp/index.html.

## REFERENCES

Alvarado, Steven E., and Douglas S. Massey. "Search of Peace: Structural Adjustment, Violence, and International Migration." *Annals of the American Academy of Political and Social Science* 630, no. 1 (2010): 137–161.

Astorga, Luis, and David A. Shirk. "Drug Trafficking Organizations and Counter-Drug Strategies in the U.S.-Mexican Context." Evolving Democracy Series, Center for U.S.-Mexican Studies, University of California. San Diego. 2010.

Becker, Andrew. "New Migrant Class Flees Mexican Drug War." Center for Investigative Reporting. March 20, 2009. http://cironline.org/reports/new-migrant-class-flees-mexican-drug-war.

### Drug-Related Violence and Forced Migration  229

Camarena, Salvador. "La guerra contra el 'narco' en México ha causado 47,515 muertes violentas." *El País*. January 12, 2012. http://internacional.elpais.com/internacional/2012/01/11/actualidad/1326317916_963041.html.

Campoy, Ana. "Mexicans Fleeing Violence Spur a Boom in El Paso." *Wall Street Journal*. October 26, 2009. http://online.wsj.com/article/SB125651480451107029.html.

Chabat, Jorge. "La Iniciativa Mérida y la relación México-Estados Unidos: En busca de la confianza perdida." Documento de Trabajo No. 195. Centro de Investigación y Docencia Económicas, División de Estudios Internacionales. 2010.

———. "Mexico's War on Drugs: No Margin for Maneuver." *Annals of the American Academy of Political and Social Science* 582 (2002): 134–148.

Dell, Melissa. "Trafficking Networks and the Mexican Drug War." Unpublished manuscript, 2011.

Engel, Stefanie, and Ana M. Ibáñez. 2007. "Displacement Due to Violence in Colombia: A Household-Level Analysis." *Economic Development and Cultural Change* 55, no. 2 (2007): 335–365.

Garza, Cecilia. "New Refugees: Mexican Businesses Moving to Laredo." Unpublished manuscript, 2009.

Ibáñez, Ana M., and Carlos E. Vélez. "Civil Conflict and Forced Migration: The Micro Determinants and Welfare Losses of Displacement in Colombia." *World Development* 36, no. 4 (2008): 659–676.

Integrated Public Use Microdata Series: Version 5.0. http://usa.ipums.org/usa.

Lozano-Gracia, Nancy, Gianfranco Piras, Ana M. Ibáñez and Geoffrey Hewings. "The Journey to Safety: Conflict-Driven Migration Flows in Colombia." *International Regional Science Review* 32, no. 2 (2010): 157–180.

Lundquist, Jennifer H., and Douglas Massey. "Politics or Economics? International Migration during the Nicaraguan Contra War." *Journal of Latin American Studies* 37, no. 1 (2005): 29–53.

Mankiw, Gregory, David Romer and David Weil. "A Contribution to the Empirics of Economic Growth." *Quarterly Journal of Economics* 107, no. 2 (1992): 407–437.

Mendoza, Enrique. "Quinto año de gobierno: 60 420 ejecuciones." *Zeta*. December 12, 2011. http://www.zetatijuana.com/2011/12/12/quinto-ano-de-gobierno-60-mil-420-ejecuciones/.

Morrison, Andrew R. "Violence or Economics: What Drives Internal Migration in Guatemala?" *Economic Development and Cultural Change* 41, no. 4 (1993): 817–831.

Morrison, Andrew R., and Rachel A. May. "Escape from Terror: Violence and Migration in Post-Revolutionary Guatemala." *Latin American Research Review* 29, no. 2 (1994): 111–132.

Olson, Eric L., and Christopher E. Wilson. "Beyond Merida: The Evolving Approach to Security Cooperation." Working Paper Series on U.S.-Mexico Security Cooperation. Woodrow Wilson Center for International Scholars, Trans-Border Institute, University of San Diego. 2010.

O'Neil, Shannon. "Moving Beyond Merida in U.S.-Mexico Security Cooperation." Prepared statement for the United States House of Representatives. 111th Congress. 2010.

Otero, Silvia. "Van 43 mil muertos en la lucha a narco: DEA." *El Universal*. October 14, 2011. http://www.eluniversal.com.mx/notas/801079.html.

Rodríguez, Catherine, and Edgar Villa. "Kidnap Risks and Migration: Evidence from Colombia." *Journal of Population Economics* 25, no. 3 (2012): 1139–1164.

Roemer, Paul. "Endogenous Technological Change." *Journal of Political Economy* 98, no. 5 (1990): S71–S102.

Sheridan, Mary B. "Drug War Sparks Exodus of Affluent Mexicans." *Washington Post*. August 26, 2011. http://www.washingtonpost.com/world/national-security/drug-war-sparks-exodus-of-affluent-mexicans/2011/08/19/gIQA6OR1gJ_story.html.

Solow, Robert. "A Contribution to the Theory of Economic Growth." *Quarterly Journal of Economics* 70, no. 1 (1956): 65–94.

Wood, Charles, Chris Gibson, Ludmila Ribeiro, and Paula Hamsho-Diaz. "Crime Victimization in Latin America and Intentions to Migrate to the United States." *International Migration Review* 44, no. 1 (2010): 3–24.

# 13 Wage Differentials, Public Policies and Mexico-US Migration

*Ernesto Aguayo-Téllez, Arun K. Acharya and Christian I. Rivera-Mendoza*

## INTRODUCTION

Economic conditions have been and will continue to be the most important driver of international migration from Mexico to the United States. Raw income differentials between the two countries have gone from 2.9 times larger in the United States than in Mexico during the 1970s to 3.2 times larger in 2010. Along with the widening of the regional economic and wage gap, the international migration from Mexico to the United States has increased from less than 120,000 migrants a year (or less than 2.4% of the total population of Mexico) in 1970 to more than 500,000 migrants a year (or more than 5.1% of the total population) in 2010.[1]

During this course of time many attempts have been made to narrow economic differences between the two countries and indirectly reduce the migration flows, and the North American Free Trade Agreement (NAFTA) is the most recent and ambitious of them. However, neither wage differentials nor migration flows have been reduced. On the contrary, the wage gap between Mexico and the United States is wider by the day, and the exodus of more than half a million Mexicans per year has become an important concern. This situation and the lack of coordinated policies between the two countries point out the urgent need of binational economic and migration strategies to provide better labor conditions in Mexico, reducing wage differentials and migration incentives in the middle run. Up to now, economic policies exclusively oriented to promote economic growth through the flow of capital and products, such as NAFTA, have not been effective to improve the labor market in Mexico, to reduce migration and to increase the total welfare of the North American region. Similarly, social policies targeted to relieve poverty and to increase the social well-being of the most disadvantaged families in Mexico have not been effective in reducing international migration either. Migration literature suggests that very poor individuals cannot afford migration costs, but when there is a slight increase in their income, they start migrating.[2] Poverty conditions should be reduced to an extent so that individuals are better off staying in Mexico than migrating to the United States, which is something current social policies in Mexico have not achieved.

232   *Ernesto Aguayo-Téllez, et al.*

Thus, this chapter reviews the effects of US-Mexico wage differentials on promoting migration from Mexico to the United States. Then, it discusses the social and economic policies adopted by the Mexican government to reduce poverty and socioeconomic inequality in the country to indirectly reduce migration. Finally, this chapter discusses some thoughts and suggestions to handle the Mexico-US migration problem and points out the urgent need of bilateral strategies to deal with one of the most important concerns of the Mexico-US relation: international migration.

## WAGE DIFFERENTIALS AND MIGRATION FLOWS

Mexican-US migration has a long history, but the dynamic of such population flow has changed through time. However, the main driver of such movements of people has always been the same: the significant difference of economic conditions between both labor markets.

International migration from Mexico to the United States started on a large scale during the middle of the twentieth century, especially after the implementation of the Bracero Program.[3] The way the Bracero Program was implemented generated a peculiar map of emigration rates in Mexico and immigration rates in the United States. Specific Mexican states such as Michoacán, Guanajuato and Zacatecas were characterized by large rates of migration to the United States, principally from rural areas. Similarly, some American states such as California and Texas received large flows of Mexican immigrants, principally to perform agricultural activities.

Nowadays, Mexicans migrate to the United States from virtually every corner of the country and live in almost every city or town of the United States. However, the strong social networks created more than half a century ago are still present, making the previously mentioned Mexican states the prevailing main source of international migrants. Such social migration networks have been—and continue to be—the main channels individuals use to find their way to the United States. So it is not surprising that very well-defined migrant enclaves exist in almost all American cities and towns and they come from specific Mexican villages and towns.[4]

Figure 13.1 shows the yearly flow of Mexican migrants to the United States since 1970 as a percentage of the total population. Migration from Mexico to the United States increased constantly during the 1980s and 1990s and only decreased slightly after 2000. During the 1970s, migration to the United States was not larger than 3% of the population a year, increasing to 4% at the end of the 1980s and beginning of 1990s, and increasing to more than 6% in the year 2000. After that year, the migration ratio decreased slightly, but at the end of 2010 it was still larger than 5% a year.

As mentioned before, labor condition differences are one of the most important drivers of international migration from Mexico to the United

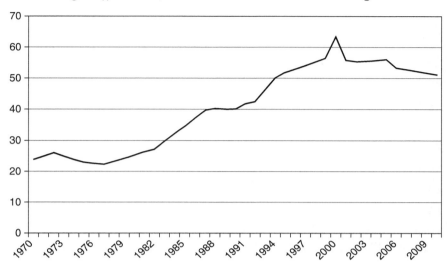

*Figure 13.1* Mexican migration to the United States, yearly migrants as share of total population.
*Source*: OECD.

States.[5] Using a multichoice model to consider simultaneously internal and international migration in Mexico and controlling for differences on observable and unobservable characteristics of migrants (such as productivity), Aguayo-Téllez and Martínez-Navarro[6] found that wage differentials are the main determinant of migration from Mexico to the United States. Reviewing the selection of Mexican migrants in the United States, Chiquiar and Hanson[7] also conclude that wage differentials are the most important determinant of migration, where the younger and less educated are the ones who present higher wage differentials. The authors also suggest that migration costs play an important role in determining who migrates, where the younger and more educated are the ones who confront lower costs.

Similarly, studying economic development and migration at the municipality level in Mexico, Unger finds that "the municipalities that exhibit higher migration [rates] are those with a large gap in economic development, living conditions, and infrastructure."[8] Stark and Taylor suggest that not only absolute income differences but also relative depravation have significant impact on migration to the United States.[9] The authors conclude that after controlling for absolute income, relatively deprived households are more likely to engage in international migration. Finally, Taylor[10] and Curran and Rivero[11] argue that social migration networks are, in addition to wage differentials, one of the main determinants of international migration in Mexico.

*Figure 13.2* National income per capita, US-MEX ratio.
*Source*: OECD.

Accordingly, taking into consideration the foregoing discussion, Figure 13.2 shows the findings of the analysis of the income differences between Mexico and the United States since 1970, using national income per capita. National income includes labor income as well as other sources of income, but it can give us an idea of raw wage differentials. It can be observed that in 1970 per capita income in the United States was 2.9 times larger than in Mexico. This ratio decreased slightly during the 1970s but increased considerably during the 1980s and 1990s, going from 2.53 in 1981 to 3.72 in 1999. During the 2000s, the US-Mexico per capita income gap decreased, although it is still larger than in the 1980s.

From Figures 13.1 and 13.2, the main conclusion we reach is that migration and wage differentials are strongly linked: when the US-Mexico income gap stretched, such as in the 1970s and 2000s, the migration rate from Mexico to the United States decreased, and when the income gap widened, such as in the 1980s and 1990s, migration increased. In the next section we will discuss the theoretical framework that links wage differentials and migration.

## MIGRATION AS A RESPONSE TO ECONOMIC INEQUALITY

Following the seminal work of Todaro[12] and Sjaastad,[13] economic theory models migration as a result of an individual utility maximization process in which the migrant decides to move only if the benefits of moving are larger than the costs. Initially, net benefits are approximated by wage differentials,

## Wage Differentials, Public Policies and Mexico-US Migration   235

although it is possible to add other nonpecuniary determinants, such as externalities, amenities and career opportunities. Harris and Todaro[14] relaxed the assumption of full employment and introduced expected probabilities of earnings rather than actual earning differentials to model the migration decision.

In principle, individuals seek to maximize the present value of their incomes by moving to places where wages are higher, expected wage differentials being the main engine for the migration decision. The existence of wage differentials drives migration flows from low-wage regions to high-wage regions. This reallocation of labor generates upward pressures on wages in the sending regions and downward pressures on wages in the receiving regions, leading to a wage convergence in the long run.[15]

As suggested by Sjaastad,[16] migration is an investment in human capital. Therefore, modeling individual migration decisions requires a migration decision function that considers not only expected wage differentials between origin and destination regions but also the associated moving costs. Individuals compute a cost-benefit analysis and depending on the skill levels, age, gender and other labor related variables such as occupation, experience and training, individuals calculate the net present value of migration and, if positive, they migrate.[17]

Refined versions of Sjaastad's[18] model, such as Polacheck and Horvath[19] and Borjas,[20] include nonpecuniary factors such as externalities, regional amenities and other long-run opportunities as migration determinants, besides the individual's wage differences and moving costs.

With relation to wage differentials, econometric studies usually depart from Mincer[21] wage equations.[22] However, in the migration case, there is a problem with estimating the wage differentials—that is, origin and destination wages cannot be observed simultaneously for the same individual. Origin wages for migrants and destination wages for residents (stayers) need to be estimated using information from the other group, providing biased results due to self-selection. Workers with identical characteristics (e.g., young, male, Mexican-born, Mexican-educated gardeners) are not randomly distributed in both countries, plus Mexican immigrants in the United States may have unobserved characteristics that make them different from the Mexicans who stay in Mexico. Such differences may encourage them to travel to the United States and stay, and even though such differences are unobserved, they do have effects on their observed wages.

To overcome the problem of self-selection and estimate comparable origin and destination wages for Mexicans in both countries, we follow the standard two-step procedure provided by Heckman,[23] bearing in mind that the relevant wage in the United States for a potential Mexican migrant that should be considered is not the average wage that an American citizen with the same characteristics may get, but the average wage that a Mexican-born migrant with the same (observable and unobservable) characteristics may obtain.

236  *Ernesto Aguayo-Téllez, et al.*

Hence, Mincer wage equations for a Mexican worker ($i$) in Mexico ($M$) and in the United States ($US$) can be defined as:

$$\ln(w_{Mi}) = \theta_{M0} + \theta_{M1}X_i + \theta_{M2}Z_{Mi} + \varepsilon_{Mi} \tag{1}$$

$$\ln(w_{USi}) = \theta_{US0} + \theta_{US1}X_i + \theta_{US2}Z_{USi} + \varepsilon_{USi} \tag{2}$$

where $w_{Mi}$ is the wage of Mexican worker $i$ in Mexico and $w_{USi}$ is the wage of the same Mexican worker $i$ in the United States. $X_i$ are her individual characteristics. $Z_{Mi}$ and $Z_{USi}$ are local characteristics for worker $i$ in Mexico and the United States respectively.

If Mexican workers are not randomly distributed on both sides of the border, wage equations (1) and (2) are missing important information (e.g., workers' productivity, entrepreneurship and other unobservable characteristics), and Ordinary Least Squares (OLS) estimation delivers biased and inefficient coefficient estimators.

Heckman's methodology inserts a selection correction variable into the regression equations (1) and (2) that controls for such missing information. Such a correction variable is called the "inverse Mills ratio" and can be proved to generate efficient and unbiased estimators for all the other parameters.[24] Inverse Mills ratios are computed for migrant and nonmigrant Mexicans using the individuals' probabilities of being part of each group. Corrected Mincer wage equations are estimated by maximum likelihood, and, according to Lee (1982), this two-stage estimation procedure results in unbiased, efficient and consistent estimates.

## ESTIMATING WAGE DIFFERENTIALS

To calculate US wages for Mexicans in Mexico and Mexican wages for Mexicans in the United States, we use a microdata set from the Mexican Survey of Occupation and Employment (ENOE) of 2008 and the American Community Survey (ACS) of 2008.

The ENOE is a quarterly survey aimed at identifying occupational characteristics from the Mexican population. It provides information about 124,000 families living in Mexico in 2008. The ENOE includes individual and family socioeconomic characteristics such as age, education, employment status, wage and hours worked, as well as some migration characteristics. The ENOE is a large database, significant for every state of Mexico and for thirty-two metropolitan areas, including the northern border cities of Tijuana, Mexicali, Ciudad Juarez, Nuevo Laredo, Reynosa and Matamoros.

The ACS of 2008 includes 1,304,000 families living in the United States in 2008 and also reports individual and family socioeconomic characteristics, as well as some migration characteristics. The ACS is significant for

## Wage Differentials, Public Policies and Mexico-US Migration    237

every state of the United States and for all communities larger than 100,000 inhabitants, including southern border cities such as San Diego, Calexico, El Paso, Laredo, McAllen and Brownsville.

Table 13.1 shows the analysis of some averaged characteristics of the populations of Mexico and the United States, paying special attention to the US-Mexico border region (all monetary numbers are in US dollars as of 2008).[25] In the table we have analyzed the information for the countries as well as for their border regions, in order to observe if there are some differences in the migration and wage gap dynamics at the border area. A smaller wage differential at the border region may imply a sort of local labor and economic integration.

As data indicates, Mexican-born migrants represent 4% of the total population of the United States and 10.8% of the total population of Mexico, but it is important to underline that migration in the border region is considerably larger—for example, Mexican-born migrants in the US border region represent 20% of the population living in that area. Together, the US-Mexico border region accounts for about 11 million people, with 6.3 million living in the Mexican border cities and 5 million living in the US border cities. The Mexican border cities represent 5.8% of the total population of Mexico, while the US border cities represent 1.7% of the total population of the United States.

On the other hand, the education levels in the two countries—and in the cities on both sides of the border—are quite different. The average schooling level of a worker in the United States is 13.4 years, while the average schooling level of a worker in Mexico is 9.7 years. The average schooling

*Table 13.1*  Mexico and US Descriptive Statistics (2008)

|  | Total | | Border region* | |
|---|---|---|---|---|
|  | US | Mexico | US | Mexico |
| Population (million) | 292.4 | 108.1 | 5.0 | 6.3 |
| Mexican-born | 11.7 |  | 1.0 |  |
| Education (years) | 13.4 | 9.7 | 13.0 | 9.6 |
| Mexican-born | 9.6 |  | 10.5 |  |
| Wage/hour (dollars) | 19.52 | 2.6 | 18.27 | 3.0 |
| Mexican-born | 12.77 |  | 12.53 |  |

*Source*: Own estimations with data from ACS 2008 and ENOE 2008.

*Note*: The border region includes the city pairs of: San Diego-Tijuana, Calexico-Mexicali, El Paso-Ciudad Juarez, Laredo-Nuevo Laredo, McAllen-Reynosa and Brownsville-Matamoros.

238    *Ernesto Aguayo-Téllez, et al.*

level of a Mexican-born worker in the United States is slightly lower than their counterpart in Mexico (9.6 years versus 9.7). The average schooling level of a worker in the US border cities is around 3.5 years higher than their counterpart in the Mexican border cities (13.0 years versus 9.6). However, Mexican-born workers in the US border cities are less educated than all workers on the American side of the border (10.5 years versus 13.0), and they are more educated than their conational workers on the Mexican side of the border (10.5 years versus 9.6).

Similarly, hourly wages are also considerably larger in the United States than in Mexico. On average, a US-born, US-educated worker in the United States earns $19.52 per hour compared to $2.60 per hour for a Mexican-born, Mexican-educated worker in Mexico (US wages are 7.5 times higher). However, such differences are not so large when comparing Mexican-born workers on both sides of the border. On average, before controlling for differences in skills and unobserved productivity, a Mexican-born worker in the United States makes $12.77 per hour compared to the $2.60 that a Mexican-born worker can make in Mexico (a ratio of 4.91).[26] Within the border region, a worker in the Mexican border cities makes, on average, $2.95 per hour while a Mexican-born worker in the US border cities makes $12.53 per hour (a ratio of 4.24). Given that Mexican-born workers on the US side of the border are more educated than Mexican-born workers on the Mexican side, this difference may get smaller when we compare the similar individuals.

To estimate composition-fixed and selection-corrected Mexican-born wages in Mexico and in the United States, we followed the standard Heckman (1979) procedure as mentioned before. In our regressions, we included both male and female Mexican-born workers between sixteen and sixty-five years old, who work at least twenty hours a week and report positive labor earnings either in Mexico or in the United States.

To analyze the selection correction variables or "inverse Mill's ratios" we run migrant probit regressions with age, age squared, gender, years of schooling, marital status, family size, number of children in the family and possession of health insurance as the independent variables.[27] We run two independent regressions: one considering the probability of moving from any place in Mexico to any place in the United States, and the other considering only the border region.[28]

With the inverse Mill's ratios computed, wage equations (1) and (2) are regressed using the following as independent variables: gender; years of schooling; years of experience; years of experience squared; the interaction of gender with schooling, experience and experience squared; and eight dummies for industry sector.[29] Coefficient estimates are presented in Table 13.2.

The first two columns of the table display wage regressions for nonmigrants, and the second two columns display wage regressions for migrants. The first and third columns display wage regressions for the countries while the second and fourth columns display wage regressions including only

### Wage Differentials, Public Policies and Mexico-US Migration    239

*Table 13.2*   Mincer Wage Regressions: Equations (1) and (2)

| | Equation (1): Nonmigrants | | | | Equation (2): Migrants | | | |
| --- | --- | --- | --- | --- | --- | --- | --- | --- |
| | Mexico to US | | Border region | | Mexico to US | | Border region | |
| Gender | 0.114 | ** | 0.007 | | 0.081 | ** | 0.250 | * |
| Education | 0.069 | ** | 0.071 | ** | 0.039 | ** | 0.070 | ** |
| Experience | 0.020 | ** | 0.016 | ** | 0.022 | ** | 0.022 | ** |
| Experience squared | 0.000 | ** | 0.000 | ** | 0.000 | ** | 0.000 | |
| Gender * education | −0.003 | ** | 0.003 | | −0.005 | ** | −0.017 | ** |
| Gender * experience | 0.006 | ** | 0.012 | ** | 0.013 | ** | 0.012 | |
| Gender * experience squared | 0.000 | ** | 0.000 | ** | 0.000 | ** | 0.000 | |
| Industry dummies | yes | | yes | | yes | | yes | |
| Border city dummies | no | | yes | | no | | yes | |
| Inverse Mills ratio | −1.212 | ** | 0.518 | ** | −0.882 | ** | −2.155 | ** |
| Constant | 0.533 | ** | −0.775 | ** | 0.705 | ** | −0.655 | ** |
| Observations | 389,368 | | 18,355 | | 49,773 | | 4,174 | |
| F-value | 4354 | ** | 281 | ** | 380 | ** | 43 | ** |
| Pseudo-$R^2$ | 0.33 | | 0.36 | | 0.15 | | 0.23 | |

*Source*: Own estimations with data from ACS 2008 and ENOE 2008.

*Note*: * and ** denote significance at 5% and 1%, respectively.

workers living in the border region. As expected, in all cases schooling and experience increase wages for both men and women. The sign and significance of the estimated coefficients of the inverse Mills ratio indicate the existence of self-selection and whether it is positive or negative. The coefficients obtained are statistically significant and suggest the presence of negative self-selection into the migrants group. Migrants from Mexico to the United States have lower earnings capabilities in the United States than nonmigrants. Into the nonmigrants group, nonmigrants are negatively self-selected but positively self-selected if they would migrate into the border region.[30] Nonmigrants have lower earning capabilities in Mexico than migrants, except within the border region.[31]

On the other hand, biased-corrected wages in Mexico and in the United States are calculated for all workers (migrants and nonmigrants) using the

240 *Ernesto Aguayo-Téllez, et al.*

estimated coefficients presented in Table 13.2. Taking into consideration the foregoing, we can compute selection-corrected wages for the same worker in Mexico and in the United States. This procedure allows us to compare average wage ratios for specific subgroups of Mexican-born workers. However, in Table 13.3 we have analyzed US-Mexico mean wage ratios in total and divided by gender and by three schooling groups.[32] The upper panel presents wage ratios for all Mexican-born workers in Mexico and in the United States. The lower panel presents wage ratios for Mexican-born workers only within the Mexico-US border area.[33] The first row of each panel presents computed wage ratios considering the wage information of all Mexican-born workers in the United States (legal and illegal, speaking English or not, etc.). However, when a Mexican worker is considering moving to the United States, she/he must compare her/his wage in Mexico with a wage she/he will obtain in the United States. The second row of each panel presents wage ratios considering wages in the United States for Mexican-born workers who are not American citizens. In the same way, the third row of each panel displays Mexico-US wage ratios considering wages in the United States for Mexican-born workers who are not American citizens and who do not speak English. Finally, the fourth row of each panel lists Mexico-US wage ratios considering wages in the United States for Mexican-born workers who are not American citizens, who do not speak English and who arrived in the United States in the last five years.

*Table 13.3*   Mean US-Mexico Wage Ratios, Corrected for Self-Selection: 2008

|  | By years of schooling | | | By gender | | |
| --- | --- | --- | --- | --- | --- | --- |
|  | 0 to 5 | 5 to 11 | 12 or more | Women | Men | Total |
| **Migration from Mexico to United States** | | | | | | |
| Mexican-born workers | 6.58 | 5.66 | 4.50 | 4.86 | 5.60 | 5.34 |
| not citizens | 6.55 | 5.43 | 4.07 | 4.58 | 5.33 | 5.07 |
| not citizens, not English | 6.64 | 5.13 | 3.51 | 4.26 | 4.99 | 4.74 |
| not citizens, not English, arrived last five years | 5.79 | 4.74 | 3.41 | 4.15 | 4.52 | 4.39 |
| **Within the border region** | | | | | | |
| Mexican-born workers | 4.94 | 4.38 | 3.57 | 3.86 | 4.31 | 4.15 |
| not citizens | 5.08 | 4.20 | 3.15 | 3.65 | 4.08 | 3.92 |
| not citizens, not English | 5.26 | 4.00 | 2.66 | 3.38 | 3.83 | 3.67 |
| not citizens, not English, arrived last five years | 4.59 | 3.83 | 2.79 | 3.08 | 3.82 | 3.55 |

*Source*: Own estimations with data from ACS 2008 and ENOE 2008.

## Wage Differentials, Public Policies and Mexico-US Migration   241

Thus from the table it can be observed that on average, after controlling for observable and unobservable characteristics, a Mexican-born worker who is not an American citizen, does not speak English and is planning to migrate to the United States will increase her/his labor earnings 4.39 times when moving from Mexico to the United States. Migration wage differentials are larger for men (4.52) and for unschooled workers (5.79). In all cases, migration wage differentials are larger for Mexican-born workers who hold an American citizenship and are English speakers. Nevertheless, results indicate that, within the border region, US-Mexico wage differentials are not that large, which may imply regional economic integration. After controlling for observable and unobservable characteristics, a noncitizen, non-English-speaking, Mexican-born worker who works on the Mexican side of the US-Mexico border will increase his/her wage 3.55 times in average just by crossing to work to the American side of the border.[34] Again, migration wage differentials are larger for men (3.82), unschooled (4.59) and English speakers. Unschooled workers have such low wages in Mexico that they are much better off migrating to the United States even if they go illegally and do not speak any English.

This analysis clearly indicates that lower wages compared to the United States and poverty in Mexico are important push factors behind the massive international migration in the country. During different phases of time both governments of the United States and Mexico have implemented plans to regulate as well as reduce migration between the two nations, which we will discuss in the following section.

## MEXICO-US MIGRATION POLICY

Immigration policy has been an ongoing subject of congressional attention in recent years and a topic of concern for the US public at large. In our earlier analysis we have observed that Mexicans are by far the largest group of US migrants, and about one in ten Mexicans now lives (legally or illegally) in the United States. Indeed, Mexico-US migration represents the largest binational migration flow in the world.

As our earlier results indicate, international migration is primarily a function of economic as well as social and demographic structural differences. Limited economic opportunities, including other social factors, encourage emigration from Mexico, while high wages and employment opportunities are the "pulling factors" within the United States.[35] In this sense, Rosenblum et al.[36] classified US-Mexico migration policies into four phases: a) Pre–World War II or limited seasonal flow, b) The Bracero Program (1942–1964), c) The origins of today's migration system (1964–1980s) and d) Heightened push-pull factors and migration controls (1980s to the present).

Between 1917 and 1920, the US Congress created the first guest worker program and allowed Mexican nonimmigrant admissions. Beginning in

242    *Ernesto Aguayo-Téllez, et al.*

1921 the US Congress exempted Mexicans and other Western Hemisphere migrants from per-country immigration limits imposed on the rest of the world. However, in 1929, US migration policy swung the other way, and there were tighter screening criteria for Mexican visa applicants, resulting in a 75% reduction in lawful permanent resident (LPR) admissions. During the Great Depression, hundreds of thousands of Mexicans and their US-born children returned to Mexico, including many who were deported. After this, Mexico also discouraged emigration (i.e., migration to the United States), with a 1926 law requiring exiting workers to obtain permission from municipal authorities, and a series of public relations campaigns to discourage outflows and support return migration. As a result, the 1930s were the only decade in which net migration in the region flowed north to south.

During World War II, there was a high demand for workers by US agricultural employers. However, American agricultural employers struggled to recruit Mexican workers as the Mexican government continued to oppose emigration. The government of Mexico viewed migration to the United States as a drain on Mexican resources and—based on the experiences of earlier migrants—as a threat to their workers' rights. In consequence, at the time of the Roosevelt administration, there was a negotiation with Mexico for a bilateral guest worker program, which became known as the Bracero Program. Under this program Mexican workers were guaranteed a minimum wage, health benefits, housing and transportation expenses. This program's peak occurred in the late 1950s, when strong constituencies on both sides of the border grew to favor labor flows. Both governments supported the program, including by developing a transportation infrastructure to move agricultural workers from the Mexican interior to the border region and beyond.

At the conclusion of the Bracero Program, Mexican workers faced difficulties on legal pathways to enter the United States. The imposition of strong anti-immigration laws affected legal migration from Mexico. As a result, illegal migration grew threefold between 1965 and 1970. By 1979, around 1.7 million unauthorized migrants resided in the United States, including 1.4 million from Mexico. After fifteen years of discussions, the US Congress passed the Immigration Reform and Control Act of 1986 (IRCA), which combined employer sanctions with a pair of legalization programs for 2.6 million illegal migrants through IRCA, which included about 2.1 million Mexican migrants.

During the 1990s and after IRCA, there was a high demand for foreign workers in new types of occupations. However, the US Congress was not interested in allowing new migration inflows and responded to these trends by passing four anti-illegal migration laws, by authorizing additional investments in border security, by restricting migrants' access to welfare and other public benefits and by streamlining procedures to remove unauthorized migrants.

## Wage Differentials, Public Policies and Mexico-US Migration 243

Border enforcement and migration control received additional attention after the 9/11 attacks, with the US Congress passing five more laws related to immigration control in 2002–2006. These immigration reforms sought to reduce low-skilled employment-based inflows, but in reality the consequences are different. Immigration reforms just act as a "wall" or "barrier" between the two nations, whose main aim is to reduce the current migration flow, not the potential migration flow. As before, 2002–2006 US immigration reforms failed to address the principal reason for Mexico-US migration: regional income inequality.

Compared to the US government, the government of Mexico has developed different social policies for the benefits of the poor that indirectly aim to reduce migration. As mentioned, in addition to geographical proximity and transnational migration networks, regional income inequality is one of the main factors underlying international migration. Hence, social policies designed by the Mexican government to combat poverty should, by reducing income inequality, lessen emigration pressures.[37]

## MEXICAN SOCIAL AND ECONOMIC POLICIES

Over the last fifteen years, the Mexican government has adopted different social policies that abandon the vision of a highly regulated economy as the main instrument against poverty. The new policies rely on state intervention in the pricing and distribution systems to ensure that the poor draw particular benefits from state subsidies. Under this new system and through prices, the federal government provides substantial subsidies to producers of staples, and provides additional subsidies to consumers in the cities. Similar mechanisms are in place in the case of fuel, electricity, mass transit systems and others.[38]

Other successful policies recently implemented by the Mexican government are *health and nutrition programs* for the poor. These programs have effectively reduced malnutrition among poor, rural and indigenous children. Recently, the government has created and re-created some social policies for the benefit of the poor that indirectly reduce migration from Mexico, such as *Solidaridad*, PROGRESA, *Oportunidades* and *Seguro Popular*.

During the 1970s, Mexican government created COPLAMAR (*Coordinación General del Plan Nacional de Zonas Deprimidas y Grupos Marginados*) and CONASUPO (*Compañía Nacional de Subsistencias Populares*). COPLAMAR was created to encourage rural development. The main objective of this program was to provide social and economic benefits to marginal zones of the country. On the other hand, CONASUPO was created to promote Mexico's economic and social development by regulating the markets of staples (or popular subsistence crops) through the elimination of inefficient and dishonest intermediaries. COPLAMAR and CONASUPO stopped operating in the early 1990s.

244   *Ernesto Aguayo-Téllez, et al.*

In the seventies and early eighties, the Mexican government created LICONSA[39] to secure the nutritional aspects of marginalized and poor people. The main objective of this program was to distribute low-cost milk to low-income families with children aged one to eleven years. Up until now, LICONSA continues operating and has been effective in reducing the prevalence of anemia in twelve- to thirty-month-old children.

Similar to LICONSA, the *Programa Nacional de Solidaridad* is arguably the most widely known poverty relief program implemented in Mexico.[40] This program was implemented for a short period of time; it started in 1989 and continued until 1994. Its main objectives were improving public service provision and development indicators. This program was the cornerstone of the government's poverty relief strategy as well as its strategy to reduce infant mortality and provide proper nutrition and caloric intake, particularly for girls, women and the old. Its resources represented, on average, 1.18% of gross domestic product (GDP) each year.

In 1997, the Mexican government implemented PROGRESA (*Programa de Educación, Salud, y Alimentación*), an integrated approach to poverty alleviation through the development of human capital. PROGRESA was part of a larger poverty alleviation strategy, and its role was to lay the groundwork for a healthy, well-educated population who could successfully contribute to Mexico's economic development, to break the intergenerational cycle of poverty and indirectly to help reduce migration. The program offered conditional cash transfers to the rural poor in exchange for sending their children to school and for regular attendance at health clinics and small group sessions focusing on health and nutrition education. The conditional cash transfers replaced many earlier programs focused on poverty alleviation through the delivery of food subsidies and other in-kind transfers, which for political and logistical reasons often did not reach the rural poor in great numbers and were largely regarded as inefficient. The conditional cash transfers were demand-driven interventions that sought to remove many of the practical barriers and opportunity costs that rural families faced in attending health clinics and sending their children to school (e.g., children were often taken out of school to earn income for the family). This program sought to work with program beneficiaries and enable them to take responsibility for their own family's welfare. Overall, the program was found to be quite successful in improving conditions of the poor.[41]

In 2002 PROGRESA was renamed *Oportunidades*. This program continues to be the principal antipoverty program of the Mexican government, and it focuses on helping poor families in rural and urban communities to invest in human capital, improving the education, health and nutrition of their children, leading to the long-term improvement of their economic future and the consequent reduction of poverty in Mexico. By providing cash transfers to households through linking to regular school attendance and health clinic visits, the program fulfills the aim of alleviating current poverty and indirectly preventing international migration.

## Wage Differentials, Public Policies and Mexico-US Migration  245

From the foregoing discussion we observe that the Mexican government has implemented a number of social programs to eliminate poverty. It is necessary to mention that through these programs, the Mexican government aim is to indirectly reduce internal and international migration. However, we should keep in mind that migration requires a minimum quantity of money to afford the costs of moving and extremely low-income families cannot afford it. Hence, increasing the income of the poorest families may promote migration, at least at the beginning.

On the other hand, looking at the enormous importance of international remittances and their potential to contribute to development, Mexican governments have designed public policies for the productive use of such capital flows. One such policy is the 3x1 Program for Migrants, which began in the state of Zacatecas in 1986. The Federation of Zacatecans Clubs, which comprised over seventy hometown associations (HTAs) located in Southern California, started to raise funds to help expatriates abroad, mostly in the event of illness or death, and to fund social and recreational projects back home. In its initial design, the (3x1) program, formerly called 1x1 program, contemplated only that the state would double the amount of money sent by migrants' associations. Although just twenty-eight projects were carried out under the program between 1986 and 1992, the initiative encouraged the Federation of Zacatecan Clubs to undertake more and more philanthropic activities.[42]

From 1988 to 1994, the Zacatecan initiative received further support, and President Salinas, interested in courting migration, created the program of International Solidarity among Mexicans, also known as the 2x1 Program. Under this scheme, not only the state but also the federation matched the contributions of HTAs. In the meantime, the initiative was replicated by the state governments of Jalisco, Durango and Guanajuato.[43]

When Vicente Fox took office in 2000, he restored the federal support to collaborative programs, created the *Instituto para los Mexicanos en el Exterior* and resurrected the matching grant program with federal support. The 3x1 Program–Citizen Initiative started in 2002, and later on became the 3x1 Program for Migrants. The main objective of this program was to increase the coverage and the quality of basic social infrastructure in localities with a high proportion of poverty, social backwardness or migration.[44] Different from the others, this program also aims to strengthen the links between migrants and its communities through collaborative development projects and the organization of migrants abroad.

As it is described earlier, many policies and programs implemented by the government of Mexico are and have been intended to increase Mexicans' quality of life, employment opportunities, education and health, and indirectly control migration flows. However, in this chapter we have discussed that the principal reason behind Mexico-US migration is the increasing wage inequality and the lack of economic opportunities in Mexico. Thus, we believe that fostering development in Mexico is the only way to diminish migratory

246   *Ernesto Aguayo-Téllez, et al.*

pressures over time. Many scholars have suggested that the United States should support development projects in Mexico to discourage emigration.[45]

Alternative strategies should also be applied. For example, Wainer suggests there should be farmer-to-farmer exchange programs to connect rural farmers' cooperatives in Mexico with Mexican farmers in the United States.[46] Another possibility would be to expand the mandate of the North American Development Bank from environmental infrastructure projects to include broader development goals. Thus, economic assistance should be a tool to reduce emigration, as it creates jobs and reduces emigration in the long run.

## FINAL CONSIDERATIONS AND RECOMMENDATIONS

Mexico is a country of emigration; nearly 18% of its workforce lives abroad. Thus, it requires some effective policies assuring that emigration benefits it, taking proactive steps to regulate migration and to ensure it meets national interests. On the other hand, the United States is a country of immigrants; almost 13% of its population is born abroad. Hence, it also requires creating fair and effective migration policies that allows the country to take full advantage of this phenomenon, not only benefiting employers and consumers but also ensuring respect for the human rights of migrants.

The last three decades have been an exceptional period in Mexico-US migration. As recently as 1970, the share of Mexico's population living in the United States was only 1.5%; by 2010, it had risen to 10.2%. As we have seen from our earlier analysis, the flow of labor across the Mexico-US border is not a new phenomenon, with previous surges occurring in the 1920s and 1950s. However, persistent mass migration between the countries did not take hold until late in the twentieth century.

During the 1960s and 1970s Mexico enjoyed sustained economic progress, but in the 1980s the country's economy stagnated. Repeated currency crises reversed the effects of short-lived expansions, leaving per capita GDP in the late 2000s more or less unchanged from two decades before. During periods of wage decline in Mexico, emigration from the country spiked. So, in this sense, our results indicate that over the period there is an increase in the migration flow, and the main reason behind it is the growing wage difference between the two nations.

Under these circumstances, the US and Mexican governments have adopted some unilateral policies: to deter immigration in the case of the United States, and to provide job opportunities to potential migrants in their places of origin in the case of Mexico. However, it seems that such unilateral efforts of both governments have not had an effect on migration flows. The ineffectiveness of such US and Mexican policies and the absence of any coordinated or binational policy to regulate migration flows or to smooth its bilateral effects have allowed the market forces to take over. In the absence of any North American institutional response to migration issues, US-Mexico

## Wage Differentials, Public Policies and Mexico-US Migration 247

labor condition and wage inequalities are, and will continue to be, the most important drive for moving people from south to north.

Mexico by itself has not been able to keep workers in its domestic market. On the other hand, the United States by itself has not been able to deter Mexican migration inflows. A natural candidate to reduce and/or to control Mexico-US migration and, at the same time, to ensure the well-being of migrants should be a binational initiative. However, the absence of any coordinated policy between the two countries can be explained by the difference in short-run objectives between the two nations. Such short-run differences seem to be stronger than the region's common interest of ensuring better jobs for Mexicans in Mexico, better jobs for Americans in the United States and better conditions for migrants.

In the short run, Mexico does not have any real interest in reducing migration to the United States. To Mexico, international migration represents the second most important source of capital inflows (smaller than oil but larger than tourism and Foreign Direct Investment (FDI) and an essential exhaust valve for the increasing labor supply that grows faster than the labor demand.

Similarly, although the government of the United States has tried to coordinate migration policies to reduce inflows of Mexicans, such policies have not been effective. Different manufacturing and farmers' associations as well as Mexican migrants' associations do not have short-run interests in reducing the inflow of Mexican workers and have put strong efforts towards preventing migration from been completely abated. Illegal Mexican immigration ensures a constant flow of cheap labor, which translates into more production and benefits, lower prices and better economic conditions.

Mexico's and the United States' long-run migration objectives should be to ensure better jobs for Mexicans in Mexico, allowing the country to generate its own income, increase its internal demand and promote sustained development. Seeking such long-run objectives can significantly reduce Mexico-US migration, while avoiding the tremendous costs many Mexican migrants have to suffer while working in the United States—costs such as risking their lives when crossing the border, being apart from their families, working under unsafe or uninspected conditions or being persecuted. In addition, seeking such long-run objectives may ensure better labor conditions for lower-income American workers, without diminishing American well-being and economic conditions.

We understand that promoting such long-run objectives may be politically costly for both the Mexican and American governments and none of the governments is willing to undertake such costs. However, a coordinated binational policy on migration issues is urgently needed to solve a problem that is getting bigger, before it becomes uncontrollable. In addition, a well-coordinated and established binational program may allow both governments to share political costs. Promoting economic integration and reducing income inequalities within the region must be the most important first steps that a coordinated binational initiative should seek. Additionally, in order for this initiative to be effective, institutional links between the two nations should be created.

248   *Ernesto Aguayo-Téllez, et al.*

The following is a list of steps that both the US and Mexican governments should coordinately adopt to stem the migration issue.

1. From this study it is clearly understood that wage differences between Mexico and the United States are a reason for migration—thus there is an urgent need for both countries to promote economic development in Mexico. It is important to notice that any increase in real wages must be large enough to make Mexican workers better off staying in Mexico and not just to give them the necessary income to afford moving to the United States.
2. Social programs like *Oportunidades*, PROGRESA and LICONSA are some of the important steps adopted unilaterally by the Mexican government to reduce poverty. However, these programs have not been effective in reducing international migration. Thus, it is essential to address how these programs can be modified to help reduce international migration.
3. The Mexican government should support returned migrants in terms of employment and ease their access to Mexican social programs.
4. The 3x1 initiative program should not be considered as a motor of regional development. Governments must invest their fiscal resources for regional development without depending on 3x1 programs.
5. The Mexican government must consider the development of the agricultural sector, creating funds particularly for the benefits of farmers.
6. The US government should provide more economic resources to help Mexico's development and job creation. The US aid may be targeted to promote education, health and technology development in Mexico.
7. Finally, the governments from the United States and Mexico should promote economic integration. As mentioned earlier, wage differences at the border region are smaller, which may suggest that economic integration reduces wage differences. A narrower wages difference reduces migration.

## NOTES

1. Source: OECD Factbook Statistics (2012), OECD iLibrary. http://www.oecd-ilibrary.org/economics/data/oecd-factbook-statistics/oecd-factbook_data-00590-en.
2. George J. Borjas, "The Earnings of Mexican Immigrants in the United States," *Journal of Development Economics* 51 (1996): 69.
3. Jorge Durand, Douglas S. Massey and Rene Zenteno, "Mexican Immigration in the United States: Continuities and Changes," *Latin American Research Review* 36 (2001): 107; Daniel Chiquiar and Gordon Hanson, "International Migration, Self-Selection and the Distribution of Wages: Evidence from Mexico and the United States," *Journal of Political Economy* 113 (2005): 239; K. Unger, "Economic Development and Mexican Out-Migration" (CIDE working paper, NBER Conference on Mexican Immigration, 2005); C. Woodruff and R. Zenteno, "Migration Networks and Microenterprises in Mexico," *Journal of Development Economics* 82 (2007); K. Unger and

## Wage Differentials, Public Policies and Mexico-US Migration   249

    G. Verduzco, "El Desarrollo de las Regiones de Origen de los Migrantes: Experiencias y perspectivas" (México: CONAPO, 2000); R. C. Jones, "Maquiladoras and U.S.-Bound Migration in Central Mexico," *Growth and Change* 32 (2001): 193; P. Ibarraran and D. Lubotsky, "Mexican Immigration and Self-Selection: New Evidence from the 2000 Mexican Census," in *Mexican Immigration to the United States*, ed. George J. Borgas (Chicago: University of Chicago Press and National Bureau of Economic Research, 2007), 159–192.

4. Durand, Massey and Zenteno, "Mexican Immigration"; David Card and Ethan E. Lewis, "The Diffusion of Mexican Immigrants in the 1990s: Explanations and Impacts," in *Mexican Immigration to the United States*, ed. George J. Borgas (Chicago: University of Chicago Press and National Bureau of Economic Research, 2007),193–228.

5. Numerous studies have discussed the effects of earning disparities (or expected earning disparities) as the main determinant of international migration from less-developed countries: M. P. Todaro, "Urban Job Expansion, Induced Migration and Rising Unemployment," *Journal of Development Economics* 3 (1976): 211; L. Yap, "Internal Migration and Economic Development in Brazil," *Quarterly Journal of Economics* 90 (1976): 119.

6. E. Aguayo-Téllez and J. Martínez-Navarro, "Internal vs. International Migration in Mexico: 1995–2000," *Applied Economics* 45 (2013): 1647.

7. Chiquiar and Hanson, "International Migration."

8. Unger, "Economic Development," 6.

9. O. Stark and J. E. Taylor, "Migration Incentives, Migration Types: The Role of Relative Deprivation," *Economic Journal* 101 (1991): 1163–1178.

10. J. E. Taylor, "Differential Migration, Networks, Information and Risk," *Research in Human Capital and Development: Migration, Human Capital and Development* 4 (1986): 147.

11. S. R. Curran and E. Rivero Fuentes, "Engendering Migrant Networks: The Case of Mexican Migration," *Demography* 40 (2003): 289–307.

12. Todaro, "Urban Job Expansion," 211.

13. L. Sjaastad, "The Costs and Returns of Human Migration," *Journal of Political Economics* 70 (1962): 80.

14. J. R. Harris and M. P. Todaro, "Migration, Unemployment and Development: A Two-Sector Analysis," *American Economic Review* 60 (1970): 126.

15. Neoclassical theory states that regional earnings differentials should disappear over the long run for various reasons. One reason is labor migration from low-wage areas to high-wage areas; however, perfect mobility of workers and perfect information should be assumed. Another reason is capital flows to regions with relatively low labor costs. In this case, perfect mobility of capital and perfect information should be assumed. A third reason is the ability to produce cheaper goods and services in the low-wage areas, which allows competitively advantaged local industries to export their products, increasing their labor demand and consequently increasing wages. In this case, perfect mobility of goods and perfect information should be assumed. However, workers, capital and goods are not perfectly mobile. Transport and legal costs may deter the flows of people, capital and goods, as may regional differences such as amenities, local taxes and cultural backgrounds.

16. Sjaastad, "Costs and Returns."

17. The individual's target function must reflect not only the wage difference between the community of origin and destination but also the associated moving costs: where denotes the individual's earnings differential in regions $m$ *(destination)* and $n$ *(origin)* at period $t$, $C_{mn}$ is the cost of moving from region $n$ to $m$, $\rho$ is the implicit discount rate and $T$ represents the length of time during which the individual remains economically active. Under this scheme, the individual chooses to migrate only when $V(t)$ is positive.

250    *Ernesto Aguayo-Téllez, et al.*

18. Sjaastad, "Costs and Returns."
19. S. Polacheck and F. W. Horvath, "A Life-Cycle Approach to Migration: Analysis of the Perspicacious Peregrinator," in *Research in Labor Economics*, ed. R. Ehrehberg (Greenwich, CT: JAI, 1977), 103–150.
20. G. Borjas, "Self-Selection and the Earnings of Immigrants," *American Economic Review* 77 (1987): 531.
21. Mincer, J. "Progress in Human Capital Analyses of the Distribution of Earnings," in *Personal Distribution of Incomes*, ed. A. B. Atkinson (London: Royal Economic Society, 1976), 136–192.
22. Following Mincer, "Progress in Human Capital Analyses," wages are mostly explained by individual characteristics such as experience, education and gender, as well as other local characteristics, as follows: where $\ln(w_i)$ is the natural logarithm of the wage of individual $i$, $X_i$ are individual characteristics, $Z_i$ are other local characteristics and $\varepsilon_i$ is the residual.
23. J. J. Heckman, "Sample Selection Bias as a Specification Error," *Econometrica* 46 (1979): 1251.
24. For a detailed explanation see Heckman, "Sample Selection Bias."
25. The Mexico-US border region includes the cities of San Diego, Calexico, El Paso, Laredo, McAllen and Brownsville in the United States and Tijuana, Mexicali, Ciudad Juarez, Nuevo Laredo, Reynosa and Matamoros in Mexico.
26. Other studies that compare earnings among different countries or specifically between Mexico and the United States present diverse results. For 1990, Chiquiar and Hanson, "International Migration," present a US-Mexico wage ratio of 10.20 for men and 7.12 for women. For 1994, M. Rama and R. Artecona, "A Data Base of Labor Market Indicators across Countries" (World Bank, Washington, DC, 2002), compound a ratio of 6.57. For 1995, R. B. Freeman and R. H. Oostendorp, "Occupational Wages around the World" (Working Paper No. 8058, National Bureau of Economic Research, Cambridge, MA, 2005), come up with a ratio of 2.78. And for 2006, A. Hoefort and S. Hofer, "Price and Earnings: A Comparison of Purchasing Power around the Globe" (Union Bank of Switzerland AG, Wealth Management Research, Zurich, 2007), calculate a ratio of 7.49 for Mexico City. Comparing wages for Mexican workers in Mexico and the United States, Chiquiar and Hanson, "International Migration," present a wage ratio of 5.60 for men and 4.98 for women in 1990 while M. A. Clemens, C. E. Montenegro and L. Pritchett, "The Place Premium: Wage Differences from Identical Workers across the U.S. Border" (Working Paper 148, Center for Global Development, 2008), compute an unadjusted wage ratio of 3.82 for 1999.
27. Given space limitations, estimated coefficients are not presented here but can be consulted in E. Aguayo-Téllez and C. Rivera-Mendoza, "Migration from Mexico to the United States: Wage Benefits of Crossing the Border and Going to the US Interior," *Politics & Policy* 39 (2011): 119.
28. The border region regression includes six city-pair dummies to control for possible regional differences along the US-Mexico border.
29. Border city-pair dummies for the border region regression and industry dummies are also included, but due to space limitations their coefficients are not displayed in Table 13.2.
30. Intuitively this means that people who actually stay earn relatively more in Mexico than migrants if such migrants were in Mexico. Similarly, people who actually crossed the border earn relatively less in the United States than nonmigrants if such nonmigrants were in the United States.
31. Negative self-selection is consistent with the findings of Aguayo-Tellez and Martinez-Navarro, "Internal vs. International Migration in Mexico"; Borjas, "Earnings of Mexican Immigrants," 69; and P. Orrenius and M. Zavodny,

## Wage Differentials, Public Policies and Mexico-US Migration 251

"Self-Selection among Undocumented Immigrants from Mexico" (Working Paper 0005, Federal Reserve Bank of Dallas, 2001). However, other authors such as Chiquiar and Hanson, "International Migration," have found positive self-selection. Aguayo-Tellez and Rivera-Mendoza, "Migration from Mexico," find that the size of the negative self-selection is smaller for the more disadvantaged groups of workers.

32. Up to five years of schooling or elementary school dropouts, six to eleven years of schooling or elementary school graduates to high school dropouts, and twelve years or more of schooling or high school graduates and above.

33. As mentioned before, the Mexico-US border area includes the cities of San Diego, Calexico, El Paso, Laredo, McAllen and Brownsville in the United States and Tijuana, Mexicali, Ciudad Juarez, Nuevo Laredo, Reynosa and Matamoros in Mexico.

34. Within the border region, wage differentials may be considerably different for different areas. For example, the San Diego area records much better wages than the Brownsville area. Aguayo-Tellez and Rivera-Mendoza, "Migration from Mexico," present wage differentials within each border city pair. Moving from Tijuana to San Diego increases the wage of a non-American, non-English-speaking, Mexican-born worker 4.12 times, while moving from Reynosa to McAllen increases her/his wage 3.16 times.

35. M. R. Rosenblum, W. A. Kandel, C. R. Seelke and R. E. Wasem, *Mexican Migration to the United States: Policy and Trends* (Washington, DC: Congressional Research Service, 7–5700, R42560, 2012) www.crs.gov.

36. Ibid.

37. A. E. Latapí, "Mexican Policy and Mexico—U.S. Migration" (Working Paper 167, CCIS, Center for Comparative Immigration Studies, University of California, San Diego, 2008).

38. Ibid.; M. Szekely, *Hacia una nueva generación de política social* (Mexico City: SEDESOL, 2002).

39. LICONSA (Leche Industrializada Conasupo, S.A. de C.V.) is a state-owned business devoted to the industrialization of milk and its distribution at subsidized prices to Mexicans under poverty conditions.

40. A. E. Latapí, "Mexican Policy and Mexico—U.S. Migration," Working Paper 167. CCIS. Center for Comparative Immigration Studies, University of California. San Diego, 2008, http://ccis.ucsd.edu/2008/05/mexican-policy-and-mexico-%e2%80%93-u-s-migration-working-paper-167/.

41. E. Skoufias, "PROGRESA and Its Impacts on the Human Capital and Welfare of Households in Rural Mexico: A Synthesis of the Results of an Evaluation by IFPRI" (International Food Policy Research Institute, Washington, DC, 2001).

42. F. Aparicio, C. Maldonado and B. Beltrán, "Programa 3x1 para Migrantes: Datos Generales de la Evaluación Externa de Consistencia y Resultados 2007" (SEDESOL, 2007).

43. K. Burguess, "Migrant Philanthropy and Local Governance in Mexico," in *New Patterns for Mexico. Remittances, Philanthropic Giving, and Equitable Development*, ed. Barbara Merz (Cambridge, Harvard University Press, 2005), 99–124.

44. S. Soto and M. A. Velázquez, "El Proceso de institucionalización del Programa 3x1 para Migrantes," in *El Programa 3x1 para Migrantes. ¿Primera Política Trasnacional en México?* ed. R. Fernández de Castro et al. (ITAM, Porrúa: Universidad de Zacatecas, 2006), 11–20.

45. About this, in 2011, the United States provided around $178 million in foreign assistance to Mexico, including about $25 million in development aid and $143 million under the Mérida Initiative. Rosenblum, Kandel,

## 252 *Ernesto Aguayo-Téllez, et al.*

Seelke and Wasem, *Mexican Migration*. However, this quantity is still very small.
46. A. Wainer, "Development and Migration in Rural Mexico," Bread for the World, January 2011, http://www.bread.org/institute/papers/briefing-paper-11.pdf.

## REFERENCES

Aguayo-Téllez, E., and C. Rivera-Mendoza. "Migration from Mexico to the United States: Wage Benefits of Crossing the Border and Going to the US Interior." *Politics and Policy* 39, no. 1 (2011): 119–140.

Aguayo-Téllez, E., and J. Martínez-Navarro. "Internal vs. International Migration in Mexico: 1995–2000." *Applied Economics* 45, no. 13 (2013): 1647–1661.

Aparicio, F., C. Maldonado and B. Beltrán. "Programa 3x1 para Migrantes: Datos Generales de la Evaluación Externa de Consistencia y Resultados 2007." SEDESOL. 2007. http://repositories.lib.utexas.edu/bitstream/handle/2152/4059/apari cio.pdf.txt?sequence=3

Borjas, G. "The Earnings of Mexican Immigrants in the United States." *Journal of Development Economics* 51 (1996): 69–98.

———. "Self-Selection and the Earnings of Immigrants." *American Economic Review* 77, no. 4 (1987): 531–553.

Burguess, K. "Migrant Philanthropy and Local Governance in Mexico." In *New Patterns for Mexico: Remittances, Philanthropic Giving, and Equitable Development*, edited by Barbara Merz, 35–41. Cambridge: Harvard University Press, 2005.

Card, D., and E. E. Lewis. "The Diffusion of Mexican Immigrants in the 1990s: Explanations and Impacts." In *Mexican Immigration to the United States*, edited by George J. Borgas, 193–227. Chicago: University of Chicago Press and National Bureau of Economic Research, 2007.

Chiquiar, D., and G. Hanson. "International Migration, Self-Selection and the Distribution of Wages: Evidence from Mexico and the United States." *Journal of Political Economy* 113, no. 2 (2005): 239–281.

Clemens, M. A., C. E. Montenegro and L. Pritchett. "The Place Premium: Wage Differences from Identical Workers across the U.S. Border." Working Paper 148. Center for Global Development. 2008.

Curran, S. R., and E. Rivero Fuentes. "Engendering Migrant Networks: The Case of Mexican Migration." *Demography* 40, no. 2 (2003): 289–307.

Durand, J., D. S. Massey and R. Zenteno. "Mexican Immigration in the United States: Continuities and Changes." *Latin American Research Review* 36, no. 1 (2001): 107–127.

Freeman, R. B., and R. H. Oostendorp. "Occupational Wages around the World." Working Paper No. 8058. National Bureau of Economic Research. Cambridge, MA. 2005.

Harris, J. R., and M. P. Todaro. "Migration, Unemployment and Development: A Two-Sector Analysis." *American Economic Review* 60 (1970): 126–142.

Heckman, J. J. "Sample Selection Bias as a Specification Error." *Econometrica* 46 (1979): 1251–1272.

Hoefort, A., and S. Hofer. "Price and Earnings: A Comparison of Purchasing Power around the Globe." Union Bank of Switzerland AG, Wealth Management Research. Zurich. 2007.

Ibarraran, P., and D. Lubotsky. "Mexican Immigration and Self-Selection: New Evidence from the 2000 Mexican Census." In *Mexican Immigration to the United*

## Wage Differentials, Public Policies and Mexico-US Migration  253

*States*, edited by George J. Borjas, 159–192. Chicago: University of Chicago Press and National Bureau of Economic Research, 2007.

Jones, R. C. "Maquiladoras and U.S.-Bound Migration in Central Mexico." *Growth and Change* 32 (2001): 193–216.

Latapí, A. E. "Mexican Policy and Mexico—U.S. Migration." Working Paper 167. CCIS. Center for Comparative Immigration Studies, University of California. San Diego. 2008. http://ccis.ucsd.edu/2008/05/mexican-policy-and-mexico-%e2%80%93-u-s-migration-working-paper-167/.

Mincer, J. "Progress in Human Capital Analyses of the Distribution of Earnings." In *Personal Distribution of Incomes*, edited by A. B. Atkinson. London: Royal Economic Society, 1976, 136–192.

OECD Factbook Statistics (2012), OECD iLibrary. http://www.oecd-ilibrary.org/economics/data/oecd-factbook-statistics/oecd-factbook_data-00590-en.

Orrenius, P., and M. Zavodny. "Self-Selection among Undocumented Immigrants from Mexico." Working Paper 0005. Federal Reserve Bank of Dallas. 2001.

Polacheck, S., and F. W. Horvath. "A Life-Cycle Approach to Migration: Analysis of the Perspicacious Peregrinator." In *Research in Labor Economics*, edited by R. Ehrehberg, 103–149. Greenwich, CT: JAI Press, 1977.

Rama, M., and R. Artecona. "A Data Base of Labor Market Indicators across Countries." World Bank. Washington, DC. 2002.

Rosenblum, M. R., W. A. Kandel, C. R. Seelke and R. E. Wasem. *Mexican Migration to the United States: Policy and Trends*. Washington, DC: Congressional Research Service, 7–5700, R42560, 2012. www.crs.gov.

Sjaastad, L. "The Costs and Returns of Human Migration." *Journal of Political Economics* 70, no. 5–2 (1962): 80–93.

Skoufias, E. "PROGRESA and Its Impacts on the Human Capital and Welfare of Households in Rural Mexico: A Synthesis of the Results of an Evaluation by IFPRI." International Food Policy Research Institute. Washington, DC. 2001.

Soto, S., and M. A. Velázquez. "El Proceso de institucionalización del Programa 3x1 para Migrantes." In *El Programa 3x1 para Migrantes: ¿Primera Política Trasnacional en México?*, edited by R. Fernández de Castro et al., 11–20. Porrúa: ITAM, Universidad de Zacatecas, 2006.

Stark, O., and J. E. Taylor. "Migration Incentives, Migration Types: The Role of Relative Deprivation." *Economic Journal* 101 (1991): 1163–1178.

Szekely, M. *Hacia una nueva generación de política social*. Mexico City: SEDESOL, 2002.

Taylor, J. E. "Differential Migration, Networks, Information and Risk." *Research in Human Capital and Development: Migration, Human Capital and Development* 4 (1986): 147–171.

Todaro, M. P. "Urban Job Expansion, Induced Migration and Rising Unemployment." *Journal of Development Economics* 3 (1976): 211–225.

Unger, K. "Economic Development and Mexican Out-Migration." CIDE working paper. NBER Conference on Mexican Immigration. 2005.

Unger, K., and G. Verduzco. "El Desarrollo de las Regiones de Origen de los Migrantes: Experiencias y perspectivas." CONAPO. México. 2000. http://conapo.gob.mx/work/models/CONAPO/migracion_internacional/MigracionOpPolitica/08.pdf.

Wainer, A. "Development and Migration in Rural Mexico." Bread for the World. January 2011. http://www.bread.org/institute/papers/briefing-paper-11.pdf

Woodruff, C., and R. Zenteno. "Migration Networks and Microenterprises in Mexico." *Journal of Development Economics* 82, no. 2 (2007): 509–528.

Yap, L. "Internal Migration and Economic Development in Brazil." *Quarterly Journal of Economics* 90, no. 1 (1976): 119–137.

# 14 Conclusion

*Gaspare M. Genna and*
*David A. Mayer-Foulkes*

This book's joint analysis allows us to take stock not only of the state of North American integration, but also of the current paradigm of US economic, political and social policy. The current US paradigm is highlighted because the strengths and weaknesses of North American integration reflect the strengths and weaknesses of the dominant policy paradigm in general. The title of the book refers precisely to the problem: while the main issues in North American integration are migration, security and development, the main obstacles to obtaining solutions is the institutional void. The institutional void, in turn, characterizes the strengths and weaknesses of the economic, political and social policy paradigm. In fact, as we shall see ahead, we could say that both the strengths and weaknesses of the institutional void are the result of implementing conservative economic and political beliefs of small government and liberalization in the democratic, market context. This is, of course, the implementation not simply of a set of philosophical beliefs, but of a set of policies shaped by economic and political interests.

The historical period of integration under examination between Canada, Mexico and the United States began with the implementation of the North American Free Trade Agreement (NAFTA) and the labor and environmental side agreements in 1994, but was then followed by little further action on the North American integration front. The North American economy was basically allowed to take its course, but little further trilateral coordination arose to deal with problems in migration and security, or to reach further levels of economic development than those promoted by free trade. For example, while NAFTA proponents had argued that free trade would lead to enough growth in Mexico to stem the flow of undocumented workers to the United States, this did not occur. In sum we demonstrate in this volume an important contraction in the development of North American integration. On the one hand, the conservative policy of economic liberalization produced a series of economic benefits, which, however, did not go as far as had been expected, but on the other hand the lack of any further economic and political actions defines an institutional void that faces a range of arising problems. This same summary could apply to the wider problems facing both the United States and countries worldwide under the current globalization resulting

Conclusion 255

from several decades of economic liberalization. The lifting of restrictions on economic activity does not of itself produce solutions to a series of problems. Once the political and economic energy liberated by liberalization has run its course, new emerging obstacles for economic growth and political harmony require political leadership through effective institutions.

On what fronts is this leadership required? What are the problems in North American integration? The various chapters of the book give a comprehensive picture of these problems. These range from general perspectives on institutional building to specific contexts in labor, migration, health and security issues.

As mentioned in the introduction, the book is divided into three sections. The first section discusses the determinants of integration, which are closely linked to the institutional characteristics of the three countries involved. Genna's examination of the overall picture of regional integration shows that regional integration and homogeneity of domestic institutions mutually promote each other. Low levels of institutional homogeneity serve to explain the current low level of North American cooperation. Thus, there is a broad scope for public policy in promoting the homogenization of institutions across North America that will yield benefits in integration.

Castro-Rea shows that much of the policy background for North American integration has been conservative ideology, which we argue here is linked in general to the institutional void facing a series of problems. Castro-Rea further argues that the conservative stance is linked with a series of social concerns such as hypernationalism and xenophobia, which are antithetical to closer regional relations and are borne out of domestic political struggles.

Norman's discussion of Hannah Arendt's notion of superfluousness and her critique of human rights shows that the lack of transnational or intergovernmental institutions dealing with labor mobility in North America effectively leaves undocumented workers as "stateless people." The impact of purely economic forces on migration, unaccompanied by effective transnational institution building, results in the erosion of the human rights. The condition of "statelessness," at present, is solvable only through unilateral action, but that is unlikely in the current political and economic environment. We are therefore faced with a dual institutional void.

García-Barrios and Mayer-Foulkes' discussion of economic paradigms explains the limitations of the neoclassical paradigm and why economic liberalization is not enough on its own to generate further economic development or a society with equal opportunities, thus exposing the limitations of the conservative economic ideology. Their discussion explains that economic liberalization needs to be complemented with government policies making technological change, human capital accumulation, urbanization and economic opportunities available for all. They include an ethical dimension in their analysis and show that ethical governance, based on a strengthened, participative democracy, is an essential basis for economic policy.

256  *Gaspare M. Genna and David A. Mayer-Foulkes*

The second section of the book gives examples in which institution building has been used to solve to problems in labor, migration and health. Nolan de García examines the institutional support of the NAFTA labor side agreement, and argues that these complementary policies to NAFTA have not been sufficiently well supported in civil society and labor unions.

Gabriel and Macdonald examine a different issue, guest worker rights in four Canadian cities. They again show how these rights have insufficient institutional underpinnings to be effective. Immigrant advocacy groups are creating institutions in order to fill a need not supplied by the lack of effective Canadian institutions. Gabriel and Macdonald demonstrate that additional state and nonstate action is required to promote and uphold migrant workers' rights.

Bayes and Gonzalez analyze the *Consejo Consultivo del Instituto de los Mexicanos en el Exterior*, a Mexican government-funded initiative to develop leadership within migrant communities in the United States. Here we have a situation in which labor mobility has not been officially sanctioned. Facing an institutional void, an institution established by the home country for promoting leadership to address health, education and business service problems related to migrants has helped to unite and construct communities.

Institutional development is also required with regard to health care. Nielan Barnes explores how the adoption of the Patient Protection and Affordable Care Act of 2010 (PPACA) would address the health care problems of Mexican migrants. She demonstrates that net North American labor mobility enters the United States, but without the PPACA, this population does not have access to basic health care due to the domestic paradigm and adds to the underclass condition. The PPACA does partially fill the institutional void, but relies on domestic and not intergovernmental decisions. Had the 2012 presidential election been decided in favor of the Republican candidate, the PPACA could have faced repeal.

The third section addresses additional economic and security issues with an important bearing on integration. Domínguez and Velázquez demonstrate that the institutionalization of the three partners' security arrangements has much more coordination between the United States and Canada. This reflects different security cultures and a polarized integration, which will tend to make these differences persist. Without a trilateral institutionalization of a security agreement, economic interdependence may not deepen.

For example, Snodgrass and Gessner analyze the enormous development of security in trade across the Canada-US border. The unilateral "thickening" of this border has led to a massive restructuring of production arrangements, especially on the Canadian side. Therefore, even with close coordination between Canada and the United States on extraregional foreign policy, there is a lack of coordination between the two on regional security, which adds costs to trade and, in turn, depresses the level of economic integration.

Even these changes are relatively coordinated as compared to the impact of the narco war in Mexico, particularly along the US-Mexico border.

Conclusion   257

Arceo-Gómez's chapter shows that the increased violence has promoted an exodus of Mexicans, including more middle-class entrepreneurs who bring with them similar or, in many cases, the same businesses they had established in their home cities. The lack of stability at home and greater economic opportunities in the United States drain the Mexican economy of talent that can facilitate greater development, producing a vicious cycle.

The last chapter notes that Mexican workers seeking employment in the United States continue to see a large wage gap. Aguayo-Téllez and Rivera-Mendoza thus show that migration will continue to be an important issue for relations in North America unless intergovernmental institutions are established to handle the development issues of North America.

The picture that emerges from this analysis is one of a piecemeal approach to issues that need to be dealt with, such as labor rights, education and health care. Clearly policies oriented exclusively to markets will not solve these issues, which require additional dimensions of social policy. This holds even for what could be regarded as a purely economic issue, the incentives for migration. A broader, more comprehensive and strategic approach, using a wider set of tools and focusing on building intergovernmental institutions, is needed to formulate policies leading more effectively to economic development across countries and social strata in North America.

# Index

3x1 Program for Migrants 245
100 Amigos (Cien Amigos) 143, 144–5

Action Plan on Perimeter Security and
 Economic Competitiveness 207
Action Plan on Regulatory Cooperation
 207
Agricultural Worker Alliance (AWA)
 121, 122, 126, 128–9
agriculture 39, 43, 100, 122
Alabama 55, 60, 62, 64, 73, 76, 77,
 137
Alianza Hispano-Americano 138
American Community Survey (ACS)
 212, 214, 216, 217, 218, 236,
 237, 239, 240
American Mexican Anti-discrimination
 Alliance (AMADA) 143, 145,
 148
American Recovery and Reinvestment
 Act 35, 201
anti-immigrant policies 39, 166
Anti-Terrorism Act (Bill C-36) 41
Arendt, Hannah 6, 52–6, 57–63
 65–71, 73–7, 255
Arizona 10, 46, 52, 55, 72–4, 76–7,
 116, 137, 142, 166, 172, 212,
 217; SB 1070 4, 6, 46, 59, 60,
 63, 64, 162
arms trafficking 213, 226
Asociación de Jóvenes Unidos en
 Acción (AJUA) 142, 143–4
Association of Southeast Asian Nations
 (ASEAN) 1, 20, 21

Basok, Tanya 119
bilateral migration policies 247
binational/border health 153
Border Enforcement Security Task
 Force (BEST) 188

Border Partnership 188
Bracero Program 139, 232, 241, 242
business openings in the US 213,
 217–19, 221, 223, 224
"Buy American" 44, 201

Calderon, Felipe 9, 136, 181, 188, 190,
 211, 213, 223
Canada Action Plan 44
Canada First Defence Strategy 41
Canada-Mexico Seasonal Agricultural
 Workers Program (SAWP) 2, 7,
 115, 116–21, 123, 126, 128,
 130
Canada-US Free Trade Agreement 24,
 200
Canadian Alliance (CA) 37
Canadian Council of Chief Executives
 (CCCE) 182
Canadian Labour Congress (CLC) 122,
 123, 124, 125
Catholic Church 37, 129
Center for Community Change (CCC)
 148
Centro de Orientación de los Derechos
 de los Migrantes 148
China i, 2–4, 43, 92, 184
Christian Coalition 38
citizenship 55, 59, 61, 63, 64, 65, 66,
 67, 115, 116, 117, 119, 121,
 125, 130, 137, 138, 139, 142,
 153, 155, 159, 161, 162, 163,
 241
citizenship rights 52, 53, 57, 59, 60, 61,
 63, 66, 68, 69, 116, 119, 120,
 128, 130
civil society 7, 108, 115, 116, 120, 121,
 122, 125, 126, 129, 130, 147,
 154–5, 157–60, 164–5, 166–8,
 256

## 260  Index

Commission for Labor Cooperation (CLC) 102, 105–6, 109
competitive security systems 179
Congreso Mexicanista 138
Congreso del Pueblo 143,147
Consejo Binacional por un México Mejor 138, 148
Consejo Consultivo del instituto de los Mexicanos en el Exterior (CC-IME) 8, 136, 137, 138, 139, 140, 141–9, 256
conservatism 6, 35, 37, 39, 45, 160; contradictions of 6, 160
Conservative Party of Canada 37
cooperative security systems 179
co-responsibility 157
cross border management 203–4
cross border suppliers 201, 204, 205, 206, 208
Customs-Trade Partnership against Terrorism (C-TPAT) 198, 201, 203

defense spending 40, 41
democracy i, 5, 7, 78, 82, 86, 87, 90, 91, 157, 158, 168, 178, 179, 255
detention 41, 59, 60, 63, 70, 77
development i, 1, 4, 5, 7, 8, 15, 16, 17, 18, 28, 29, 35, 45, 68, 78, 79, 87, 88, 89, 90–1, 92–3, 123, 155, 156, 157, 168, 178, 181, 182, 213, 226, 233, 243, 244, 245, 246, 247, 254, 255, 256, 257
Development, Relief and Education for Alien Minors Act (DREAM) 4
dispute resolution 35, 99, 102–4, 106, 108–9, 111
drug(s) i, 4, 6, 8, 9, 34, 40, 41, 42, 44, 58, 78, 92, 136, 181, 183, 184, 187, 188, 189, 190, 191, 211, 212, 213, 214, 223, 226
Drug Enforcement Agency (DEA) 187
dual-bilateralism 34, 178

Economic Freedom of the Word index (EFW) 20, 21, 22, 23, 24, 25, 26, 27
economic growth 2, 7, 78, 79, 86, 87, 88, 89, 91, 156, 168, 169, 213, 226, 231, 255
employment insurance 116, 120, 126, 128
environmental 1, 101, 105, 152, 153, 246, 254

ethical 7, 79, 80, 82, 83, 84, 85, 86, 87, 90, 91, 92, 255
Europe 2, 3, 22, 23, 54, 55, 56, 57, 59, 61, 62, 63, 65, 78, 83, 86, 87, 178
European Union (EU) 1, 4, 25, 26, 61, 100, 136, 153, 158, 161, 178, 180, 181, 182
exchange rates 21, 28, 203, 205
exclusion 34, 46, 51, 52, 55, 56, 65, 109, 124, 125, 131, 134, 155, 164, 167, 194

Fast and Furious Operation 187
Federación de Clubes Michoacanos en California Lázaro Cárdenas del Río 148
federal and provincial responsibilities (Canada) 124–6
Fox, Vicente 40, 140, 141, 148, 181, 190, 245
Free and Secure Trade (FAST) 185, 198, 203, 208
freedom of association 102, 104, 105
Frontier College 121, 122, 127–8
Fundación MEX-I-CAN 143, 147

GI Forum 138
Gini coefficient 35
globalization 2, 36, 53, 55, 57, 67, 78, 79, 81, 83, 88, 89, 90, 92, 115, 160, 254
Golden State Fence Company 39
growth theories 213, 226
Grugel, Jean and Nicola Piper 116–17, 120, 130
Gulf Cooperation Council (GCC) 20, 21

health i, 5, 6, 8, 20, 39, 90, 91, 102, 104, 116, 118, 120, 126, 138, 139, 140, 143, 144, 149, 152–69, 185, 198, 219, 238, 242, 243, 244, 245, 255, 256, 257
Health Initiative of the Americas (HIA) 142, 143, 148, 163, 164, 167, 168
High Level Contact Group 188
human capital 7, 29, 85, 86, 88, 89, 90, 91, 156, 226, 235, 244, 255
Human Development Index (HDI) 20, 21, 22, 23, 24, 25, 26, 27, 82
humanity, concept of 52–3, 55, 66–7, 73, 75, 79, 80, 85, 87, 90

*Index* 261

human rights 6, 7, 47, 49, 51–77, 80,
101, 110, 113, 122, 123, 127,
152–60, 165–8, 228, 246, 255;
framework 125, 152–4, 155,
156–7, 166, 159; and health
155
hypernationalism 6, 35, 160, 255

identity 5, 6, 18, 46, 49, 54, 57,
62, 63, 64, 71, 73, 77, 137, 147,
157, 179
ideology 6, 37, 91, 160, 255
immigrant health 143, 152, 153, 155,
163, 166, 167, 168
(im)migration *i*, 1, 3, 5, 7, 9, 15, 16,
28, 29, 35, 36, 40, 41, 43, 51, 52,
55, 57, 61, 65, 66, 68, 91, 92,
100, 108, 123, 128, 136, 137,
144, 146, 147, 149, 152, 158,
167, 180, 181, 183, 184, 190,
211, 212, 213, 214, 215, 219,
220, 221, 222, 223, 224, 226,
231–5, 236, 237, 240, 241–243,
244, 245–248, 254, 255, 256,
257; illegal (qv undocumented,
unauthorized immigrants,
illegal migration) 2, 4, 6, 39, 44,
58, 59, 60, 62–3, 64, 67, 69,
76, 115, 117, 119, 120, 124,
125, 133, 153–4, 160, 161–6,
169, 170, 171, 173, 174,
241, 242, 247, 251, 253, 254,
255
Immigration Reform and Control Act
of 1986 (IRCA) 242
inclusion 1, 57, 101, 134, 177
India 4, 87
individualistic systems states 179
institutional void 1, 28, 29, 35, 26, 45,
53, 68, 91, 152, 166, 177, 178,
207, 254, 255, 256
Integrated Border Enforcement Team
(IBET) 186
interdependent linkages 199
International Labor Affairs Bureau
(ILAB) 107
International Labor Organization (ILO)
102, 122–3
international law 53, 57, 59, 60, 63,
65, 66, 154
institutionalization 5, 6, 8, 108, 109,
148, 155, 156, 169, 256
Instituto de los Mexicanos en Canadá
138

Instituto de los Mexicanos en el
Exterior (IME) 138, 139, 140,
141, 143, 144, 145

KAIROS 121, 122, 124, 125
Keen, Steve 81, 84
Keynes, Milton 7, 79, 84, 85, 89, 90

labor mobility 2, 3, 6, 19, 26, 57, 100,
115, 152, 154, 255, 256
labor unions 7, 106, 163, 168, 256
League of United Latin American
Citizens (LULAC) 139, 148
Leamington, Ontario 116, 121, 122,
124, 126–9
liberalization *i*, 2, 4, 7, 35, 37, 42, 43,
78, 82, 83, 88, 90, 91, 156, 168,
178, 180, 254, 255
Liga Protectora Latina 138–9

*maquila* 101
manufacturing 2, 4, 29, 39, 81, 101,
136, 247
Marshall, T. H. 116
Marx(ist) 7, 79, 85–7, 89, 90
Merida Initiative 152, 181, 188, 213,
226
Mexican American Coalition (MXAC)
143, 146, 148
Mexican American Student
Organization (MASA) 139
Mexican American Youth Organization
(MAYO) 139
Mexican Survey of Occupation and
Employment (ENOE) 236, 237,
239, 240
migrant rights 102, 104, 106, 116, 122,
123, 124, 142, 146
Migrant Workers Community Program
(MWCP) 121, 122, 126–7, 129
Mincer equations 235, 236, 239
ministerial agreements 102, 105
ministerial consultations 103, 104, 105
money laundering 187, 213
moral majority 38
Mutualistas 138

narco 8, 256
National Action Party (PAN) 37, 38,
40, 211
National Council of La Raza (NCLR)
139, 148
National Program of Public Security
2008–2012 (NPPS) 185

## 262 Index

National Rifle Association (NRA) 42
National Security Strategy 2010 (NSS) 184
National Administrative Offices (NAO) 102–104, 106–108, 109
Nationalism 6, 35, 44, 46, 160, 255
neoclassical economics 7, 35, 79–83, 84, 85, 86, 88, 89, 90, 91, 92, 211, 255
neoliberalism 36, 168
neopanismo 37
NEXUS 201, 208
North American Aerospace Defense Command (NORAD) 186, 200
North American Agreement on Labor Cooperation (NAALC) 99, 101–8; and Bush Administration 107–8, 110, 112; and Obama Administration 108–9
North American community 9, 177, 180, 182
North American Free Trade Agreement (NAFTA) i, 1, 2, 3, 6, 7, 9, 21, 24, 25, 26, 27, 34, 35, 40, 42, 43, 44, 57, 58, 92, 99, 100, 101, 102, 103, 104, 105, 108, 109, 115, 123, 136, 137, 148, 152, 156, 158, 177, 180, 181, 182, 189, 200, 201, 203, 206, 207, 231, 254, 256; NAFTA Plus 46, 181; Chapter 16 46, 115
North American Leaders Summit 190

Obama, Barack 38, 63, 106, 107, 115, 147, 149, 165, 181, 190, 207, 213
Occupational Health and Safety Act (OHSA) 126
Oficina Presidencial para Mexicanos en el Extranjero (OPME) 140, 141
Omnibus Crime Bill C-10 42
Operation Casablanca 187, 188
Operation Falcon 188
Operation Intercept 187, 188
Oportunidades Program 244
Organización Espejo 138, 148

paradigm 7, 35, 78–90, 160, 254–6
parental benefits 128
path dependence 36
Patient Protection and Affordable Care Act of 2010 (PPACA) 8, 153, 154, 155, 159, 160, 162, 163–8, 256

Personal Responsibility and Work Opportunity Reconciliation Act (PRWORA) 161, 162
physical capital 213, 226
pluralistic security community 178
political identity 18, 62
Populism 38
Powell Memorandum 38
Programma para las Comunidades Mexicanas en el Extranjero (PCME) 139, 140, 141, 143
PROGRESA 244
Progressive Conservative Party (PCP) 37
Protecting Canada's Immigration Act (Bill C-31) 40, 159
Public Health 152, 154, 155, 157, 158, 159, 164, 166, 167, 185
Public Safety Act November (2002) 41

real wages 43, 85, 248
Red Mexicana de Líderes y Organizaciones Migrantes 148
Red de Mujeres Mexicanas en el Exterior (REMAX) 142–143, 144
red Toryism 37
Reform Immigration 4 America (RI4A) 142, 148
Reform Party 37
refugee(s) 40, 47, 49, 54, 56–8, 60, 64, 70, 71, 75, 76, 124, 165, 166, 183, 189, 227, 229
regional integration 1, 2, 3, 4, 5, 6, 7, 8, 15, 16, 17, 18, 19, 20, 21, 22, 24, 25, 26, 27, 28, 29, 34, 35, 36, 51, 57, 63, 65, 66, 79, 91, 92, 100, 101, 108, 115, 123, 136–7, 138, 148, 149, 160, 177, 178, 180, 181, 182, 189, 190, 200, 207, 237, 241, 247, 254, 255, 256
regionalism 19, 155, 158
religious right 38
remittances 40, 137, 139, 140, 245
Republican Party 37, 38
right-wing 35, 36, 37, 38, 41, 44
Roma 47, 61–2, 72, 74, 75, 76, 77

Salinas, Carlos 139, 180, 245
Secretariá de Relaciones Exteriores (SRE) 139, 140, 144
Secure Fence Act (2006) 39
*Securing an Open Society* 185

## Index   263

security community 178, 180, 190
security cooperation 177, 180, 182, 183, 184, 186, 189, 190, 213, 226
security policy 40, 185, 196
Security and Prosperity Partnership (SPP) 3, 149, 152, 181, 189, 190
self-deportation 62, 73, 77
self-selection 235, 239
September 11, 2001 attacks (9/11) *i*, 3, 35, 40, 136, 152, 169, 181, 186, 189, 198, 200, 243
Shared Vision for Perimeter Security and Economic Competitiveness 207
Smart Border 149, 182, 185, 186, 198, 201
socioeconomic inequalities 43
Solidaridad 244
sovereignty 47, 49, 51, 52, 53, 54–60, 65–8, 69, 70, 72, 76, 105, 107, 185, 189, 190, 201
spaces of humanization 156, 158
State Children's Health Insurance Program (SCHIP) 161, 162
State Employees International Union (SEIU) 148
stateless 6, 54, 55, 56, 59, 60, 67, 70, 154, 160, 255
*Strategy to Combat Transnational Organized Crime* (2011) 184
superfluousness 55–6, 57, 59, 62–64, 67, 68, 255
supply chains 8, 198–200, 201, 202, 204–5, 206, 207, 208
supranational institutions 6, 16, 19, 43, 65, 100, 106, 154, 158
sustainability 85, 90, 91, 93

Temporary Agricultural Worker visa (H-2A) 119
Temporary Worker Advocacy Group (TWAG) 121, 124–5
Tennessee Immigrant Rights Coalition 148
terrorism 3, 8, 34, 40, 41, 58, 177, 181, 182, 183, 184, 185, 189, 190, 198

terrorist 3, 40, 41, 185, 198, 200
Texas-Mexico Automotive Supercluster (TMASC) 207
thickening of the border 8, 198, 200, 256
Todaro's migration model 234, 235
transnational solidarity 62, 63
trade policy 42
"Tres por Uno" 139

United Food and Commercial Workers (UFCW) 121, 122, 123, 125, 126, 128, 129
Universal Declaration of Human Rights (UDHR) 53, 54, 59, 66, 68, 154
University of Texas Center for Hispanic Achievement (LUCHA) 148
U.S. Department of Defense 188
U.S. Department of Homeland Security 41, 200
U.S. Department of Labor 107, 108–9, 110
U.S. drug demand 213, 226
U.S. Northern Command (NORTHCOM) 186
U.S. Purchasing Managers 204, 205, 206
U.S. Supreme Court 60, 64, 72, 76, 77
USA PATRIOT Act 41
US-Mexico 21st Century Border Action Plan 189
US-Mexico wage ratios 240

violence *i*, 4, 6, 9, 42, 57, 60, 67, 86, 136, 144, 183, 184, 188, 189, 191, 211–16, 219–24, 226, 257; homicide rates, 212, 214, 215–216, 219, 220, 223, 226; in Mexico 189, 211–30

war on drugs 78, 92, 211, 212, 213, 223, 226

xenophobia 6, 35, 123, 125, 145, 160, 255

AuQ1

## Author Query

1. There are several terms that overlap here: smart borders, Smart Border Accord, and Smart Border Declaration. Perhaps specify or make subentries.

CPSIA information can be obtained
at www.ICGtesting.com
Printed in the USA
JSHW011454201219
3107JS00006B/140